The Nine Keys

*A Guide Book to Unlock Your Relationships
Using Kundalini Yoga and the Enneagram*

Published 2018
ISBN: 978-0-9971831-7-7

For information, please contact:
Rasayan Center, LLC
111 Captain Road
Longmeadow, MA 01106

Acknowledgements:

While the Enneagram material and content in this manual is my original work, the information about the Enneagram system is largely based on the work of the following authors (listed alphabetically):
- Beatrice Chestnut
- Russ Hudson
- Peter O'Hanrahan
- Helen Palmer
- Don Riso

The testimonial stories referenced in all Enneagram type combinations are real. In all but two instances, names and in some cases identifying details have been changed.

Copyright
Lynn Roulo and Rasayan Center, LLC 2018

Copyright
The Teachings of Yogi Bhajan 2018

All rights reserved. No part of this publication may be reproduced, distributed, or transmitted in any form or by any means, including photocopying, recording, digital scanning, or other electronic or mechanical methods, without the prior written permission of the publisher, except in the case of brief quotations embodied in critical reviews and certain other noncommercial uses permitted by copyright law. For permission requests, please contact Lynn Roulo through www.lynnroulo.com.

All teachings, yoga sets, techniques, kriyas and meditations with the exception of Heart's Delight are courtesy of The Teachings of Yogi Bhajan. Reprinted with permission. Unauthorized duplication is a violation of applicable laws. ALL RIGHTS RESERVED. No part of these Teachings may be reproduced or transmitted in any form by any means, electronic or mechanical, including photocopying and recording, or by any information storage and retrieval system, except as may be expressly permitted in writing by the The Teachings of Yogi Bhajan. To request permission, please write to KRI at PO Box 1819, Santa Cruz, NM 87567 or see www.kriteachings.org.

The Kundalini Yoga Kriya Heart's Delight is based on "Transitions to a Heart Centered World", Second Edition, copyright 2014 Guru Rattana, Ph.D. and is used with kind permission of the copyright holder.
Yoga Technology - http://www.yogatech.com

Always consult your physician before beginning this or any other exercise program. Nothing in this book is to be construed as medical advice. Neither the author nor the publisher shall be liable or responsible for any loss, injury or damage allegedly arising from any information or suggestion in this book. The benefits attributed to the practice of Kundalini Yoga and meditation stem from centuries-old yogic tradition. Results will vary with individuals.

The Nine Keys

*A Guide Book to Unlock Your Relationships
Using Kundalini Yoga and the Enneagram*

Lynn

PREFACE

When I was 23 years old, I moved from Los Angeles, California to Boston, Massachusetts to be part of a new East Coast office for the CPA firm I was working for at the time. Shortly after arriving, I started dating an attractive Boston chef. He was charming, affectionate and attentive and since we met as housemates, we were always together. And then, about 7 months into our relationship, I learned he was stealing money from me. He would take checks from my checkbook, forge my signature and then steal my bank statements so I wouldn't understand what was happening.

On the day it all came to light, it was a huge shock that left me blindsided and emotionally confused. I was angry with him especially as I learned he was stealing money from me to pay for our Florida vacation and the Dalmatian puppy he bought me as a gift. I was angry at myself - I couldn't understand how I had missed all the warning signs. But above all, I was confused. I didn't understand why he would steal money from me - who he said he loved - to buy things we didn't need.

At about this same time, I stumbled across the Enneagram, a system of psychology that helps explain why people act the way they do. I randomly bought an Enneagram book in a bookstore. I had never heard of the system, but I liked the book cover. Little did I know that random purchase would become so useful.

Like most people, I started reading the book most interested in learning my own type. But as I sunk deeper into the material, I started seeing other people in my life too. And eventually, I found what I thought was a match for the lying chef. Through reading the personality profiles, the motivations, the personality blind spots and all the levels of

development, I was finally able to piece together what had happened – why he had stolen from me and how I had missed it.

I'm an Enthusiast (7), wired to see the positive, so it was easy for me to miss warning signs. My mind wasn't looking for them and didn't want to see them anyway. Why were his rent checks bouncing? Why was he changing jobs a lot? Why was there always confusion around money? None of this ever bothered me. There were weekend getaways, delicious dinners, puppies and holidays. I was happy. No questions asked.

And I understood he was an extremely unhealthy Achiever (3). His image was everything – even more important than honesty. In his mind, the top priority was to have the image of the perfect boyfriend. And if that meant he had to steal money from me to maintain that image, that was the price.

I won't say I healed quickly from the whole experience, but I did heal, and I credit a lot of that to the Enneagram. It helped me to understand what was otherwise baffling behavior. And it helped me move on without a lot of scarring because I understood very clearly what had happened, both my own behavior and the chef's behavior.

I wrote this book to share what I've learned about the Enneagram and to introduce an equally powerful system, the technology of Kundalini Yoga as taught by Yogi Bhajan®. Together, these two systems offer a roadmap to understanding and a path to healing.

My hope is that this book is of benefit to you.
Lynn

*"May the long time sun shine upon you,
All love surround you,
And the pure light within you,
Guide your way on."*

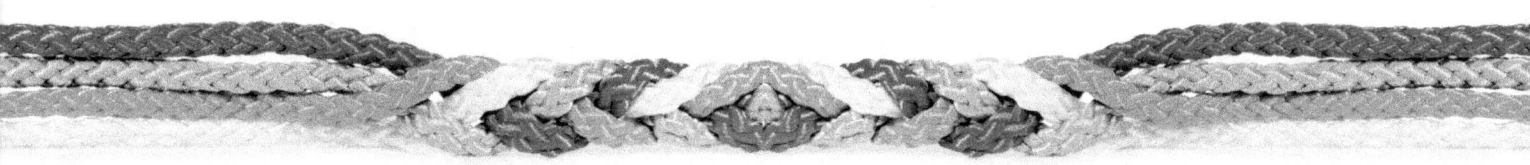

INTRODUCTION

This book weaves together two technologies shrouded in mystery that have made their way into the mainstream over the last 50 years.

Kundalini Yoga, the yoga of awareness, was taught in secrecy until the late 1960s when a Kundalini Yoga master from India named Yogi Bhajan brought the practice to the West and began teaching it openly. Now, there are thousands of Kundalini Yoga teachers worldwide sharing this technology with the masses.

The exact origin of the Enneagram is unclear, and it too was taught in secrecy until the information leaked out in the 1970s. The first books hit the mainstream market in the 1980s, and the system has been gaining popularity ever since. In 2005, a yearlong study conducted by well-known aptitude and psychometric test provider Saville & Holdsworth reported that the Enneagram is on par with the Myers-Briggs system, the Big Five and other well-known and widely-accepted psychological systems.[1]

As Kundalini Yoga and the Enneagram have gained in popularity, they have found their way into boardrooms and classrooms, churches and doctor offices, homes and rehabilitation centers. Both systems offer practical tools for living in the modern world. Both offer a path to higher consciousness, increased awareness, better communication and greater compassion. Individually, both systems are effective. Combined, they are a powerhouse.

This book interlaces these systems together in the context of intimate interpersonal relationships. Over 100 people came together to share their partnerships in this book. Their wisdom totals over 1,500 years of relationship experience. The age of respondents ranges from 21 to 77. The relationships range from 3 months to 57 years. They include straight, gay and bisexual couples. The respondents came from all over the world from Africa to the Americas, from Europe to Australia. Some stories are heart-warming. Others are heart-breaking. They are all real.

The thread of Kundalini Yoga and the Enneagram offers tools to turn these stories into wisdom. Combined, these systems offer a path to greater understanding, compassion and happiness. My hope is that the tools and insight in this book lead us to a path of greater harmony, peace and understanding.

---

(1) David Bartram and and Anna Brown of SHL Head Office, Research Division, published 2005 "Relationships between OPQ and Enneagram Types"

The Nine Keys
Table of Contents

TABLE OF CONTENTS

HOW TO USE THIS BOOK 11

THE ENNEAGRAM 12

PERFECTIONIST (1) 32

HELPER (2) 80

ACHIEVER (3) 122

INDIVIDUALIST (4) 166

INVESTIGATOR (5) 208

LOYALIST (6) 252

ENTHUSIAST (7) 296

LEADER (8) 340

PEACEMAKER (9) 380

THE BRIDGE BETWEEN THE ENNEAGRAM AND KUNDALINI YOGA 424

KUNDALINI YOGA KRIYA FOR ELEVATION/MEDITATION
FOR GURUPRASSAD 443

THE FEELING TYPES/HEART TRIAD: HEART'S DELIGHT KRIYA
AND MEDITATION TO CREATE SELF-LOVE 452

THE THINKING TYPES/HEAD TRIAD: KRIYA FOR RELAXATION AND TO
RELEASE FEAR AND MEDITATION TO OVERCOME FEAR OF THE FUTURE 460

THE INSTINCTIVE TYPES/BODY TRIAD: KRIYA TO BURN OUT ANGER
AND MEDITATION TO BURN OUT INNER ANGER 472

CLOSING 482

APPENDIX OF KUNDALINI YOGA KRIYAS AND MEDITATIONS 486

SUMMARY OF TERMS 488

RECOMMENDED RESOURCES 490

THANK YOU 491

ABOUT THE AUTHOR 492

REFERENCES 494

How to Use this Book

This book weaves together Kundalini Yoga and the Enneagram system of psychology. Individually, both systems are effective. Combined, the total is more than the sum of the parts. If you are unfamiliar with either system, this book provides an overview of both. To get started, read the two overview chapters: The Enneagram and Kundalini Yoga. These chapters give you the background and a brief education in these two technologies. After you feel you have a basic introduction to the systems, follow the guidelines below.

Guidelines

- To get the most out of this book, learn your type and if possible, the type of your partner or ex-partner. The Enneagram chapter discusses how you can learn your type.

- Read not only your type combination but also the entire chapter of your type and the type of your partner. You will get clues about yourself, your partner and your dynamic when you study your types from all angles. This is the value of the 360-degree review.

- Try the Kundalini Yoga kriyas and meditations specific for your type but also read and consider trying the sets that are assigned to other types. While the kriyas and meditations are mapped to specific core Enneagram types, the Enneagram system is complex, and there are many connecting points. Experience is your best guide. Find out what works for you.

- There is some repetition in this book. The theory for each type combination is the same, but it is presented in each of the type chapters. For example, the same theory for Perfectionist (1) with a Helper (2) is found in the Perfectionist (1) and Helper (2) chapters. This repetition is intended to improve the flow of the material.

The Enneagram

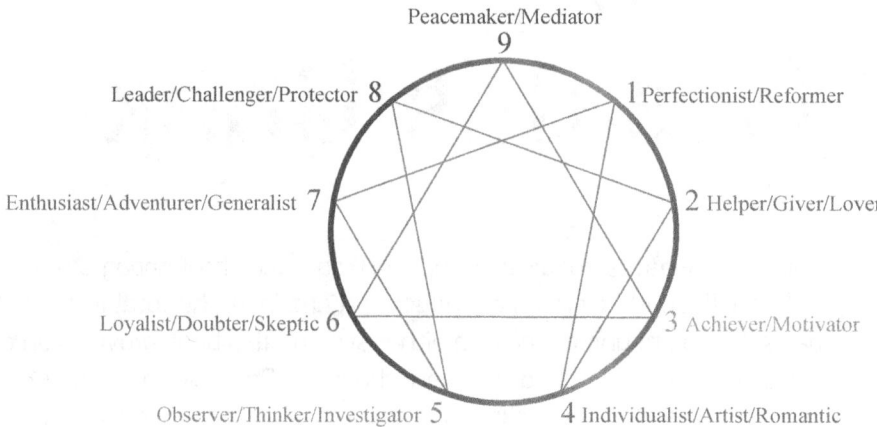

What is the Enneagram?

The Enneagram is a system of human personality that helps explain why people behave the way they do. It is essentially a map of personality, behavior and motivation. It has been referred to as the "GPS of wisdom." I think of it as a tool for compassion.

The Enneagram asks the question: Where does your attention go? The direction is referred to as your habit of attention or attention bias. Your attention bias dictates how you experience the world and your interpretation of events.

The system outlines nine core areas that your attention moves towards. These habits of attention are assigned numbers and labels as follows:

Type 1: Perfectionist/Reformer
Attention goes to what needs correction or improvement. Attention moves away from leaving things as "good enough."

Type 2: Helper/Giver/Lover
Attention goes to how to be helpful, useful or likable. Attention moves away from your own personal needs.

Type 3: Achiever/Motivator
Attention goes to how to be successful, particularly in the eyes of others. Attention moves away from failure or potential failure.

Type 4: Individualist/Artist
Attention goes to what is missing, what you don't have and what you long for. Attention moves away from what you do have.

Type 5: Investigator/Observer/Thinker
Attention goes towards self-sufficiency and conserving resources including time, energy, money and so forth. Attention moves away from dependencies from others and external demands.

Type 6: Loyalist/Skeptic/Doubter
Attention goes towards dangers and potential threats to your security. Attention moves away from positive or more moderate outcomes.

Type 7: Enthusiast/Adventurer/Generalist
Attention goes towards the positive, what could be fun, new, exciting. Attention moves away from the negative.

Type 8: Leader/Boss/Protector/Challenger
Attention goes to power and power dynamics. Attention moves away from feelings of vulnerability.

Type 9: Peacemaker/Mediator
Attention goes to harmony and maintaining a peaceful environment. Attention moves away from conflict.

Once you learn your attention bias, your own behavior begins to make more sense. And once you learn the Enneagram type of someone else, their behavior begins to make more sense. This attention bias also explains how two people can be in the same situation and have radically different interpretations of what happened.

The Origins of the Enneagram

The origins of the Enneagram symbol itself are vague. Variations of the symbol have been found in the sacred geometry of the followers of the Greek philosopher Pythagoras dating back 4,000 years. Others believe the origins of the Enneagram symbol can be traced from within the Sufi tradition of Central Asia. While the exact origins of the symbol may never be clearly known, there is more agreement about the modern application. The modern-day application of the Enneagram is largely credited to three individuals:

• **G.I Gurdjieff** (Jan 13, 1886-Oct 29, 1949): Born in Russian Armenia, Gurdjieff was a mystic, philosopher and spiritual teacher who spoke of the symbol of the Enneagram and presented a practical teaching path to greater consciousness called The Fourth Way.

The Fourth Way is an approach to self-development that combines and harmonizes what Gurdjieff saw as three established traditional "ways" or "schools": those of the mind, emotions and body or of yogis, monks and fakirs (Sufi ascetics) respectively. His teachings related to the Enneagram focused on the three centers of intelligence. These centers are described later in this book.

Gurdjieff wrote:

"Man is a machine, but a very peculiar machine. He is a machine which, in right circumstances, and with right treatment, can know that he is a machine, and having fully realized this, he may find the ways to cease to be a machine."

Gurdjieff believed that only through intense self-observation could man break out of the mechanical, repetitive behavior that makes us like a machine. He believed only through intense self-awareness can you choose your behavior.

• **Oscar Ichazo** (Jun 24, 1931-living): Born in Bolivia, Ichazo founded the Arica School and is largely credited as the first person to offer a detailed description of the nine distinct Enneagram types. The origin of his knowledge is not transparent, though he mentions Aristotle and Neoplatonism as sources. It is believed that his knowledge came from his studies in the near and far East, particularly in Afghanistan. Among other things, his Arica School teaches the concepts of the Enneagram.

Per Ichazo, the aim of the Arica school is to have the complete and entire knowledge of our psyche to enable us to handle our problems faster, easier and more clearly.

• **Claudio Naranjo** (Nov 24, 1932-living): Born in Chile, Naranjo learned the Enneagram model from Ichazo in 1970 when he went for an Arica School training. Shortly after, Naranjo created a group called SAT (Seekers of Truth) and shared his learnings there. Naranjo integrated Ichazo's work with his own broad view of human development and offered even more refined descriptions of the personality types. He asked the members to keep the information secret, but the material leaked out. The first mass-market books describing the nine distinct Enneagram personality types were published in the 1980s. The majority of these Enneagram books is based on the teachings of Naranjo.

The Symbol of the Enneagram

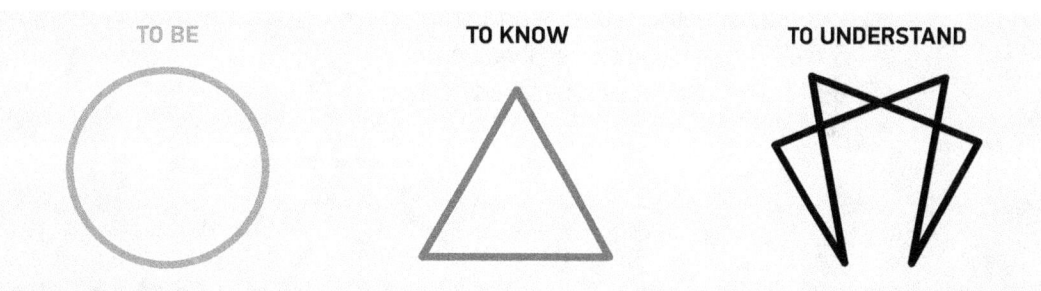

The symbol can be deconstructed as a circle, triangle and an irregular hexagon. Each shape has an esoteric spiritual meaning. The symbols map to laws that are referred to as laws of the universe or laws of cosmology.

Unity: The circle of the Enneagram symbolizes oneness, unity and wholeness. It represents the Law of One which maps to completeness and the everlasting quality of love.

Trinity: The inner triangle of the Enneagram represents the Law of Threes. This universal law states that three forces guide everything: active, passive and neutral. It is seen in many religions. For example, Christianity has the Father, the Son and the Holy Spirit and Hinduism has Brahma, the Creator, Vishnu, the Preserver and Shiva, the Destroyer.

THE NINE KEYS

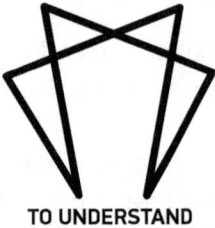

TO UNDERSTAND

Sequence: The irregular six-point hexagon represents the Law of Seven. This universal law reveals the way things happen in terms of process or a sequence of steps. It is illustrated in the spectrum of light (the seven colors of the rainbow), the spectrum of sound (seven fundamental tones in an octave), sequence (seven days in a week) and energy (seven chakras in the body).

The symbol of the Enneagram is a circle divided by nine points. The points are numbered from 1-9. All points are equal in meaning and status. No number is better or higher or lower value than any other number.

There are triads typically used with the Enneagram symbol for the types. Each triad group has three types arranged into three groups in a consistent way. The most foundational triad depicts the grouping for the three centers.

2-3-4: The feeling types/Heart Center
5-6-7: The thinking types/Head Center
8-9-1: The instinctive types/Body Center

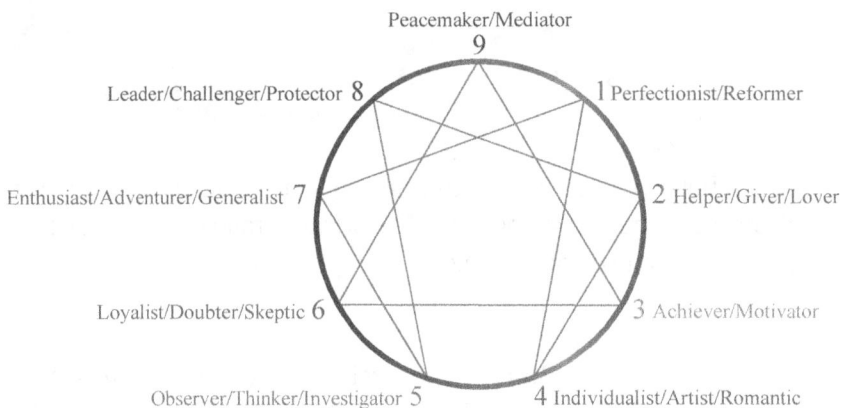

Six basic facets of the Enneagram system

Level One: The Nine Types
Level Two: The Three Centers
Level Three: The Wings
Level Four: The Subtypes
Level Five: The Stress and Security Points
Level Six: The Levels of Awareness

level 1:
THE NINE TYPES

Perfectionist (1)
The Correcting Pencils of the Enneagram
Perfectionists/Reformers are typically realistic, conscientious and principled. They strive to live up to their high ideals. This person sees the world in black and white, right and wrong, perfect and imperfect. It is difficult for them to leave things in an imperfect state.

Things Perfectionist (1)s say:

Q: *If you take a test and get 95 out of a 100 correct, how do you feel about that?*

A: Perfectionist (1)s focus on the 5 they got wrong and would want to know which 5 they missed.

Q: *On a scale of 1-10, how self-critical are you?*

A: Most Perfectionist (1)s score themselves as 8, 9 or 10. When I ask what they criticize themselves about, they typically reply "Everything. What I said, what I didn't say, what I ate, what I didn't eat, the list is endless."

Helper (2)
The Big Hearts of the Enneagram
Helper (2)s are typically warm, concerned, nurturing and sensitive to the needs, preferences and desires of the people around them. They proactively look for ways to be helpful, useful and likeable. They have high emotional intelligence, give thoughtful gifts and remember your food preferences. Personal boundaries are difficult for them.

Things Helper (2)s say:

Q: *Is it hard for you to say no to a request for help, even if it is something you really don't want to do?*

A: Helper (2)s generally have difficulty with personal boundaries. They find it hard to say no to requests, because they feel like it is their duty to offer help and if they don't, it reflects poorly on them.

Q: On a scale of 1-10, how important is it for you to help other people?

A: Most Helper (2)s score themselves as 9 or 10 and often say they feel helping others is the meaning of life. It is how they define themselves, and they feel it is the right thing to do.

Achiever (3)

The Energizer Bunnies® of the Enneagram

Achiever/Motivator (3)s are typically energetic, optimistic, self-assured and goal-oriented. Gifted at focusing on goals and achieving them, Achiever (3)s embody "human doing" rather than human being. This person is highly productive, efficient and can be extremely motivating to others. They want to be the best in any situation and can be overly concerned about the opinions of others.

Things Achiever (3)s say:

Q: Are you competitive? What types of things are you competitive about?

A: Achiever (3)s are typically very competitive about a wide variety of things ranging from professional status to casual games and even walking faster than the people around them. This may be covert or overt, but it is in their minds.

Q: On a scale of 1-10, how much time do you spend thinking about what other people are thinking about you and hoping they see you in a good light?

A: Achiever (3)s typically report a high number as much of their time is spent focused on what other people are thinking about them. Their focus goes out to others as their self-image is seen only in the reflection of others. They want to be well regarded by others. They also report that their reputation is extremely important.

Individualist (4)

The Owners of the Emotional Spectrum

Individualist (4)s are original, authentic with intense feelings spanning the entire emotional spectrum. They feel great highs, great lows and everything in between. This is a person who favors intensity, both positive and negative, over commonplace, bland and routine. They are drawn to what is missing and spend a lot of time thinking about what they don't have. They experience longing. They value authenticity.

Things Individualist (4)s say:

Q: Have you had periods of happiness and contentment or do you usually feel like something is missing?

A: The attention of Individualist (4)s goes out to what they don't have and what is missing in their life. As such, they may have periods of happiness and contentment, but these tend to be brief as their mental wiring refocuses them on what they don't have.

Q: If we were trying to average out your emotional state over the span of your entire life would you say you have spent more time in the brighter or darker emotions?

A: Most Individualist (4)s place themselves on the lower part of the spectrum. While they often report memories of happy times, their overall experience is more colored by the darker emotions.

Investigator (5)

The Owls of the Enneagram

Investigator (5)s are typically introverted, curious, analytical and insightful. These are the owls of the Enneagram with a very boundaried approach to life. This person is quite observant and curious but generally likes to observe from a distance, slightly out of the group. Eventually, they get bored or lonely and join the group. But joining the group often provokes anxiety and triggers a tendency to withdraw. They are constantly asking the question "Should I engage?" or "Should I withdraw?" Their instinct is to withdraw. Investigator (5)s usually come across as quiet – they have many things in their heads, but they rarely share all that they think.

Things Investigator (5)s say:

Q: How important is it for you to get time alone every day on a scale of 1-10? 10=it is essential I get time alone

A: Investigator (5)s report high, usually 8, 9 or 10. When I ask what happens if they don't get time alone, they have a pretty intense reaction. They flinch and become visibly uncomfortable, and some have reported they will have a breakdown if they don't get time alone.

Q: When you are making a major decision, how important is it to get facts and information before you decide?

A: Most Investigator (5)s rely heavily on their intellect and reasoning to make decisions, so they report that it is an important part of their decision-making to get full facts and information. They gain a certain comfort and sense of safety in data and information.

Loyalist (6)
The African Gazelles of the Enneagram
Loyalists (6)s are typically responsible, reliable, trustworthy and value security and loyalty. These are the gazelles of the Enneagram — scanning and on high alert for danger at all times. This person can quickly and easily identify what could be dangerous or problematic in a situation and starts preparing for that outcome. They align with the values of duty and loyalty and often feel responsible to step in during challenging situations. It can be difficult for them to believe in positive outcomes and more moderate scenarios. They don't trust people easily and often have a small, closely-knit group of friends they have had for many years.

Things Loyalist (6)s say:

Q: How frequently do you experience anxiety or anxious thinking?

A: Most Loyalist (6)s have anxious thoughts regularly – daily, weekly and in some cases constantly. They fear an unpredictable and unsafe future. They are prone to anxiety, and many have had actual panic attacks.

Q: On a scale of 1-10, how easy is it for you to imagine the worst-case scenario, what could go wrong or what could be dangerous about a situation?

A: Loyalist (6)s typically rate high in this question. They also describe how it isn't a thought exercise for them, but they see the worst-case scenario as though it is really happening, like a high definition movie.

Enthusiast (7)
The Rose-Colored Glasses of the Enneagram
Enthusiast (7)s are typically energetic, lively, adventurous and optimistic. These are the experience junkies of the Enneagram – curious, positive and often bold, they are drawn to try nearly anything they haven't done before. This person has a very easy time imagining what could go right and what could be amazing. They have a very difficult time imagining what could go wrong. They often underestimate danger and sometimes get themselves into difficult situations because of their overly positive nature. They can be avoidant of

the negative, and their mind automatically reframes negative data as positive. They can be trapped in sunshine. A lack of focus and lack of discernment are often themes for Enthusiast (7)s.

Things Enthusiast (7)s say:

Q: *How are you with rules and limitations?*

A: Personal freedom is extremely important to Enthusiast (7)s, and they are generally uncomfortable with rules and limitations. For this question, they typically report that they don't like rules and limitations and may show physical discomfort at the thought.

Q: *On a scale of 1-10, how easy is it for you to imagine the best-case scenario?*

A: Enthusiast (7)s rate high in this question. They think positive, and they know it.

Leader (8)
The Soldiers of the Enneagram

Leader (8)s are typically resourceful, self-reliant, self-confident and protective. Tough, direct, prepared for combat and comfortable with confrontation, this person instinctively understands power dynamics. Straightforward, honest and blunt, Leader (8)s have a strong internal compass. Justice is important to them. They follow their own code of ethics, but they take this personal code of conduct very seriously. In communication, they can be like a bull in a china shop. They sometimes get feedback that they are "too much" or that their aggressive communication style is overwhelming to others. Expressing vulnerability is not easy for them. Instead of expressing vulnerability, they often express anger.

Things Leader (8)s say:

Q: *What makes you really angry?*

A: Injustice or unfair treatment of vulnerable groups, particularly children and animals, is a trigger point for Leader (8)s. They often have jobs that relate to protecting these groups.

Q: *On a scale of 1-10, how uncomfortable is it for you to express your more vulnerable emotions?*

A: Leader (8)s typically answer high (8, 9 or 10) reporting that it is hard to express vulnerability even to people they are close to.

THE NINE KEYS

 **Peacemaker (9)**
The Comfortable Armchairs of the Enneagram
Peacemaker (9)s are typically soothing, receptive, good-natured, supportive and accepting of others. They are gifted at understanding the viewpoints of others and are so good at leaning into other people's agendas and perspectives, they sometimes lose their sense of themselves. Tranquility is their main focus. They are very conflict avoidant, and change typically doesn't come easily for them. They often stay in unhappy jobs, relationships, living situations and so forth much longer than other people would. Indecision, procrastination and stubbornness can be themes for Peacemaker (9)s.

Things Peacemaker (9)s say:

Q: Do you procrastinate?

A: Peacemaker (9)s have a tendency to put off important things and focus instead on unimportant things. They need to change jobs but rather than updating their resume, they will clean the garage. They may stay busy, but their important priorities are often put off.

Q: On a scale of 1-10, how comfortable are you with conflict (10=I like to fight, 1=I will give up things that are important to me to avoid conflict).

A: Most Peacemaker (9)s report very low, and when asked what they might eventually get into a conflict over, it is usually to defend someone else. They have a hard time advocating for themselves.

If you are unsure of your Enneagram type, typing interviews are one useful tool to help you uncover your core motivations and your type. You can learn more at www.lynnroulo.com. To set up a typing interview, email me at lynn@lynnroulo.com.

level 2: THE THREE CENTERS

Within the Enneagram, the nine primary types are grouped into three centers. The centers determine physically and energetically how each of the types first receives information. Each center also points to a central psychological, sensitive issue – a pain point – facing the personality. This pain point also shows a growth path for each type. The three centers and their related types are:

Center	Types	Pain Point
Heart / Feeling	2,3,4	Shame
Head / Thinking	5,6,7	Anxiety
Body / Instinctive	8,9,1	Anger

In all nine types, there is a characteristic that causes the attention to move too much in one direction. This characteristic also provides a clue to the path back to balance.

The Heart/Feeling Types

(Sensitive Issue: Shame)
The heart/feeling types first receive and process information through their emotions and feelings. They experience the energy of emotion before the information flows to their bodies and minds. The central issue each of the heart/feeling types deals with is shame.

Helper (2): Pride → Humility

On a subconscious level, Helper (2)s feel a certain pride in being helpful to others and in needing very little themselves. This is a reality distortion. Helper (2)s are at their best when they acknowledge their own needs and practice a high degree of self-care. The path back to balance is humility.

Achiever (3): Deceit → Authenticity

On a subconscious level, Achiever (3)s struggle with a fair and balanced presentation of themselves and their situation. They tend to filter out the negative elements and overemphasize the positive elements, presenting an incomplete and somewhat false picture. Achiever (3)s are at their best when they accept themselves and are comfortable with the negative aspects of themselves. The path back to balance is authenticity.

Individualist (4): Envy → Equanimity

On a subconscious level, Individualist (4)s have a hard time seeing the positive things in life that they have as their attention naturally shifts to what they don't have. This is typically seen through comparison with others and leads to envy. Individualist (4)s are at their best when they have a more level-headed view of themselves and their circumstances. The path back to balance is equanimity.

The Head/Thinking Types

(Sensitive Issue: Anxiety)

The head/thinking types first receive and process information through their intellect and mind. They process information mentally before the information flows to their feelings and their body. The central issue each of the head/thinking types deals with is anxiety.

Investigator (5): Avarice → Non-Attachment (Sharing)

On a subconscious level, Investigator (5)s have a sense they do not have enough resources including time and energy. This leads them to "hoard" or conserve what they do have, including even words and verbal communication. When they are at their best, they share more, move in flow and feel less anxious and restricted about outside attachments. The path back to balance is non-attachment.

Loyalist (6) Fear → Courage

On a subconscious level, Loyalist (6)s fear an uncertain future. Their minds naturally gravitate to the worst-case scenario, and this leads to anxious thinking. When they are at their best, they can imagine more moderate outcomes and feel confident in their ability to deal with whatever the future holds. The path back to balance is courage.

Enthusiast (7): Gluttony (for Experience) → Sobriety (Discernment)

On a subconscious level, Enthusiast (7)s are driven by gluttony or excess. They are easily excited by almost anything that is new, and this excess excitement clouds their ability to focus. When they are at their best, they manage this drive, apply discernment and act from a place of moderation. The path back to balance is sobriety.

The Body/Instinctive Types

(Sensitive Issue: Anger)

The body/instinctive types first receive and process information through their bodies. They process information somatically before the information flows to their minds and emotions. The central issue each of the body types deals with is anger.

Leader (8): Lust → Innocence
On a subconscious level, Leader (8)s feel they are in an unsafe world where they must be strong and powerful to survive and thrive. When they are at their best, they are able to drop their protective armor and come forward in an open and vulnerable way. The path back to balance is innocence.

Peacemaker (9): Sloth → Engagement
On a subconscious level, Peacemaker (9)s fear stepping into their power may disrupt their harmonious environment. This leads them to cut off from their power, drains them of their energy and results in sloth or inaction. When they are at their best, they engage in right action. The path back to balance is engagement.

Perfectionist (1): Anger → Serenity
On a subconscious level, Perfectionist (1)s have a need to correct that is fueled by repressed anger. They tend not to connect with or express their anger directly, and it manifests instead as an intense drive to fix, correct and improve things. When they are at their best, they engage in wise acceptance and know what to improve and what to appreciate as is. The path back to balance is serenity.

level 3: THE WINGS

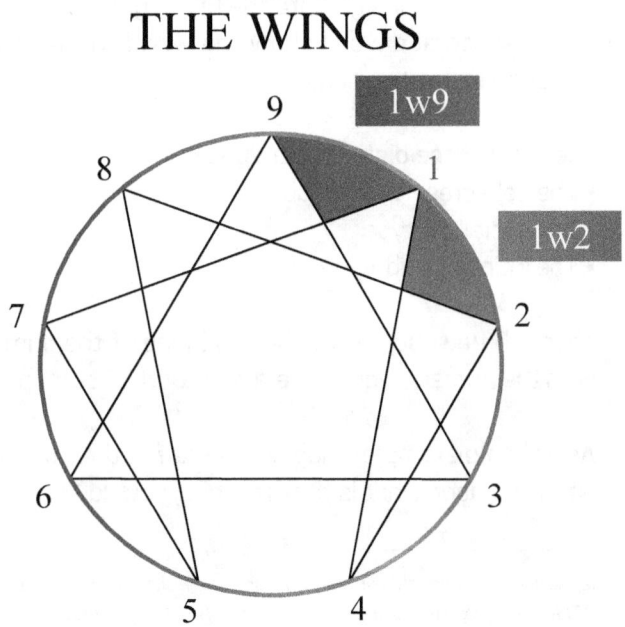

The Enneagram system includes a third level of insight and nuance called wings. Each Enneagram type is influenced by one of the types numerically next to it. This relationship is called a wing. For example, a Perfectionist (1) is influenced either by the Helper (2) or Peacemaker (9) behavior. In Enneagram shorthand, this is a 1w2 or 1w9.

Each combination has characteristics that are unique to that wing + type pairing. For example, the 1w2 is called the Advocate, and the 1w9 is called the Dreamer.

People often ask if they can have both wings or if they can change their dominant wing over time. One theory in the Enneagram community is that you begin your life with one dominant wing and in the second half of your life, your other wing begins to develop more.

This book doesn't delve into the subject of the wings, but it is an interesting topic ripe with nuance.

level 4: THE SUBTYPES[2]

A fourth level of insight into the Enneagram system is the subtype. The subtype describes your instinctual drive for how the world works. It isn't a conscious choice you make but rather an instinctive sense.

There are three distinct subtypes:
- The self-preservation subtype
- The social subtype
- The intimate subtype.

These three subtypes apply to all nine of the primary Enneagram types. When combined with the primary type, there are in total 27 subtype variations.

As a simple example, imagine yourself at the front door of a party of a casual friend. As you enter the door, what is the first thing you do?

---

(2) All subtype information in the Enneagram type chapters has been paraphrased from Beatrice Chestnut, PhD, published 2013, "The Complete Enneagram: 27 Paths to Greater Self Knowledge".

Self-preservation: Some people scan the room looking for the food, the drinks, noticing the layout, wondering where they will put their coat and so forth. Their energy goes to meeting their basic needs.

Social: Other people glance around for the host or hostess. They look for their friends and take in the social dynamics of the party. Then they decide who they will say hello to first. Their energy goes to social connections.

Intimate: And other people scan the room to see who they think is the most interesting person at the party. After they have zeroed in on who they think will be interesting, they start to imagine how they will be introduced to or approach that person. Their energy goes to intense connections.

This exercise isn't definitive of your subtype, but it helps to give you an idea of where the instinctive energy goes.

Subtype	Emphasis	Worldview
Self-Preservation	Personal needs and interests	"I am responsible for myself, you are responsible for yourself, and we all understand these rules."
Social	Group or community interests	"The world functions better when we all get along."
Intimate	Intimate or one-on-one connections	"You and me against the world."

The subtypes are described more specifically in each type chapter.

You may see elements of yourself in all three subtypes. The question is more "which aligns with you the most?" You can think of the subtype as a pie chart. Most of us are 50% or more of one of the three subtypes.

level 5: STRESS AND SECURITY POINTS

People behave differently when they are stressed and anxious and when they feel relaxed and expansive. The Enneagram system recognizes this and offers an explanation through the use of stress and security points.

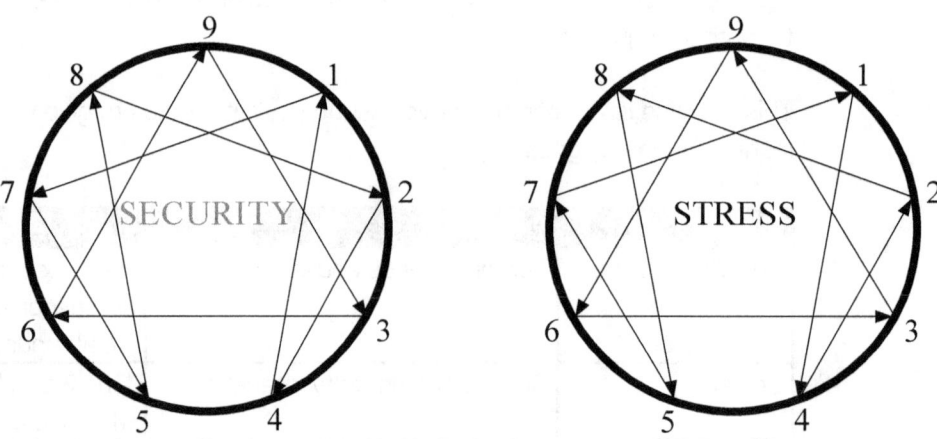

The image above illustrates the connection points between primary types and their stress and security points. The core motivation always remains with the primary type, but the behavior may adopt patterns for the type connected to the stress point and security point.

For example:
A Perfectionist (1) goes to Enthusiast (7) when they feel relaxed and expansive. While their core pattern is still focused on correction, their behavior becomes more playful, carefree and daring. And a Perfectionist (1) goes to Individualist (4) when they are under stress. Their behavior becomes more dramatic, their moods are more intense, and they may focus on what is missing or what they long for.

level 6:
LEVELS OF AWARENESS

The levels of awareness are general guidelines for how much the habit of attention has been relaxed. We may experience multiple levels of awareness during each day depending on the amount of stress we experience, our ability to be self-reflective and many other factors. The goal is to keep the habit of attention relaxed as much as possible and to operate from the higher levels of awareness.

In relationships, most problems occur in the middle or lower levels of awareness. In this book, these levels are described as the type with "tightening defenses" and the type when "fixated." How do you recognize when you are slipping into lower levels of awareness? The first signs of stress show each type tightening their basic defense systems. Fixated refers to fixated on the type's habit of attention. This is described in more detail in each of the type chapters.

One factor in maintaining the higher levels of awareness is a somatic one, a strong nervous system. To move from the lower to the higher levels of awareness, exercises to strengthen the nervous system and breathwork can be extremely effective.

Learning Your Enneagram Type

There are several ways to learn your Enneagram type. Often, people are able to read through the type descriptions and recognize themselves. There are many websites and Enneagram books to help you through this process. I've outlined some of these in the Appendix under "Recommended Resources." If reading the type descriptions is inconclusive, you can schedule an Enneagram typing interview with someone trained in the Enneagram typing process. These typing interviews are designed to help uncover motivation. It can be extremely useful to have an objective, knowledgeable person guiding you through the process. There are also online tests. These can be helpful, but a limitation to many online tests is that the questions often address behavior rather than motivation. They can be a useful data point, but they may not give you an accurate, definitive answer.

Self-typing
A key element in the Enneagram is the idea that you self-type. This means you decide which

Enneagram type you are. No one else can tell you. The Enneagram speaks to motivation, not behavior, and only you can say why you did what you did. The Enneagram is about your thoughts. It asks the question, where does your attention go?

What were you like when you were 25 years old?

Try to remember your behavior when you were in your mid 20s. As we mature, we start to modify our behavior based on our personal experience of what works and what doesn't. In our mid 20s, most of us don't yet have enough life experience to be heavily modifying our behavior, so in a sense, we're at our most "raw." This can make it easier to self-identify. If you are past your mid 20s, try to remember yourself at 25 years old and see which of the nine descriptions fits the best.

Are you most of the things most of the time?

Remember that to be an Enneagram type, you are most of the things most of the time. It is unlikely you will be 100% of the description 100% of the time. Each person continues to be a completely unique individual, and there may be specific traits of your Enneagram type that don't fit your particular personality. That's normal. Your type is when you are most of the things most of the time.

Mistyping

You may mistype yourself. If that happens, that's part of your journey. I once did a typing interview with a woman who for over 20 years thought she was a Leader (8). She strongly identified with the anger and controlling traits of the type, and this led her to assume she must be a Leader (8). And for 20 years, this worked for her. It helped her understand her behavior, manage her anger response, try to express softer emotions and so forth. But she was a Perfectionist (1). She asked for a typing interview because she was starting to have some doubts. When she learned her responses to the interview questions suggested she was closer to a Perfectionist (1), she visibly relaxed. I can usually tell when someone finds their type because a look of relief comes over them, and they physically relax. It wasn't a bad thing that she had misunderstood her type. She gained benefit in all those years of believing she was a Leader (8), and when she was ready to step into who she really was, she was able to identify herself correctly.

Blind spots

Consider asking for input from people who know you well. We all have blind spots. Blind spots are character traits we ourselves can't see. For example, as an Enthusiast (7), I can be unrealistically optimistic. But it is a blind spot for me because I truly feel my optimism is reality. I don't experience myself as optimistic. To me, I feel I'm being realistic. I need other people to point out to me that my thinking is too positive.

If you have narrowed your Enneagram type down to two or three options, you may want to ask people closest to you how they experience you. You can read the type description to people who know you well and ask which seems most aligned with your personality. I knew a Leader (8) who thought she was a Peacemaker (9). Despite the fact she would get into conflict on a regular basis, she felt she was conflict-avoidant, mellow and harmonious. It took other people explaining to her that they experienced her as angry and confrontational for her to understand she wasn't a Peacemaker (9). External feedback can be helpful and in some cases, crucial in correctly identifying yourself.

The following chapters address the next part of the conversation: within the 45 type combinations, what are the common strengths and weaknesses?

Type One
PERFECTIONIST/ REFORMER (1)
(seeks improvement and perfection/avoids leaving things as imperfect)

 ## Overview

Perfectionist (1)s are typically realistic, conscientious, loyal and principled. They strive to live up to their high ideals. This person sees the world in black and white, right and wrong, perfect and imperfect. It is difficult for them to leave anything in an imperfect state. They have a tendency to analyze, and sometimes overanalyze, things. They have high standards and often find themselves in charge of projects or initiatives because they have a sense that "it will only be done right if I do it." They feel a great deal of personal responsibility for things they are involved in. Critical of others, they are even more critical of themselves.

This is a person with a lot of unspoken beliefs about how others should behave. When fixated, they can be rigid in their thinking and judgmental in their approach.

In an intimate relationship, partners appreciate that their Perfectionist (1) is conscientious, efficient, responsible, loyal, detail-oriented, organized, pragmatic, honest, committed, hard-working with a strong work ethic and a person of high integrity. Partners often say that their Perfectionist (1) "pushes me to be a better person." This is usually a relationship in which work comes before play, and efficiency and a drive for perfection can be emphasized over the emotional world.

Partners report they are challenged by the fact that their Perfectionist (1) can be rigid, inflexible, critical, lost in the details, missing the big picture and unemotional or emotionally detached. In the drive to get all the details right, the big picture is often lost. In the quest to be efficient, the emotional side of life is often minimized.

• Attention Bias/Habit Of Attention:
Their attention goes to what needs improvement and what needs correction. The Perfectionist (1) mind is almost like an automatic correcting machine, seeing what needs to be fixed and making note of it. Their attention moves away from the current state as good enough.

• Emotional Style:
Contained, measured, sincere.

• Communication Style:
Precise, teaching, preaching, informing, facts and information focused, practical problem-solving over emotional fluency.

• Brings To The Relationship:
Organization, efficiency, attention to detail, thoroughness, reliability, desire to do good and be good, strong work ethic, idealism, a practical approach, loyalty, an ability to get things get done.

• Unique Strengths:
Problem-solving ability. These are the folks to bring in for practical solutions. Realistic and focused, Perfectionist (1)s plan carefully and stay committed and detail-oriented to achieve positive outcomes.

• Challenges:
Rigidity in thinking, intolerance of ambiguity or multiple "right" ways to do something, seeks a concrete solution and has a harder time letting things flow and unfold. Perfectionist (1)s have difficulty seeing the big picture and can get lost in the details. Feelings and the emotional world are often overlooked in a quest for efficiency and perfection.

• Stability And Security:
"I feel stable when I have order, structure and efficiency in my life. Being "right" makes me feel secure. When everything runs smoothly and goes exactly as planned, I feel wonderful."

• Instability And Insecurity:
"When order, structure, systems and efficiency break down I can feel confused and unstable. When I am "wrong" or do something improper, I feel insecure. I feel terrible when I make a factually incorrect statement."

• Path Of Growth:
Serenity
The path is from critical mind to curious mind and then to compassionate mind. Anger and irritation transform to compassion. Judgment, criticism, rigidity dissolve first to curiosity (allowing for multiple "truths" or alternate ways) and then to compassion (accepting multiple "truths" or right ways). The journey is to joyful tranquility.

• Energy:
Contained, solid, stoic, rigid, elegant.

• The Kundalini Yoga Connection:
Perfectionist (1)s have an excessively critical mind and can cut off from their heart connection. They forget that true wisdom is based in compassion. To be at their best, Perfectionist (1)s need to move from critical mind to compassionate mind. Energetically, this requires their nervous system to be strong enough so they can tolerate the idea of multiple truths. Kundalini Yoga kriyas and meditations that help burn off anger, open the heart and strengthen the nervous system are beneficial.

The Perfectionist (1) Subtypes

"Worry" Self-Preservation Subtype:
The self-preservation Perfectionist (1) turns their attention for improvement to themselves. To the outside world, this person is warm, kind, tolerant and decent. Internally, they are often very self-critical and filled with worry. This is a person who has a drive to control their environment, plan everything out and keep things under control. Extreme attention may be paid to detail in living spaces, food, cooking, practical household tasks, bill paying and so on. The attention goes to behaving well and correctly. They have the title "Worry" because of a constant drive, expressed through worry, to achieve perfection, to avert misfortune or disaster and to avoid blame.

The self-preservation Perfectionist (1) is the stereotypical perfectionist, striving to do everything right and being particularly hard on themselves when they miss the mark of their own high standards. In intimate relationships, partners usually don't feel as judged by a self-preservation Perfectionist (1) as the habit of attention is focused on the Perfectionist (1) themselves and not their partner.

Self-preservation Perfectionist (1)s are wired to believe love and support are not freely given. Instead, they must be earned by good behavior. This is a person for whom anger and worry go hand in hand. They may have an energetic warmth to them.

On the positive side, this is someone who tries hard to behave appropriately and to be a good, supportive partner. They admit their failings and can be forgiving of others when they get a sincere apology. They are reliable and loyal.

On the less positive side, this is someone who can be filled with worry, anxiety and repressed anger. They are highly sensitive to being blamed or criticized and can become rigid and unyielding.

"Non-Adaptability" Social Subtype:
The social Perfectionist (1) turns the attention for improvement to become a model of behavior for others. This is a person who strives to be extremely appropriate and correct and wants the group to emulate them. This person often expresses irritation that others don't act "as they should." To the outside world, this person can seem a bit detached, introverted or "above it all." Internally, they feel a lot of irritation and typically don't feel completely comfortable in the groups they frequent. They have the title "Non-Adaptability" because of their predisposition to believe there is one right way to do things, and they know that way. This is a type that often tires themselves out in their quest to be a model for others.

Less than a stereotypical perfectionist, this person strives to be correct. They want to act correctly, speak correctly, think correctly and so forth. In intimate relationships, the social Perfectionist (1) expresses a deep need to be right and may have a school teacher type of mentality. They may have an energetic coolness to them.

On the positive side, this is someone who naturally gravitates to the role of teacher and who truly tries to be a good example for other people. They can be fair, inspiring, wise and discerning. They practice what they preach and have a sense that modeling and demonstrating is just as important as their spoken word.

On the less positive side, partners may experience very rigid thinking and observe that their

Perfectionist (1) partners can't easily take in new information. In extreme rigidity, the mind closes completely and is unable to accept and absorb new information. It is important to understand the root of this inability is a concern that new information could shake the entire foundation of the belief system shattering the stability of correctness. New information can feel threatening. This can also be someone who comes across as superior and a "know-it-all" often without realizing it. It is very important for them to be right.

"Zeal" Intimate Subtype:

The intimate Perfectionist (1) turns the attention for improvement towards their intimate relationships and partner. This is a person who has an intensity and drive to correct which is more exaggerated than in the other two subtypes. To the outside world, this type looks more like a reformer than a perfectionist. Internally, this person feels more direct anger than the other Perfectionist (1)s and is driven to action with a sense of urgency. They have the title "Zeal" because of this intense drive to correct. This is a special intensity of desire that can have a flavor of righteousness to it. This person may feel they must have their desire for correction met immediately.

In intimate relationships, this zeal is directed at their partner. This is the type most likely to be directly frustrated by their partner's "imperfections," and the intimate subtype Perfectionist (1) expresses more intense anger and frustration directly towards their partner's behavior. This zeal can extend to anyone in the Perfectionist (1)'s intimate circle. This person may have an energetic heat to them.

On the positive side, this is someone who legitimately wants to help their partner make genuine and helpful improvements. The intimate Perfectionist (1) doesn't question themselves too much, and their energy goes into making others into what they feel they should be.

On the less positive side, the intimate Perfectionist (1) can be hypocritical, demanding improvements in others but not holding themselves to the same standards. There is an emotional intensity in this Perfectionist (1), and situations and behavior can quickly escalate to the pitch of "This must stop now!"

Perfectionist (1)—Levels of Awareness

Perfectionist (1) When Self-Aware

Perfectionist (1)s become wise, discerning, accepting and compassionate. They exude joyful tranquility and acceptance. Realistic, humane and inspiring, they exercise good judgment knowing when to take action and when to let things be as they are. They have a strong desire to be rational, reasonable, mature and moderate. Extremes are avoided although a strong sense of right and wrong remains. They become accepting, though maybe not agreeing, of other perspectives and views. Perfectionist (1)s at this level of awareness are intensely principled with a focused aspiration to be fair and objective. Their primary values are truth and justice. They have a deep sense of personal responsibility and a sense of answering to a higher authority. Personal integrity, diligence and determination are observable.

Perfectionist (1) With Tightening Defenses

Demanding and disapproving of both their self and others, the Perfectionist (1) becomes more judgmental, harsh and rigid. Their thinking becomes narrow as they believe they alone know the right way things should be done. Reality feels imperfect and disappointing. The drive to improve can be directed at causes, people or their own environment. Fear starts to present itself as the Perfectionist (1) becomes deeply afraid of making a mistake or acting improperly. They become orderly and well-organized in the extreme and can seem emotionally contained, rigid, serious, detached and at times robotic. Workaholism may be a factor as the Perfectionist (1) feels a heightened sense of responsibility for everything in their environment. They have an opinion and a critique about everything. Impatience and dissatisfaction set in at this level along with scolding, reprimanding, correcting, blaming and chastising. Anger may start to present itself.

Perfectionist (1) When Fixated

The Perfectionist (1) becomes self-righteous, rigid, closed-minded and dogmatic. Black and white thinking dominates with little or no room for compassion. A strong sense of moral superiority and righteousness begins to prevail along with harsh judgments and rigid self justifications. There is little to no flexibility in their thinking. The Perfectionist (1) becomes obsessive about perfection and completely intolerant of any perceived wrongdoings of others. Uncompromising, adamant, severe, and fixed in their positions, the Perfectionist (1) may start to isolate and alienate themselves from others. They start to have a reality distortion, projecting wrongdoing into benign situations. The Perfectionist (1) becomes cruel and punishing towards others. They won't tolerate any behavior that doesn't conform to their standards and can be unapologetically harsh in their judgments. Depression and nervous breakdowns are possibilities.

Keys If You Are In A Relationship With A Perfectionist (1)

The relationship keys are a result of the 360 degree review - partnership with a Perfectionist (1) from the perspective of each the nine types. The keys are a summary of some common themes.

"I have a relentless drive for perfection that tires even me out. Help me find non-personal ways to talk about it."

John, Perfectionist (1) married in an 18-year relationship with Anne, Leader (8)

"As someone who is wired to seek perfection, it is difficult to overstate how overwhelming my inner drive to perform and to achieve perfection - or at least improvement - can be. I don't think that anyone who doesn't share this wiring can fully grasp the pressure that puts me under. It's totally pathological and can be exhausting!

What has helped over our 18-year relationship is that my wife and I have a framework and vocabulary for discussing our negative traits that make it less personal. We both get a daily email "Enneathoughts" from the Enneagram Institute, and we often share these with each other, asking questions such as "Do I really look like that?" "Do I really do that?" "Is that how other people might see me?" ...or sometimes "Oh dear... that really is what I do, isn't it?" This openness that we have created becomes a safe space for us to point out when we start moving towards the negative side of our habit of attention.

When I'm getting rigid, my family has learned to use humor to point it out without causing me to feel humiliation or failure. For example, several years ago my children were breaking one of my "rules," and I told them "I'm getting really cross!" My daughter, about 10 years old at the time, totally defused the situation by her unexpected response, saying, "Oh you are, are you!?" with a huge smirk on her face! This worked like a charm."

Clark, Perfectionist (1)

"When I get home from a trip, it is unimaginable to me that I would just hang out or go to bed without getting the house in order for the next day. I want to unpack my things, start the laundry, change the bed sheets, check my schedule and so forth. Having things in their place relaxes me, and I feel anxious - or at least uncomfortable - when my living area is disorganized. It is like a part of my brain isn't available to me until I know everything is in its right place..."

The Perfectionist (1) mind seeks structure, organization and efficiency. Many Perfectionist (1)s will say they can't sleep if there are dirty dishes in the kitchen sink and that they can't think straight when the house is a mess. This is because of the way their brain is wired. Until "things are in order" the Perfectionist (1) mind doesn't have the mental bandwidth to give other issues mindshare. This drive is directed to different areas for different Perfectionist (1)s.

Some people don't care about a messy house but need the checkbook balanced before they can relax. Whatever the manifestation is, until their drive for order is satisfied, they may feel distracted and anxious.

If you are a Perfectionist (1):

Understand you have this tendency and don't get angry with yourself about it. Work to strengthen your nervous system (see Kundalini Yoga kriyas and meditations for Perfectionist (1)s) so that the drive for order, improvement and correction feels a little less intense. And understand that not everyone has the same attention to order that you have. Your partner may not even notice the dirty dishes in the sink.

If you are with a Perfectionist (1):

Don't take their drive for order personally! Your partner isn't trying to ignore you or prioritize cleaning over you. Your Perfectionist (1) feels like they can't relax and really focus on you until a structured environment is in place.

"If you ask feedback, I will give you criticism. I assume that is what you are asking for."

Marta, Enthusiast (7) married in a 12-year relationship with Dietrich, Perfectionist (1)

"My husband wants perfection in everything, and this can be challenging. For example, a few weeks ago I went to him with a presentation I had created for work. I knew it was good and was really just looking for confirmation and maybe a bit of praise. But instead of positive feedback, he found a few things I had missed and a couple of areas that could be improved. This can be frustrating..."

Daphne, Leader (8) married in a 12-year relationship with Antonio, Perfectionist (1)

"In our relationship, differences in communication style have been challenging. When we were first married, he would get so angry if I didn't do the laundry or the dishes - which is just weird to me! And while it is very helpful to have a partner who can give me constructive feedback on something 95% of the time, sometimes I just want reassurance or praise. I've learned his criticism isn't personal. It is just the way his brain works. He is also more interested in being socially appropriate than I am. I make inappropriate jokes, and I react if I hear something offensive. I'm not interested in putting on a show of propriety in public, and this sometimes embarrasses my husband."

When you ask for feedback from your Perfectionist (1), prepare for criticism. If you are actually looking for affirmation or reassurance, make that 100% clear to your Perfectionist (1) partner. Asking for open-ended feedback will invite criticism or recommendations for improvement. Why? Because their attention goes to the fine details you missed, and they feel compelled to point these out to you. These fine details are actually very big in their mind. You may get this critical input without asking.

If you are a Perfectionist (1):
Before you give feedback to your partner, pause and ask them directly if they want to hear constructive criticism or just praise. Try to balance your constructive criticism with positive feedback. Your partner will be more receptive to your suggestions for improvement if you also include some positive comments.

If you are with a Perfectionist (1):
Be careful when you ask for feedback. The Perfectionist (1) tendency is to focus on the 5% you didn't get right, not the 95% that you did. Make sure you really want constructive criticism before asking for feedback. If you only want praise, ask for praise, not feedback.

 "Being "right" makes me feel stable and secure"

Stelios, Investigator (5) in 2-year relationship with Marie, Perfectionist (1)

"My girlfriend doesn't let things go, no matter how insignificant they are. I imagine it is just part of her black-and-white thinking, but it is amazing how she will beat a topic to death. I like to argue things too, but she takes it to a whole new level. We might have a friendly debate about something, and she'll follow it up with an email with scientific support the next day. It is imperative for her to be right. It doesn't necessarily have a negative impact on our relationship, but it is a big difference in communication styles."

Georgina, Peacemaker (9) married in a 18-year relationship with Henry, Perfectionist (1)

"While I love my husband's integrity, the rigid side of his beliefs can by trying, and sometimes I have to ignore his beliefs entirely to maintain harmony. Our denomination is officially "Open and Affirming" meaning that we totally accept people as they are, regardless of anything, including sexual orientation. My husband doesn't agree with this. He feels so strongly that he told me that if I were to become a pastor at an "Open and Affirming" church, that he would refuse to become a member or attend there. I found this unacceptable. It hurts me

so much that I have had to tune it out completely. Our young adult son once overheard us arguing about homosexuality and the Bible and became so angry at his father that it was incredibly stressful for me. I feel all the time like I have to be the mediator between the two of them."

You may at times feel like your partner would rather be right than happy. This isn't the full picture – your partner feels stable when they are right. When it seems like they may be wrong, your Perfectionist (1) feels unstable and insecure.

If you are a Perfectionist (1):
Understand that you have a drive to be "right" that can be astonishing to other people. Reflect on why it is so important to you. Would you rather be right or happy? Why?

Understand that you feel unstable if you aren't firmly entrenched in your "right" corner, but that others don't experience this and in fact, might experience you as rigid and closed-minded. Try to open the door to more flexible thinking and the idea that multiple "rights" can exist.

If you are with a Perfectionist (1):
Try to have compassion that your partner's drive to be "right" isn't about what it seems. It is about feeling stable and secure. Adding humor can help to lighten the heaviness that comes with this drive to prove you wrong.

"My focus on efficiency takes my focus off the emotional world. I am not trying to be insensitive. I just don't have mental space for the emotional world until my drive for perfection and efficiency is met."

Charles, Helper (2) married in a 6-year relationship with Eden, Perfectionist (1)

"The focus on efficiency and optimization has often meant that my feelings and the feelings of others are not understood and in fact not even on the radar... For example, my wife's mother, who lives in a different country, had a major health issue come on very quickly. My wife was focused on whether her mother would be able to make an upcoming trip to visit us. It was as though she completely forgot her mother's actual physical well-being and her emotional state until I reminded her. When I did remind her, it was like it all clicked, and my wife got on the next flight to go be with her mother. It isn't that she doesn't care - she loves her mother deeply - it is just that her attention goes to efficiency and getting the details right."

TYPE ONE **THE REFORMER/PERFECTIONIST**

Marta, Enthusiast (7) married in a 12-year relationship with Dietrich, Perfectionist (1)

"My husband can forget the big picture when he is really focused on his detailed goals. For our wedding, there was a tremendous amount of preparation involved, but the night before the big day, I sat down with my mom and sisters to enjoy the evening with a glass of wine. My husband became very agitated that I would take time out when we still had so much to do – but for me, the point was to be happy, not necessarily get every detail right."

Your partner's drive for efficiency and correctness doesn't always leave a lot of space for the world of emotion, especially during times of stress. Recognize that this is an area your Perfectionist (1) may just miss and that you will need to remind them of the value of the emotional world and that emotional needs must be taken into decision-making. While obvious to many, this isn't always in the field of vision of a Perfectionist (1), so they frequently need to be refocused.

If you are a Perfectionist (1):
In times of stress, try to pause, step back and ask for feedback. While your mind is wired for the details, there might be a larger picture you are missing. As this is a blind spot of yours, you will need feedback from others to see it.

If you are with a Perfectionist (1):
In times of stress, help your Perfectionist (1) see the bigger picture. While the Perfectionist (1)'s way of feeling stable is to get the details right, this doesn't mean the world of emotion should be ignored. Help your partner refocus so they can see the bigger picture.

360 DEGREE REVIEW

The next section features the 360 degree review--partnership with an Perfectionist (1) from the perspective of each of the nine types.

1:1 Perfectionist (1) with Perfectionist (1)

Gail, Perfectionist (1) in a relationship for less than one year with Joshua, Perfectionist (1)

"Joshua is honest, thoughtful, kind, generous to a fault and has integrity in all he does.

Treating each other with fairness, honesty and kindness has been at the foundation of our relationship and from that base, we are able to work out any issues. We easily and naturally understand each other's quirkiness, especially around everyday things like food, cleaning and work. We don't demand each other be different because we see our own quirky habits and ways.

We are generally objective and fair with each other, until something triggers us to cross the line into judgment. For example there was a situation recently where Joshua thought my position on a topic was immoral, and he simply couldn't reconcile with it. It still bothers him, and we've agreed not to speak about that topic.

Joshua's overwhelming sense of responsibility puts a lot of pressure on him. In the beginning of our relationship, he was striving so hard for everything to be perfect for me, and it created an unsustainable amount of discontent for him. Now we communicate much better and are both more aware of being responsible for ourselves, as well as the other...

As it relates to issues, it is easy for me to see imperfection, and I can be condescending and sarcastic. This happened once in our relationship, and I felt horrible afterwards. I will try very hard to make sure this doesn't happen again.

We also can bottle our anger, letting it build into resentment until it comes out sideways. Since we both understood this as a potential issue, we regularly check in with each other to make sure we're ok and to air our grievances immediately before they have a chance to fester and grow.

Our biggest relationship challenge is the tendency to put work and practical responsibilities before fun and play. We work extremely hard all week and end up drained with little energy for socializing. We use our limited time off together to rest and recover for the next brutal week of work. Putting work before play is automatic for both of us. Unfortunately, this pattern is too familiar to me. In my previous marriage, we both worked 70-hour weeks. In 20 years together, we took maybe 4 weeks of vacation. It nearly killed me. Now I see this in Joshua... He's younger so he can handle it physically, but he has a huge lack of work/life balance. He feels hyper-responsible for everything at work and self-sacrifices to reach as close to a level of perfection as possible. The result is we don't have any time to play together. We only have time to recover. This is hard for me. I'm hoping we can find a way to bring that important rest and downtime into our lives. I learned that lesson the hard way.

Work aside, I'm so incredibly grateful for this amazing man in my life. I adore him. He understands me, loves me, sees my struggles and successes and is right there with me. Our similar traits make it easy to get along and have compassion and kindness for each other. It's hard to have such high standards all the time. It can be painful. Thankfully we can help each other see this, and sometimes it takes pressure off. And as a bonus, he is a most excellent, skilled lover. As with all things he does, he approaches sexuality with attention to detail, aiming for perfection. This makes for a very exciting and satisfying sex life."

Joshua, Perfectionist (1) in a relationship for less than one year with Gail, Perfectionist (1)

"I value everything about my girlfriend because she's perfect for me. I appreciate her discipline and that she is so conscientious about the way she lives and takes care of herself. She is an inspiration to me and being with her is helping me to become more disciplined.

Early in our relationship, my biggest challenge was feeling that I didn't measure up to her standards. As time has passed, with love and understanding from her and with self-improvement of my own, this has become less of a concern.

A personal challenge is that I often feel a great deal of responsibility for things I care about, and this is even more so in my intimate relationship. I want to make sure I treat her with integrity and love constantly. I'm trying to find a better balance between my responsibilities and our relationship. This is my challenge."

1:1: The Theory

1:1 When In Balance

Two Perfectionist (1)s share the traits of integrity, honesty, efficiency and reliability. They inherently understand and agree about the importance of hard work, responsibility and honoring social contracts. Both value a strong work ethic and strive to live "correctly." Work comes before play, and work is taken very seriously. Both partners are pragmatic, rational and gifted problem solvers. This couple may be sought after in their various social and professional circles for their organizational ability and practical solutions.

Fairness, honesty, objectivity and acting responsibly are foundational elements in this pair. This couple gives each other a lot of latitude for personal quirks around cleanliness, organization and so forth since they generally recognize these tendencies in themselves. Both look to each other for inspiration on how to become a better person. They also seek to be that inspiration for their partner. Both partners strive to be reasonable, respectful and appreciative of each other. There can be a serious flavor in this dynamic as work and other practical responsibilities may dominate the lives of both partners.

As Perfectionist (1)s tend to bottle their anger, finding non-threatening ways to express the full range of emotion is important. Unexpressed anger can present itself as sarcasm, biting comments and indirect attacks. Successful Perfectionist (1) couples talk about using regular check-ins with each other and other forums in which they can discuss their grievances before negative energy builds.

When in balance, this is a highly supportive, understanding and loving couple.

1:1 The Downward Spiral

As a couple, learning to prioritize restorative rest, deep relaxation and play can be a challenge. When too much tension builds, defenses tighten, and themes of judgment, inflexibility and isolation enter the picture. Rigid thinking, harsh interpretations and a sense of righteousness can trigger the downward spiral.

This rigid thinking and judgmental attention can go in several directions. In some dynamics, one partner will become harsh and judgmental towards the other, creating a toxic environment void of support and acceptance. In other instances, the couple may align around shared values but narrow their thinking to exclude anyone who doesn't strictly adhere with their code, creating an environment of isolation and superiority. Both environments are typically void of true compassion, and the ability to speak from the heart is lost. With an unsupportive environment and a lost heart connection, the relationship may collapse.

1:1 The Lighthouse

Because the Perfectionist (1) type structure can become so rigid, maintaining a strong heart connection, both to self and others, is vital. In an unhealthy state of awareness, the attention becomes completely focused on improvement and criticism of others allowing no space for compassion. In addition, the ability to engage in deep, healing relaxation is important. Perfectionist (1)s push themselves hard, are self-critical and struggle to relax completely. Learning healthy, sustainable ways to quiet the mind and relax the body can be helpful in allowing the full flow of emotion and of healing energy.

1:1 The Kundalini Yoga Connection

Perfectionist (1)s must make the journey from critical mind to curious mind and then to compassionate mind. Their path is to joyful tranquility. Ideally, a Perfectionist (1) can relax the urge to correct and improve and instead enjoy things as they are.

Kundalini Yoga kriyas and meditations that emphasize relaxation, anger release and connection to the heart center can help create space for compassion and creativity. Relaxing their external and physical rigidity helps Perfectionist (1)s relax their internal rigidity as well. Nervous system work is useful to make the path to change less daunting and to help relax the habit of attention.

See the appendix for Perfectionist (1) recommended Kundalini Yoga kriyas and meditations.

1:2 Perfectionist (1) with Helper (2)

Charles, Helper (2) married in a 6-year relationship with Eden, Perfectionist (1)

THE NINE KEYS

"I value Eden's high ideals, solid values and that she has a strong, unwavering internal compass. I love the way she treats her parents and friends. She will drop everything and fly across the world to be with a sick parent. She will focus the full force of her energy to achieve an outcome that benefits someone she loves. She is very affectionate with me and makes it clear I am number one in her life.

She thinks very differently than I do and gives me a fresh perspective. I can give a hundred examples - ranging from world politics to how to deal with a wayward friend - in which she presents a critical point of view that I may never have considered. This helps me to clarify, modify and evolve my own point of view. Her ability to see a range of possible outcomes, the potential problems inherent in a decision or path, and the 'optimal' direction or choice is a huge help to me.

I admire her smart sense of humor, playfulness and ability to laugh at even the most serious or difficult situations. The recent death of her mother was a terrible loss, but throughout such a difficult period, Eden's ability to see the humorous aspects of the ordeal meant that the darkest moments were tempered with laughter.

In our dynamic, my wife reminds me of my inherent integrity, conscientiousness, responsibility and consistency. She is like my 'inner coach', and pushes me in areas where I am prone to laziness. It isn't that I don't know that I possess those qualities myself - but Eden keeps me true to my higher purpose.

She has at times seemed obsessive-compulsive, with all-consuming attention to what seems like a minor point, but in fact represents some huge principle for her. For example, the one time out of a thousand that I will accept a store owner not giving me a receipt, meaning the transaction goes unreported and untaxed, to her represents my participation in corruption and everything that is wrong in the world.

In our dynamic, we are in a constant push-pull between the balance of her efficient nature and my generous nature. I can be a people pleaser and want to make everyone happy. Eden reminds me to value my own time, to set boundaries and to say no. I might lend money to my cousin without a lot of thought, but my wife reminds me to think through if my cousin can pay me back, if this loan will really solve his problem and so forth. This is a constant push-pull renegotiation. She prioritizes efficiency and concrete outcomes while I prioritize enjoyment and human connection. Should we spend money on a nice dinner, or save the expense?

We work hard to find balance. My instinct for being generous with time or money is certainly not comfortable for her, and I must constantly justify my case in order to avoid conflict. As much as I value the input and support in trying to save money or help me be a 'better me', I often wish she could see more easily that feeling better is sometimes a more important outcome than being better. Efficiency and optimization are not enough on their own to ensure a happy relationship and a happy life. Work may come before play, but play is equally important and often more so.

Overall, I am very happy in my relationship. I trust in the fundamental character of my wife and in our ability to work through our differences. She brings playfulness, companionship, joy, wisdom, a fresh perspective and commitment to my life. I feel that as the years have passed, we move towards each other more and more, and I enjoy sharing our differences as gifts."

1:2 The Theory

1:2 When In Balance

The Perfectionist (1) and Helper (2) can be a very balancing and symbiotic match combining the cool, rational thought and problem-solving abilities of the Perfectionist (1) with emotional warmth, empathy, helpfulness and genuine concern for others of the Helper (2). Both partners tend to direct their attention outwards, either towards improving the world or their environment or in offering help or assistance to others. With this outward focus, there can be a flavor of independence and autonomy in this dynamic. This can be a powerful, effective couple who can make a meaningful and lasting mark on their environment and the people in their social circles.

This pair shares a respect of one another's core values. They feel intrigue and interest around their differences and have shared vision of a harmonious future. Because they come at situations from very different perspectives, they can teach each other a lot. Perfectionist (1)s model logic, long-range thinking, rational thought and practical solutions. They show the Helper (2) how to set healthy boundaries and help disassociate from the emotional charge that often clouds the thinking of their Helper (2). They can offer sage advice, an alternative perspective and objectivity to their Helper (2). The Helper (2) brings warmth and a human touch to the often precise, mechanical thinking of their Perfectionist (1). They help show value of human relationships, emotions and interdependence. Together, this couple combines compassion with discernment and cool logic with warm concern. When their values are aligned, and they are respectful of their differences, this couple uses their opposite habits of attention as a strength.

1:2 The Downward Spiral
The habit of attention of the Perfectionist (1) and the Helper (2) point in very different directions and if the two partners aren't able to find balance that respects these differences, the downward spiral can begin. In a stressed or fixated state, the Perfectionist (1) becomes frustrated with the weak boundary setting of their Helper (2), and the Helper (2) becomes disappointed with disregard of the emotional world by the Perfectionist (1).

Perfectionist (1)s value efficiency and planning, rarely wanting to deviate from the predetermined course of action. The emotional world is minimized in exchange for mechanical, rational thinking. This thinking differs sharply with the Helper (2) who often values the satisfaction of others above their own. The feelings of other people factor largely into the Helper (2)'s thoughts and decision-making. They may be inclined to sacrifice their own happiness, or by extension the happiness of the partnership, to meet the needs of others. This triggers the Perfectionist (1) who feels this is unjust, unfair and wrong.

Both types may not be able to express their needs very clearly or directly, focusing on the difference in values instead of their own unmet needs. Instead of "I want more of your time" the Perfectionist (1) may say "I can't believe you once again answered your boss's email at midnight!" They may feel the Helper (2) is generous with their time and attention with everyone but the Perfectionist (1). And the Helper (2) may start to see the Perfectionist (1) as cold and uncompassionate. Instead of saying "I want you to speak from your heart and think of what it's like for that person" the Helper (2) may say "I don't care if we didn't agree to spend it, we're donating to that charity!"

If the downward spiral gains momentum, each person gets more frustrated with their partner. The Perfectionist (1) gets irritated and angry at the Helper (2)'s people-pleasing behavior. The Helper (2) gets fed up with the Perfectionist (1)'s criticism and rigid thinking. Arguments escalate, and anger intensifies. Both become disillusioned with the other. This continues until respect for one another is lost, and the relationship itself is threatened.

1:2 The Lighthouse
Different values around efficiency and human connection are the basis for discord in this relationship. Tolerance of these differences is the path back to connection. Perfectionist (1)s need to honor that their Helper (2) has a different sense of personal boundaries and a different priority around the emotional world. Helper (2)s need to honor their Perfectionist

TYPE ONE THE REFORMER/PERFECTIONIST

(1)'s drive for efficiency. These differences need to become balancing and not polarizing.

 1:2 The Kundalini Yoga Connection
The path back to balance for this couple is an awareness and respect of their differences around efficiency and the emotional world. To come forward and accommodate these differences, both types need to strengthen their nervous systems.

Helper (2)s need to get in touch with their own needs and place a priority on self-care. Energetically, Helper (2)s are usually out of touch with their bodies and physical, emotional and energetic needs. Kundalini Yoga kriyas and meditations that increase body awareness and that build energy are helpful for Helper (2)s.

Perfectionist (1)s need to open their heart and connect with the emotional world, both their own emotions and the emotions of others. Kundalini Yoga kriyas and meditations with heart opening and energy awareness exercises are helpful for Perfectionist (1)s.

See the appendix for Perfectionist (1) and Helper (2) recommended Kundalini Yoga kriyas and meditations.

1:3: Perfectionist (1) with Achiever(3)

Rory, Achiever (3), formerly in a 17-year relationship with Cindy, Perfectionist (1)

"Cindy was very competent and disciplined with a strong work ethic. She always tried to do her best, and I appreciated her hard work and high standards.

We were an extremely effective team. For example, I helped her run a major conference that garnered her significant professional esteem and praise. Without my energy, she would never have undertaken the project. In return, she helped me to become more professional in my job by critically analyzing my output and bringing it to a much higher standard. We successfully built a house together and raised two caring and compassionate boys.

While we were an effective couple in terms of practical matters, we were less successful on the emotional front. We rarely celebrated the results of our hard work and our successes, and if we did, it was emotionally dry. Our work efforts made us tired and exhausted, and when children were introduced, the expectations became too great. My wife had more internal guilt and felt even more external expectations. It was just too much to keep up with, like a pressure cooker.

My big challenge in the relationship was in trying to build an emotional connection with Cindy and dealing with her feelings of guilt, judgment and control. She was driven to have perfection in everything, and her desire to control eventually smothered everything else. I wish she had understood that compassion and forgiveness allow for imperfection. Love just is."

Marietta, Achiever (3) married in a 28-year relationship with Peter, Perfectionist (1)

"I love my husband's dedication and sense of responsibility. He is an extremely committed physician, working countless hours to make sure his patients receive quality care and the best treatment protocols. Peter is organized, systematized and efficient in his ability to optimize his schedule and performance. At the same time, he is very patient and open-hearted, especially with animals and children. It is sweet to watch a natural sense of serenity wash over him when he's around our dogs or when he's interacting with kids. With me he's very thoughtful, from starting the coffee pot in the morning before I get up to making sure I'm protected when bikes fly by us on our walking trail.

As a couple, we have always made a great team, and we get stuff done! We have similar values around respect, responsibility, follow-through and integrity. We maintain a clean, comfortable, organized home. When we are focused on a goal, we can get just about anything done including selling our home and most of our belongings, moving across the country and starting a new life in a new place within a couple of months. We both like to keep active with exercise, hiking, walking our dogs, doing tasks, cooking, errands, traveling, exploring new places and seeing movies. Scheduling vacations has always been a priority for us because we work hard all year round.

As it relates to issues in our relationship, one of my biggest pet peeves is the constant reminder of how things could be made better. This focus on improvement ranges from recipes and meals to opening a jar to how to walk the dog correctly. Very few things are ever good enough, something can always be made or done better...

At times my husband's need for routine and structure is extreme. Running out the door to do an errand requires two hours of preparation to make sure he is well groomed, and things are set before we leave. Spontaneity is almost out of the question. This can be frustrating.

Our communication styles can present challenges. My husband has an intense need to be right so while it is important to him that he finish his thought and not be interrupted, he's the first to interrupt me and shut me down when we are debating something heated. And he will emotionally withdraw and refuse to discuss things further at times.

We both had a watershed moment earlier this year. We were becoming emotionally distant and frustrated, not really enjoying each other's company. We realized at the root of our discontent was that neither of us felt accepted for who we are – we both can be critical of each other, knowing ways each of us could improve and can easily become detached and condemning. We promised to be nicer to each other, to be more open and accepting of each other's struggles, and this has brought us closer together.

We've learned over the years that it is critical for us connect at a heart level on a regular basis. For both of us, it's so easy to detach and go into "do" mode. Relaxing, enjoying each other's sheer presence and essence of being is essential for our healthy relationship. We've found establishing a gratitude practice, showing appreciation for all the little things each day can move mountains and reestablish heartfelt connection."

1:3 The Theory

1:3 When In Balance

The Perfectionist (1) and Achiever (3) can be an effective, efficient, goal-oriented team. Both are disciplined and hard-working, and this couple shares a focus on the achievement of tangible, practical goals. Both can be seen by the outside world as classic overachievers, and both can be highly accomplished.

In their relationship, they offer compensating traits. The Achiever (3) boosts the confidence of their Perfectionist (1), encouraging them to become more adaptable, consider different approaches, stretch for their potential and share their talents more widely. Achiever (3)s can be motivating and inspiring, and they want to bring out the best in their partner. This dovetails nicely with the Perfectionist (1)'s drive for self-improvement. It is as though the Perfectionist (1) has their own personal coach in their Achiever (3).

In return, the Perfectionist (1) improves the quality of their Achiever (3)'s output, focusing less on image and appearances and more on depth, substance and the finer details. The Perfectionist (1) shows the Achiever (3) how to slow down and do things intentionally and purposefully. The Perfectionist (1) resists cutting corners and insists the integrity and true quality of the work be high. They are also good at demonstrating authenticity and can help their Achiever (3) move away from people-pleasing behavior.

The foundation of this pair is mutual respect, admiration and shared goals and values. This couple is highly supportive of each other as it relates to concrete topics in the material world. Each understands the workaholic tendency of the other. Because the focus of attention tends to be outward and practical, relating more as "doing" rather than "being," cultivating a sustainable, intimate, emotional connection is key to the true success of this partnership. Sharing time together in stillness and appreciating each other's essence helps develop this connection. When this pair has a strong emotional connection, their differences can serve as assets rather than triggers. When balanced, this can be an almost unstoppable team who effectively and efficiently overcomes all obstacles to reach their shared goals.

1:3 The Downward Spiral
In an unaware state, the distinctly different habits of attention of these two types can lead to the beginning of the downward spiral. This couple may also lock horns around issues of not feeling heard or seen by each other, feeling unappreciated and ultimately feeling disrespected. As respect is a foundational element of this couple, feeling disrespected can create fissures in their foundation.

The Perfectionist (1) mind seeks integrity and improvement. When fixated, the defenses tighten, and the Perfectionist (1) mind becomes rigid, harsh and judgmental. They may direct this rigidity at their Achiever (3) partner, judging them too competitive, too achievement-oriented and too concerned about the opinion of others.

The Achiever (3)'s mind seeks achievement and success. When fixated, the defenses tighten the mind to become even more focused on achievement and external validation. They may start to see their Perfectionist (1) as too rigid, too judgmental and too lost in the details. Frustration builds, and respect erodes. Achiever (3)s are triggered by any character attack and building criticism from their Perfectionist (1) may cause them to shut down and withdraw.

Both types are practical so an eroding relationship may appear intact to the outside world. However, whether the split is internal or external, the emotional connection is lost.

1:3 The Lighthouse
Because both of these types are goal-oriented and serious in their pursuit of achievement, taking time to reconnect at a heart level is extremely important for this relationship. Both people need to slow down and spend time connecting with their emotional world, to experience "being" instead of "doing." This can be a challenge for both Perfectionist (1)s and Achiever (3)s.

TYPE ONE THE REFORMER/PERFECTIONIST

 1:3 The Kundalini Yoga Connection

Both Perfectionist (1)s and Achiever (3)s struggle with stillness so cultivating the ability to relax, unwind and just "be" is important. For both partners, Kundalini Yoga kriyas and meditations that incorporate breathwork can be very beneficial in cultivating stillness. Since these are types who prefer to be in motion, breathwalk (walking meditations) can be a great way to incorporate meditation into daily life. This is also a practice they can do together.

Perfectionist (1)s are often blocked from their heart center so Kundalini Yoga kriyas and meditations to open their heart, connect with the energy of emotion and burn out inner anger are helpful.

Achiever (3)s are often cut off from their heart with their extreme focus on achievement so Kundalini Yoga kriyas and meditations to develop self-love, self-acceptance and an open heart are beneficial.

See the appendix for Perfectionist (1) and Achiever (3) recommended Kundalini Yoga kriyas and meditations.

1:4 Perfectionist (1) with Individualist (4)

Antony, Individualist (4) married in a 15-year relationship with Margaret, Perfectionist (1)

"I love Margaret's pureness, idealism and her drive to do the right thing. Integrity is innate in her nature, and I never have to question it. I value Margaret's practical, solution-based approach to life. While I spend a lot of time thinking about things I will probably never actually do, she is the opposite and tends to stay constantly on the go with house cleaning, bill paying, organizing travel and schedules and meeting daily goals. Although it must be tiring for her to be constantly occupied with daily minutiae, it means I don't have to think about the practical, mundane tasks because she's taking care of all of those things.

Our differences can come out in how we want to spend our time. We'll come home from a weekend holiday, and my wife immediately starts to organize the house, review the bills and prepare for the upcoming week. I'd rather sit around, relax and process the whole weekend experience, but she is on the go and keeps the practical things moving forward. I know she won't be able to sleep until the house is in order and the next day is planned. Getting her to relax is hard and getting her to go with the flow is nearly impossible. I think in her mind, the flow is something she has to create.

A challenge in our relationship is that I like to talk about my feelings quite a bit, and Margaret doesn't necessarily speak the language of emotion as fluently. We've been together 15 years, and it has improved tremendously, but even now, I feel like there are parts of my life that go unshared with her. She tries to listen to me, but she is so focused on solutions and efficiency, she has difficulty holding the emotional space for me. This isn't for lack of honest effort. It is more like an underdeveloped muscle."

1:4 The Theory

1:4 When In Balance

The Perfectionist (1) and the Individualist (4) bring many complementary personality traits to the relationship and when self-aware, they balance each other's blind spots and appreciate each other's strengths.

The foundation of this pair is shared core values layered with very different operating styles. Perfectionist (1)s offer efficiency, order, logic, purpose and rational thinking. They can provide a stable, organized environment for the Individualist (4) and model self-discipline, follow-through, emotional containment and self-sacrifice for the greater good. They can help the Individualist (4) get out of their fantasy world and ground them back down to the material world. Perfectionist (1)s are action-oriented, and their structured, disciplined approach to life can be balancing for the Individualist (4).

Individualist (4)s offer emotional awareness, sensitivity, creativity and a more intuitive approach to life. They have high emotional fluency and can help their Perfectionist (1) partner access a wider range of emotions. Individualist (4)s can see the deeper subtext of situations and offer wise counsel to their Perfectionist (1), who tends to be more literal in their interpretation of events. They also help the Perfectionist (1) to slow down and not feel guilty just "being." This can be healing and helpful for the Perfectionist (1) who naturally feels driven to stay on the go accomplishing their various tasks.

Together this couple combines intuition and rational thought, efficiency and sensitivity, strategic focus and attention to detail. When approaching life together, they successfully blend intuitive and practical operating styles.

1:4 The Downward Spiral

Like a logician and an empath, these two types see the world from very different vantage points and have very different emotional responses to situations. When fixated, their balancing traits can become trigger points, and intolerance, disappointment and frustration build. This can set the downward spiral into motion.

Both handle their emotions and their emotional reactions differently. Individualist (4)s seek to allow themselves to feel the full spectrum of feelings, and this requires them to have time to process and absorb their experiences. Perfectionist (1)s are driven by efficiency and don't want or require as much time to "feel." If these differences aren't understood and accepted, problems arise. To the Individualist (4), the Perfectionist (1) starts to feel stiflingly rigid and controlling. They resent the never-ending "to do" lists and long for a deeper emotional connection. And to the Perfectionist (1), the Individualist (4) starts to seem wallowing, self-absorbed and in need of copious amounts of unstructured time. They are mystified by their Individualist (4)'s desire to "do nothing" and to relax and hang out. When one or both starts to resent these differences in each other, the downward spiral begins.

As each type starts to get rigid in their interpretation of events, the Individualist (4) may feel unseen and misunderstood. This triggers an intense emotional response and more need for time to process their feelings. The Individualist (4) may start to feel drained and judged by their Perfectionist (1). The Perfectionist (1) may resent or take personally the Individualist (4)'s need for time alone. They interpret this as self-absorbed, wallowing, self-pitying and in extreme cases, pathetic. This triggers the Perfectionist (1) to become more rigid and critical in their reaction. The downward spiral gains momentum.

Both can be spiteful and unforgiving, tracking past grievances and emotional wounds. If the relationship continues its downward trajectory, it ends in bitter frustration, mutual disrespect and nasty arguments until it finally splits apart.

1:4 The Lighthouse
Keeping a strong heart connection and minimizing feelings of disappointment are key to stopping the momentum of the downward spiral in this relationship. Remembering common values and mutual respect can take the sting off the differences. A shared gratitude practice can help bring this couple closer together.

1:4 The Kundalini Yoga Connection
The growth path for the two types in some respects heads in different directions so they can use this to their advantage and to balance each other. The Individualist (4) needs to move towards equanimity and being more neutral in the face of intense emotions. The Perfectionist (1) needs to move towards serenity and tranquility. They need to resist the

urge to try to improve things. They must learn stillness.

The Individualist (4) needs to strengthen their nervous system so they don't feel as overwhelmed by their intense emotional responses. While letting themselves fully feel their emotions is important, managing the energy of emotion is also key in maintaining personal stability and balance. Kundalini Yoga kriyas or meditations that lower anxiety, cultivate self-love and to promote neutral mind and stability are beneficial.

Perfectionist (1)s need to connect to and speak from their heart. They need to wake up to their inner compassion. Expanding their emotional fluency and range can help them connect to the emotional world of the Individualist (4). Kundalini Yoga kriyas and meditations that promote energy awareness and heart-opening and burn out anger can help bring forward their softer feelings.

See the appendix for Perfectionist (1) and Individualist (4) recommended Kundalini Yoga kriyas and meditations.

1:5 Perfectionist (1) with Investigator (5)

Anne, Investigator (5) formerly in a ~2-year relationship with Mason, Perfectionist (1)

"I admired Mason's intellect, objectivity, logical thinking, honesty and independence. I knew I could trust him to act with integrity, regardless of our relationship status. He stuck to his principles, had high self-confidence and self-esteem and was deliberate in thought and deed.

In our relationship, we had a very stimulating intellectual connection. Unlike most of my past relationships, we never had a dull conversation. We would often just sit and discuss life, current events and our values, understandings and beliefs. We enjoyed having thought experiments and particularly "nightmare hypothetical" situations which we would debate and share our opinions on.

We would also discuss our jobs and co-workers, analyzing their behavior, trying to understand who they were, their deeper motivations and so forth. I would come at the conversation from pure curiosity and in an attempt understand my work environment and myself better. Mason was different. His signature phrases were "that's not the way it should be done!' and "what are these people thinking!" He wanted them to behave differently.

TYPE ONE **THE REFORMER/PERFECTIONIST**

Our relationship was slow to develop, which was different than most of my past relationships. Mason had lots of very firm mental, emotional and physical boundaries so we grew closer slowly, and even at the end of the relationship, it felt like the ice was still thawing out...After almost two years together, I was still left wondering if "maybe I just needed to give it more time.." But I just couldn't.

Our differences started to surface when we would talk about the future. Mason was rigid in his ideas about marriage, children and family, ideas which were fairly different than mine. He discussed how if he had the means, he wanted to provide for his children with trust funds, college education and so forth. To him, it was just "the right thing to do." This was the opposite end of the spectrum of my ideas - I'm not convinced funding all of those things is what's best in the long run. I felt like he would listen to me but not really hear my side. His mind was already made up. This issue intensified near the end of our relationship when we were talking about the future and he stated, "My children will never be average! That would be unacceptable!" This really struck me and made me pause because not only did it focus too much on "perfectionism," but it also seemed too absolute. Would I like my future children to be more than "average"? Sure. Is this an absolute that is a core belief I hold? Absolutely not. There are too many variables for me to put that kind of pressure on myself and my future kids. I think it would be detrimental to my mental health as well as that of my children to hold an absolute expectation like that. This fundamental difference played a big role in our breakup. Some of our basic philosophies were incompatible, and we were each too stuck in our respective corners to be able to come together to find common ground.

The other big issue we couldn't resolve was that our emotional connection was tenuous at best. We had very different understandings of what vulnerability was, and I never really felt like I saw Mason fully. At one point I told him, "I don't feel as though you are completely emotionally vulnerable with me..." to which he replied, "What are you talking about!? I have given you so much information, you could make a few phone calls and ruin my life in 5 minutes if you wanted to!" To him, personal information was vulnerability. I meant emotional vulnerability in terms of letting his guard down, expressing his deeper feelings, his fears and so forth. I struggled because when I tried to be really open and raw with him, I got the impression that he felt I was being irrational.

It was hard for either of us to "make the first move" in regards to vulnerability, even in simple, seemingly benign things like taking each other's hand in public. They say in a relationship every person is either a "flower" or a "gardener." We were both "flowers" that wanted to be tended, but there was no "gardener" to do so.

Our connection was more mental than emotional and left me feeling cold and distant at times. This, coupled with our very different ideas of how to live and what we wanted for our respective futures, made our connection even weaker. Eventually there just wasn't enough to keep the relationship together, and we split up."

Stelios, Investigator (5) in a 2-year relationship with Marie, Perfectionist (1)

"I appreciate how mindful Marie is of my personal boundaries. I never feel crowded, smothered or pressured by her. The fact that she is so respectful of my boundaries actually helps me to share more with her, since I don't feel pressure to offer more than I'm ready to.

At one point early in the relationship I got a job offer in a different country. I wasn't really sure how I felt about the whole thing and couldn't answer her questions about what I wanted to do. To her credit, she asked, but never pressed the issue and that space allowed me to come forward and talk the situation through with her, which in turn helped me sort out my own feelings about it. Now I use her as a sounding board for all types of things, since I trust she will give me the space I need to think and process my feelings at my own pace."

1:5 The Theory

1:5 When In Balance
The Perfectionist (1) and Investigator (5) share many traits and values that make for a steady, satisfying partnership punctuated by mutual respect, independence and shared interests.

Values of personal freedom, respect, integrity and pursuit of knowledge are the foundation of this pair. Both are interested in facts, data and being well-informed and correct. Together they enjoy verbal sparring and lively discussion. They share an attraction to each other's intellect, and this can be a highly cerebral couple. Both partners value objectivity and try to avoid drama. They are highly respectful of personal boundaries and are generally contained with their emotions. They work hard to allow each other personal space and freedom as this is seen as a foundational element to their relationship.

Their differences offer opportunities for growth. Their thirst for knowledge is different, and they can learn a lot by observing each other. Perfectionist (1)s seek fairness, justice and correctness. They tend to have a more rigid perspective, and this absolutism can be intriguing to their Investigator (5). Investigator (5)s are more relative, open-minded and on a never-ending quest for knowledge. When in balance, this open-mindedness can offer a growth edge for the Perfectionist (1), inviting them to be more flexible in their thinking.

Both types tend to manage time differently. Perfectionist (1)s are structured, organized and precise in their time commitments and time management. They are schedule oriented and often have future plans carefully laid out weeks or months in advance. This can be a growth opportunity for Investigator (5)s who resist making concrete long-range plans with others since they have difficulty predicting their energy levels or appetite for social engagements. When these differences are seen as opportunities to cultivate flexibility, compromise and compassion, they can be an asset to the relationship.

Overall, this is a sweetly contained, affectionate and even-keeled couple. Their devotion to each other is evident and inspiring to those around them.

1:5 The Downward Spiral

When in a fixated or unaware state, the same differences that offered growth opportunities can trigger the downward spiral of the relationship. When Perfectionist (1)s tighten their defenses, they become more critical, rigid, harsh and close-minded. When Investigator (5)s tighten their defenses, they withdraw, disengage and shutdown. This polarization triggers the downward spiral.

Perfectionist (1)s may become critical and judgmental about their Investigator (5)'s less structured approach to life and their sometimes radical intellectual ideas. Investigator (5)s may start to see their Perfectionist (1) as rigid, close-minded and focused on the details at the expense of the bigger picture. Criticism, stonewalling and a lack of respect may enter the picture. As both types are highly contained with their emotions and respectful of personal boundaries, open fighting may be rare. However, the warm bond the couple shared weakens, and coolness and isolation set in. Both may craft fairly independent lives for themselves, so while the relationship may appear intact to the outside world, true intimacy is lost. At this stage, an eventual breakup is likely.

1:5 The Lighthouse

As isolation and coldness characterize the path of deterioration in this pairing, connecting on an emotional level is the path to healing. Sharing time and space together and reconnecting around their shared interest and hobbies can help break the momentum of the downward spiral. Moving the energy out of the head and into the heart is the path back to balance.

1:5 The Kundalini Yoga Connection

Both Perfectionist (1)s and Investigator (5) can relate very much from their intellect and much less from their heart center. Ultimately, a head connection alone may not be enough to maintain a long-term intimate relationship. Both types need to learn to connect to and speak from the heart so heart opening Kundalini Yoga kriyas and meditations are beneficial. Kundalini Yoga kriyas and meditations for strengthening the nervous system help both types relax their habit attention.

For Investigator (5)s, a powerful and precise physical practice to bring focus to the body can be effective. Strengthening the immune system is helpful as Investigator (5)s can feel overwhelmed easily. And as the emotional world can sometimes feel foreign to Investigator (5)s, energy awareness exercises can be helpful.

Perfectionist (1)s need to burn out anger and irritation so they can become less rigid and more flexible in their thinking. Kundalini Yoga kriyas and meditations to relieve anger, strengthen the nervous system and open the heart are beneficial.

See the appendix for Perfectionist(1) and Investigator (5) recommended Kundalini Yoga kriyas and meditations.

1:6 Perfectionist (1) with Loyalist (6)

Willem, Loyalist (6) in a 3-year relationship with Tess, Perfectionist (1)

"Tess is naturally gifted in seeing and attracting truth, beauty and love into her life and the lives of others. I appreciate her trust, gratitude, love and dedication to me and to our relationship. She is open to new adventures and growth.

In our relationship, Tess is more decisive than I am, and we work to balance each other. She is more practical, taking care of the details of scheduling, logistics, social arrangements and so forth. I take on the more traditional "male" duties of making sure our space is safe, secure and guarded. Our relationship has a certain stability to it that I really value and even in challenging times I feel this stability.

As it relates to issues, Tess can be a workaholic, becoming very serious, focusing almost obsessively on the details and trying to get everything right. This drive for perfection can extend out to me, and it creates a pressure in our relationship that can be difficult. I shut down and begin to feel a lot of doubt and anxiety which triggers Tess to become more demanding and frustrated. If we don't catch ourselves as we start to fall into this pattern, it can be quite dark and difficult. Fortunately, we are both committed to self-awareness so we have been able to catch ourselves falling into this pattern and break out of it before it becomes too severe.

For us, selfishness is a concept that can be good or bad. It helps us both maintain a certain beneficial independence, but we need to keep it balanced. For me, I can use this selfish independence to find my own inner authority. For her, she has the freedom to pursue her higher truth and goals for perfection. However, we both have to watch a tendency to create too much distance in our relationship by living in our own worlds where we miss each other. In its unconscious state we become blind to each other and instead bring lots of blame. This is when we lose touch with the gifts we bring.

I really value this relationship. We are entering a new phase of finding more of the gems in ourselves and each other rather than just the issues. This new chapter really touches my heart. And as expected, this unchartered territory brings another wave of anxiety and relief, connection and fear. But each wave brings more awareness."

1:6 The Theory

1:6 When In Balance

The Perfectionist (1) and Loyalist (6) have a blend of shared qualities and balancing differences. In a self-aware state, this can be a steadfast, stable, loyal and committed pair.

Both types have a strong work ethic and sense of duty and responsibility. This is a couple where work comes before play, decision-making is thorough and methodical, and practical issues may dominate the shared landscape. Foundational elements of trust, respect, fairness, reliability and stability are at the core of this relationship.

To the dynamic, the Perfectionist (1) brings precise thinking, decisiveness, order, logic, clear thought and efficiency. They are action-oriented and don't like to stay frozen in indecision. They have a mental framework to follow that gives them guidance, self-confidence and the ability to act with assurance. Their internal compass is strong, and when they act, they act with conviction.

Loyalist (6)s are more doubtful, insecure and indecisive. These qualities make them relatable and bring warmth, approachability, vulnerability and a more human touch to the dynamic. The Loyalist (6) brings an eye for potential pitfalls to the relationship and helps ensure security and safety. As they spend a lot of time considering all possible risks, their decision-making tends to be slow but reliable. This is something their Perfectionist (1) comes to value.

When self-aware and aligned, this is a committed, grounded, loving team.

1:6 The Downward Spiral
When in a fixated or unaware state, the stability and security that were hallmark of this couple become threatened. When Perfectionist (1)s tighten their defenses, they become more critical, rigid, harsh and close-minded. As Loyalist (6)s tighten their defenses, they become more negative, indecisive, insecure and frozen in worst-case scenario thinking. The Perfectionist (1) leans forward with criticism, and the Loyalist (6) pulls back to try to avoid their Perfectionist (1)'s attack.

Perfectionist (1)s have a keen sense of fairness and efficiency and when fixated, their thinking narrows. They may become critical of their Loyalist (6) or the relationship itself on any variety of topics ranging from household chores, life decisions, personal growth and so forth. This criticism, either direct or indirect, is very anxiety-provoking for the Loyalist (6) who begins to project a worst-case scenario. Contempt and criticism from the Perfectionist (1) and stonewalling and avoidance by the Loyalist (6) enter the picture. What the Loyalist (6) needs is reassurance, but if neither partner can break the momentum, reactivity intensifies with the Perfectionist (1) becoming increasingly critical, and the Loyalist (6) becoming increasingly insecure and indecisive. Stability erodes, and without of reversal of the momentum, the relationship becomes increasingly distant and may eventually end.

1:6 The Lighthouse
Opposite stress responses of the two types is at the base of the downward spiral so learning to manage stress is a key to healing for this hard-working couple. Taking time out to relax, reconnect and feel expansive is important to help mend the relationship. Reconnecting at the heart level is also important as both types can be overwhelmed with anger and anxiety.

1:6 The Kundalini Yoga Connection
This couple needs to work hard to stay in balance. Loyalist (6)s experience more self-doubt, and Perfectionist (1)s can assume a leadership role in a way that stifles the development of their Loyalist (6) partner. The Perfectionist (1) must learn to leave things as they are. The Loyalist (6) must learn to find their own inner guidance.

For the Loyalist (6), Kundalini Yoga kriyas and meditations, particularly breathwork, to help manage anxiety are beneficial. Kundalini Yoga kriyas and meditations to strengthen the nervous system are also helpful so they don't feel as overpowered by worst-case scenario thinking and as fearful of the future.

The Perfectionist (1) needs to burn out anger and irritation so they can drop some of their harshness and rigidity. Kundalini Yoga kriyas and meditations to release anger are helpful. They should also strengthen their nervous system to help them resist the urge to correct things. They must learn stillness.

See the appendix for Perfectionist (1) and Loyalist (6) recommended Kundalini Yoga kriyas and meditations.

1:7 Perfectionist (1) with Enthusiast (7)

Marta, Enthusiast (7) married in a 12-year relationship with Dietrich, Perfectionist (1)

"After 12 years together, I still feel like my husband is the perfect fit for me! He's supportive, and it's fun to tell him about all my new ideas because often he gets quite excited as well. He is very organized, he has excellent follow-through, and he wants everything he does to be of high quality.

Where I see more of the big picture, he notices the details. For example, we love to travel and while I often pick the city or country, he'll start searching for the most beautiful places in the area to go. He even researches when the light is at its best point to have perfect pictures. In the end, we see wonderful places and leave with gorgeous pictures to keep beautiful memories of what we saw.

In our dynamic, I come up with ideas, and he takes over and maps everything out in a very detailed way so we reach better results. My husband brings a better structure to big projects that I plan. I used to think I was a good planner, but my husband brings planning to a whole new level. When we wanted to remodel our home, I made a rough sketch of my ideas. Then he created a scale model with the new furniture placed in the areas we were thinking about. Of course, the end result is amazing when there is so much attention to detail.

Overall, I'm very happy in my relationship. It feels like we are meant to be together, supporting each other in every step of our life. Sometimes it can be difficult that he always

THE NINE KEYS

believes things must be perfect, and my work is not as good as his but this is the area we work to balance. And our relationship is never boring since he's always open to trying my new discoveries."

1:7 The Theory

1:7 When In Balance
The detail-oriented, practically-minded Perfectionist (1) and brainstorming, big picture Enthusiast (7) enjoy a symbiotic, balancing relationship with both offering valuable traits the other generally lacks. When self-aware and in balance, they complete each other. This can be a highly complementary pairing. Perfectionist (1)s bring order, efficiency, tactical thinking, practicality, follow-through and commitment to high standards. Enthusiast (7)s offer high energy, a positive outlook, resilience, strategic thinking and an orientation towards fun and adventure.

Perfectionist (1)s help Enthusiast (7)s stay the course and remain focused in the face of difficulties and obstacles. The Perfectionist (1)'s attention to detail and practical thinking means projects and initiatives get done well with favorable results. They are methodical, thorough and more contained with their energy, and this can be helpful for the excitable Enthusiast (7).

Enthusiast (7)s bring joy and playfulness to the relationship and can help make sure things don't get too heavy, balancing the seriousness of the Perfectionist (1). They remind the Perfectionist (1) to have fun, to relax and to enjoy life. With their insatiable belief in a brighter future where all things are possible, the Enthusiast (7) inspires new projects, new trips and new adventures for the couple.

Both types can admire each other. Enthusiast (7)s appreciate the Perfectionist (1)'s methodical and systematic approach to life as well as their reliability. They are happy to have a detail-oriented person at their side as most Enthusiast (7)s are aware that attention to detail is not their forte. Perfectionist (1)s admire the Enthusiast (7)'s high spirits, joy and sense of fun and adventure. Enthusiast (7)s charge enthusiastically forward in life, and this can be balancing for Perfectionist (1)s who sometimes hold back and get overly involved in the details.

When aligned and in balance, this can be a mutually satisfying, fulfilling relationship.

1:7 The Downward Spiral

When fixated or in low stages of awareness, this can be a frustrating and difficult match riddled with misunderstanding and misaligned goals.

Under stress with tightening defenses, Perfectionist (1)s become more rigid, judgmental, irritated and blaming. They start to resent the playful, high-spirited Enthusiast (7) who is rarely interested in details or a methodical approach to situations. Perfectionist (1)s see the Enthusiast (7) as pleasure-seeking, unfocused, impractical and with a lack of commitment to high standards. It may feel as though a social contract has been broken, and the Perfectionist (1) may start to take this behavior personally, as though it were directed at them.

Enthusiast (7)s, on the other hand, get frustrated with the rigidity and seriousness of the Perfectionist (1). They start to feel penned in and trapped by what feels like a relentless "work before play" attitude. They can see the Perfectionist (1) as a strict schoolmarm who brings them down, limits them and drains their enthusiasm.

Conflicts between the two usually stem from their different approaches—Enthusiast (7)s have an immediacy of wanting to enjoy life to its fullest, and Perfectionist (1)s want to make sure all practical responsibilities are met before they allow themselves to relax and enjoy life. Enthusiast (7) start to feel like the Perfectionist "just doesn't get it" while Perfectionist (1)s see the Enthusiast (7) as irresponsible and immature. If the downward spiral gains momentum, the differences they share start to polarize the couple. The Enthusiast (7) may feel worn down and frustrated by the Perfectionist (1)'s continual criticism and dissatisfaction. They look for pleasant distractions to make themselves feel better. The Perfectionist (1) gets even more frustrated with the Enthusiast (7)'s way of dealing with the situation. Their Enthusiast (7) partner begins to seem unreliable, scattered and hedonistic, someone with whom it is very difficult to imagine a positive future. The Perfectionist (1) might start developing feelings of contempt for the Enthusiast (7). With a panicking and frustrated Enthusiast (7) and a disillusioned, contemptuous Perfectionist (1), the connection falters, and the relationship is in trouble.

1:7 The Lighthouse

Tightening defenses move in the opposite directions in this couple so coming back to the center is key to stopping the downward spiral. The Enthusiast (7) needs to resist the urge to flee in the face of rising anxiety and stress. The Perfectionist (1) needs to resist the urge to lean in and try to control too much of the environment. And for both partners to change directions, they need to strengthen their nervous systems.

1:7 The Kundalini Yoga Connection

The Enthusiast (7)'s underlying anxiety can benefit a lot from Kundalini Yoga kriyas and meditations that incorporate breathwork. Practices that require grit and determination and that lower anxiety are particularly helpful.

The Perfectionist (1)'s frustration can be released with Kundalini Yoga kriyas and meditations to burn inner anger and to open the heart. Any practice that connects the Perfectionist (1) with their softer emotions is beneficial.

See the appendix for Perfectionist (1) and Enthusiast (7) recommended Kundalini Yoga kriyas and meditations.

1:8 Perfectionist (1) with Leader (8)

Gloria, Leader (8) married in an 18-year relationship with Michael, Perfectionist (1)

"My husband is a man of his word and fiercely loyal. He is reliable, committed and driven to make a difference in the world and for those around him. He is willing to look at himself and to face difficult issues to improve himself and the world around him. As a father, he is loving and fun and has adapted his style to connect to our children. Throughout our community, people come to him for his gentle humble wisdom.

Our relationship started as a shared vision to change the world. The thing that drew us together was a shared desire to serve God overseas. With the perspective of years, I now see that the vision, commitment and drive to change the world was bigger than the intimate connection between us. We wanted to change things for the better and give people who were underdogs and vulnerable a better chance at life, to show people how things could be. We were willing to give up careers and move away from home to a developing country to do something better with our lives than join the rat race, and while others thought we were brave and amazing, we just followed our instincts. And we did it together.

We have been married 18 years and are more like friends than lovers. Intimacy is difficult for both of us so this is not entirely surprising, but we get on very well as people, and we are able to maintain a very strong partnership.

When we disagree, however, it can be very uncomfortable as we seem to be at polar opposite views. He can seem very rigid to me at times, and I probably seem quite threatening to him. For example, this difference came up dealing with a family health issue--he refused to consider alternative medical treatment for our daughter, despite my own personal positive experience with the same treatment. I felt his attitude was extremely rigid, but eventually I backed down to avoid a bigger battle about it. I was aware that he often goes with what I want to avoid conflict, and I need to give in sometimes too.

In our dynamic, we try to balance his rigidity with my boundary pushing. I lost my faith over the last few years, and the result is I am slowly starting to question the boundaries imposed by that faith. This has created challenges for my husband, since his perspective hasn't shifted quite as much. I've questioned the very concept of marriage - what it is, what it looks like and involves - and faith in all sorts of ways. I swear much more than I used to and am quite willing to shock others with what I say to provoke a response. Sometimes he finds this amusing, but sometimes he finds it really hard.

One thing that provides a foundation for us as we navigate life's changes is that we continue to do hard work on ourselves in our personal development journeys. We are both fairly private people, so opening up to one another about intimate and painful issues can be challenging. But we are both committed to the work and the process.

Overall I find it a great relationship. If there were romance as well it would be perfect. But for a partner to share my life and raise a family with, I am very content."

Daphne, Leader (8) married in a 12-year relationship with Antonio, Perfectionist (1)

"I love my husband's ability to see areas for improvement in basically everything. He's an artist, and I think his drive for perfection is what makes his work stand out. He's incredibly hard on himself, but at the end of the day this produces artwork that is above and beyond what others are creating.

I love his sense of adventure and how he can convince me to try things I would never normally consider doing. He's playful and fun with our young daughters and can be emotionally expressive with me. At the same time, my husband is just as strong-willed as I am, and this has helped me learn to back down when necessary. I respect him for standing up to me and holding his opinion even when it's hard.

In our relationship, differences in communication style have been challenging. When we were first married, he would get so angry if I didn't do the laundry or the dishes--which is just weird to me! And while it is very helpful to have a partner who can give me constructive feedback on something 95% of the time, sometimes I just want reassurance or praise. I've learned his criticism isn't personal, it is just the way his brain works. He also is more interested in being socially appropriate than I am. I make inappropriate jokes, and I react if I hear something offensive. I'm not interesting in putting on a show of propriety in public, and this sometimes embarrasses my husband."

1:8 The Theory

1:8 When In Balance

This pair shares many fundamental values while adopting very different approaches. When self-aware and aligned in their goals, the common values serve as a solid foundation and the stylistic and energetic differences keep the partnership interesting and vibrant.

Shared values include a determination, grit and a willingness to work hard to overcome adversity for a higher cause. Both can be fierce, tough, focused, self-sacrificing and unswayed by the opinions of others. Truth, justice and a strong moral compass are key traits and values of both partners.

Energetically the two types are quite different, and this can be balancing, with the Leader (8) bringing a passionate and powerful presence contrasted against the Perfectionist (1)'s more contained, reserved and rigid manner. The Perfectionist (1) appreciates the presence, the big energy and the directness of the Leader (8). The Leader (8) admires the values, convictions and the uncompromising nature of the Perfectionist (1). Like a Mafia boss and a head nun, both embody their beliefs. When balanced and respectful of their differences, this is a powerful and impactful couple.

1:8 The Downward Spiral

Fundamental philosophical and energetic differences can be the trigger for the downward spiral of this couple. Their temperaments and approach to life are different and, in some ways, opposite. When fixated on their habit of attention, the differences can cause challenges. Perfectionist (1)s are methodical, rational, cool-headed and restrained. Work comes before play and self-denial lines up neatly with their values. This is a sharp contrast with the Leader (8) who uses their energetic presence to their advantage to get what they want and further their cause.

Leader (8)s are self-referencing and feel no shame or restraint in their pursuit of what they want. This can offend the Perfectionist (1) who values model behavior as part of their idealized world. The Perfectionist (1) starts to see the Leader (8)'s boldness as crude, unpredictable and untrustworthy. The initial attraction of the powerful, assertive Leader (8) descends into criticism, disdain and contempt.

Conversely, Leader (8)s don't appreciate feeling judged and begin to view the Perfectionist (1) as rigid, nitpicking, delusionally idealistic and hypocritical. Rather than feel controlled by the Perfectionist (1) in any way, the Leader (8) may start to act out, becoming more outrageous, rebellious and irreverent. As the downward spiral picks up momentum, anger, either open or convert, enters the picture. Without a mechanism to stop the momentum, the partners polarize and may eventually split.

1:8 The Lighthouse
Ironically, one of the core areas of work between these two energetically different types is the same: to open the heart. Both of these types have a lot of emotional armor, particularly in the heart center. When the downward spiral begins, the heart connection is lost. To reconnect, they need to dissolve their emotional armor and reconnect from the heart.

1:8 The Kundalini Yoga Connection
Both partners can have issues around control and both have a strong internal compass and sense of themselves. To bridge their distance, they need to rediscover their common ground and shared values.

The Leader (8) needs to manage their anger response and their drive to control. This helps them reconnect to their heart. Long deep breathing and Kundalini Yoga kriyas and meditations for relaxation that require energy and breath control are beneficial. Heart opening practices are also important.

The Perfectionist (1) needs to burn out anger and frustration so they can access their heart once again. They need to learn stillness and acceptance. Kundalini Yoga kriyas for relaxation, releasing anger, opening the heart and cultivating compassion are beneficial and help them drop some of their rigidity.

See the appendix for Perfectionist (1) and Leader (8) recommended Kundalini Yoga kriyas and meditations.

1:9: Perfectionist (1) with Peacemaker (9)

Henry, Peacemaker (9) married in a 17-year relationship with Prisha, Perfectionist (1)

"I love so many things about my wife... Prisha sets high standards and lives by them. Her integrity is unquestionable. She can be the most considerate and thoughtful person I have ever known. She has a bubbly, self-effacing, charming sense of humor that could never offend anyone. She is both spontaneous and funny! She has great taste in clothing, decorating and furnishing. My wife is extremely well organized and keeps clutter to a minimum. Prisha inspires others with her vision and her charisma. She is an excellent public speaker.

Professionally, Prisha is very accomplished as a master trainer in adult 'soft skills' education and from my perspective, she has no peer. What I respect the most about her work is that people who take her training walk out with skills they apply in the real world. She has been a huge positive influence in many people's lives. With all of her talents, she remains humble, almost to a fault, which makes self-promotion nearly impossible for her. With her time and money, she is generous and is willing to sacrifice her personal interests for the good of the community. She works hard to advance community interests.

I have learned so much from Prisha that I cannot begin to thank her for her influence. I attribute a huge portion of my personal development to her innate wisdom. For example, at the age of 64 I finally got over my fear of public speaking and found myself able to conduct a one-hour presentation with full audience participation. It went comfortably and flawlessly.

In our relationship, Prisha and I initially shared a burning interest in understanding people. We were both self-described seekers. For our first eight years together, I felt very supported by my wife and for most of our marriage, Prisha gave people the benefit of the doubt. We socialized normally and were happy together.

However, over the last years, things have changed, and our relationship is deteriorating. In retrospect, there were some red flags along the way, but I didn't recognize them as indicators of a bigger problem. For example, Prisha moved to the United States to marry me, and it took her about ten years to make her first friend here.

In the last decade, despite all her accomplishments and talents, she has become more insecure which triggers a recurring pattern. She begins to find everyone in her life untrustworthy which provides the basis for cutting them out of her life. She talks about a place inside herself which she calls 'The Pen.' This is where she places people she has written off. When I asked her how anyone could ever get out of The Pen, she simply replied, "The very fact that they could have done what they did, means they are the kind of person to whom there is no point in talking."

The first time I saw her do this was with her oldest friend Jennifer, whom she had known for over 35 years. Because Jennifer lives in a different country, they don't see each other frequently, but Prisha took a trip during which she met with Jennifer to catch up. Upon her return Prisha announced that Jennifer was lost to her. My wife was no longer interested in having her as a friend, because Jennifer had 'put her whole life into taking up political causes.'

This behavior continued, and Prisha gradually cut herself off from all the friends I had introduced her to, perhaps in judgment or perhaps out of insecurity. At about the ten-year mark, she commented: "I have caused you to lose all of your friends." I swept this comment under the rug, minimizing it.

As the years waxed on, Prisha became increasingly rigid in her judgments: "A lie is a lie is a lie." I estimate the tipping point, when she began to mistrust me, was when I came up to our apartment via the elevator instead of directly ascending the stairs. She asked me why, and I replied that I had some trash to dispose of. She stated flatly, "You're lying." That began an interrogation, by the end of which I admitted I had actually hidden her Christmas present in the storeroom. She expressed feelings of betrayal: "You told me you would never lie to me."

The paranoia intensified. At the thirteen-year mark we planned a 'Second Honeymoon' in Hawaii. While we were planning it, she shared that she had been there many years before with her friend Jennifer and loved it. I shared that I had visited Hawaii on vacation with my first wife, as I recalled that trip vividly since we went to see my relatives living in Hawaii.

Prisha and I had a wonderful time on our vacation. I planned the entire event to be a deluxe occasion and surprised her with one incredible experience after another. One day we took a helicopter tour where we flew over volcanoes, and the same day we sailed on a catamaran in the sea. The trip was amazing, one incredible memory after another.

It was, as Prisha described later, the last good time we would ever have together. Shortly after our return, at Thanksgiving, we visited my second ex-wife, with whom Prisha had become friends. Martha, my second wife, disclosed to Prisha that she had been to Hawaii with me, though this was more than 30 years before.

Although Martha and I had done nothing anywhere near as spectacular there, Prisha decided our Hawaii honeymoon was based on a lie, and now meant nothing to her. She didn't speak to me once during the 2 1/2 hours driving back to our home, nor for 9 weeks afterward. It soon became evident after that point that Prisha considered everything I had ever told her to be based on lies.

Several months later she announced, "You no longer have access to the 'Me' of me. From now on, we are just roommates." In my heart, I heard a dungeon door slam shut.

My strategy until very recently has been to accept continual rejection, 'taking the hits' while staying engaged. I have continually reached out to bridge the silence, offering to resume conversations and work things out. Prisha has for years now refused my suggestions for marriage counseling and individual therapy, even though in her early adulthood she took full advantage of counselors. She replied to my most recent offer for counseling, "I'm not interested in renewing our marriage." It was then I knew for certain I had been assigned to The Pen.

Further compounding the situation, Prisha has become increasingly critical. If a 5:1 ratio of positives to negatives is generally needed to sustain a relationship, her ratio of communications to me became closer to 1:5, with a predominance of unsolicited criticism and unrelenting disapproval and rejection. This culminated in Prisha taking sides against me in a dispute I was having at work. I felt totally emotionally undermined. By contrast, I have always stood up for Prisha as her advocate. On the very few times I have critiqued Prisha's behavior, not her person, she has become angry, sometimes to the point of rage.

Prisha, when hurt, becomes almost totally uncommunicative. When I wait sufficient time for her to process her feelings and attempt to bring up the subject again for resolution, she generally continues to stonewall. She says things like, "There is no use in talking. Talking can't fix this."

As the years have worn on, Prisha's terms for relationship became non-negotiable. She considers any compromise as 'compromising herself.' "If people think I'm picky and sensitive, well I am. I won't give up my standards. Not for anyone."

I wish Prisha would understand that life is by definition a dynamic process. In any truly alive relationship including with self, the relationship must also be dynamic. Thus integrity is always being renegotiated – and always thereby restored. Once there are too many aspects of a relationship that have become non-negotiable, your relationship calcifies and dies.

You will then discover in your dance of relationship, once you dispel illusion: You are now dancing with the bones of a skeleton."

Nancy, Peacemaker (9) married in an 18-year relationship with Roger, Perfectionist (1)

"My husband is reliable, committed, steadfast, generous, giving, highly focused on community groups and has good morals. I love all these things but above all I value his reliability. He never yells and never gets angry with me, even when I try to push his buttons on purpose.

We both share a desire to change the world. He serves as the chaplain for the local fire department and is very involved in the Masonic Lodge on the local and state levels. Both my husband and I are church pastors and have moved five times during our marriage.

In our relationship, striking a balance of give and take requires effort and can be a challenge given my drive for harmony and his sometimes rigid views. For our last move, I wanted to go back to New England, but I knew that my husband's more conservative outlook would not be a good match with churches there and that he would have a hard time, even though I might be happier. He was willing to follow my church call this time, and I had several interviews. However, in the end, my energy petered out, and I became frustrated with the dysfunction in some of the search committees with whom I interviewed. I began to feel like moving for my call would be too overwhelming and require too much energy on my part. I decided the stress of my husband's possible unhappiness was too much for me to handle and so I told him to start interviewing instead. We ended up moving west to Ohio for his call, as we always have, instead of east to New England for my call.

Our differing beliefs can present challenges in the relationship, but our shared values and mutual love and respect for each other provide a solid foundation for us to fall back on. We've been together 28 years and have weathered many differences during that time. And as another, somewhat entertaining, part of our foundation, we have our dog. We both love our dog. We often talk more to the dog than to each other! It's almost like the dog is in a triangular relationship with us, where we are very aware of his needs, and he in turn is a great comfort to us and often the most important family member."

1:9 The Theory

1:9 When In Balance

Perfectionist (1)s and Peacemaker (9)s offer each other a blend of shared and compensating personality traits. Both can be altruistic, working in the service of others and subjugating their own needs for the greater good. Both can be committed to improvement and growth, albeit with large energetic differences. Neither type need the spotlight, and both can stay focused on the task at hand, leaving their ego to the side to focus on concrete goals. And with these foundational shared values, they also have many balancing differences.

Peacemaker (9)s bring an accepting, nonjudgmental nature, steadiness and a human focus to their interactions. They are kind-hearted, good listeners with a soothing, easy presence. They easily and naturally accommodate multiple viewpoints and perspectives making others feel unconditionally accepted.

Perfectionist (1)s bring clarity, rational thought, an action-oriented approach, and precise and critical thinking. They are ethical, fair and driven to improve themselves and their environment.

In the relationship, the Peacemaker (9) softens the rigidity of the Perfectionist (1) and helps mute the Perfectionist (1)'s drive to be right. They can broker compromise and help maintain harmony. Perfectionist (1)s give inspiration to the Peacemaker (9). They may push their Peacemaker (9) outside their comfortable zone, helping them to achieve more of their full potential.

This can be a highly idealistic, hospitable, altruistic couple who create good in the world and bring out the best in each other.

1:9 The Downward Spiral

The downward spiral of the relationship begins because of the opposite way the two types behave when fixated, with Perfectionist (1)s expressing criticism and contempt and Peacemaker (9)s stonewalling and becoming stubbornly avoidant. With tightening defenses, Perfectionist (1)s become more openly critical, frustrated, prickly and dissatisfied. This can be directed at themselves, their partner, their other relationships and their environment. They become fixated on finding fault and determining who is to blame. They become increasingly rigid in their views and disconnected from their hearts. Isolationism can occur with no one meeting the harsh standards strictly set by the Perfectionist (1). Compassion is usually nowhere in the picture.

In this environment, Peacemaker (9)s head in the opposite direction and become more shut down, withdrawn, internally confused and uncomfortable. They numb out as a strategy to deflect the criticism and dissatisfaction of the Perfectionist (1). Internally, they try to convince themselves that nothing is wrong or it is a phase the couple is going through.

This further triggers the Perfectionist (1) who feels the Peacemaker (9) isn't addressing the issue. The two partners polarize with the Peacemaker (9) resisting the situation even more, becoming more passive and more withdrawn. The Perfectionist (1) interprets this as passive defiance. The Perfectionist (1) starts to lose respect for the Peacemaker (9), and the Peacemaker (9) starts to lose confidence and trust in the Perfectionist (1).

If the downward spiral continues, the Perfectionist (1) becomes even more condemning, disdainful and critical of the Peacemaker (9). The Peacemaker (9) reacts by becoming more unresponsive, passive, resigned and withdrawn. To the Perfectionist (1), they feel they are merely living up to their own internal high standards. To the Peacemaker (9), they feel they are accommodating their very frustrated partner in the best way they know how. To the outside world, this couple may be hard to be around because of the barely suppressed anger seething from the Perfectionist (1) and the unresponsive passive energy of the Peacemaker (9).

Once the couple reaches this stage, any heart connection is lost. Because of the Peacemaker (9)'s resistance to change, the relationship may continue for long periods in this state before it ends.

1:9 The Lighthouse
The downward spiral starts because of the different and opposite way both partners deal with conflict. Peacemaker (9)s withdraw and shut down. Perfectionist (1)s become more harsh and rigid in their thinking. If both people can break their patterned responses, there can be real healing between these two. Strengthening the nervous system to accommodate alternate reactions to conflict is beneficial.

1:9 The Kundalini Yoga Connection
Both types must shift their energetic patterns to bridge their gap. Peacemaker (9)s need to resist the urge to withdraw and hope that time passing will fix their problems. This inertia is a response to the discomfort of conflict. They must confront this discomfort. Perfectionist (1) need to break free of their tendency to judge harshly and to polarize in their opinions. They need to move to less rigid, more flexible thinking.

THE NINE KEYS

Because the Perfectionist (1) type structure can become so rigid, maintaining a strong heart connection, both to self and others, is vital. In an unhealthy state of awareness, the attention becomes completely focused on improvement and criticism of others allowing no space for compassion. Kundalini Yoga kriyas and meditations to burn out anger and connect to and open the heart can help create this space.

Peacemaker (9)s energetically numb out as a strategy to avoid conflict. For Peacemaker (9)s, conflict is extremely anxiety-provoking and can feel like annihilation. Peacemaker (9)s need to wake up to their anger and discontent. They need to risk conflict. Kundalini Yoga kriyas and meditations to build the navel center (third chakra) and to burn anger are helpful.

See the appendix for Perfectionist (1) and Peacemaker (9) recommended Kundalini Yoga kriyas and meditations.

This book is a living document. We will be updating it periodically with new information. If you are or were in a relationship with a Perfectionist (1) , and you would like to participate in the related relationship survey, please email me at lynn@lynnroulo.com.

Type Two
HELPER/GIVER/LOVER (2)

(seeks satisfying needs of others/avoids own needs)

Overview

Helper (2)s are typically warm, concerned, nurturing and sensitive to the needs, preferences and desires of the people around them. They proactively look for ways to be helpful, useful and likable. This person is the stereotypical perfect host or hostess with an almost sixth sense for the needs of others. Helper (2)s often report having boundary issues and having a very difficult time saying no to a request, even if they really don't want to do what is being asked of them.

In a relationship, they can be very focused on the needs of their partner and often want to be the central person in their partner's life. They seek environments where they will be needed and appreciated.

Partners say they value their Helper (2)'s kindness, open-heartedness, generosity, social graces, helpfulness, caring, nurturing, their high emotional intelligence and ability to make others feel welcomed. Helper (2)s are often attracted to relationships with obstacles, which subconsciously serves to keep the attention off their own needs.

Partners say challenges with their Helper (2)s include overcommitting to others, an inability to say "no" to requests, a sense of being smothered, a weak sense of personal boundaries and a lack of self-care. They have to be mindful of not getting overly involved in dealing with their partner's issues and taking them on as their own. Codependency or dysfunctional dependency can develop due to the Helper (2)'s natural inclination to try to be helpful.

• Attention Bias/Habit Of Attention:
Their attention goes to the needs of others or to being liked and likable. They see the wants and preferences of other people and work to gain their appreciation. This can manifest as offering help and assistance to others or presenting themselves in a likable manner. Their attention moves away from their own needs.

• Emotional Style:
Warm, inclusive, connected.

• Communication Style:
Heartfelt, friendly, attentive, relational, complimentary, social, expansive, sensitive.

• Unique Strengths:
Connect easily with others and can typically reach even emotionally distant or unavailable people. Helpers (2)s are capable of a deep heart connection.

• Challenges:
Helper (2)s typically have personal boundary issues and have difficulty saying "no." They can overextend themselves trying to care for and help others. They are often unaware and disconnected from their own needs and may have difficulty with self-care. This is someone who has difficulty advocating for themselves. They can be emotionally needy or smothering. They can be subconsciously manipulative, giving to get something in return.

• Stability And Security:
"I feel stable when I am told I am helpful, useful and when I can tell you like me. Feeling appreciated by you helps me feel secure. Knowing you need me and like me makes me feel stable."

• Instability And Insecurity:
"I feel insecure when I think you might be disappointed or displeased with me. It can be difficult for me to take a hard, confident stance for myself because I worry you might like me less. I can advocate for you, but I can't advocate very well for myself. Being in an environment where no one needs or wants anything from me can feel disorienting, and I might feel unstable. If this happens, I'll try to imagine what you need next."

- **Path Of Growth:**
Humility
Helper (2)s must learn to drop the illusion of not having personal needs. They must start to make their own needs a priority. They can use self-nurturing and self-love to dissolve shame.

- **Energy:**
Nurturing, warm, inclusive, sticky.

- **The Kundalini Yoga Connection:**
Helper (2)s have a hard time containing their energy and focusing it inward. Their attention and energy naturally gravitate out to others. This disconnects them from their own needs and has the potential to create unhealthy bonds with others. Kundalini Yoga kriyas and meditations to raise body and energy awareness are helpful because they turn the attention away from the outside world and back to the Helper (2). Helper (2)s get additional benefit from doing a Kundalini Yoga practice privately so they can stay connected to themselves without external distractions.

The Helper (2) Subtypes

"Privilege" Self-Preservation Subtype:
There is an inherent cuteness and charm to the self-preservation Helper (2). To the outside world, this is a person with a somewhat childlike appearance. They can be less trusting and more reserved than the other two subtypes, adopting a sometimes helpless, me-first attitude. Internally, this person feels anxious about self-reliance and gravitates to situations where others will take care of them. Their need for love is quite naked. They have the title "Privilege" because this type can be self-indulgent and hedonistic with an underlying unconscious belief that others must care for them. They may enjoy parties, shopping, drinking and socializing as a subconscious distraction from a deeper connection to themselves.

In relationships, they often fall into a childlike role with a more "adult" partner taking care of their needs. This is the Helper (2) who expresses a drive to be likable over a drive to be helpful and may adopt a strategy of being helpless to gain love and attention. This Helper (2) is less "other" referencing and may want to be the center of attention. In the self-preservation Helper (2), humor, playfulness, irresponsibility, charm and self-importance are in the foreground. When fixated or less self-aware, the thought of taking charge of themselves fills them with anxiety.

On the positive side, this is a youthful, charming, sweet person who is positive and playful, often uplifting the mood of others.

On the less positive side, this is someone who can be very reluctant to take control of their own lives and act independently. They are the most guarded and fearful of the Helper (2)s.

"Ambition" Social Subtype:

The social Helper (2) expresses a drive to be helpful and useful in groups, companies and social settings. This is a person who is keenly aware of power and influence and naturally aligns with situations where they are influencing powerful people. To the outside world, this Helper (2) can look like a leader and someone who is comfortable in the limelight. This is a more adult, "Power" Helper (2). Internally, this type is (either subconsciously or consciously) supporting others from a desire to gain loyalty and reciprocity. They have the title "Ambition" because this type is highly driven towards success and competence.

The social Helper (2) tends towards workaholism. Work is a large focus in their lives, and they typically have a highly positive sense of their career and their goals. This Helper (2) can be powerful, influential, protective of others and oriented to the big picture. Vulnerable emotions like shame, fear, jealousy and envy are hard for them to recognize and process. They can become emotionally confused, thinking they are displaying vulnerability when they aren't and denying shame when they are in fact feeling it. They tend to overcommit and then get stressed out.

On the positive side, this is a highly effective, accomplished person. They often rise to positions of leadership and are well-connected in their chosen field or social sphere.

On the less positive side, this is someone who can misunderstand their own emotions and motivations. They can be calculated in their relationships without consciously realizing it.

"Aggressive/Seductive" Intimate Subtype:

The intimate Helper (2) expresses a drive to be helpful, likable and desirable to particular individuals. This is a person who is more driven to direct seduction and as such cultivates an attractive appearance. They can have an almost irresistible quality. To the outside world, this person is like the classic "femme fatale" (or homme fatale). Internally, this person feels they are seeking love, and that search justifies all behavior. They tend to put a lot of energy and focus on relationships and can have a hard time letting go if the relationship doesn't work out. They have the title "Aggressive/Seductive" because they actively pursue seduction of intimate partners or potential partners. This is the almost too adult Helper (2).

TYPE TWO HELPER/GIVER/LOVER

In a relationship, this may be someone who wants their partner to give them everything and wants to be everything to their partner. They subconsciously solve their issue of denying their own needs by having a strong bond with somebody who will give them anything they want. They have a need to be desired that fuels the need to be seductive.

On the positive side, this is a passionate and seductive Helper (2) who puts a great deal of energy into making relationships happen. They can be very flexible, generous and attentive to their partner.

On the less positive side, being alone can be hard for this Helper (2), and they have a deep need to be desired. They can lose themselves in their drive for attention.

Helper (2)—Levels of Awareness

Helper (2) When Self-Aware
Helper (2)s are humble, altruistic, direct and pure. They share their gifts with the world and can offer unconditional love. These Helper (2)s are kind, compassionate, caring and interested and concerned in the lives of others. They offer empathy, sincerity, generosity, and they strive to respond to others in a balanced way. They have a high capacity for forgiveness. They are supportive, encouraging, grateful and giving. Helping others is a priority, but it is balanced with genuine self-care. They can see the spark of beauty and potential in each person.

Helper (2) With Tightening Defenses
Helper (2)s are warm, friendly and emotionally demonstrative in a somewhat indiscriminate way. They become more people-pleasing and less authentic in their behavior, deviating from what they really think to be more likable. They have a give-and-take relationship with flattery, applause and approval. Self-containment can be difficult. Relationships with others are their top priority. They begin to become more intrusive, invasive and interfering with their behavior, confusing love with helping. Their self-sacrificing becomes imbalanced, and their self-care suffers. They have a complicated relationship with dependency and giving, subconsciously giving to get and creating dependencies to ensure a place in the receiver's life. They may start to experience a reality distortion around their own sense of self-importance feeling they are indispensable to others and overestimating the positive impact of their efforts. When entranced, they may experience an almost obsessive drive to find needs to fill as a way of feeling useful and valued. They can become controlling and bossy with an attitude of superiority.

Helper (2) When Fixated

This Helper (2) may be subconsciously manipulative using guilt and blame to get attention. Their behavior can turn sharp and aggressive, reminding others they are "owed" for all the things the Helper (2) has done. They may have a reality distortion around how contentious their behavior is and may subconsciously start to undermine those they meant to help. They may seek outside outlets (food, medication, shopping and so forth) to fill unmet emotional needs. They may demonstrate a gross lack of respect for the personal boundaries of others. Behavior at this level is highly manipulative. Helper (2)s don't recognize their manipulative and controlling behavior. Bitter resentments, anger and rage come to the surface. Health problems, including depression, may develop as a result of a low self-esteem and emotional imbalance.

Keys If You Are In A Relationship With A Helper (2)

"My drive to make other people happy is relentless and can cloud my thinking."

Margarita, Helper (2) married to David, Perfectionist (1)

"My husband and I rent apartments on Airbnb. I handle all of the guest communications, and he handles the logistical elements. We had one Australian group come to our city in Spain for the annual marathon. They made a mistake with their arrival time and had let me know they would need help getting their running bibs before the registration desk closed. Of course, this was completely outside of our duty as Airbnb hosts, but I really wanted to help them. They sent me all the information, and I agreed we would do the work for a small fee. The registration turned out to be a total nightmare for my husband. He had to run all over town standing in lines, picking up running bibs, showing paperwork, passport copies and so forth. He was willing to do it but was pretty frustrated at the effort involved. Then, when the guests arrived, and I gave them the bibs, they offered to pay the fee, but I said "No, really, it's fine!" I'm not exactly sure what came over me, I just wanted so much for them to have a good experience. Of course, when I told my husband I had waived the fee, he hit the roof...."

Francine, Helper (2)

"I was at a trade show in Los Angeles, and it was my first time presenting my product, a gym bag made from recycled material. I was getting positive feedback from the attendees, and then someone asked me directly how much the gym bag cost. I completely froze. Of course, I knew the price I had set, but my mind raced to "What if he doesn't like that price?

TYPE TWO HELPER/GIVER/LOVER

I want him to be happy with me and with my gym bag…" I couldn't actually answer the question at that moment, and a friend of mine who was with me gave me an odd look and took over explaining the pricing…"

Helper (2)s are driven by a desire to be liked and likable. It is part of their innate wiring that helps defend against feelings of being unlovable. They can be cautious about doing anything that they fear might jeopardize a friendly status with someone. This can easily get distorted into chronic people-pleasing behavior.

If you are a Helper (2):
Become aware of your compulsion of wanting others to be happy with you. You might believe you people-please because you want others to be happy, but this is not the full picture. Why is it so important that other people like you? What would happen if someone's opinion of you was less than positive?

If you are with a Helper (2):
Understand that your Helper (2)'s desire to be liked by others triggers automatic behavior. It is actually quite draining and anxiety-provoking for your Helper (2) to imagine someone might not like them. Try to be compassionate when you observe people-pleasing behavior.

> "I see you, my partner, as an extension of me. Like myself, it is easy to put the needs of others before me, you and us. You are still the most important person in my life."

Stavros (3) Achiever, married in a 20-year relationship with Athena, Helper (2)

"A challenge in our relationship is that I feel the love and generosity that she so easily dispenses to everyone else is given more sparingly to me. She helps everyone but herself, and I have become an extension of her by virtue of being her husband and being married to her for so long. She tells me she loves me all the time, but I sometimes feel that her actions do not match her words. She doesn't do things to hurt me, per se, but she's not as overly generous to me as she is with, say, her friends. Luckily, she's super loving to my son, and I bathe in the reflective glow of that love."

Helper (2)s have issues around self-care, and after they have been in a committed relationship for some time, they often start to experience their partner as an extension of themselves. This may mean their attention goes to the needs of others and not to themselves or their partner. Partners often report frustration that their Helper (2) seems to put everyone else's needs above their own.

If you are a Helper (2):
Remember that your partner is not you and wants your attention just as much as other people in your life. Consider reassessing your priorities to make sure the important people in your life get the majority of your time and focus.

If you are with a Helper (2):
Understand your Helper (2) compulsively wants to offer assistance to others, and this often means the neediest get your Helper (2)'s time and energy. Try to help your Helper (2) understand the impact this has on you. Your partner may not understand how serious of an issue their time allocation is.

"It isn't that I want you dependent on me. I want you to appreciate me."

Joseph, Helper (2)

"It is very natural for me to create dependencies with the important people in my life. I see this most clearly in my work situations. This isn't deliberate or calculated as much as wanting to make sure I am highly valued. In a work environment, for example, I want to be seen as the 'go to' guy and the 'what would we ever do without him?' team member. I see this drive as high-level performance in my role and with a potential benefit of higher pay, better promotions and so forth."

Appreciation is like oxygen for Helper (2)s, and Helper (2)s typically have a complicated relationship with giving and dependency. It isn't that they want the important people in their life to be dependent on them as much as they want a steady supply of appreciation and to feel valued.

If you are a Helper (2):
Try to honestly determine the motivation behind your giving, especially to important people in your life. What would happen if you turned that giving energy back to yourself and exercised more self-care?

If you are with a Helper (2):
If your Helper (2) is starting to "over" give or does too much, remind them that you appreciate their generosity and their character, confirm that they are an important person in your life and firmly tell them you are ok, and you have everything you need. Helper (2)s value connection and appreciation, so try to give them this without the entanglement of giving.

TYPE TWO HELPER/GIVER/LOVER

HELPER (2)
360 DEGREE REVIEW

The next section features the 360 degree review--partnership with a Helper (2) from the perspective of each of the nine types.

2:1 Perfectionist (1) with Helper (2)

Eden, Perfectionist (1) married in a 6-year relationship with Charles, Helper (2)

"I really admire my husband's generosity – and I mean that in all senses of the word. He's generous with his time, with his emotional support and sometimes even his finances. He truly gets pleasure seeing other people happy, so he'll invest whatever it takes to make that happen. Yesterday, for example, he was having a really busy day at work, but his good friend Rudie called for help with a personal issue, and he dropped everything to help Rudie work through his dilemma.

This generosity applies to finances too. In our six years together, he has lent or given money to his cousin, his brother, his father, without analyzing the potential negative impact on his personal finances or whether those individuals can repay him. He does it for the sake of seeing others happy or at least to see them suffer less.

My husband connects to the creative, aesthetic and artistic side of life in a way that I cannot. He can achieve an almost romantic connection to music, to art, a beautiful interior and so on. He can spend hours window shopping, observing the textures of fabrics, the quality of the construction, the cut, the work put into it – valuing the 'love' that went into a piece rather than seeing it as just a product. His world comes alive.

I also admire his personal evolution and development to become the person he is. Instead of feeling resentful and angry about a difficult past, he decided to consciously become the best he could be, accepting, acknowledging and forgiving others and himself.

Charles helps me to soften and relax my drive to do things "right." For example, when we go on vacation, I'm entirely focused on getting the best flight connections, the optimal accommodation, visiting sites at the best time to avoid line-ups, so on. Most of the time I forget that the reason we're there is to enjoy ourselves. He forces me to slow down and shift my focus away from efficiency and the master plan and to sit down to enjoy a cup of coffee. I need and appreciate that.

One of our challenges is that it is difficult for my husband to say no to requests for help from other people in his life. It isn't a confusion about priorities – it is a philosophical difference. He says other people's needs ARE his priority. But it is hard to watch him physically, emotionally and energetically exhaust himself by spreading himself too thin trying to make other people happy or based on a sense of duty that he must step up to help.

One of my personal challenges in the relationship is that Charles is always willing to put his own needs on hold to satisfy mine. He is completely flexible in day-to-day decisions, which often means that I get my way, allowing me to remain in my own rigid comfort zone. From the outside, it may seem like a wonderful situation to have such an accommodating partner, but without a lot of conscious awareness, it can actually end up as an unhealthy codependency.

Overall, I'm very happy in my relationship. I feel like we push each other to be better people, and we share a deep love and respect for one another."

2:1 The Theory

2:1 When In Balance

The Perfectionist (1) and Helper (2) can be a very balancing and symbiotic match combining the cool, rational thought and problem-solving abilities of the Perfectionist (1) with emotional warmth, empathy, helpfulness and genuine concern for others of the Helper (2). Both partners tend to direct their attention outwards, either towards improving the world or their environment or in offering help or assistance to others. With this outward focus,

TYPE TWO HELPER/GIVER/LOVER

there can be a flavor of independence and autonomy in this dynamic. This can be a powerful, effective couple who can make a meaningful and lasting mark on their environment and the people in their social circles.

This pair shares a respect of one another's core values. They feel intrigue and interest around their differences and have shared vision of a harmonious future. Because they come at situations from very different perspectives, they can teach each other a lot. Perfectionist (1)s model logic, long-range thinking, rational thought and practical solutions. They show the Helper (2) how to set healthy boundaries and help disassociate from the emotional charge that often clouds the thinking of their Helper (2). They can offer sage advice, an alternative perspective and objectivity to their Helper (2). The Helper (2) brings warmth and a human touch to the often precise, mechanical thinking of their Perfectionist (1). They help show value of human relationships, emotions and interdependence. Together, this couple combines compassion with discernment and cool logic with warm concern. When their values are aligned, and they are respectful of their differences, this couple uses their opposite habits of attention as a strength.

2:1 The Downward Spiral

The habit of attention of the Perfectionist (1) and the Helper (2) point in very different directions and if the two partners aren't able to find balance that respects these differences, the downward spiral can begin. In a stressed or fixated state, the Perfectionist (1) becomes frustrated with the weak boundary setting of their Helper (2), and the Helper (2) becomes disappointed with disregard of the emotional world by the Perfectionist (1).

Perfectionist (1)s value efficiency and planning, rarely wanting to deviate from the predetermined course of action. The emotional world is minimized in exchange for mechanical, rational thinking. This thinking differs sharply with the Helper (2) who often values the satisfaction of others above their own. The feelings of other people factor largely into the Helper (2)'s thoughts and decision-making. They may be inclined to sacrifice their own happiness, or by extension the happiness of the partnership, to meet the needs of others. This triggers the Perfectionist (1) who feels this is unjust, unfair and wrong.

Both types may not be able to express their needs very clearly or directly, focusing on the difference in values instead of their own unmet needs. Instead of "I want more of your time" the Perfectionist (1) may say "I can't believe you once again answered your boss's email at midnight!" They may feel the Helper (2) is generous with their time and attention with everyone but the Perfectionist (1). And the Helper (2) may start to see the Perfectionist (1) as cold and uncompassionate. Instead of saying "I want you to speak from your heart and think of what it's like for that person" the Helper (2) may say "I don't care if we didn't agree to spend it, we're donating to that charity!"

If the downward spiral gains momentum, each person gets more frustrated with their partner. The Perfectionist (1) gets irritated and angry at the Helper (2)'s people-pleasing behavior. The Helper (2) gets fed up with the Perfectionist (1)'s criticism and rigid thinking. Arguments escalate, and anger intensifies. Both become disillusioned with the other. This continues until respect for one another is lost, and the relationship itself is threatened.

2:1 The Lighthouse
Different values around efficiency and human connection are the basis for discord in this relationship. Tolerance of these differences is the path back to connection. Perfectionist (1)s need to honor that their Helper (2) has a different sense of personal boundaries and a different priority around the emotional world. Helper (2)s need to honor their Perfectionist (1)'s drive for efficiency. These differences need to become balancing and not polarizing.

2:1 The Kundalini Yoga Connection
The path back to balance for this couple is an awareness and respect of their differences around efficiency and the emotional world. To come forward and accommodate these differences, both types need to strengthen their nervous systems.

Helper (2)s need to get in touch with their own needs and place a priority on self-care. Energetically Helper (2)s are usually out of touch with their bodies and physical, emotional and energetic needs. Kundalini Yoga kriyas and meditations that increase body awareness and that build energy are helpful for Helper (2)s.

Perfectionist (1)s need to open their heart and connect with the emotional world, both their own emotions and the emotions of others. Kundalini Yoga kriyas and meditations with heart opening and energy awareness exercises are helpful for Perfectionist (1)s.

See the appendix for Perfectionist (1) and Helper (2) recommended Kundalini Yoga kriyas and meditations.

2:2: Helper (2) with Helper (2)

Karl, Helper (2) formerly in a 4-year relationship with Jiya, Helper (2)

"Jiya was kind, generous, giving, nurturing of her family and friends and gifted at identifying what other people needed in a situation. She had strong family values and was dependable. She had very high emotional intelligence and could shapeshift to meet her audience. With a company CEO, she could talk at that level. And with a delivery person, she could talk at their level too to make them feel comfortable. She had an almost chameleon-like way about her that didn't seem phony. At the same time, she could be very concerned about what others thought of her. She was very afraid of being judged and had a deep sensitivity to rejection.

In our relationship, we had great communication as it related to what we felt but neither of us was as good at identifying what we wanted or needed. On one level, we connected deeply, and on another, we completely missed each other. We come from different cultural and racial backgrounds, and this brought in a unique set of issues to our dynamic. Jiya was committed to our relationship, but she wasn't ready to risk rejection by her family, friends and community, so our relationship remained hidden. In the beginning, I didn't object, but as time passed, I started to feel rejected myself. As the years passed, I felt angry and humiliated that I was being kept secret, but at the same time, I was trying to accommodate her. Neither of us was great at expressing direct anger so it would come out more like frustration and indirect confrontation.

As time passed, I became disillusioned with the relationship. We both had goals and dreams for our future, and I began to feel that the finish line to even basic goals was just too far away and with too many hurdles to get there. Eventually, we split up.

In retrospect, I think the fear of rejection by her family and friends was more than her temperament could tolerate. With hindsight, I recognize our relationship must have been tremendously hard for her because with me, by the very nature of my origins, she was trying to build an uncertain future.

This was many years ago, and I've gone on to marry a woman who is much better suited to go head to head with her family and friends if she wants something. We too have an interracial relationship, and while it has raised its share of issues, we've been able to navigate them successfully and are happy together. I appreciated my time with Jiya and learned a lot about myself from the relationship."

Elizabeth, Helper (2) married in a 4-year relationship with John, Helper (2)

"John is loyal and communicates well in a way that leaves me feeling loved. He affirms me constantly and reminds me that he values me and our relationship. We share many values

and see the world similarly. We both love time with friends and time together. We get joy from many of the same activities.

Our dynamic is very affirming. We are warm and affectionate with each other, constantly touching and playing together. We both want the other to feel wanted. We ask each other if the other is ok multiple times a day. And we seek reassurance from each other by asking "Do you love me?" And I ask, "Do you think I'm pretty?" We both know the other will respond right away with "Yes."

Self-esteem can be a challenge for both of us. My husband struggles with feeling incapable, worthless, broken and defective beyond repair. He has a hard time accepting compliments especially when he is feeling low. When I say kind things to him or compliment how well he is performing at work, he refutes my compliments faster than I can say them. It is like he cannot accept that he is valuable and important. At times he compares himself with me, and this is difficult. We both have stressful jobs, but he perceives me as able to handle stress much better than him, and that makes him feel deficient. He also struggles with physical illnesses. He frequently needs my help and support to get through the challenges of his illness. For example, John can't carry anything over 5 pounds so even simple things like opening heavy doors or carrying luggage or groceries can be a challenge requiring my help. I think this need compounds his feelings of defectiveness.

Self-esteem issues manifest differently for me. I struggle with feeling my worth is intrinsically tied to how I look, my weight and my beauty. It is hard for me to untangle these issues and see myself more holistically. I feel like my appearance determines my value.

While we have our struggles, I love our relationship. I feel life is joyful when we choose to be grateful, accept compliments and have perspective in how we react to difficult situations. It could be worse. And God is kind to us. We have so many blessings. We have one another. I try to focus on that and be grateful rather than letting small annoyances ruin my attitude. And I try to share this perspective with my husband."

2:2 The Theory

2:2 When In Balance

Two Helper (2)s make a kind-hearted pairing who place a high value on the relationship itself and are willing to work hard to make it successful and fulfilling. They strive to make the other feel loved and supported. Both partners have high emotional intelligence and are comfortable talking about their feelings so establishing a certain level of intimacy generally comes easily in this relationship. They both share the traits of being attentive, caring, nurturing, kind and reassuring.

As a couple, they are generous with time, energy and material support, trying to make the world a better place and to lessen suffering. When both partners are self-aware and in balance, they are extremely affectionate and connected while at the same time having a healthy sense of themselves and respect for personal boundaries.

Together, this is a generally loyal and stable partnership. Because both partners have such a drive to offer help, they may use their supportive, stable relationship as a foundation to bring in others that they can support and nurture. They create a supportive, healing environment and may invite the less fortunate to share this space with them. Together, this can be an altruistic, sweet, affirming and inspiring couple.

2:2: The Downward Spiral
When fixated, the Helper (2) defenses tighten around fear of rejection, feelings of low self-worth and a need for appreciation and validation from others.

Fear of rejection can come out in various ways with either or both partners accommodating behavior they are not really comfortable with. It can be hard for Helper (2)s to know their own needs and under stress, this disconnect intensifies. They may be deeply connected on some emotional and physical levels but miss each other completely on core needs and desires. There also may be issues of low self-esteem and indirect competition. The success of one partner may make the other feel worse about themselves.

This can bleed into questions of attractiveness and desirability. When fixated, Helper (2)s seek attention and admiration from others as a way to feel stable and to bolster their low self-esteem. As the downward spiral gains momentum, they may develop unhealthy dependencies on one another, and boundary issues develop. The more this continues, the more isolated and lonely each partner becomes threatening a once loving and supportive relationship.

2:2 The Lighthouse
Unmet needs signal the beginning of the downward spiral for this couple, so learning to identify and ask for what they need is key to reversing the momentum and healing the relationship. Self-care and self-nurturing by each partner are critical for the health of this relationship.

2:2 The Kundalini Yoga Connection
Energetically, both partners need to find balance within themselves. Their habit of attention sends their energy out to others as a way of supplying self-esteem. This is a trap. They must find self-esteem internally.

Because of the complicated relationship between pride and shame, both Helper (2)s need to admit, accept and appreciate their own needs. Kundalini Yoga kriyas and meditations for body awareness, energy awareness, creating self-love and balancing energy taken versus energy given are beneficial for Helper (2)s.

See the appendix for Helper (2) recommended Kundalini Yoga kriyas and meditations.

2:3: Helper (2) with Achiever (3)

David, Achiever (3) married in a 12-year relationship with Stephanie, Helper (2)

"My wife has a natural interest in people and instinctively wants to understand and help them. She brings thoughtfulness and a personal touch that I admire. Early on in our relationship, I learned something from her that in hindsight seems so obvious, and yet wasn't at the time given my level of awareness when I was younger. Through observing her, I've learned that to build genuine relationships with other people, I need to intentionally ask them questions about themselves when in conversation. She is amazing this way. It just comes naturally to her. She challenges me to think outside of myself and my needs.

In our relationship, we make a natural power couple. She engages well with intimate, personal connections while I drive things at a higher level. Often in the same setting, we alternate between these levels, giving each other breathing room and also the freedom to dabble as little or much as possible in the other person's zone. This allows us both to stretch our comfort zone and to retreat when needed. We have before been told, "You are attractive people!" with the context being relational as well as physical.

Together, we socialize well and balance each other. For example, recently, we entertained my work colleagues in our home. I shared many common interests with our guests, which made for lively conversation fodder. My wife engaged them directly with different questions, drawing out deeper feelings and insights that I would never have reached. Eventually, she had a prolonged, personal conversation with one guest, learning information of his somewhat strained family relationships and exposing him to helpful new reading material for these relationships. All the while I was absent from this conversation yet helping to entertain our other guests – and to re-engage the entire party when the time was right. She can establish intimacy quickly in a way that isn't as natural for me.

While I am not extroverted, I do enjoy the spotlight via accomplishment, from musical and academic competitions as a child to being perceived as an all-star in the corporate environment. She not only tolerates this but enthusiastically supports me in the spotlight.

TYPE TWO HELPER/GIVER/LOVER

In our relationship, we've had conflicts arise from her need for more recognition and appreciation from me. When I am unaware, I can be so focused on my own needs that there isn't always time and energy left for her interests. We try to talk at the end of the day, and I tend to direct conversations towards our end-goals: how are our finances looking? How are our practical needs like home, food and so forth being met? How will we spend our time? I will dominate our together-time with these topics, leaving us both exhausted, and at the end, there is little time or energy on my part for her interests. Naturally, this is frustrating for her.

Our pace is different. A fast pace of achievement is important, or at least natural, for me. I tend to act before I think, wanting to accomplish a task or project before considering a broader context. I thrive off these victories and yet rarely slow down enough to appreciate them. This is much different than her slower, more deliberate and emotionally connected pace. She wants to see, understand and experience all the emotional reactions and tends to focus her attention more on interpersonal dynamics than practical achievements.

We fight differently. In a conflict, I like to get to the point and a conclusion, either through tangible outputs or intangible relations. When we argue, I want us to understand each other with the explicit goal of resolving an issue. In contrast, it is more important for her that we understand each other emotionally. The outcome is less of a priority. Because we are different, I sometimes want to move beyond a topic before she is ready. I am generally uncomfortable with criticism from her, and in the past, I have tended to walk out on conversations that are heading towards what I see as unfair criticism. It is very hard for me to sit in negative emotional space. When confronted with a situation that I judge to be broken, my solution may be to burn it down. She is more cautious and considerate. These different styles can lead to conflict between us.

I hope my wife understands that despite how much I work, I do truly appreciate intimate personal connections. I have become absorbed in my career now because of my sense of obligation to provide for my family, not because I love work. To be fair, however, the desire to win and accomplish has always been there for me and is part of my character. I feel my best when I am achieving..."

Stavros (3) Achiever, married in a 20-year relationship with Athena, Helper (2)

"My wife is the most generous person in the world. Everyone loves her, which is easy to do since she emotes kindness and sincerity. She has almost an innocence to her, and there isn't a false bone in her body. She offers unconditional love, especially to our son. I really appreciate that she doesn't nag.

We complement each other well. We are both very social, outgoing and extroverted. I started a Greek-American social club after college, and that's where Athena and I met and when we started dating. These days, we continue to be very comfortable in a social scene and work well as a team. When we go to a party, we tend to split apart, socialize separately during the evening, touching base with each other throughout the party, and then leave together and share our highlights. We do not pout about being left alone, like I had experienced with girlfriends who were more introverted.

Our way of socializing also highlights some of our differences. Athena likes small, intimate parties with 5-30 people where everyone has a great time. It can be very upsetting for my wife if even one person is not enjoying themselves. She's super-detailed oriented for her parties to ensure a 100% satisfaction rate among her guests. I, on the other hand, take a more utilitarian approach to party-planning. I believe "the more, the merrier," and I used to plan parties for hundreds of people for my social club. My philosophy is that you can't please everyone, so I practice the 80/20 rule: as long as 80% of the people are happy with 20% of the effort and cost, I believe that the party is a success. This illustration carries over into our daily-decision making on a smaller scale.

I have worked very hard in my career, and I appreciate that my wife has always been extremely understanding of my travel, and amazingly flexible at picking up and moving our family for my career. Now and then she pushes for more quality time with the family, but I've worked hard at finding a good work-life balance, so this has been a manageable issue for us. Athena is interested in self-development, and I've learned a lot of it from osmosis – she's talks about this stuff all the time!

One of our central challenges is that we have a different perceived value of money. For my wife, money is very low on her list of needs, wants and concerns. Because of this, she makes decisions without factoring in how much things cost. From her perspective, I focus on money too much. Financially we have enough, and Athena doesn't spend huge amounts buying luxury goods and so forth, but we still often argue about the "worth" of something. I give her credit for teaching me to spend money on memories and intangibles instead of material things, but this has been a long, slow lesson."

2:3 The Theory

 ### 2:3 When In Balance

The Helper (2) and Achiever (3) can be a very supportive, charismatic and socially adept combination. While both can be outwardly focused, in their highest levels of development, both focus inward more. The Helper (2) takes more time for self-care, and the Achiever (3) is content just being, instead of doing. This deepens their emotional connection. Externally they can be a powerful combination with the Achiever (3) offering motivation, charisma and leadership, and the Helper (2) offering more in-depth connection and emotional support. Together, they can be well-regarded, charming, generous, positive and high-spirited. In their social circles, this is often a popular couple. They work well together in part because of their balancing differences.

Helper (2)s place a higher value on the emotional world and bring an empathetic personal touch and more individual focus to their interpersonal connections. They are thoughtful and considerate, generous and loving. Their pace is slower, and they speak more directly from the heart. Their goal is a true connection.

Achiever (3)s bring adaptability, charm, charisma and an orientation towards goals and achievement. They strive to be successful in the eyes of others, and Helper (2)s appreciate and respond well to this effort. Achiever (3)s have a faster pace and a greater desire to keep the mood high and positive. They seek achievement and to motivate and inspire others.

When in balance, the Helper (2) feels appreciated by their Achiever (3), and the Achiever (3) feels admired by their Helper (2). When both partners are self-aware, this can be an amazingly effective and accomplished couple, radiating charm, charisma, magnetism, helpfulness, kindness and grace. At their best, themes of quiet altruism may be present.

2:3 The Downward Spiral

Appreciation and admiration are like oxygen to the Helper (2) and Achiever (3). If either partner feels a scarcity of their oxygen, problems can arise. With tightening defenses, the Helper (2) may do more than they should and become overengaged and intrusive in the lives of others. They begin to feel underappreciated and worn out by their subconscious efforts to be appreciated thereby triggering the downward spiral. Conversely, with tightening defenses, the Achiever (3)s try to do and achieve more with a subconscious goal to gain admiration. This may trigger workaholism and a disconnect from the relationship itself and their own emotional needs. Both partners may begin to resent the other for not recognizing their efforts and indirectly for not meeting their emotional needs.

The Helper (2) may grow impatient at the drive to achieve and gain admiration that takes the Achiever (3) away from the relationship and a deeper emotional connection. The Helper (2) is highly aware of how image conscious their Achiever (3) is, and this can become a source of discord in the relationship. As the Helper (2) seeks a more authentic connection, the

Achiever (3) may feel threatened that their autonomy to pursue their goals is at risk. Both partners polarize, the Helper (2) leaning in for more focused time and attention and the Achiever (3) pulling away to achieve more goals as a way to feel stable.

Conversely, the Achiever (3) may start to resent the amount of time the Helper (2) lavishes on the needs of others feeling this attention is given more sparingly to them and to the relationship itself. The Helper (2) may see the relationship as an extension of themselves, and attention for the relationship may take a back seat for other priorities. The underlying issue is that when fixated, both Helper (2)s and the Achiever (3) disconnect from themselves. In a fixated state, Helper (2)s can't set healthy personal boundaries, and they lose connection with themselves. In a fixated state, Achiever (3)s focus exclusively on goals and achievement and lose connection with themselves. In both environments, the relationship suffers.

When fixated, the Helper (2) has lost touch with themselves and the Achiever (3) is in denial of their own emotions and self-worth, using constant achieving as a way to feel better about themselves. Misunderstandings become central themes in the dynamic. Unless the partnership finds a way to repair, the connection weakens and breaks apart, and the relationship drifts off course.

2:3 The Lighthouse
Unmet needs for attention, admiration and appreciation can be the downfall of this couple, so cultivating self-love can help break the downward momentum. Helper (2)s need to manage the drive for external appreciation and instead turn inward to find their sense of worth and value. Cultivating self-care and independent hobbies are helpful, healing and balancing. Achiever (3)s need to observe their compulsive drive to achieve and stay on the go. Learning stress and anxiety management tools can be beneficial in cultivating the ability to slow down. From this slower pace, emotions can come forward, and Achiever (3)s can communicate more directly from their hearts.

2:3 The Kundalini Yoga Connection
As Achiever (3)s connect with their heart and relax the need to continuously achieve, they become more present to themselves and others and less reliant on outside admiration and approval. Kundalini Yoga kriyas and meditations to cultivate a heart connection and develop a tolerance for stillness are helpful.

As Helper (2)s cultivate feelings of self-love, their drive to meet everyone else's needs diminishes. Behind the drive to help others is a subconscious sense of shame, a belief that on their own, they are not lovable. With the cultivation of self-love, this shame can dissolve. Kundalini Yoga kriyas and meditations to develop self-care and self-love are beneficial.

See the appendix for Helper (2) and Achiever (3) recommended Kundalini Yoga kriyas and meditations.

2:4: Helper (2) with Individualist (4)

Crystal, Individualist (4) married in a relationship for one year with Philippe, Helper (2)

"Philippe is selfless, compassionate, loving, sensitive and focused on the needs of others. He is generous and wants everyone in the world to be happy. He has a soft heart and is self-sacrificing. His friends know this and are protective of him. He is amazing with children – fatherly and very comfortable with them. Because he is so kind, he is loved and welcomed everywhere he goes. He gets along really well with my friends. He supports my relationships with other people and isn't jealous or threatened by my outside relationships.

I love that he has a soft heart and is not afraid to show his emotions – when we see a puppy, he gasps at how cute it is. When his father was gifted a motorcycle by his friends for his birthday, Philippe saw the post online when we were together at a restaurant, and he cried in public. I love that he wears his heart on his sleeve and is not self-conscious or ashamed of it.

Our relationship is life-giving as we can openly share our feelings and thoughts with each other. I feel secure with his warmth, knowing I don't have to worry about where I stand with him. I appreciate that he is so supportive. I'm not good at asking for help, but I still need it, especially as I struggle with Hashimoto's, a chronic autoimmune disease that drains my energy. He tries to be helpful from offering emotional support to buying groceries for me, even if he doesn't have groceries at his own house. He is relaxed and easy going, and we both feel like we belong and are at home with each other. Philippe is very physically affectionate, which I love and need, and his warmth allows me to be affectionate in return.

In our relationship, we offer each other balance. I bring emotional honesty, and as I am hypersensitive to any arising conflicts, I am usually the one who brings up difficult issues. It is very hard for me to leave things unaddressed. Philippe has said he's aware of the issues in the back of his mind but doesn't see an urgency to address them or even acknowledge them because "we're okay," meaning we're both committed to the relationship. I appreciated that when I voice my concerns, he usually addresses the issue immediately. A simple example is him looking at his phone too much when we are together. I brought it up as an issue, he took it seriously as a concern of mine, and now he's much more mindful. This is so important to me because it shows me he's committed not just to me but to the health of our dynamic together.

Through example, Philippe teaches me to look outside myself and to consider others more. Though I see the suffering of people I know and want to alleviate their pain, I often end up making the situation about me. He helps me to keep the focus on others and not fall into the trap of self-absorption. And conversely, I help him face his own needs. He is great at focusing on others but has a harder time focusing on himself. I help him to notice himself, and if I see something that I know he needs but isn't asking for, I try to meet that need.

As it relates to issues, our communication styles are different. Due to my autoimmune disease, I often feel extremely drained and low energy, but despite this, it is very hard for me to ask for help. My default pattern is to secretly hope my partner will see my suffering without me having to point it out. When I am noticed and seen, I feel loved. It is hard for me to be direct about my pain – it makes me feel vulnerable and weak. Philippe doesn't always notice my suffering, despite the fact I know he loves me deeply. We've had issues with simple things like cooking dinner. Sometimes I'm so tired that I'll ask him just to decide what we should eat so I can make it, but he doesn't want that responsibility. And often he will leave the dishwashing and so forth to me even though I'm exhausted. I've tried to ask him to ask me more about myself, but he feels uncomfortable and doesn't know how to ask questions. He feels inadequate and vulnerable in this area. So, this is an area we actively work on – me being more direct about my pain and him being more tuned in to my suffering. Despite how open we are with each other, we are both naturally shy and need a lot of time and trust to feel comfortable being openly vulnerable. Both of us have this challenge in all our relationships, romantic or not. We are getting there; it is just taking time.

It is so important to me that he truly sees me. I often think of this quote:
"To be loved but not known is comforting but superficial. To be known and not loved is our greatest fear. But to be fully known and truly loved is, well, a lot like being loved by God. It is what we need more than anything. It liberates us from pretense, humbles us out of our self-righteousness and fortifies us for any difficulty life can throw at us."

-Tim Keller, pastor

Overall, I am extremely happy in my relationship. I recognize with my push-pull nature, some of my attention will always be drawn to our issues. I know to honor that but to not buy into dissatisfaction too much. I admire and respect Philippe so much as a person and a partner, and I feel so lucky to be with him. He's fascinating, incredibly attractive, magnetic and so good at loving. He makes me very happy, and I am excited to spend my life with him."

Claire, Individualist (4) in a relationship for less than one year with Robert, Helper (2)

"I really value Robert's emotional availability, his communication skills, his ability to connect deeply, the way he sees the needs of others and responds and the value that he places on me and relationships in general. I also love how he notices and remembers little things – what I like or visual details of a place and so on.

Warmth and passion are the strengths that drew me to this relationship. I sensed warmth, safety and passion almost immediately and felt no hurdles of intimacy. Within the first week, he scheduled a massage for me, and he is constantly talking about ways that he wants to help me. Though that feels good to me, it's uncomfortable too; I don't know how to respond or what to do in return. He likes to give gifts, which I love. But again, I don't know how to respond.

What I appreciate about this relationship is the opportunity to really pour my love into someone that feels safe and who receives it. For my part, I've never been so affectionate or openly caring in a romantic relationship before. He says that he really cares for me, and I think that authenticity and presence is something I can give him. I appreciate that he's able to feel it and receive it.

This is a new relationship, so we haven't had a lot of issues yet. That said, while I don't find him saccharine, sometimes the flattery does make me uncomfortable, and I question his sincerity. I wonder if he could easily say the same things to anyone, just as earnestly. Even though I don't sense this from him, I worry that at some point he will want things from me that he won't say. I don't always know how to give to him, or whether I'm showing love in the way that he wants or needs.

One funny, ironic and sort of sweet dynamic we have is that when I'm trying to explain some way in which I'm broken or flawed, he just skips to the next thing as if he either doesn't understand or won't acknowledge it. On reflection, I realize this is probably very good for me. I don't need a partner who will perpetuate the "I'm broken" loop."

2:4 The Theory

2:4 When In Balance
The Helper (2) and Individualist (4) make a closely bonded, supportive, caring and loving combination. Both have high emotional fluency, and the world of feelings is center stage in this relationship. They openly share their thoughts, impressions and emotional responses with each other and can spend hours recounting the events of the day, their reactions and so forth. Together they create a safe haven to be real and authentic, and this can be a very healing relationship for both partners.

Helper (2)s are typically outward facing, social and comfortable interacting with a wide range of people. They can give the Individualist (4) confidence and energy to do the same by joining them socially. They are thoughtful, encouraging, patient, kind and considerate. They can make their Individualist (4) feel seen, something that is deeply healing for the Individualist (4).

Individualist (4)s bring emotional fearlessness, creativity, humor and broad picture thinking. They seek emotional honesty, and as they tend to be highly sensitive to arising conflicts, they are often the ones to bring up thorny issues. Individualist (4)s are deeply intuitive and can read the subtle undertones of a situation. They offer wise counsel to their Helper (2). More self-referencing, they give the Helper (2) permission to get in touch with their own needs and make themselves a priority.

Together they create a positive feedback loop, both admiring and appreciative of what the other brings. Both seek deep emotional connection, and they find it in each other. This is a couple known for its closeness.

2:4 The Downward Spiral
When fixated with tightening defenses, the emotional connection and intensity they share polarizes this couple. As both crave intimacy, they can spend a lot of time and energy processing small grievances and minor misunderstandings. Under stress with tightening defenses, this intensifies, and themes of insecurity, shame and blame enter the picture. Without a healthy mechanism to come back into balance, an endless loop of misunderstandings can begin, thus triggering the downward spiral.

The two types express their emotional needs very differently. Individualist (4)s are guided by their feelings, and their feelings are ever-changing. They need a lot of downtime to process their experiences and emotional energy, and this can be frustrating to the Helper (2) who wants a more engaged partner. With time, Helper (2)s can start to feel the Individualist (4) is self-absorbed, temperamental, testy and emotionally unpredictable. They may tire of the Individualist (4)'s negative self-image and difficulty accepting the nurturing the Helper (2) wants to provide.

The Individualist (4) can become suspicious of the Helper (2), as they see through their people-pleasing behavior and question its authenticity. They may feel smothered by the Helper (2), finding them needy and overly-involved. And because Individualist (4)s can be quite intuitive, they may tire of the often-unspoken need for appreciation coming from the Helper (2).

If the downward spiral gains momentum, the Helper (2) starts to feel increasingly unappreciated, and the Individualist (4) starts to feel increasingly misunderstood and alone. Both find each other emotionally needy and draining. Eventually one or both start to feel they would be better off without the relationship, and the relationship is in danger.

2:4 The Lighthouse
Because both Helper (2)s and Individualist (4)s are so charged with the energy of emotion, energy management is essential to break the momentum of any downward spiral. Both types are very emotionally driven so learning to balance the ever-changing fluctuations of emotional current is key to the health of the relationship. Under stress, they move in opposite directions, the Helper (2) leaning in for connection, and the Individualist (4) pulling back to conserve what little energy they have. To break the momentum of the downward spiral, each partner needs to learn to stay energetically still.

2:4 The Kundalini Yoga Connection
When the downward spiral starts, Helper (2)s need to get in touch with their own needs and place a priority on self-care. They need to resist the urge to lean forward into the energetic space of the Individualist (4) as the Individualist (4) typically wants to withdraw to process their feelings. Kundalini Yoga kriyas to build the nervous system, that center and balance the energy centers and that cultivate self-love and self-acceptance are helpful for Helper (2)s.

Individualist (4)s need to cultivate feelings of trust and self-love. They need to learn to honor their emotions while resisting the urge to withdraw. They grow as they become more balanced. Kundalini Yoga kriyas and meditations that promote a strong nervous system and a consistent breathwork practice to build stability, equanimity and neutral mind are beneficial.

See the appendix for Helper (2) and Individualist (4) recommended Kundalini Yoga kriyas and meditations.

2:5 Helper (2) with Investigator (5)

Moses, Investigator (5) married in a 15-year relationship with Lucy, Helper (2)

"My wife is smart, thoughtful, moral, principled and extremely caring and concerned about the feelings and happiness of others. She is sensitive and has keen insight into people's preferences and desires. She is a wonderful mother and friend, and I admire how much she cares about others. She is incredibly patient and tolerant of my quirks. And she is always up for an adventure. Lucy and I are generally aligned with values, principles and lifestyle preferences, but when we don't agree on something, her position always still seems reasonable. In debates and discussions, I appreciate her perspectives and that she rarely gets defensive. She's quite open-minded and curious.

Lucy has improved my life in countless ways through her nurturing, her emotional intelligence and her wisdom. I live in a much cleaner apartment, I dress better, and I eat better than I did before I met her. Because of her in influence, I now act in much more socially appropriate ways, and my ability to connect with people has improved dramatically. I often think "What would Lucy do?" and find a better response than my natural reaction. I really admire that she's an incredible "preference collector" - someone who notices what people love and value, and then finds a gift or makes a thoughtful gesture based on that observation. She's given me dozens of gifts that I didn't even know I wanted but once I got them, I couldn't believe I ever lived without them.

One key value in our relationship is that we respect each other's time and space. Lucy is extremely respectful of my need to have independent time when I can read, listen to music, go down internet rabbit holes and so forth. I love going to see live music and go to over 100 concerts per year. As long as we plan in advance, so it doesn't disrupt her schedule, she is very supportive of this passion of mine. And I give her lots of space to pursue her activities.

I do sometimes sense tension, frustration and resentment on her part that she has less free time than I do. But we both recognize that this is because she fills her time helping others – writing the weekly school newsletter for our daughter's school, keeping up with her wide network of friends, taking on extra work of her co-workers to help them out and so forth. She spends a lot of energy doing things for other people to try to make them happy, and this often leaves her tired and drained. Occasionally I get frustrated at her overcommitments since they take away from the relatively little time we have to do things as a couple.

She has a reluctance to let me help that is puzzling to me. She generally declines my offers for assistance if I volunteer to do something that will make her life easier. Instead, she insists on doing it herself. And interestingly, she rarely thanks me for doing things around the house when I do pitch in. I probably should do more, and lately, I have been making an effort to take more initiative, but if she expressed more appreciation, I think I would feel more motivated. This is an issue we're actively working on and one in which compromise can seem challenging. Sometimes we both would rather be "right" than happy, and we continue to work on this.

I love my wife, and I wish she would take more time for herself and for us as a couple than she does. I wish she understood there is nothing wrong with healthy amounts of self-care and that it's OK to say no to a request from someone else if saying yes to them will negatively impact your ability to take proper care of yourself. But, in the same way that she has come to terms with the choices I make, I have to accept the ones she makes as well.

Another core difference centers around our values about money. I value saving money more than my wife, and I sometimes feel that she is overly generous to her friends. She'll buy them expensive gifts or pay for more than her share of dinner while I view that money as something for our daughter's college education or our future retirement. We try to meet in the middle on this, but it is a difference.

Overall, I'm very happy in my relationship. My wife is a wonderful partner whom I love, respect and admire. She balances me and brings me many of life's gifts that I would never find without her. I'm very grateful to have her as my wife."

2:5 The Theory

 ### 2:5 When In Balance

The Helper (2) with the Investigator (5) is a classic example of opposites attracting, the social butterfly with the reserved wallflower. Their differences form not only the initial attraction but the longer-term bond between the two. Together, this couple balances each other.

Helper (2)s are socially adept with high emotional intelligence, charm, warmth and engaging, friendly behavior. They value personal relationships highly and seek deep connection with others. They are at home in the world of feelings, emotions and social connections. In contrast, Investigator (5) prefer to minimize their connection to others as they seek to preserve what they experience as very limited energy. They value self-sufficiency, limited demands and personal freedom. They are at home in the world of logic, facts, information and reason. Blended, this couple creates a home that values both logic, facts, feelings and relationships.

The Helper (2) offers the Investigator (5) caring, nurturing, concern, attentiveness and an introduction to the soft skills in life: communication, emotional fluency and social graces. Investigator (5)s report their life becomes upgraded with the influence of their Helper (2). Their home is cleaner, they dress better, they eat better, they understand other people more and so forth. In return, the Investigator (5) offers a solid foundation to their Helper (2). Less clouded by emotion, the Investigator (5) brings clear analysis, rational thought and logic to the decision-making of the Helper (2). They help calm emotional storms and are a stable rock for the Helper (2) who can get drawn into interpersonal dramas.

Successful negotiation of time spent together and independently is key in this relationship. Investigator (5)s and Helper (2) set their personal priorities differently, and successful couples report giving each other a lot of personal freedom to pursue things that are important to them.

Together, this is a highly balancing couple who share a deep bond of affection, commitment and loyalty.

2:5 The Downward Spiral
A key difference between Investigator (5) and Helper (2) is their sensitivity to personal boundaries (including time alone) and the different way they express love and affection. Investigator (5)s feel stable and secure when they are isolated and left to their individual pursuits. Helper (2)s feel stable and secure with constant, consistent personal connection. Investigator (5)s express love indirectly, though loyalty, consistency, good listening and problem solving. Helper (2)s are more openly affectionate and verbally expressive. These differences are fundamental and can create conflicts when either partner is fixated.

The Helper (2) may get frustrated and feel rejected by the Investigator (5)'s desire for solitude and lack of emotional expression. This triggers the downward spiral, with the Helper (2) trying harder to connect with their Investigator (5) who now feels their stability threatened. The more the Helper (2) leans in, the more the Investigator (5) shrinks back. The Helper (2) may not understand how their interest is interpreted as intrusion the same way the Investigator (5) may not realize how their isolation is interpreted as rejection.

Or conversely, the Helper (2) may start to withhold care and nurturing as a passive aggressive way of expressing dissatisfaction over the lack of attention they feel from their

Investigator (5). This may be confusing to the Investigator (5) who feels their desire for time alone is healthy and acceptable. They feel rejected without cause.

How far the downward cycle goes depends a lot on each person's self-awareness and tolerance for discomfort. If there is awareness of the disconnect, it may be mended. If the fixation continues, both partners polarize, and the relationship may end.

2:5 The Lighthouse
Differences in stress responses characterize the downward spiral of this pair, so both partners need to notice their opposite push-pull response and come into balance. Both partners experience personal boundaries very differently. They each need to gain an awareness and understanding of the other person's experience around these boundaries.

2:5 The Kundalini Yoga Connection
The Helper (2) needs to stand more firmly in their own energetic space and resist the urge to lean forward into the space of their Investigator (5), who may feel this as intrusive. Self-care, self-acceptance and self-love must be cultivated. Helper (2)s have a strong drive to send their energy outward and to focus on others. Kundalini Yoga kriyas and meditations to develop physical awareness, self-love, self-acceptance and balance are beneficial for Helper (2)s.

The Investigator (5) needs to stay engaged with others and resist the impulse to withdraw for security, as this triggers insecurity and stress in their Helper (2). Kundalini Yoga kriyas and meditations to build the nervous system, to move the energy out of the head and into the heart and to cultivate energy awareness are helpful.

See the appendix for Helper (2) and Investigator (5) recommended Kundalini Yoga kriyas and meditations.

2:6: Helper (2) with Loyalist (6)

Paul, Loyalist (6) married in a 12-year relationship with Karen, Helper (2)

"I admire my wife tremendously – she is extremely intelligent without being overbearing. One of the things I value the most is her counsel. She analyzes and calculates situations from all angles, and she always gives me the best advice.

Our relationship is based on mutual support and caring. I get anxious under stress, but she knows just how to handle me, offering support while also letting me have my feelings and experience. And while I'm not the most verbal guy ever, I hope she knows and feels how much I love her. I think she is a wonderful partner."

2:6 The Theory

2:6 When In Balance
The Helper (2) with the Loyalist (6) have foundational values of mutual support, dependability and deep caring. This is a kind, nurturing couple in which both partners know they can rely on each other. Stability, both at home, at work and in their community is important to them and something they actively cultivate. With this as the base, they have some balancing differences.

Helper (2)s seek positive human connections and are warm, generous and kind. Protective and observant of those they love, they offer their sometimes anxious and reactive Loyalist (6) sage advice and a more rational, objective perspective. Because of their high emotional intelligence, they can often understand the subtle undercurrents of a situation, and this is balancing for the Loyalist (6) who has more narrow, worst-case scenario thinking. They work hard to create a nurturing, loving, supportive environment, and this effort is noticed and appreciated by the Loyalist (6).

Loyalist (6)s are hardworking, diligent, reliable, responsible and committed. They have an eye for danger and work hard to make sure threats to the home and the relationship itself are minimized. Helper (2)s appreciate this is someone who they can depend on through thick and thin, and this helps relax the Helper (2)'s fear of abandonment. The Loyalist (6)s can be affectionate and playful, and humor may be an important element in this couple's dynamic.

Together this can be a sweet, steady, straightforward pair. They respect each other's values and share an easy enjoyment of each other's company. This relationship grows and deepens over time. Dependability and commitment are at the core of this couple, and they can share an enduring, enjoyable partnership.

2:6 The Downward Spiral
The anxiety response of these partners can be the trigger for the downward spiral. With tightening defenses, Loyalist (6)s freeze or become erratic, and Helper (2)s lean in to

help. This creates an environment of confusion, resentment and misunderstanding. In times of stress, Loyalist (6)s become highly anxious, worried, panicky, suspicious and confused. Their thinking becomes circular and clouded leaving them unable to make clear, firm decisions.

As the Loyalist (6) freezes, the Helper (2) pushes to assist. Under stress with tightening defenses, they may become overly involved and domineering without realizing it. The Loyalist (6), prone to suspicion and anxiety, doesn't appreciate this behavior and the feeling they are being controlled. Resentment and confusion on both sides builds. The more the Helper (2) tries to get involved, the more the Loyalist (6) gets resentful. As the downward spiral gains momentum, there can be cycles of anxiety, anxious decision-making, resentment, apology, forgiveness and more anxiety.

The line between how much or how little the Helper (2) should get involved can be blurry and ever moving. Helper (2)s don't always understand that their efforts aren't appreciated, and with tightening defenses, Helper (2)s can become needy and demanding. The self-confidence of the Loyalist (6) can wax and wane with cycles of independence followed by neediness. The Loyalist (6)'s fears of being controlled are interwoven with the Helper (2)'s fears of rejection. Continuing downward, the Helper (2) can enter into a power struggle, threatening withdrawal if their partner doesn't change. With each cycle, the Helper (2) tries to come closer, and the Loyalist (6) tries to pull further away. If left unchecked, the downward momentum continues to build with exhausting cycles of dependency and rejection. Without a mechanism to break the momentum, the relationship suffers and may split.

2:6 The Lighthouse
Different responses to anxiety and fears of rejection are at the core of this couple's downward spiral. Loyalist (6)s worry about an uncertain future. Helper (2)s lean too far forward to try to become indispensable. To heal and break the downward momentum, both partners need to learn to become still and stay present in the face of anxiety and discomfort.

2:6 The Kundalini Yoga Connection
Helper (2)s need to manage their impulse to be overly involved in the lives of others and to get more in touch with their own needs. Kundalini Yoga kriyas that increase body awareness are helpful for Helper (2)s. Doing a yoga or meditation practice independently can be very beneficial to keep them focused on their own experience.

Loyalist (6)s need to manage their anxiety so their thinking becomes clear. Breathwork to change the body's response to stress and meditations to connect with inner guidance are a good first step. Kundalini Yoga kriyas and meditations to address anxiety and self-authority are beneficial.

See the appendix for Helper (2) and Loyalist (6) recommended Kundalini Yoga kriyas and meditations.

2:7: Helper (2) with Enthusiast (7)

Justin, Enthusiast (7) married in a 12-year relationship with Winter, Helper (2)

"My wife is the most compassionate, tolerant and caring person I have ever met. She feels gratitude for everything she has and is always willing to help others. She has a great work ethic and is always looking for new ways to be useful and helpful. Most of all, I value her spiritual path. Her commitment to her spiritual community and her spiritual path amazes and inspires me.

My wife brings people together, and through her, my social life has been expanded and enriched. At the same time, she never pressures me to socialize when I want down time. She brings balance to my life as well as supporting my emotional and physical needs. I feel her love and her commitment to our marriage.

We are lucky, in our twelve years together, we don't have a lot of big challenges in the relationship – more minor stuff like I wish Mary were neater and more organized. I think we both feel satisfied with our level of intimacy and the balance between that and our independence. I am the happiest I've ever been in my life and know that my wife and I can face life's challenges together."

2:7 The Theory

2:7 When In Balance
The Helper (2) and the Enthusiast (7) are a high energy, social, engaging and outgoing couple who enjoy creating a positive environment to share with those around them. Both share a lust for life and a natural curiosity about the world and other people.

While their external behavior can look similar, their habit of attention and internal world are very different. Helper (2)s are more other-oriented with a sensitivity to the feelings and conditions of others. They offer emotional depth to the relationship and are genuinely concerned about other people. This is inspiring to their partner and can help awaken the sometimes-latent capacity for compassion in their Enthusiast (7).

Enthusiast (7)s bring positive energy, a thirst for adventure, a bold "can-do" attitude and a sense of endless possibilities. Enthusiast (7)s generate excitement in their environment and uplift others with their joy, humor and storytelling. Helper (2)s admire this and appreciate the happiness their Enthusiast (7) brings to them and those around them. Enthusiast (7)s are self-referencing, and they can help their Helper (2) establish clearer personal boundaries. By example, they show the Helper (2) how to advocate for themselves and make their own desires a priority.

Both types can be idealistic and get pleasure sharing their abundance with others. This can be a highly altruistic, generous and inspiring pair. They make others feel warm, welcomed, loved and included.

2:7 The Downward Spiral

Their different habits of attention can become a source of conflict under stress with tightening defenses. Helper (2)s seek a deep, intimate connection to feel stable whereas Enthusiast (7)s seek personal freedom and an absence of limitations for their sense of stability. Under stress or in an unaware state, the Helper (2)'s fear of rejection may trigger clingy and dependent behavior. They lean forward towards their Enthusiast (7) wanting more connection and more assurance that the relationship is stable. The Enthusiast (7) may sense their personal freedom is at risk and begin to turn their attention to new possibilities. The degree to which the Helper (2) can manage their urge to lean in and the degree to which the Enthusiast (7) can resist their urge to flee determines how much momentum the downward spiral gains.

The Helper (2) can also become disillusioned with the self-referencing nature of the Enthusiast (7). The Helper (2) longs for a deep, stable emotional connection and as they start to understand the degree that their Enthusiast (7) focuses on themselves, they may start to doubt the chance of a happy future together. When fixated, Enthusiast (7)s adopt a "me first" attitude, and this can be disappointing to their Helper (2). The downward spiral can be triggered through themes of rejection and limitation. Once this couple starts to polarize, it can be hard to break the momentum.

2:7 The Lighthouse
Differences around core fears and core desires are what start the downward spiral for this couple. Helper (2)s fear rejection, and Enthusiast (7)s fear limitations on their freedom. As fears get triggered, they begin to move in opposite directions energetically – Helper (2)s moving towards the Enthusiast (7), and Enthusiast (7)s running away from the Helper (2). To break the downward momentum, both types need to learn to stay still.

 2:7 The Kundalini Yoga Connection
A strong nervous system will help both the Helper (2) and Enthusiast (7) cultivate stillness and to act, not react.

Helper (2)s need to stay centered and turn their attention back to themselves when they start to get triggered by fears of rejection. Self-care is important, and Kundalini Yoga kriyas and meditations that cultivate self-love, self-acceptance and raise body and energy awareness are beneficial for Helper (2)s. It is beneficial for Helper (2)s to do their practice independently so they can fully focus their attention on themselves.

Enthusiast (7)s need to connect with their heart and to lower their anxiety around perceived limitations. Enthusiast (7)s can have a physical response to limitation, a contraction, that triggers stress and anxiety. Kundalini Yoga kriyas and meditations for heart opening, anxiety management and decreasing stress are helpful. Breath management exercises, particularly long deep breathing, can be helpful for Enthusiast (7)s.

See the appendix for Helper (2) and Enthusiast (7) recommended Kundalini Yoga kriyas and meditations.

2:8: Helper (2) with Leader (8)

Charlotte, Leader (8) married in a 20-year relationship with Oliver, Helper (2)

"We were 26 years old when we met and each going through difficult times. His kindness, softness and tenderness, despite my constant resistance, was what won my heart... He knew somehow that my hard shell was just that, a shell. He saw through it, whereas other people didn't. Or others saw it, decided they could not break it and walked away. He was persistent. And that won me over. Somehow, I felt he passed the test.

My husband is stable, reliable, self-sacrificing and wants the best for his family. He's always willing to help others, and I love that he's the one who runs to help an old lady crossing

TYPE TWO HELPER/GIVER/LOVER

the street. He's passionate and very comfortable expressing his soft side. I feel safe being vulnerable with him. He broke my tough shell and can handle me. He is forgiving and takes my bluntness without getting too hurt by it. He forgets fights between us quickly, not taking my harshness and anger to heart for very long. He is always trying to please me and works hard to make me happy. I love being his queen and being waited on by him! We are best friends and enjoy each other's company.

Our parenting styles are different and in many ways we have the opposite of traditional male/female roles. He's more in touch with the kids' emotions than I am and in that regard is more like the "mom." As the kids get older, I am more understanding of their needs as teenagers and give them more space and freedom. We've learned ways to respect, accept, love and celebrate the differences, and I actually think as parents we provide a healthy balance.

One central issue we had to work through was finding the right balance of dependency in our relationship. My husband is very giving and wants to do everything for everyone in his family. When the kids were younger, he would get them ready in the morning, take them to school, go grocery shopping, manage the house, pay the bills, bring me coffee at my bedside every morning and so forth. But then, he'd go away on a business trip leaving me alone with the children, and I would rage at how dependent they were, expecting me to do all the things their father did for them. It was extreme – my seven-year-old expected his toothpaste to be squeezed on his toothbrush for him. I had no idea that my husband was squeezing their toothpaste! I would call and scream at him for leaving me with these problems. My poor husband felt so guilty, and it took me a while to realize my accusations weren't helping the situation. But my anger would take over again. This cycle went on for many years with me blaming him for doing too much and him not feeling appreciated for all he was doing.

And then, there was the tuna incident. One day right before leaving on a business trip, he noticed there was no tuna in the pantry. In his mind, it was his responsibility to make sure the pantry was full in case, God forbid, we urgently needed something. Like tuna. He was about to leave to go to the store when I finally broke down yelling I wasn't interested in TUNA, and I would rather he spend time with me before he went away on his trip. This was a huge moment for both of us, a shock for him that I actually wanted him, and not the things he does, and for me to get him to understand that we needed to find a healthy balance.

We continue to fine-tune the dependency balance, but my kids understand that Dad and I are different. They can't expect the same treatment. My husband has gotten more in touch with his needs and doesn't feel as compelled to do everything for everyone. And my urge to fight has decreased, so we have more peace in our environment.

In many ways, he is everything I am not. We've been together 20 years and are much more settled into the understanding of who we are, both individually and as a couple. He has stuck with me through thick and thin, and I feel a tremendous amount of love and appreciation to have him by my side. If two people with opposite trigger points can grow together, it's a real soulmate thing. And that's what I feel with him."

Vlad, Leader (8) married in a 10-year relationship with Stasia, Helper (2)

"My wife has an ability to forgive which I admire, particularly since I have almost none of that ability. She easily expresses kindness to others and always has a willingness to show up for others – emotionally, practically and sometimes even financially. My wife easily and authentically expresses love. This is especially true with our children – I feel like she literally smothers them in love – in a healthy way, and they can sense it. It makes me happy to know they feel this protective and supportive cocoon around them from her."

2:8 The Theory

2:8 When In Balance

The Helper (2) and the Leader (8) combination can have an archetypical flavor to it with the Leader (8) embodying many of the traditional masculine or yang traits and the Helper (2) embodying the more feminine or yin traits. This can be a successful and enduring couple in which responsibilities are clearly delineated, and both partners complement and support each other.

Helper (2)s are more interested in the welfare of others while Leader (8)s tend to be more self-interested. Helper (2)s are more directly connected to the emotional world. They value emotions highly and can identify, discuss and process their feelings and the feelings of others. They can reach even emotionally remote people. This is an important trait in breaking through the Leader (8)'s tough emotional armor. Leader (8)s can be very vulnerable and sensitive on the inside, but this is rarely presented to the outside world, and it takes someone with great empathy and an open heart to reach them. Helper (2)s are affectionate and adoring, and Leader (8)s enjoy basking in their care.

Leader (8)s are tough, practical and results-oriented. They balance out the Helper (2)'s softness and make sure concrete priorities get done. They have few or no issues with personal boundaries, and Helper (2)s can learn a lot from watching their Leader (8) partner. Leader (8)s are hard-working, resourceful, resilient and make sure the couple's concrete needs are met. Helper (2)s notice this and appreciate and admire their Leader (8)'s hard work and sacrifice.

Together, this can be a strong-willed, effective, supportive couple who accommodate each other's blind spots and accentuate each other's strengths.

2:8 The Downward Spiral
Helper (2)s and Leader (8)s value the emotional world very differently and have very different communication styles. With tightening defenses, these differences can trigger the downward spiral.

Helper (2)s place importance on feelings, relationships and emotional responses. Leader (8)s value the tangible, practical world more highly, and in average-to-lower levels of awareness can have a casual disregard for the emotional world. This difference manifests as dramatically different interpersonal styles. Leader (8)s are direct and independent with a potentially harsher way of dealing with people and situations. In average levels of awareness, they fall back on logic and reason, often stripping emotion out of decision-making. They can take pride in this approach. In contrast, average Helper (2)s become highly attached to people. Situations are loaded with emotion. Helper (2)s are more other-oriented in their thinking and feel they can't be at ease if they know someone close to them is suffering. Leader (8)s feel they can't relax if those close to them can't learn to take care of themselves.

Both types can polarize about their approach to interpersonal problems. Helper (2)s want to be overly involved whereas Leader (8)s demand independence. Helper (2)s see their Leader (8) as hard-hearted, confrontational, cold and self-centered. Leader (8)s lose respect for their Helper (2) seeing them as weak, manipulative and creating unnecessary dependencies with others. Fights around value differences can pepper the relationship, with neither side feeling they can move too much into the middle without a loss of their core values. They can be mutually confused by the other's position.

The cycle continues with the Leader (8) losing respect for the Helper (2), finding them people-pleasing and manipulative, and the Helper (2) feeling their Leader (8) is hard-hearted and controlling. Without a break in the momentum, the relationship is at risk, and the partners may split.

2:8 The Lighthouse
Different values around human connection and different communication styles start the downward spiral of this couple so coming back into the center is the way to stop the

downward momentum. Helper (2)s need to try to connect with their Leader (8)'s fear of being vulnerable and the accompanying aggression to hide vulnerability. Leader (8)s need to respect their Helper (2)'s orientation towards feelings and emotions.

 2:8 The Kundalini Yoga Connection
Both types need to strengthen their nervous system, so the communication style differences don't feel as threatening.

Helper (2)s need to manage their impulse to be so involved in the lives of others and to get more in touch with their own needs. Kundalini Yoga kriyas and meditations that increase body awareness, that cultivate self-love, self-acceptance and balance are helpful for Helper (2)s. Doing a yoga or meditation practice independently can be very beneficial to keep them focused on their own experience.

Leader (8)s need to connect with their heart and to learn the value of the emotional world, both their own emotions and the emotions of others. They need to learn to contain the energy of anger and to manage their aggressive communication style. This aggressive style is likely damaging their relationships. And they need to learn the power of vulnerability. Kundalini Yoga kriyas and meditations with heart opening and breath management exercises can be helpful for Leader (8)s.

See the appendix for Helper (2) and Leader (8) recommended Kundalini Yoga kriyas and meditations.

2:9: Helper (2) with Peacemaker (9)

Fotini, Peacemaker (9) married in a 23-year relationship with Thodoris, Helper (2)

"I love my husband's wisdom, insight, generous spirit, clarity and personal strength. I appreciate his masculine energy, his ability to get things done, his decisiveness, and the fact that he brings interesting people and experiences to our lives. Thodoris creates a loving, safe space for me and others. I feel adored and fully accepted by him, and he has a gift for holding a healing emotional space for people as they face their deepest truths and fears. He is also extremely gifted with words and language.

Together, we are a nurturing, helpful, hospitable, easy-going, positive couple. Thodoris brings energy and initiative, and I offer a quiet steadiness and uncomplicated directness. We are very accepting, supportive and considerate of each other and have experienced a psychic link, often calling each other at exactly the same time or knowing what the other is thinking or having intuitive knowledge about one another.

TYPE TWO HELPER/GIVER/LOVER

Our professional lives center around providing acceptance, support and personal insight to others. We lead small groups in our home, helping people become more conscious, suffer less and have better relationships. People love our approach, and several people have told us they wish they were our children. We also teach workshops about having better relationships, and often people come because they see our partnership and want to learn our secrets.

We are a blended family with six children, both of us coming to our marriage with children from prior relationships. The combined family is big, with significant others and grandchildren, and we love being together. Thodoris and I enjoy providing a nurturing, supportive environment for the extended family.

As it relates to issues, we both have to be mindful of our personal boundaries and not giving our power away. It is easy for each of us to go along with what the other one wants, and neither of us wants to be the bad guy, which has caused issues in our parenting. At various times I have thought Thodoris was too lenient with his own children, and vice versa.

When I am upset about something, I sometimes withdraw and get passive aggressive, and Thodoris feels rejected and criticized. I can also get reactive when he gives too much of himself to others, either feeling like it threatens our connection or just that it is not right, offending my sense of fairness. But we learned early in our relationship to speak openly and honestly with each other. We are passionately committed to being connected, so we don't let much time pass before we talk through our issues.

We are a happy couple – I love being with Thodoris, and he loves being with me. Because we became a couple later in life and are both passionately committed to personal growth and self-awareness, I think we have avoided some of the pitfalls that we might have experienced if we had met earlier. The fact that we are both focused on the other and less self-focused has also been good for us. I feel seen and valued, and he feels appreciated. I've very grateful for my relationship and how we've found a good balance between giving and receiving."

2:9 The Theory

2:9 When In Balance

The Helper (2) with the Peacemaker (9) make a warm, loving, accepting and nurturing couple who enjoy each other's company and create a supportive, healing space for others. Both are other-referencing and place a high value on harmony so this a relationship with little direct conflict. Both can be accommodating, low-key and compassionate, seeing the pain in others and wanting to help alleviate suffering. With these foundational similarities, there are also some balancing differences.

Helper (2)s are generally more social, engaging, decisive and extroverted. They bring energy and initiative to the dynamic, and they may drive the social calendar of the couple. Relationships are important to them, and they gain a lot of happiness from their interactions with other people. With this consistent drive to connect, they need less alone time than their Peacemaker (9).

The Peacemaker (9) offers steadiness, uncomplicated directness and a relaxed, easygoing attitude. They are adaptable and can be comfortable in a lot of different environments and situations. More low energy and less decisive than their Helper (2) partner, they take more time to putter, process their feelings and just generally relax.

Together, this can be an easygoing, sensitive, kind and altruistic pair. They support each other in a variety of ways ranging from affirmation, acts of service, physical presence and kind gestures. Both strive to be sensitive to the needs of the other and harmony and support are top priorities for both partners.

 2:9 The Downward Spiral
This couple's avoidant tendencies and confusion around personal boundaries can be the trigger for the downward spiral. With tightening defenses, both Helper (2)s and Peacemaker (9)s can avoid bringing up difficult subjects relating to the relationship and may instead make unspoken agreements to let difficult issues go unaddressed. This means important problems go unresolved, building walls of unhappiness and resentment setting the stage for the downward spiral.

Alternatively, weak boundary awareness can be an issue in this couple. Both types have a tendency to merge, and in the case of the Helper (2), this can manifest as a desire to get overly engaged in the issues of their Peacemaker (9) partner. The Helper (2) leans in to help as a way of expressing love and a subconscious strategy to gain appreciation. However, the Peacemaker (9) may resent these efforts, experiencing their Helper (2) as bossy and controlling. Both partners are triggered but their reaction moves in different directions. The Peacemaker (9) becomes more withdrawn and disengaged, and the Helper (2) gets more demanding and involved. Thus begins a repeating toxic loop of help and withdrawal.

As the defenses tighten, so does the intensity of the polarization. The Helper (2) seeks appreciation, and as this need goes unmet, their increase their efforts. The Peacemaker (9) numbs out and can feel internal confusion. Because both types avoid conflict, the relationship may continue but both types may fall into a depression or experience other physical manifestations of an unhappy relationship. Eventually one or both partners may decide to get their needs met elsewhere or end the relationship.

2:9 The Lighthouse
Indirect communication and a lack of clarity around their own needs and desires mark the beginning of the downward spiral for this pair, so becoming clearer on both fronts is the way to break the downward momentum. A strong navel point and a powerful Kundalini Yoga breathwork practice will help these types.

2:9 The Kundalini Yoga Connection
Energetically, confusion around personal boundaries is an issue this couple needs to address. Both partners may have difficulting identifying where each individual starts and ends. Developing a strong self-awareness is helpful for both.

Helper (2)s need to manage their impulse to speak for the Peacemaker (9) and to instead refocus on their own needs. Kundalini Yoga kriyas that increase body awareness, self-care and self-acceptance are helpful for Helper (2)s. And cultivating stillness is helpful for the dynamic so the Peacemaker (9) feels less of an urge to withdraw.

Peacemaker (9)s need to connect to their own power and learn to be direct instead of passive-aggressive. This starts with them understanding their needs and desires. They need to cultivate a sense of themselves and to develop their power center. Kundalini Yoga kriyas and meditations to build a strong navel center, a strong nervous system and to raise their energy are helpful for Peacemaker (9)s.

See the appendix for Helper (2) and Peacemaker (9) recommended Kundalini Yoga kriyas and meditations.

This book is a living document. We will be updating it periodically with new information. If you are or were in a relationship with a Helper (2) and you would like to participate in the related relationship survey, please email me at lynn@lynnroulo.com

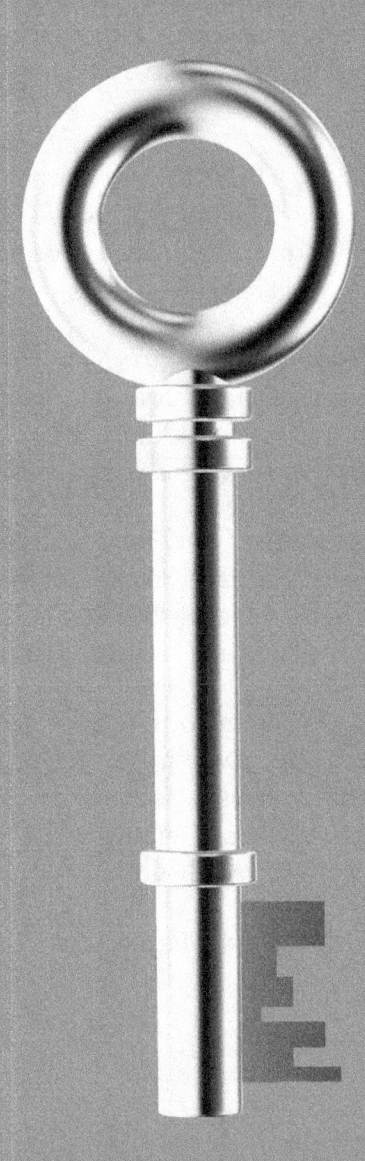

3

Type Three
MOTIVATOR/ ACHIEVER (3)
(seeks success/avoids failure)

 ## Overview

Achievers/Motivators are typically energetic, optimistic, self-assured and goal-oriented. This is the Energizer Bunny® of the Enneagram. This person is highly productive, efficient and can be extremely motivating to others. This type is a very action-oriented, often successful person who naturally presents a positive image to the outside world. Gaining the admiration of others is important to them, and they put a lot of energy into the achievement of their goals. A desire to be the best in any situation is a hallmark of Achiever (3)s.

Image matters a lot to Achiever (3)s, and they work hard to make sure they and their relationships are presented in a good light. In a relationship, partners say they value that their Achiever (3)s are driven, energetic, accomplished, adaptable, responsible, easy to admire, charismatic, adventurous yet stable and dedicated to excellence. Achiever (3)s value achievement, so they tend to get a lot done, often bringing their partners along for the ride.

On the positive side, the drive for excellence often encompasses the partnership itself, and Achiever (3)s can bring an almost magical quality to their relationships.

On the less positive side, this magical quality can be based on an image consciousness that can create relationship tension. Partners say they are challenged by the fact their Achiever (3) is goal-oriented to the point of sacrificing their personal life, excessively competitive, image-conscious to the point of being insecure, shapeshifting and overly concerned about the opinions of others.

• Attention Bias/Habit Of Attention:
Their attention goes towards being successful in the eyes of other people. They see what brings success and approval from others. Their attention moves away from anything that could be recognized as a failure, particularly in the eyes of others.

• Emotional Style:
Positive, upbeat, desire to spin the situation into a win, focus on excellence, avoidant. Love is fused with an appearance of well-being.

• Communication Style:
Motivational, encouraging, inspiring, positive, business-like, directive, charming, impatient, professional, polished.

• Brings To The Relationship:
Drive, a desire to win and succeed, optimism, motivation, networking with others, determination, perseverance and hard-working nature often leading to material success, stability.

• Unique Strengths:
Brings out best in self and in others, inspirational and motivating, able to set and achieve concrete goals and make a difference in the world.

• Challenges:
Overly goal-oriented, sacrificing family time, emotional connection and personal health to achieve professional goals. Can be overly competitive, overly concerned about the opinion of "others," may walk away from or abandon situations and relationships where they feel they cannot be successful. This may include intimate relationships.

• Security And Stability:
"I feel stable when I know other people are speaking and thinking well of me. I feel my best and most secure when I am working, winning, being recognized as the best, being popular and achieving external markers of success. When I achieve an important goal, and others recognize it, I feel wonderful."

• Instability And Insecurity:
"I feel insecure when I think other people might be speaking poorly of me. I feel unstable when I'm not achieving and being productive. Sometimes this shows up as impatience. I feel terrible if I am associated with failure in any way."

• Energy:
Kinetic, radiating energy, bright on the outside but more subdued, darker on the inside, difficulty with true stillness.

• Path Of Growth:
Authenticity

Self-acceptance is the growth path leading to authenticity, allowing for imperfection and personal failure. Shame dissolves to self-acceptance and self-love.

• Kundalini Yoga Connection:
Despite being part of the Heart/Feeling Triad, Achiever (3)s can be very cut off from their emotional world and from their heart center. Their drive to achieve and avoid shame is so strong they often sacrifice the emotional world in their pursuit of goals. Kundalini Yoga kriyas and meditations to balance the head and heart, connect with their heart center and cultivate stillness are beneficial.

Kundalini Yoga is particularly well-suited for Achiever (3) because the practice generally requires the practitioner to keep their eyes shut and their focus internal. For such an externally focused type, this is beneficial and potentially healing.

The Achiever (3) Subtypes

"Security" Self-Preservation Subtype:
The self-preservation Achiever (3) expresses a focus on achievement and a drive to succeed in an understated, humble way. This is a person who considers it bad manners to openly brag about accomplishments, although most self-preservation Achiever (3)s privately admit they do enjoy public praise and admiration.

To the outside world, this is hard-working, successful, humble person who excels professionally in their chosen field. This Achiever (3) goes beyond wanting the image of success. It is important to them that they actually are good in their respective fields and roles. Internally, this person is often experiencing a great deal of anxiety. They address this anxiety by working harder in an attempt to achieve more security. They have the title "Security" because of their preoccupation with work, efficiency and security.

Self-preservation Achiever (3)s are motivated to work very hard to achieve security. On the positive side, there is a certain genuine quality with self-preservation Achiever (3)s as their drive for excellence extends beyond the image. They put in long hours and much effort to be truly great at their chosen goal.

On the less positive side, with so much energy focused on work and security, there can be little mental and emotional space left for these Achiever (3)s to engage deeply with others. Though they may work hard to maintain relationships, they may have trouble making deep connections. Partners need to learn to deal with workaholism. These Achiever (3)s struggle with expressing vulnerability and getting help from others. They are fiercely autonomous.

"Prestige" Social Subtype:
The social Achiever (3) expresses a focus on achievement by outwardly seeking admiration and highlighting their achievements and successes. They want to shine in front of the whole world. This person can be a social chameleon, shape -shifting to impress as much as possible in whatever environment they are in. To the outside world, this is someone who can look socially brilliant and adaptable. They want to be accepted, so feeling sociable with others is critical.

Internally, this person has a lot of anxiety about being overexposed, and criticism can be devastating to them. They sometimes express a fear that if they look too deeply inside, they will find there is nothing there. This type is titled "Prestige" because of their desire to have the approval and applause of others. Image matters a lot for the social Achiever (3). This is the most externally competitive Achiever (3), and they are concerned about appearances and what looks good.

On the positive side, they can make an externally dazzling partner. They are often accomplished, attractive and work hard to present themselves well.

On the less positive side, they can have difficulty cultivating intimacy because they want so much to make a good impression and to be seen in a positive light. They are reluctant to reveal themselves, particularly their flaws, faults and shortcomings. Because they are good at numbing out their feelings, in extreme circumstances they can be cold and lack empathy.

"Charisma" Intimate Subtype:
The intimate Achiever (3) expresses a drive for achievement and recognition through intimate relationships. This is a person that focuses energy on being attractive and

desirable. More shy, sweet and reserved than the other Achiever (3)s, this person can be uncomfortable with direct recognition and instead focuses their energy on promoting someone or something else.

To the outside world, this is an attractive, sometimes seductive person who often offers enthusiastic support to others. They are highly helpful and supportive, often striving to be the perfect role model – for example, the perfect husband or wife. Internally, this person often feels a deep sadness or emptiness and sometimes fantasizes about a perfect mate and a happy future. This type is titled "Charisma" because of their intense focus on their desirability and attracting the devotion of others.

These Achiever (3)s are helpers and pleasers generally in support of someone else and working hard to make someone else look good. They may work hard to promote their partner or a shared venture with their partner.

On the positive side, they tend to be very helpful, though subconsciously this is a way to prove their lovability. Like all Achiever (3)s, they are goal-oriented, but their goals center around attaining love or desire from others and what they achieve within relationships.

On the less positive side, this Achiever (3) can have a profound disconnection from themselves and from others. They often report feeling an emptiness or a void. This is the most emotional of the Achiever (3)s, and this is someone who is more in touch with their sorrow. There can often be a deep sadness within them.

Achiever (3)—Levels of Awareness

Achiever (3) When Self-Aware
Self-accepting, authentic and real, the Achiever (3)'s image, inner world and reality align. They are humble, honest and able to speak from the heart. Compassionate and kind, their influence benefits others. Self-assured, effective, energetic and efficient, the Achiever (3) goes after their goals while remaining connected to their heart and the emotional world. They are flexible, charming, polite and accepting of others. They radiate genuine self-esteem and self-acceptance. This Achiever (3) is highly goal-oriented and seeks to embody success in their chosen field. High-achieving, talented, inspiring and collaborative, the Achiever (3) motivates others to reach their potential.

Achiever (3) With Tightening Defenses
Focus is on achievement and establishing themselves as the best. The Achiever (3) feels some anxiety about not measuring up. Fear of failure fuels more hard work. They become

highly competitive with a strong desire to be "the best." They constantly compare their performance and status to others. They display workaholic tendencies. Image-conscious and insecure about the opinion of others, they shapeshift to try to make the most positive impression in various environments. The drive to look good outstrips the need to be authentic. They are practical and efficient but can also be calculated and transactional. They have difficulty with intimacy and credibility as they fear exposing their full self. The Achiever (3) seeks a supply of external validation as a means to feel good about themselves. They may brag, self-promote and over-promise as a way to impress others. They may envy the success of others.

Achiever (3) When Fixated

The Achiever (3) can become ruthlessly exploitative as a means of dodging failure and humiliation. They exhibit a lack of empathy, and they feel envy and begrudge the success of others. Maintaining a sense of superiority takes priority and influences their behavior. The desire to maintain a positive image replaces reality. Deception, lies and devious behavior is prominent in the picture. Mistakes, shortcomings and failure are hidden. This Achiever (3) is like the classic Dorian Gray character. They become delusional in their envy of others. Ruthless and malicious in their attempt to destroy the happiness of others, Achiever (3)s at this level become obsessive about whatever reminds them of their own failures and shortcomings.

Keys If You Are In A Relationship With An Achiever (3)

The relationship keys are a result of the 360 degree review - partnership with an Achiever (3) from the perspective each of the nine types. The keys are a summary of some common themes.

 "Help me with my workaholic tendencies"

Maria, Achiever (3) married in a 12-year relationship with Marc, Achiever (3)

"My husband left on a business trip on March 15th and returned August 17nd. I saw him 6 days during that period – and we have a toddler! When he was home for two months straight, he worked every day. But as a fellow workaholic, I understand that goals are very important and helping him achieve these goals is important for a healthy relationship between us. I also know that both of us can become too goal-oriented, to the point in which we miss out on life.

As it relates to the big picture, Marc truly loves his work, and his happiness is a real booster for us. When I get frustrated, I try to focus on that. On the day-to-day issues of workaholism, one important element I've learned is to be realistic about what is possible. I don't ask my workaholic husband to promise to be home by 5:00 pm because I know there is no chance he'll do it. I know better than to set him up for failure since it makes him feel bad. And as I share workaholism as a mindset, I know we workaholics are also consumed with a certain amount of guilt. If we fail at an objective, for example, if we said we would be home by 5:00 pm and we aren't, we feel bad, so when we do get home, we're not happy.

Since I understand this, I know it is better to assume he won't be home at 5:00 pm. Then, instead of frustrated, I am pleasantly surprised if he does make it. We are both happiest when we meet our priorities. If I fail in too many goals, I feel unfulfilled, and you won't want to be around me. My husband is the same way. I actually think we can make ourselves physically depressed over not meeting goals. It is that intense for us.

As a workaholic, I also appreciate when others in my life help me see that there is more to life than achieving my goals! Last week I was at my gym in my dance class with a girlfriend of mine. After class she suggested we take a special treatment of a sauna, cold bath and electrolights. At first, I said no because I have my program – I always take a second class and then go to work. But somehow, she convinced me by suggesting that it would be something different, something special and so I said yes. For me, that was a radical decision. My day is planned. I have a million things to do. I don't take saunas, and baths and non-essential stuff like that. But it was possible to get me gently off my objective by proposing in a non-threatening obligatory way, an alternative, which by the way, I really enjoyed. As a workaholic, this friendly nudging is helpful for me."

Achiever (3)s are typically workaholics and define themselves by their achievements. Meeting their goals energizes them. Spending time on things that aren't achievement oriented can feel like a waste of time, and in some cases, it can be anxiety provoking.

If you are an Achiever (3):
Try to appreciate that there is more to life than work and professional achievement. Try to push yourself to be more flexible with your schedule. Notice if you become anxious when you aren't spending time pursuing your goals. Ask yourself why stillness is so difficult. Consider a practice to cultivate stillness and to quiet your mind.

If you are with an Achiever (3):
Understand your Achiever (3) may not get the same pleasure out of relaxing, hanging out and "enjoying life" as you do. Time not spent pursuing a goal can be anxiety-provoking for

them. And not meeting goals can be even worse. Set realistic, reasonable goals for non-work time so you can set up your partner for success.

 "Image matters a lot to me. Don't make me look bad!"

Alisa, Loyalist (6) married in a 39-year relationship with Sasha, Achiever (3)

"Sasha is very sensitive about his image and never wants the appearance of our marriage tarnished in any way to the outside world. Once we had a huge fight in the car – I thought he was driving dangerously, he felt he was driving efficiently. It escalated to the point where I had him drop me off, and I took a train back to Odessa and spent the night in a hotel. The next weekend we were having dinner with friends, and as they were good friends, I began to recount the story. I still remember the look on Sasha's face – he was so horrified I would share our marital issues with our close friends."

Dorothy, Helper (2) married in a 9-year relationship with Alex, Achiever (3)

"Alex is very image-conscious; this is both an asset and a challenge at times. He is very careful to do what will be impressive, both for me and others. He can come across as compatible and caring. At other times his image sensitivity can seem silly or even be challenging. A playful example is a way he will change his outfit to match the different activities we engage in over the course of the day. We may start our day with morning yoga, then go play golf and in the later afternoon take a hike or play tennis. He will change his complete outfit to "look" the part he is playing. I may just change footwear and have to wait for his ensemble change, which often doesn't look that different to me."

Achiever (3)s fuse love with the appearance of wellness. They have a hard time separating their image from their true self. As such, anything that threatens their positive external image can feel destabilizing to them. It is very important to them that they look good, and others speak well of them.

If you are an Achiever (3):
Understand that you have a deep sensitivity to the opinions of others and that others may not share this sensitivity. Others may be more focused on their own internal truth and internal interpretation of events. Try to tune into your inner compass and see if you can separate your truth from the interpretation of outsiders. Your conscience ultimately doesn't rule by majority.

If you are in a relationship with an Achiever (3):
Understand that your Achiever (3) has a deep concern about the opinion of others. Recognize that anything you do that makes them "look bad" may leave them feeling unstable and insecure. Try to be sensitive to this issue.

 "If I've decided I can no longer be successful, I can abandon something or someone."

Maria, Achiever (3) married in a 12-year relationship with Marc, Achiever (3)

"I recall speaking to my husband about an old project he was working on that he had walked away from. He went to great lengths to reconcile the decision in his own mind – that dumping the project on another poor soul was the absolute right thing to do. I was thoroughly shaken by the complete lack of ethics in the process, at the very least, but there was no changing of his mind. Today if you were to ask him, he'd tell you it was the absolute right thing to do. Not a bit of guilt."

Achiever (3)s focus their attention on success. They like to be associated with winners and having a positive image makes them feel stable. Their attention moves away from failure. To be associated with failure can trigger shame and other intense emotions. It can almost feel like annihilation. As such, the Achiever (3) mind can perform a lot of mental gymnastics to remove themselves from "losing" situations. This can be shocking and can feel cold and heartless to those around them.

If you are an Achiever (3):
Understand that you have an intense aversion to failure and anything that might make you look bad to others. This aversion is related to shame and may trigger justifications for walking away from the negative scenario. Recognize this. Try to connect the abandonment back to your own feelings of shame.

If you are with an Achiever (3):
Understand your Achiever (3) has a reality distortion around winning and losing. They experience it much more intensely than you probably do. Try to help your Achiever (3) understand that you love many things about them that have nothing to do with their achievements. Helping them feel totally accepted can help them begin to dissolve shame.

ACHIEVER (3)
360 DEGREE REVIEW

The next section features the 360 degree review--partnership with an Achiever (3) from the perspective of each of the nine types.

3:1 Achiever (3) with Perfectionist (1)

Katharina, Perfectionist (1) married in a 29-year relationship with Lucas, Achiever (3)

"My husband is highly intelligent, confident, goal-oriented, exceptionally hard-working and has an almost uncanny ability to read other people accurately. He started his life from almost nothing and has achieved amazing things based on his talent and hard work. He is mature — he sees the big picture and has the wisdom not to sweat the small stuff. He is a strong, decisive leader who doesn't waste time with regret or anger. He is generous to a fault, though privately in a low-profile way. I have been shocked when people tell me about the amount of help he has offered them, all without me knowing! As a father, he is gentle and loving, and my children and I all feel deeply cared for by him.

As a couple, we have many similarities. We're both goal-oriented and can be relentless in completing a project, regardless of the cost in time or energy. When we met, we immediately recognized this aspect of each other. It is a helpful shared trait because we don't need to explain or defend ourselves in this regard. For example, he IS a workaholic, but I understand how goal-oriented he is, and I respect that and support him. When we both worked in the

CHAPTER THREE MOTIVATOR/ACHIEVER

corporate world, at different companies, we each won Presidential Citations/President Club status for being recognized as the highest performers in the company. Individually, we are highly self-motivated, high achievers, and we both find ourselves in leadership roles professionally and socially.

In our relationship, I appreciate that he is so supportive. He gives me room to be who I am, and I cannot think of one time when he has told me "no" when I wanted to do something. I'm very independent with an active social life, and I have a large group of women friends who get together often and who sometimes even travel together on tennis trips. It amazes me when some of my friends say their husbands don't like them going out for our dinners and other social occasions and instead want them to stay home with them!

Lucas has always been supportive of my independent lifestyle. He travels extensively for work, so this connection with friends was my sanity as I raised the kids when he was absent on business trips. And in balance, I cannot think of a time when I complained about his travel. I understand it is his job and what makes him successful – he loves getting in front of clients, and I know it lights him up!

He balances me. I am a planner and a rule follower, and he is the exact opposite. I admire his spontaneity, and I wish I could be more like him that way. There is NEVER a dull moment with him. He brings adventure to my once very carefully controlled life.

We work well as a couple. When we were raising children, we divided up the responsibilities of parenthood easily and effectively. I handled all school-related issues, and he took on sports, especially for my son who was a gifted athlete. My husband made my son's competitions a priority and would rarely miss a game, arranging his travel around it. I take care of all things emotional and relating to family life, and he is a solid provider. This worked well for us.

As it relates to issues, we do have differences. While he is not a law-breaker by any means, he puts achieving at the top of the list, and that can mean compromising. He can be hard on his employees and can be condescending. He is usually the smartest person in the room, and he is easily frustrated if people don't agree or understand. I see this as an integrity issue, and it drives me crazy.

While I have always been supportive, his job and business have always been a top priority in his life. Spending time with me is often whittled down to the weekends only, so it is good that I am independent. We have ALWAYS had date night on Saturday night, and Friday often when there were no commitments, even before we had kids. He initiated this idea telling me that it was essential that we spend that time as a couple each week and to also go on a trip together without the kids once a year to re-connect. He's right — this time together has been crucial in keeping us connected. That said, I do sometimes feel he puts work first. He defines himself by how well he provides and was self-aware enough to actually admit to this once. I appreciated his candor but was still a bit shocked to hear that directly – I love so many things about him that have nothing to do with his earning potential.

As it relates to issues in the relationship, my biggest challenge is dealing with his need to be right all of the time. When I disagree with Lucas about something, he interprets it as a personal attack and becomes condescending. He has actually told me that if there were 100 people in a room — hearing both of our opinions, they would ALL agree with him. Of course, I found this funny and ridiculous...but at times the attitude is condescending and really pisses me off! This is especially challenging because I too have a need to be right! Usually, I end up getting frustrated because he stops listening even if I concede to some of his points. He just bulldozes over me sometimes, so I end up just dismissing the whole conversation. The saving grace for us is that we are both able to quickly let things go. We don't carry anger or grudges – which I know is rare and something I feel very fortunate to have in my relationship. There are also times when he will concede a point to avoid the conflict. We go back-and-forth in regards to who will back down. We have actually laughed about this whole having-to-be-right with our adult children. Both of my kids have said that my husband usually thinks he's right 99.9% of the time...

He is also not very good at expressing his emotions. I feel loved by him, but this is not a result of his verbal or physical expression. He can cover outside issues perfectly well and is happy giving his opinion to anyone who will listen, but he holds his own emotions very close to the chest. For me, it is difficult not to have any reassurance, positive feedback or compliments. He tells me he just doesn't think that way. He sees any positive behavior as fulfilling his expectation. I've dealt with this by turning to myself for validation and lessening the search for outside validation. I know better than to try to change him, and this validation vacuum has pushed me to grow. At the same time, it would be so nice to have more physical and verbal affection from him...

I wish we could have more of a spiritual relationship. He is admittedly not very introspective. I am in the constant pursuit for self-improvement. We were both raised Catholic so when I began my spiritual "quest" around the age of 32, he was very threatened by that. He has slowly come to tolerate it, and I have learned his boundaries. He has never told me not to do it, but he is not of the same mind!

He is very uncomfortable talking about relationship issues and generally just agrees to avoid conflict. I am a big communicator and always strive for resolution, so I have had to learn to respect this part of him...especially because he does acquiesce and is motivated to make things better. Unfortunately, some issues are just swept under the rug and have caused a disconnect at different times in the marriage. However, we never go to bed angry, never carry resentments into the next day and have a strong and enduring marriage.

Overall, I am very happy in my marriage. I love, admire and respect my husband tremendously. The areas where we are challenged have become growth edges for me, as I learn forgiveness, acceptance and the true meaning of unconditional love. I feel like there is a Divine perfection in our relationship, and I feel very grateful to share my life's journey with my husband."

3:1 The Theory

 ### 3:1 When In Balance

The Perfectionist (1) and Achiever (3) can be an effective, efficient, goal-oriented team. Both are disciplined and hard-working, and this couple shares a focus on the achievement of tangible, practical goals. Both can be seen by the outside world as classic overachievers, and both can be highly accomplished.

In their relationship, they offer compensating traits. The Achiever (3) boosts the confidence of their Perfectionist (1), encouraging them to become more adaptable, consider different approaches, stretch for their potential and share their talents more widely. Achiever (3)s can be motivating and inspiring, and they want to bring out the best in their partner. This dovetails nicely with the Perfectionist (1)'s drive for self-improvement. It is as though the Perfectionist (1) has their own personal coach in their Achiever (3).

In return, the Perfectionist (1) improves the quality of their Achiever (3)'s output, focusing less on image and appearances and more on depth, substance and the finer details. The Perfectionist (1) shows the Achiever (3) how to slow down and do things intentionally and purposefully. The Perfectionist (1) resists cutting corners and insists the integrity and true quality of the work be high. They are also good at demonstrating authenticity and can help their Achiever (3) move away from people-pleasing behavior.

The foundation of this pair is mutual respect, admiration and shared goals and values. This couple is highly supportive of each other as it relates to concrete topics in the material world. They understand the workaholic tendency of the other. Because the focus of attention tends to be outward and practical, relating more as "doing" rather than "being," cultivating a sustainable, intimate, emotional connection is key to the true success of this partnership. Sharing time together in stillness and appreciating each other's essence helps develop this connection. When this pair has a strong emotional connection, their differences can serve as assets rather than triggers. When balanced, this can be an almost unstoppable team who effectively and efficiently overcomes all obstacles to reach their shared goals.

3:1 The Downward Spiral
In an unaware state, the distinctly different habits of attention of these two types can lead to the beginning of the downward spiral. This couple may also lock horns around issues of not feeling heard or seen by each other, feeling unappreciated and ultimately feeling disrespected. As respect is a foundational element of this couple, feeling disrespected can create fissures in their foundation.

The Perfectionist (1) mind seeks integrity and improvement. When fixated, the defenses tighten, and the Perfectionist (1) mind becomes rigid, harsh and judgmental. They may direct this rigidity at their Achiever (3) partner, judging them too competitive, too achievement-oriented and too concerned about the opinion of others.

The Achiever (3)'s mind seeks achievement and success. When fixated, the defenses tighten the mind to become even more focused on achievement and external validation. They may start to see their Perfectionist (1) as too rigid, too judgmental and too lost in the details. Frustration builds, and respect erodes. Achiever (3)s are triggered by any character attack and building criticism from their Perfectionist (1) may cause them to shut down and withdraw.

Both types are practical so an eroding relationship may appear intact to the outside world. However, whether the split is internal or external, the emotional connection is lost.

3:1 The Lighthouse
Because both of these types are goal-oriented and serious in their pursuit of achievement, taking time to reconnect at a heart level is extremely important for this relationship. Both people need to slow down and spend time connecting with their emotional world, to experience "being" instead of "doing." This can be a challenge for both Perfectionist (1)s and Achiever (3)s.

3:1 The Kundalini Yoga Connection
Both Perfectionist (1)s and Achiever (3)s struggle with stillness so cultivating the ability to relax, unwind and just "be" is important. For both partners, Kundalini Yoga kriyas and

meditations that incorporate breathwork can be very beneficial in cultivating stillness. Since these are types who prefer to be in motion, breathwalk (walking meditations) can be a great way to incorporate meditation into daily life. This is also a practice they can do together.

Perfectionist (1)s are often blocked from their heart center so Kundalini Yoga kriyas and meditations to open their heart, connect with the energy of emotion and burn out inner anger are helpful.

Achiever (3)s are often cut off from their heart with their extreme focus on achievement, so Kundalini Yoga kriyas and meditations to develop self-love, self-acceptance, and an open heart are beneficial.

See the appendix for Perfectionist (1) and Achiever (3) recommended Kundalini Yoga kriyas and meditations.

3:2: Achiever (3) with Helper (2)

Dorothy, Helper (2) married in a 9-year relationship with Alex, Achiever (3)

"My husband is responsible, focused, adaptable, diverse in his interests and a wonderful mix of stable and adventurous. Alex has a huge heart and is a truly kind and caring person. He is a great partner; very conscious of his actions and decisions and how they impact me, us and our flow.

He can be very sensitive, expressive, affirming and affectionate. He is often a great listener and when fully focused, shares heartfelt responses. He has high self-esteem and a strong drive to be the best in all he does, including our relationship. He easily resets to a positive outlook and frequently shares his appreciation for me, our partnership and our life together.

We both office in our home. Alex can work long hours with a very diligent focus. I sometimes tease him that he would not notice if the house was on fire until the fire was under his chair. Most of the time, if I need him for something, I can distract him. I am, however, respectful of his need to accomplish, and I sense when he is eager to get back to his task or can't take a break.

He is extremely competitive and makes a game of everything he does. We play many sports and games like cards, Scrabble and Othello. He also enjoys competing against himself and playfully changing the rules or purpose of the competition to make sure he wins.

Despite being competitive, he is genuinely supportive of his peers and seems to glow when they mention him as being helpful and motivating. An example of his mix of competition and supportiveness is when we play golf. He will challenge me for a monetary amount on each hole: if I owe him anything at the end of the game, he will make up another additional competition so I can win and not owe him anything. He gains the thrill of winning and ensures I feel like I won too. Very sweet.

Alex is aware and good at creating a balance between work and play. An example of this is that we often travel. We may take a vacation, and he will work some or we might combine a business trip with a vacation. He is good at balancing work and doing a fun activity or exploring the new place with me. I am patient when he has to work, as I can do my work and passions via the internet too.

I frequently teach and host groups, classes and workshops in our home. When Alex chooses to participate in any of them, he is the perfect host. He warmly welcomes people, shares handshakes and hugs, easily chats and establishes commonality through genuine inquiry. I am more practical in that my welcoming includes informing them of their options for seating and food, and sharing where the restroom is located, and so forth. Alex is very supportive and complimentary to me as a facilitator and a teacher. At times he likes to share in more depth, or be in the spotlight, always keen on how he can be impressive.

Our communication styles are different. I express my feelings and opinions more freely and openly; I bring up the elephant in the room, lay my cards on the table as the saying goes and bring up more challenging topics. I can dig deeper into what might be considered things that are more personal. When I'm stressed, my voice rises, and my body tenses – I call it passion. I get bored with chit-chat and seek depth.

Alex is more reserved, careful, private and compliant. He seems to me to be more focused on maintaining a particular image. When stressed, he goes into stubborn defense or what feels like a dance of detaching and deflecting. It is most often short-lived, as he resets to the positive. He seems to have a smaller variance in his emotional world than I do, he prefers the status quo, familiarity and safety.

Alex is capable of deep emotional conversations that are delicious to me, but only when he is feeling very safe and in private. It is much easier for him to share his accomplishments, stories about our great life and how good things are.

All conflicts in our relationship, when we honestly root down to the core are about image. Alex has a strong concern with what he thinks others might think about him, and I can be *oversensitive in seeking appreciation, honesty and depth. Alex is sensitive to rules, feeling safe and being compliant – to not stand out. I am more rebellious and willing to be the outcast for what is right. We are both careful about what we perceive the other thinks about us, and when we are on opposite ends of a particular view, it definitely helps to repeatedly reassure each other of our basic love, respect and value for each other. From there we can better navigate any issue.*

At times our focuses are very different, and this creates periods of time when we may be apart or together, but not connected. Alex can have a work focus where nothing else is in his awareness at times, and I can get deeply involved with my classes, writing or others in intense emotional explorations. We are both good at self-entertaining and also being aware of when we need to make time for reconnection, fun, adventure, and explorations. Alex is more of a planner, and I am better at spontaneity.

My biggest challenge in the relationship is having patience when he becomes defensive, detached and distracted. It can feel like a brick wall has gone up between us. I need to remind myself to give him time and space and that he will reset to a place where we can connect again. Equally, I think his biggest challenge with me is when I get very passionate, righteous, a bit loud and what feels like to him, argumentative. He has to soften his concerns and be real with me, knowing I will quiet down if I feel heard.

I am so very proud of Alex and all he does, including his ability to adapt and show up as an impressive person. I believe he works hard to ensure I am proud of him, as I also do for him. I acknowledge and appreciate his efforts to be the "best" in all he does, including being the best partner to me. I truly appreciate how his radar is active to perform in ways that will please me. I know he is committed to me, our relationship and our future together.

I also know and feel that Alex appreciates my support; from bringing him food when he gets so focused on his work, to taking care of all the things that keep our family and home looking good! I feel very safe and loved in our relationship."

3:2 The Theory

3:2 When In Balance

The Helper (2) and Achiever (3) can be a very supportive, charismatic and socially adept combination. While both can be outwardly focused, in their highest levels of development, both focus inward more. The Helper (2) takes more time for self-care, and the Achiever (3) is content just being, instead of doing. This deepens their emotional connection. Externally they can be a powerful combination with the Achiever (3) offering motivation, charisma and leadership, and the Helper (2) offering more in-depth connection and emotional support. Together, they can be well-regarded, charming, generous, positive and high-spirited. In their social circles, this is often a popular couple. They work well together in part because of their balancing differences.

Helper (2)s place a higher value on the emotional world and bring an empathetic personal touch and more individual focus to their interpersonal connections. They are thoughtful and considerate, generous and loving. Their pace is slower, and they speak more directly from the heart. Their goal is a true connection.

Achiever (3)s bring adaptability, charm, charisma and an orientation towards goals and achievement. They strive to be successful in the eyes of others, and Helper (2)s appreciate and respond well to this effort. Achiever (3)s have a faster pace and a greater desire to keep the mood high and positive. They seek achievement and to motivate and inspire others.

When in balance, the Helper (2) feels appreciated by their Achiever (3), and the Achiever (3) feels admired by their Helper (2). When both partners are self-aware, this can be an amazingly effective and accomplished couple, radiating charm, charisma, magnetism, helpfulness, kindness and grace. At their best, themes of quiet altruism may be present.

3:2: The Downward Spiral

Appreciation and admiration are like oxygen to the Helper (2) and Achiever (3). If either partner feels a scarcity of their oxygen, problems can arise. With tightening defenses, the Helper (2) may do more than they should and become overengaged and intrusive in the lives of others. They begin to feel underappreciated and worn out by their subconscious efforts to be appreciated thereby triggering the downward spiral. Conversely, with tightening defenses, Achiever (3)s try to do and achieve more with a subconscious goal to gain admiration. This may trigger workaholism and a disconnect from the relationship itself and their own emotional needs. Both partners may begin to resent the other for not recognizing their efforts and indirectly for not meeting their emotional needs.

The Helper (2) may grow impatient at the drive to achieve and gain admiration that takes the Achiever (3) away from the relationship and a deeper emotional connection. The Helper (2) is highly aware of how image conscious their Achiever (3) is, and this can become a source of discord in the relationship. As the Helper (2) seeks a more authentic connection, the Achiever (3) may feel threatened that their autonomy to pursue their goals is at risk. Both partners polarize, the Helper (2) leaning in for more focused time and attention and the Achiever (3) pulling away to achieve more goals as a way to feel stable.

Conversely, the Achiever (3) may start to resent the amount of time the Helper (2) lavishes on the needs of others feeling this attention is given more sparingly to them and to the relationship itself. The Helper (2) may see the relationship as an extension of themselves, and attention for the relationship may take a back seat for other priorities. The underlying issue is that when fixated, both Helper (2)s and the Achiever (3) disconnect from themselves. In a fixated state, Helper (2)s can't set healthy personal boundaries, and they lose connection with themselves. In a fixated state, Achiever (3)s focus exclusively on goals and achievement and lose connection with themselves. In both environments, the relationship suffers.

When fixated, the Helper (2) has lost touch with themselves and the Achiever (3) is in denial of their own emotions and self-worth, using constant achieving as a way to feel better about themselves. Misunderstanding become central themes in the dynamic. Unless the partnership finds a way to repair, the connection weakens and breaks apart, and the relationship drifts off course.

3:2 The Lighthouse
Unmet needs for attention, admiration and appreciation can be the downfall of this couple, so cultivating self-love can help break the downward momentum. Helper (2)s need to manage the drive for external appreciation and instead turn inward to find their sense of worth and value. Cultivating self-care and independent hobbies are helpful, healing and balancing. Achiever (3)s need to observe their compulsive drive to achieve and stay on the go. Learning stress and anxiety management tools can be beneficial in cultivating the ability to slow down. From this slower pace, emotions can come forward, and Achiever (3)s can communicate more directly from their hearts.

3:2 The Kundalini Yoga Connection
As Achiever (3)s connect with their heart and relax the need to continuously achieve, they become more present to themselves and others and less reliant on outside admiration and approval. Kundalini Yoga kriyas and meditations to cultivate a heart connection and develop a tolerance for stillness are helpful.

As the Helper (2)s cultivate feelings of self-love, their drive to meet everyone else's needs diminishes. Behind the drive to help others is a subconscious sense of shame, a belief that on their own, they are not lovable. With the cultivation of self-love, this shame can dissolve. Kundalini Yoga kriyas and meditations to develop self-care and self-love are beneficial.

See the appendix for Helper (2) and Achiever (3) recommended Kundalini Yoga kriyas and meditations.

3:3 Achiever (3) with Achiever (3)

Maria, Achiever (3) married in a 12-year relationship with Marc, Achiever (3)

"I admire my husband's dogged perseverance, his problem-solving ability and the fact that he is a great strategist. I love he is adventurous, a risk-taker and yet at the same time dependable. It is easy to admire him.

Both of us strive to avoid drama in our relationship and give each other space to pursue our own interests and self-development. For example, Marc launched a nonprofit organization to address climate change shortly after the birth of our first child. Initially, I was a little taken aback by his commitment which took him away from our home and our toddler, but once I realized how important this was for him and for the world, I decided to support him. This emotional support has really helped him and given him the strength and energy to succeed.

In our relationship, we're a fabulous couple as long as we want the same thing. When we have different objectives, it can be an impossible struggle to get him to agree to pursue my objective instead of his.

I have had to reset my expectations. Workaholism is definitely an issue – he is on the road for months on end, and even when he's back, he's always working. After the birth of our daughter, I eventually came to the conclusion that I neither could nor wanted to force Marc to do something he had clearly decided wasn't of interest. Caring for our daughter was no longer a goal of his since he just wasn't connecting with her. And to be honest, neither was I. It's not popular to admit, but parenting is hard, and toddlers can be boring – and that's when they're not annoying you, which they often are.

But then I made a conscious choice to change my perspective. My goal became to make up for my husband's absence and to be the best mom I could possibly be. Instead of focusing on what was missing, I focused on what I have – an amazing place to live with a supportive mom who lives close by, a wonderful job, a husband pursuing meaningful work and so forth. I was able to find many reasons to get over my negative feelings and look on the bright side. After feeling hurt and disappointed for many months, one day I woke up and decided to change my perspective. I haven't looked back since.

I can be very rational at the end of the day. I reasoned my way through my challenges and left the emotions behind. Then I built new positive emotions around my newfound pride and admiration for what my husband was trying to accomplish. And this has worked for me."

3:3 The Theory

3:3 When In Balance

Two Achiever (3)s are hard-working, goal-oriented, and high energy with a focus on practical, concrete issues. This is an accomplished, motivating, often charismatic couple with an outward facing focus. Both understand one another's competitive nature, desire to be the best (in whichever category they have placed themselves) and focus on efficiency and accomplishment. When in balance, this couple is highly supportive of each other's efforts and can become one another's best cheerleader. As they have the energy, drive, focus and ambition to overcome many obstacles, this couple is almost unstoppable when they are aligned in their goals. Both strive for a low drama, low conflict environment. With their shared habit of attention, the issue of workaholism may have less of a sting as both partners understand the drive to be achieving constantly.

Together this is an impressive, polished, supportive and loving couple. Demands from the outside world take priority over demands within the relationship, freeing both partners to focus on external achievement. This couple is admired by many.

3:3 The Downward Spiral

As long as the Achiever (3) couple is balanced and aligned, they are highly supportive of one another's goals. They admire and feel pride in their partner's accomplishments and understand each other's drive to achieve. If their goals fall out of alignment, however, problems arise. Support may be withdrawn. An unhealthy competitive edge may enter the relationship, and resentment may start to build. Thus begins the downward spiral.

Both partners can be competitive and petty comparisons may arise: salaries, titles, prestige and so forth. The foundation of support erodes to one of one-upmanship. Alternatively, when their goals are unaligned, one or both partners may start to grow resentful of time away from their quest to achieve. Compromise doesn't come easily to Achiever (3)s particularly if their goal is at risk. Time invested in the relationship can feel like a waste of time particularly if they start to feel the relationship cannot be a clear success. In this environment, emotional connection is lost.

It can be hard for Achiever (3)s to know their true feelings. The drive to achieve is so strong in both of them that self-reflection and emotional processing are often bypassed. They can metaphorically put their emotions in a box to be dealt with later. Generally, neither are particularly fluent in the language of emotion. They may see strong feelings as a potential source of shame, humiliation, failure or rejection as well as a distraction from work. In this environment, intimacy suffers, and one or both partners may start to feel isolated and lonely. As image is important to both, externally this couple may continue to impress, but behind closed doors, there can be a disconnect and sadness. If the downward momentum continues, alienation intensifies until the relationship drifts so far apart, it eventually ends.

3:3 The Lighthouse
The drive to achieve can take priority over intimacy and emotional connection and can trigger the downward spiral for this couple. Finding ways to reconnect on an intimate and emotional level is part of the healing. Speaking from the heart and cultivating feelings of self-love and self-acceptance are helpful for both partners.

3:3 The Kundalini Yoga Connection
Balancing the head and the heart is essential for Achiever (3)s. They are part of the Heart Triad and have the capacity for powerful love, compassion, tenderness and empathy, but this energetic flow gets blocked by shame which manifests as a compulsive drive to achieve. Kundalini Yoga kriyas and meditations to balance the head and heart, to cultivate stillness, self-acceptance and self-love are beneficial.

See the appendix for Achiever (3) recommended Kundalini Yoga kriyas and meditations.

3:4 Achiever (3) with Individualist (4)

Aiden, Individualist (4) formerly in a 3-year relationship with Marisa, Achiever (3)

"Marisa was brilliant and knew how to develop her talent. She was very goal-oriented, focused, organized and efficient. She not only became a therapist, but she also became a cutting-edge leader in mind-body awareness, bringing her clairsentient and clairvoyant talents to her clients as a healer. She wanted to know everything she could about consciousness because being the best therapist possible was her agenda. And she achieved it. She had high standards in what she wanted yet was playful and thoughtful with her children. She worked hard to put her children in a school that valued nature and tried to keep them young as long as possible.

CHAPTER THREE MOTIVATOR/ACHIEVER

In our relationship, she cultivated parts of me that were already there but maybe more latent. We both enjoyed nice homes, and she ramped up my appreciation of art and my social skills. I loved the world expansion from 3D reality to 5D that she taught me, moving from the physical world of matter to the metaphysical world of consciousness. I visited my first energy worker when we were together, and this launched me into a new world of thought and vitality in my future life.

I loved her experimental mind and her unique approach to God and the divine. Her drive and vision expanded so many horizons for me.

As it relates to issues, I needed more attention than she did. We met in Co-Dependents Anonymous, so we were both working on ourselves and in therapy. We shared introspection, and at the same time, we were both dealing with a lot. When we were together as a couple, she was in school training to become a psychotherapist while raising two children as a single mom, so her free time was limited. Her response was to be super organized.

Both of us were working through a lot of family issues around shame, and that intense shame can become fairly lethal. I have heard it said that Individualist (4)s with my habit of attention can "take their experiences and dip them into the toxic fondue of our family of origin." To some extent, I did that.

There was a lot of unhealthy behavior, and neither of us really knew how to hold the space for the other. When things got tough, it was hard to hold our centers with so much shame to process. We both worked hard on it, but I think eventually it was all too raw to sustain the relationship.

Growing up in our dysfunctional family systems, we both watched and lived and acted out a lot of unhealthy behavior. When we were dating, we were early in our recovery and processing quite a bit. I had a hard time dealing with her shut-down nature. She would go into efficient overdrive to get things done and avoid being overwhelmed by my feelings and my sometimes diva-like behavior. And when she would shut down her feelings, I would go ballistic.

Our behaviors polarized, hers becoming more shut down and mine becoming even more fiery and emotional. Having my feelings go unacknowledged was a huge trigger point for me. I was less self-aware at the time and didn't understand that feelings are not facts. Now I am more aware that feelings are like a weather pattern over my heart, ever-changing.

It was hard to love her because it was hard for me to love myself at that time. Despite our challenges, I am very grateful to her for many things, especially how much she expanded my horizons and pointed me to a larger world."

3:4 The Theory

3:4 When In Balance

The Achiever (3) and Individualist (4) approach the world from different directions, the Achiever (3) seeking their identity from the outside in, and the Individualist (4) seeking their identify from the inside out. When in higher states of awareness, these fundamental differences can be balancing, intriguing and can offer growth opportunities for one another.

The Achiever (3) models confidence, polish, goal-setting, discipline and a practical focus on achievement. They value efficiency and organization and show the Individualist (4) how to march on in the face of their ever-changing emotional world. Achiever (3)s help the Individualist (4) stay present and grounded in the practical world. More emotionally-contained than their Individualist (4) partner, they use achievement as their guideposts of how to behave and where to put their energy. All of these traits can be helpful and balancing for their Individualist (4) who sees the world from a very different lens.

Individualist (4)s are well-versed in the language of feelings and place a much higher value on the emotional world. They value authenticity, creative expression and originality. They seek to be understood more than they seek approval. They help their Achiever (3) partner pinpoint and discuss their feelings and emotional responses. They can help their partner cultivate empathy, compassion and open-heartedness. The Individualist (4) offers the Achiever (3) a safe container to explore hurts, wounds and past failures, and the Achiever (3) generally feels held and supported as they move this previously uncharted emotional territory.

When self-aware and accepting of their very different ways of relating to the world, this can be a pair who really feel they complete each other and keep each other in balance. When their differences are understood and respected, this has the potential to be a long-lasting and symbiotic match.

3:4 The Downward Spiral

Because both types approach the world from such different angles, it can be easy for needs to go unmet and for both to feel misunderstood. Both share a sensitive issue of shame, and both can have a fragile sense of themselves. With tightening defenses, Achiever (3)s cut off from their emotions, and Individualist (4)s sink more deeply into their emotions. These reactions can trigger the downward spiral in one another.

Achiever (3)s may grow weary of the Individualist (4)'s focus on their own deficiencies and perceived shortcomings. Achiever (3)s want to focus on practical matters, the positive and the image of success. The low self-esteem of the Individualist (4) can be wearing on the Achiever (3). The more the Individualist (4) laments, the more the Achiever (3) turns their attention away from the Individualist (4).

Feeling unseen, unheard or misunderstood is a huge trigger for the Individualist (4) who responds by either withdrawing or getting angry. Like salt on an open wound, having feelings go unacknowledged can prompt an immediate and intense response in the Individualist (4). These reactions can be mystifying to the less emotionally driven Achiever (3). Both partners start to polarize. The Individualist (4) may vacillate between needing more time alone to process their feelings and wanting more of their Achiever (3)'s attention. The Achiever (3) start to see their Individualist (4) as needy, dramatic and emotionally draining and unstable.

As the downward spiral gains momentum, both partners become a source of irritation to each other. The respect and admiration they both shared evaporates and is replaced by disgust and disdain that is potentially undermining. The relationship may end, leaving both partners bitterly disappointed.

3:4 The Lighthouse

Feelings of inferiority mark the beginning of the downward spiral for this couple. Both types have a sensitivity towards shame, though the Individualist (4) is much more in touch with this emotion. Shame and a lack of self-love is often at the forefront of the Individualist (4) experience. Conversely, Achiever (3)s don't always directly relate to shame. Instead, they under-process this emotion by staying on the go to achieve, with the subconscious belief that enough achievement will prove their worth.

To dissolve shame, both partners need to cultivate self-acceptance and self-love. This balances the dependence on the outside world and external factors. With self-acceptance and self-love, both types can feel stable independently.

3:4 The Kundalini Yoga Connection

Both types need to manage their reactivity and cultivate heart-opening.

Achiever (3)s need to learn to sit still, to listen deeply and to speak from the heart. This requires nervous system work since their natural reaction to stress is to stay active. They are generally uncomfortable remaining in negative emotional spaces for long periods of time, so they need to cultivate a tolerance for discomfort. Kundalini Yoga kriyas and meditations to build the nervous system, open the heart and to balance the head and heart are beneficial.

Individualist (4)s need to learn self-love and to resist the temptation to withdraw when they feel overwhelmed. Nervous system work is helpful to allow them to stay outside their comfort zone. They overidentify with their flaws and undervalue their talents, so Kundalini Yoga kriyas and meditations to cultivate a neutral mind, inner balance and self-acceptance are helpful.

See the appendix for Achiever (3) and Individualist (4) recommended Kundalini Yoga kriyas and meditations.

3:5 Achiever (3) with Investigator (5)

Tim, Investigator (5) formerly in a relationship for less than one year with Bob, Achiever (3)

"Bob had a commitment to excellence in everything he did. I admired the way he could connect with people easily and express emotions in an embodied way – in his voice, his eyes, his body language – without needing to say many words.

In our relationship, we were a good balance. He could easily see and respond to the big picture whereas I was more inclined to get lost in deep focus on details. I was the one who would patiently and meticulously research and plan our travel itinerary. He, on the other hand, could be responsive in the moment of travel and adjust plans on the fly without getting stressed out.

I appreciated his ability to take my raw intellectual ideas and quickly translate them into simple, relatable words. His presence was a gateway for me out of being "in my head" and into a more heart-based and relational space.

While we were a good balance, we also had some significant differences. I can be very meticulous about following rules and living in integrity and honesty. Bob was more comfortable playing fast and loose with the rules. He felt it was okay to break the rules as long as he could get away with it. It boiled down to a difference in values as my standards are less based on other people's perceptions and more about personal integrity.

He was much more interested in fashion and his appearance than I was. His Facebook posts were mostly attractive selfies, whereas my posts were mostly links to newspaper and magazine articles. During our time together, I got inspired to put more effort into my grooming, clothes and appearance, which I had previously considered too superficial to care about.

While ultimately the relationship didn't last, I learned a lot from Bob and our differences. I appreciated his human touch, and he appreciated the depth of my listening and ability to hear and understand things that he was not able to articulate.

I always wondered what he would have been like if he had had some sort of meditation practice so he could cultivate a comfort in being still, in just being and not always doing."

3:5 The Theory

3:5 When In Balance

The Achiever (3) and Investigator (5) share many core values and interests though their habit of attention is quite different. Both are interested in intellectual pursuits, gaining knowledge and expertise and becoming well-regarded in their chosen fields. Both value discipline and are willing to work hard. They seek to make a positive impact on the world. Both tend to be emotionally contained and while they may feel things deeply, this rarely conflicts with their pursuit of tangible, concrete goals. Beneath it all, there is a practical, logical undercurrent in both partners.

To the dynamic, the Achiever (3) brings a focus on image, polish and good communication skills. Achiever (3)s tend to be outwardly facing and have a high awareness of the impression they are making on others. This can be a point of learning for Investigator (5)s who generally are less interested in appearances and who tend to prefer written, rather than interpersonal, communication skills. Achiever (3)s are also more spontaneous than the Investigator (5) counterpart. They model for their Investigator (5) how to wing it, go with the flow and work out unexpected issues in real time. This can be helpful and inspiring for the Investigator (5).

Investigator (5)s offer depth of insight, a focus on details and planning and a more methodical, rational approach to situations. They are interested in satisfying their curiosity more than in getting to a specific outcome. This allows them to be more flexible in their thinking and more thorough in their approach. This difference can be balancing for their Achiever (3) who in their drive to succeed may be tempted to cut corners or take a less comprehensive approach.

As a couple, they can be proud of and admire each other. They may feel they have found their perfect match – someone who can keep up with them intellectually, who gives them sufficient personal freedom, who supports their endeavors and who they can show off to the outside world. This can be a successful, enduring match.

3:5 The Downward Spiral
While this couple has many similarities, they also have some key differences that can trigger the downward spiral. Their lifestyle pace is different, with the Achiever (3) on the go like an Energizer Bunny® and the Investigator (5) more like the tortoise with a slow but deliberate pace. Both are interested in being competent and successful in their chosen fields and in a fixated state with tightening defenses, there can be a competitive element in this relationship. And as both types tend to underemphasize the emotional world, important issues can go unaddressed.

In a fixated state, one or both partners may start to get frustrated with the other. The Achiever (3) may feel their Investigator (5)'s lifestyle pace is slow and threatening their ability to achieve their goals. They may mock their partner's careful and deliberate planning for all various scenarios. Likewise, the Investigator (5) may start to lose respect for their Achiever (3), feeling they are overly concerned about image and achievement and all to willing to sacrifice depth for appearance. One danger this couple has is that their connection can be largely mental, professional and pragmatic. If they aren't strongly connected at the heart, the lack of an emotional connection can create distance in the relationship that is hard to recover. As the downward spiral gains momentum, they may become harsh, hard-hearted and arrogant with each other. If this couple can't find a way to get out of their heads and into their hearts, the relationship can drift apart or end abruptly.

3:5 The Lighthouse
A lack of a truly heartfelt connection is ultimately what starts this pair into a downward spiral. Both partners need to find ways to connect more deeply to their emotional world and to communicate from their heart. Both need to learn to place value on interdependence and collaboration.

3:5 Kundalini Yoga Connection
Achiever (3)s need to slow down, connect with their heart center and stay collaborative. If they put the partnership before self-interest, the deterioration of the relationship may reverse. Kundalini Yoga kriyas and meditations to cultivate stillness and to balance the head and heart are particularly good.

Investigator (5)s need to learn to share more of their feelings with their Achiever (3). While open emotional expressions may not come easily for most Investigator (5)s, a practice to open the heart and move the energy out of the head and into the body can be useful. Kundalini Yoga kriyas and meditations to open the throat chakra and to cultivate gratitude are beneficial.

See the appendix for Achiever (3) and Investigator (5) recommended Kundalini Yoga kriyas and meditations.

3:6 Achiever (3) with Loyalist (6)

Alisa, Loyalist (6) married in a 39-year relationship with Sasha, Achiever (3)

"I admire my husband's optimism, motivational skills and his ability to connect with others. I appreciate his determination and his refusal to be bested. Without his grit and hard work, we wouldn't have the homes we do, our children would not have had the education they received, and we would not have had the lifestyle we have now. Above all, I love that he really wants to be with me and makes sure we have regular time together on our own. This has always been a priority of his even when we had three children under the age of four.

As it relates to issues, we can both be competitive. When we were both training to be psychotherapists, we behaved like a couple of rivalrous siblings – which is hysterical, considering the nature of our training! Over the years this has become less of an issue, but when we were younger, it was part of the picture.

I wish Sasha could understand that the journey is just as important as reaching the goal. He can be obsessively goal-oriented, and I feel this causes him to miss out on some of life's simple pleasures. Also, even though I recognize that I can never have enough reassurance, I still want him to give me more reassurance!

Part of the key to the success of our 39-year partnership has been personal growth and finding the Enneagram. The Enneagram has helped me understand that my husband's style is just his way of being in the world and not to take things personally.

Overall, I am very happy in my relationship. I have a husband I respect, admire and love tremendously, and we've shared a good part of this life journey together. I feel very grateful to have Sasha as my husband."

3:6 The Theory

3:6 When In Balance

This couple shares the values of hard work, discipline, determination and a drive for comfort and security. Both are willing to put in effort, energy and sacrifice to their reach targets. They share many fundamental values and have a high degree of respect and admiration for each other.

Achiever (3)s bring optimism, a can-do attitude and a sense of expansion and possibility. They present confidently to the outside world and communicate positively and easily with others. They give the relationship polish and a drive to be the best. With their relentless focus on success, their efforts go a long way in establishing practical comforts in this couple's shared life.

Loyalist (6)s offer reliability, caution, a strong sense of duty and responsibility and an eye for potential pitfalls. They remind their Achiever (3) to be more cautious and realistic and of the value of human relationships and connection with other people. With their collaborative, interpersonal approach, they can take the edge off their Achiever (3)'s competitive drive.

When in balance and connecting at the heart, this is a stable, supportive partnership. Both can be each other's best cheerleader, and they highly value the life they have built together.

3:6 The Downward Spiral

In the lower levels of awareness, these types can bring out the worst in each other.

Both partners share a competitive nature and when under stress, this may be directed towards each other. Both have the potential to be workaholics and to look outside themselves to feel secure and valuable. It is easy for them to lose their own internal compass and to get lost in the opinions and impressions of others. Both may avoid deep introspection, making it difficult for true motivations and desires to be discussed or even acknowledged.

Each type has a different stress response and can become irritated watching the other, thus triggering the downward spiral. Achiever (3)s see their Loyalist (6) as anxious, over-reactive and unnecessarily pessimistic. They feel their Loyalist (6) is taking the wind from their sails, bringing them down and creating an unnecessarily negative environment. The Loyalist (6) may grow frustrated at the relentless orientation towards goals of their

Achiever (3). They may feel their partner is missing out on the truly important things in life and can grow weary with the Achiever (3)'s need to constantly achieve. They can also get irritated at their Achiever (3)'s desire to put a positive spin on everything, feeling this is disingenuous.

With tightening defenses, each feels their stability slip, and the downward spiral gains momentum. They may begin to lose respect for each other and become evasive and withdrawn. The relationship takes on a lifeless flavor as deeper, more meaningful issues are avoided, and both partners craft independent lives for themselves. Because both value security so highly, the relationship may continue, with the Achiever (3) presenting a mask to the world and the Loyalist (6) keeping quiet, afraid to rock the boat. The relationship may coast along in a stable yet zombie-like state until eventually some outside force enters the picture and exposes the truth. At that point, the partners are either forced to deal with previously repressed issues, or the relationship splits.

3:6 The Lighthouse

Differing responses to stress are usually the trigger for the downward spiral, and the fact the heart connection gets broken helps the downward spiral gain momentum. To break the momentum and begin to mend the relationship, both partners need to learn healthy ways to handle stress and anxiety. And to come back together, both partners need to learn to become still and speak from their heart.

3:6 The Kundalini Yoga Connection

Because both partners need to break their patterned reactions, Kundalini Yoga kriyas and meditations to strengthen the nervous system are beneficial to both.

Achiever (3)s need to get in touch with their deeper feelings and to learn to cultivate stillness. The drive to constantly achieve has a negative impact on their intimate relationships. Kundalini Yoga kriyas and meditations to cultivate stillness, to move from the head to the heart and a deepen the heart connection are helpful. Cultivating self-love is also important to help relax the drive for achievement.

Loyalist (6)s need to manage their anxiety and the accompanying worst-case scenario thinking. They need to relax their tendency to project into situations and quiet their overactive mind. Kundalini Yoga kriyas and meditations to lower anxiety, to manage stress and to cultivate a neutral mind are helpful.

See the appendix for Achiever (3) and Loyalist (6) recommended Kundalini Yoga kriyas and meditations.

THE NINE KEYS

3:7 Achiever (3) with Enthusiast (7)

Louis, Enthusiast (7), married in 12-year relationship with Angelina, Achiever (3)

"My wife gets things done! She is focused and relentlessly works on her list and her goals. I appreciate that she has also become able to be incredibly present to herself and to those close to her. She's learned to let her heart be touched, and this is when she is the most beautiful to me.

As a couple, we are extremely high energy. Our friends often ask "How do you get all those things done?" and our children ask "Can we just hang out more?" For us it is natural to be on the go, achieving, enjoying, exploring and so forth.

Whereas I see the world as a place filled with opportunity, my wife brings a more practical focus. For example, she is very intent on us achieving our financial goals. She meticulously plans and manages how we spend all of our money. When we agree on a plan, I can begin to feel constrained and limited even though I agreed to it – a budget makes me feel trapped. But we work together to find a great balance of being flexible, having fun and meeting our financial goals.

As it relates to issues, ironically our high energy level can be a challenge. We have learned, especially with our children, that we have to be very careful about the number of things we plan as a family. We have heard them on several occasions ask if we could not "do" something and instead just "hang out" at home. We work on this as it is natural for both of us to stay on the go.

Neither of us wants to dwell on negative emotions, failures or shortcomings in any way, and we both work diligently to avoid failure. While we intellectually understand the benefit of failure, that it can be a catalyst for growth, it still isn't a topic we sit with long. That said, I've learned that sharing my failures and negative feelings with my wife brings greater intimacy in our relationship.

Overall, I think we're a great match. Part of the key to our success is that we've done a lot of work to be self-aware and self-reflective. The outcome is a thrilling relationship full of fun and opportunity."

Emma, Enthusiast (7) married in a 24-year relationship with Thomas, Achiever (3)

CHAPTER THREE **MOTIVATOR/ACHIEVER**

"My husband is decisive and clear-thinking. He carries through on his plans even when he is unsure of the outcome. He is loyal – if you are his friend, you can do no wrong. And he can be absolute – if he decides he doesn't like you, you can do no right. He is a natural leader with a strong personality and an opinion on everything.

As a husband, he is supportive and brings a sense of adventure to my life. I love that he accepts me even at my most frustrating and that he looks for ways to make my life easier, even if I am not asking for it. He is a constant support in all that I do.

We started off as colleagues, hosting workshops and presentations together. We were friends for ten years before becoming a couple. He was 50 years old and had never been married when we wed.

As a couple, we balance each other. He is more outwardly-focused and sensory so he would be responsible for the workshop content, the event pacing and the mechanics of the sound and visuals. I'm more intuitive and relationship-focused, so I connect with the audience, usually through humor, and sometimes soften the delivery of our material. I admire his skill with people and group dynamics. And he admires my compassion and sensitivity.

Thomas and I are both social and enjoy diverse people and great conversations. My husband is more verbal and articulates easily what we both might be feeling or thinking. In a group, he connects easily with others and can get even the most introverted person to talk. I say I can take him anywhere, and he will get into a conversation with someone. My style is more cautious and reserved. I like to get a feel for the group before I jump in. I'm not always sure of my position, so I love hearing the different sides of a subject. We both can speak with great authority, even if we aren't really sure of our position and have sometimes been called a "power couple." I don't know that we see ourselves that way, but I do think we're a great team.

Like all couples, we have our differences. As we both like to story tell, we occasionally try to talk over each other, and I'll have to insist, "I'm telling the story!" I correct him more than he corrects me, but we do it humorously.

We both have had serious, long-term careers and the related stress that comes with that responsibility. He confronts me when I get too volatile, and I do the same for him. That's not to say it's perfect. After over 20 years of marriage, I still, at moments, get mad and stomp around. Then he does his little things to make himself feel better, and we move on. We both understand the other's weak points and try to be present for each other in ways that make both of us feel seen and heard.

Overall, I am extremely happy in my marriage. We have a tremendous amount of admiration, respect and love for one another. The fact that we both had a great deal of life experience prior to our marriage has helped our relationship immensely. He loved the fact I came with a full family and that he has become an indispensable father figure to my children. The grandchildren adore him. And so do I."

3:7 The Theory

3:7 When In Balance

The Achiever (3) with the Enthusiast (7) make an extremely high energy couple, and this can be a complementary match as both have ample energy to keep up with each other. Both are extroverted, positive, social, lively, outgoing with full schedules and multiple activities. They share a can-do attitude and a belief in a brighter future that can be uplifting to those around them.

To the dynamic, the Achiever (3) brings a practical orientation, a sense of priority and a concern about appearances. They have a heightened concern about what others might think and spend time and energy to make sure the couple is appropriate, accomplished and well-regarded in the community.

Enthusiast (7)s are driven by a sense of adventure, a desire for fun and an appetite for the new, and thus they are less concerned about the opinions of others. Resilient and not overly concerned about failure, they can be spontaneous and outrageous, traits that are both balancing and sometimes healing for the Achiever (3).

The two complement each other with the Achiever (3) bringing a focus on goal achievement and practicality, and the Enthusiast (7) bringing a sense of fun and adventure, boldness and good cheer. They work as a team with the Enthusiast (7) generating the ideas and plans and the Achiever (3) stepping in to make sure the plans are well executed. This couple can be almost legendary in its energy level with others marveling at how they keep it up.

3:7 The Downward Spiral

Both Achiever (3)s and Enthusiast (7) are likely to stay on the go and instinctively turn their attention to the positive. With so much energy focused outward, it can be challenging for this couple to slow down enough to look at deeper issues and examine real problems. There can also be an air of superficiality to this relationship. The couple may look great together but lack true intimacy. Without the ability to drop the masks, slow down and share weaknesses and vulnerabilities, the emotional connection may be lost. In this environment, the downward spiral can be triggered in a variety of ways.

Avoidant behavior can inadvertently trigger the downward spiral if the partners hurt each other without realizing it. Enthusiast (7)s reframe negative situations into positive ones. The defense mechanism of the Achiever (3) is to work harder in negative situations. Since neither is particularly skilled in directly dealing with negative issues, problems can pile up with minor resentments growing, frustrations building and concerns going unaddressed. Without learning to slow down, to sit quietly together and to honestly discuss real issues and the relationship itself, the intimacy the couple once shared becomes eroded.

Alternatively, competing agendas can be an issue. Both Achiever (3)s and Enthusiast (7)s are self-interested and when their personal goals fall out of alignment, it can be difficult to reach compromise. With tightening defenses, both dig in their heels, the Achiever (3) focusing more on their goals and the Enthusiast (7) focusing more on their freedom. Both partners may have the instinct to run, feeling their life priorities are at risk. Without a mechanism to put the relationship first and break the momentum, this couple may put individual interests ahead of the partnership, leading to a split.

3:7 The Lighthouse
Difficulty facing negative emotions can be the start of the downward spiral for this pair so learning to hold the full spectrum of emotions can help to break the momentum. Both types have drive and energy and stay on the go as a subconscious strategy to avoid deeper feeling. Achiever (3)s avoid shame. Enthusiast (7)s run from anxiety. Both types need to cultivate stillness and to learn to slow down so the full range of emotions can be processed. To break their ingrained pattern, strengthening the nervous system is a critical first step.

3:7 The Kundalini Yoga Connection
Achiever (3)s need to relax the drive for constant achievement and face shame, feelings of inadequacy and low self-worth. They must cultivate self-love and self-acceptance so their identity is felt internally, and they aren't as reliant on the opinion of outsiders. The goal is to cultivate a strong sense of self that includes self-acceptance and compassion. Kundalini Yoga kriyas and meditations to get out of the head, to connect with the heart and to cultivate self-love are helpful.

Enthusiast (7)s need to face pain and the darker emotions like sadness, despair and melancholy. They need to sit still, let all their feeling arise and manage their avoidant tendency. They grow when they learn they can tolerate negative emotions, and in fact, see the benefit of feeling and processing these emotions. Kundalini Yoga kriyas and meditations to lower anxiety, cultivate stillness, open the heart and quiet the mind are helpful.

See the appendix for Achiever (3) and Enthusiast (7) recommended Kundalini Yoga kriyas and meditations.

3:8 Achiever (3) with Leader (8)

Margaret, Leader (8) formerly married in a 29-year relationship with Stanley, Achiever (3)

"In our 29-year relationship, which ended almost 10 years ago, I experienced both the strengths and the weaknesses of our differences.

Stanley is very pragmatic, charismatic and well-educated with the ability to write and speak well in front of others. He has a strong drive to succeed and achieve, and it is important to him that people see him as a success. He is comfortable in a leadership role and enjoys creating new breakthroughs and inventions in medicine and business. He is a kind and gentle person with his kids, family, patients and friends.

We were an amazing team who navigated many major life challenges successfully, and despite some very intense obstacles, we raised four exceptional kids who are all thriving in their lives. One of our challenges occurred when our oldest daughter, at the age of 14, was diagnosed with a very rare and serious cancer. Stanley, an orthopedic surgeon, rallied to bring the best of western medicine to support our daughter, while I brought the best of complementary medicine and spiritual support. It was an epic healing journey. Our daughter not only survived the cancer but went on to become a film director and is happily married with a baby son.

While together, Stanley and I also founded a very successful independent high school that all four of our children attended. Stanley was the head of the board of trustees, and I was the visionary leader. We built a diverse board, hired a head of school, raised $50 million and built a state of the art new campus that opened in 1998. The school continues to be successful and highly ranked.

While we achieved a significant amount, we also suffered a tremendous amount of stress. Our daughter lost her leg, and this was extremely difficult for Stanley, who, as an orthopedic surgeon put people's legs back together. It was out of his control to prevent it, and this was extremely painful to all of us, but particularly to him. It felt like a failure.

In addition, the school we created encountered some resistance from conservative factions in the community, creating more stress and tension. And at this same time, my parents split up after 42 years of marriage which led to less financial security for us as a family.

Somewhere during all of this, we lost our way, and the support that we previously shared deteriorated. He had an affair with a nurse with whom he worked. I lost trust in him. He began to see me as controlling and too strong. He became competitive with me. I became suspicious and felt deep abandonment. The relationship deteriorated, and we split up ten years ago.

With perspective and the knowledge of the Enneagram, I now see that we were operating from a level of being unevolved and unaware when under stress. I was always seeking authenticity, regardless of appearances and image. He was always trying to maintain the look of success, regardless of authenticity. I was undermining his stability, and without his stability, expressions of my strength felt threatening to him.

Ten years have passed, and I now understand why things broke down. I also appreciate that we were really good partners and achieved some amazing things. I hope at some point I can have an opportunity to say all this to Stanley in a way that doesn't leave him feeling defensive."

3:8 The Theory

3:8 When In Balance

The Achiever (3) and the Leader (8) make an effective, formidable couple who achieve their shared goals while sharing a deep emotional connection. Both are action-oriented, intense, assertive and practical — they see what they want and go after it. Both are high energy, competitive, disciplined and willing to work hard to further their cause. They can clearly and effectively divide up the duties of running a household or a company, both understanding the other's strengths and weaknesses. And both types are able to put their emotions to the side to stay focused on practical outcomes. With these shared traits, they also have some balancing differences.

Achiever (3)s bring a focus on image, a more diplomatic approach, balanced communication and a greater sensitivity to the way things are being perceived. Practical with a focus on their goals, they bring polish and tact to the dynamic. They strive to be the best in their field, and success is important to them. The Leader (8) finds it easy to admire their Achiever (3) partner, and this admiration brings the couple closer together.

Leader (8)s bring directness, decisiveness, grit, fearlessness and a strong internal compass. They are largely unswayed by the opinion of others and are less image-conscious than their Achiever (3). Honor, honestly, determination and integrity are hallmark Leader (8) traits, and these can be balancing for Achiever (3)s who can be swayed by concerns over image and failure. Leader (8)s have almost legendary willpower and stamina and don't flee in the face of failure. This can offer a growth opportunity for the Achiever (3) who is more inclined to remove themselves if they sense failure on the horizon.

Together this is an impressive, capable, influential couple. Outsiders see them as confident and bold. Once trust is established, this couple is almost unstoppable.

3:8 The Downward Spiral

Both Achiever (3)s and Leader (8)s are focused on practical goals and success so this couple can have a tendency towards workaholism. While this workaholic tendency doesn't usually trigger the downward spiral, it weakens their emotional connection and creates an environment of reactivity.

Tightening defenses cause the Achiever (3) to become more insecure and image-conscious. Situations that would have felt like setbacks start to feel like failures, and the Achiever (3) starts to look for areas where they can score a clear success. Authenticity may be sacrificed as the Achiever (3) becomes fixated about appearances and maintaining a positive external image. This may trigger a breach of trust for the Leader (8) who pushes for authenticity. If authenticity proves evasive, the Leader (8) responds by becoming more controlling and domineering. The downward spiral gains momentum. As both partners polarize, the Achiever (3) becomes more evasive, slippery and avoidant. This prompts an intense reaction in the Leader (8) who seeks to control their environment and wants answers now.

With trust, a common vision and shared goals gone, this couple has lost its way. Intense fights over control and personal agendas may erupt. Without a dramatic change in momentum, the relationship ends, sometimes very bitterly.

3:8 The Lighthouse

Reactions to stress trigger trust issues which mark the beginning of the downward spiral in this team. Trust is a foundational element in this pairing, and any fissures in trust can quickly escalate. As such, rebuilding trust is key to repairing this relationship. To do this, both partners need to go outside their comfort zone and manage their stress reaction differently. Leader (8)s need to learn vulnerability and how to share the full spectrum of emotions, including fear, sadness, melancholy, loneliness and so forth. Achiever (3)s need to speak from their heart, not from their head. They also need to learn self-love so they can dissolve shame and their intense fear of failure.

3:8 The Kundalini Yoga Connection

Both types need to strengthen their nervous system so that going outside their comfort zone feels less threatening. Achiever (3)s need to resist the urge to walk away from what feels like a potential failure. Leader (8)s need to resist the urge to press for immediate resolution.

Achiever (3)s must energetically balance their head with their heart and learn self-acceptance and self-love. With true self-acceptance, the threat of failure feels less intense. Kundalini Yoga kriyas and meditations to cultivate self-acceptance, to connect with feelings of love and gratitude and to strengthen the nervous system are helpful.

Leader (8)s need to learn to share their vulnerability in a heartfelt and raw way. They need to experience the power of their vulnerability. Kundalini Yoga kriyas and meditations to manage anger, to open the heart and to connect with gratitude are helpful.

See the appendix for Achiever (3) and Leader (8) recommended Kundalini Yoga kriyas and meditations.

3:9 Achiever (3) with Peacemaker (9)

Martin, Peacemaker (9) in a 3-year relationship with Claire, Achiever (3)

"Claire is energetic, persistent, determined and motivated. I value her drive for efficiency and her ability to set and achieve long-term goals. She brings spontaneity, high spirits and a positive attitude to the relationship.

In our relationship, we both try to avoid difficult, contentious issues, and this can be a challenge as it means some topics don't get addressed. Our needs can be different. She has an incredible need for admiration and approval which I recognize in her but don't have myself. Tempering this need can be draining. Our pace is different. I need a lot of time to process my thoughts, sort out my feelings and develop my opinions. Her process is much faster, and she can become impatient and short-tempered at times. She's much more impulsive than I am. Sometimes we experience this as positive spontaneity, and other times it is the lack of forethought that leads to difficult situations.

Overall, I'm happy in my relationship. I enjoy my girlfriend's high energy, her positivity and her drive. We're a good balance."

3:9 The Theory

3:9 When In Balance
The Achiever (3) and the Peacemaker (9) can make a very supportive and balancing match bringing each other important personality traits the other generally lacks.

Peacemaker (9)s bring support, acceptance, encouragement and an unflappable sense of calm. Because they are less image-conscious and less concerned about the opinion of others, they offer the Achiever (3) a firm base from which to jump. The Achiever (3) correctly senses the Peacemaker (9) will support them through thick and thin, and this gives the Achiever (3) greater self-confidence to pursue their goals. Peacemaker (9)s enjoy the simple things in life and can help remind their Achiever (3) to slow down and smell the roses. Achiever (3)s like to be admired, and the Peacemaker (9) finds it easy to be proud of their Achiever (3).

In return, Achiever (3)s help the Peacemaker (9) to wake up to all that life has to offer. Achiever (3)s bring a high energy, drive, ambition and a fast-paced, "can do" attitude that helps motivate and focus the Peacemaker (9). With their Achiever (3) at their side, Peacemaker (9)s may stretch themselves to try new things, go places they haven't been and to break out of their comfortable routine. They sparkle in the face of their new experiences and enjoy a broader worldview.

Energetically, this couple has the potential to be balancing. The Peacemaker (9) gives the Achiever (3) permission to relax, and the Achiever (3) helps the Peacemaker (9) to get going. The easy acceptance of the Peacemaker (9) and the enthusiastic drive of the Achiever (3) can be healing for both partners. When self-aware and in balance, this can be a successful and enduring match.

3:9 The Downward Spiral
This couple can run into trouble by being too conflict avoidant. Peacemaker (9)s feel threatened by conflict, and Achiever (3)s feel threatened by a negative image, so both people tend to sweep issues under the rug. With tightening defenses, the Achiever (3) gets

more attached to the image of a perfect relationship, and the Peacemaker (9) gets more withdrawn to maintain harmony.

Peacemaker (9)s feel extreme anxiety in the face of conflict and will often stonewall or shut down to avoid the related stress they feel from a loss of harmony. They prefer to wait, hoping that time passing will somehow resolve the issue.

Achiever (3)s are very interested in maintaining a positive image. Love is fused with the appearance of wellness, and it is hard for them to separate the two. To feel stable, they want the image of the "perfect marriage" and to honestly deal with an issue might shatter that image.

As both people polarize into their corner of denial the relationship weakens, though to the outside world everything may appear fine. Dinner parties continue, holidays seem bright and happy to outsiders, school functions have both parents in attendance, but behind closed doors, the relationship is cold and distant. Both partners are unhappy but unwilling to face reality. Instead, they craft separate lives for themselves and continue down their path of avoidance.

The downward spiral gains momentum. The Achiever (3) has many unmet needs of being admired and appreciated. They may fall into a depression or go outside of the relationship to get their needs met. The Peacemaker (9) may start to resent the falseness of the Achiever (3) and the mask that is presented to the outside world. They experience the Achiever (3) as attention seeking, self-centered and phony. The lives may continue to drift apart as the couple becomes like distant housemates.

Often, some life crisis such as an affair or a major health challenge brings the deterioration of the relationship into awareness. If the core issues remain unaddressed and unresolved, the relationship may collapse.

3:9 The Lighthouse
Issue avoidance is the root of the downward spiral for this couple. Feelings of shame and anxiety trigger avoidance, so dealing with these two issues on a somatic level can help break the momentum of the downward crash.

In addition, the Achiever (3) needs to recognize how anxiety-provoking conflict is for a Peacemaker (9). Stonewalling is often a way to avoid anxiety, so unthreatening ways to address issues are the most effective. And Peacemaker (9)s need to acknowledge how image conscious their Achiever (3) is. Achiever (3)s are better able to address sensitive issues when they are feeling very safe, secure and their image is not in jeopardy.

 ### 3:9 The Kundalini Yoga Connection
Feelings of shame result in the Achiever (3) sacrificing reality for an image. Achiever (3)s can cut off from their emotions, leaving them often with a polished external world but a sad and unfulfilling inner world. Kundalini Yoga kriyas and meditations that cultivate heart opening, self-acceptance and self-love are beneficial for Achiever (3)s.

Peacemaker (9)s need to strengthen their nervous system and their navel center/third chakra to activate their power center. The anxiety of conflict feels less overwhelming with a strong nervous system. A strong navel point gets the Peacemaker (9) in touch with their needs allowing them to advocate for themselves better. Kundalini Yoga kriyas and meditations to build their nervous system and the navel center are highly beneficial for Peacemaker (9)s.

See the appendix for Achiever (3) and Peacemaker (9) recommended Kundalini Yoga kriyas and meditations.

This book is a living document. We will be updating it periodically with new information. If you are or were in a relationship with an Achiever (3) and you would like to participate in the related relationship survey, please email me at lynn@lynnroulo.com

Type Four
INDIVIDUALIST/ ARTIST

(seeks individuality/avoids the mundane)

 ## Overview

Individualist (4)s are original and authentic, with intense feelings spanning the entire emotional spectrum. They have felt great emotional highs, deep emotional lows and can feel everything in between on a daily basis. This person favors intensity, either positive or negative, over commonplace and routine.

Drawn to what is missing, Individualist (4)s spend a lot of time thinking about what they don't have and experiencing longing. This person is capable of profound creativity. Individualist (4)s want to be seen as special and may exaggerate their differences to minimize feelings of being ordinary or mundane.

Individualist (4)s bring an emotional richness and fluency to their relationships. No feeling scares them, so they fearlessly explore the emotional world. They can have a push-pull relationship with their partners, longing for them when they are distant or unavailable but pulling away from them when they are available. Partners appreciate their Individualist (4)'s sensitivity, expressiveness, creativity and originality. Partners are challenged by their

Individualist (4)'s tendency to withdraw, low energy, impulsiveness, lack of objectivity and need for lots of time to process feelings.

• Attention Bias/Habit Of Attention:
Attention goes to what is missing, distant or unavailable. They see what they don't have and long for it. Their attention moves away from what they do have and from feelings of satisfaction and fulfillment.

• Emotional Style:
Verbal, colorful, intense, accessible, dark, fearless.

• Communication Style:
Expressive, sensitive, vivid, lyrical, emotional, intense, empathetic, kind.

• Brings To The Relationship:
Creativity, authenticity, intensity, the ability to access, understand and process the emotional world, sensitivity, originality.

• Unique Strengths:
Individualist (4)s are emotionally expressive, able to detect and analyze the fine details of their own and others' internal world. They are typically very empathetic, able to connect with others easily and are often profoundly original thinkers. They can be gifted at creating a safe space for others to share their vulnerabilities. They can be truly innovative in their pursuits and may offer original concepts and creations to the world.

• Challenges:
Individualist (4)s have a tendency to focus on what they don't have or what is missing. Their emotional intensity can distort reality and rational thinking. They can be prone to depression.

• Stability And Security:
"I feel stable when I feel authentically understood and accepted. I feel secure when I can express my intense emotions and when I harness my creative energy in a productive way. When my creative expressions are truly understood, I feel wonderful."

• Instability And Insecurity:
"I feel unstable when I feel misunderstood, unseen or when I don't fully understand my own emotional state. I feel insecure when my emotional intensity is dismissed or ridiculed. I

feel terrible when I am told I am too dramatic, too sensitive or when my feelings are ignored or minimized."

- **Path Of Growth:**
Equanimity
Individualist (4)s grow when they learn to stay in balance despite intense and ever-changing emotions. The journey is to compassionate neutrality.

- **Energy:**
Fluid, flowing, emotionally charged, melancholy.

- **The Kundalini Yoga Connection:**
Individualist (4)s are more connected to the emotional world than many other types. This has its benefits, but emotions are constantly changing and in flux. They don't serve as reliable guides for decision-making if they aren't balanced with more stable factors as well. Learning to hold the energy of emotion without getting swept into it is important in establishing a path to balance. Kundalini Yoga kriyas and meditations for energy management, for stability and for cultivating neutral mind are helpful.

The Individualist (4) Subtypes

"Tenacity" Self-Preservation Subtype:
The self-preservation Individualist (4) expresses emotional intensity more stoically than the other subtypes. This is a person who suffers in silence and is sometimes referred to as the "Sunny" Individualist (4).

To the outside world, this person can seem reserved and introspective. Internally, this person is often feeling a wide range of intense emotions on a regular basis. However, this intensity is often not expressed to others. They have the title "Tenacity" because of their tendency to hold it all together, to suffer in silence.

In intimate relationships, the self-preservation Individualist (4) may subconsciously link stoic suffering with love and acceptance. This is a less dramatic, more autonomous Individualist (4) who is less likely to involve others in their mood swings. While this Individualist (4) may have a masochistic element, to the outside world, they are empathetic, nurturing and sensitive.

On the positive side, this is someone who channels feelings of inadequacy into working hard to be successful.

On the less positive side, this can be an Individualist (4) who struggles with workaholism and self-sabotage and who has a difficult time ever feeling secure enough.

"Shame" Social Subtype:
The social Individualist (4) openly expresses the emotional intensity of the type, feels things deeply and presents the sense of shame closer to the surface than the other subtypes. This is sometimes called the "Sad" Individualist (4).

To the outside world, this is someone who communicates suffering openly and regularly. Others may see this person as dramatic and overly emotional. Internally, this is a person who feels a lot of suffering and whose attention goes naturally to their own deficiencies. They have the title "Shame" because this type openly experiences and identifies with shame more than the other subtypes.

This Individualist (4) needs to have their suffering witnessed and validated. Unlike the self-preservation Individualist (4), this is someone who relies on others to get their emotional needs fulfilled.

On the positive side, because this Individualist (4) talks more about their emotions, they can bring emotional awareness and emotional processing to the relationship. This is someone who helps their partner pinpoint, discuss and process emotions.

On the less positive side, this Individualist (4) can over-identify with their suffering and can have a difficult time being happy or content.

"Competition" Intimate Subtype:
The intimate Individualist (4) expresses emotional intensity and envy through competition and an attempt to establish superiority. This type has been characterized as the angriest type in the Enneagram, and this person typically has a colorful, vivid personality. It is hard to forget an intimate Individualist (4). This type is sometimes called the "Mad" Four.

To the outside world, they appear intense, opinionated, strong-willed and sometimes angry. Internally, this person is feeling misunderstood, competitive and a mix of inferiority and arrogance. Conversely, this type can also express great sensitivity, understanding and tenderness. This person is a study in contrasts. They have the title "Competition" because of their keen focus on competition and being the best.

In intimate relationships, intimate Individualist (4)s can have an "all or nothing" attitude that their partners may experience as demanding.

On the positive side, this person likes and needs emotional intensity, and this can open up a new world to less emotionally driven partners. Intimate Individualist (4)s are colorful and direct and can shake their partners awake.

On the less positive side, anger and competition can be central themes as can a push-pull relationship. Because the emotional intensity is so externalized in intimate Individualist (4)s, partners often can't avoid being drawn into the mood swings.

Individualist (4)—Levels of Awareness

Individualist (4) When Self-Aware
Deeply creative, original and expressive, Individualist (4)s are able to share their authenticity with the outside world in a profound way. Healing, inspiring and regenerating, they harness their intense emotional energy in a positive way. They are highly self-aware, self-reflective and balanced. They are sensitive to others, compassionate to themselves and able to experience self-love. They start to recognize some of their talents and accomplishments. Individualistic, self-revealing but not self-wallowing, they come forward honestly and clearly. They become easier to relate to because their emotions, while intense, are more managed. They may be funny and ironic with a beautiful balance of emotional strength and vulnerability.

Individualist (4) With Tightening Defenses
They are poetic and sensitive in their approach to life, feeling deeply touched by small things and with a heightened sense of reality. Emotional intensity, passionate feelings and ever-shifting moods characterize their experience. In an attempt to stay connected to their feelings, they begin to internalize everything. Their imagination and fantasy world become very rich and vivid, making reality dull by comparison. They are moody, introverted, hypersensitive and self-absorbed with a tendency to take everything personally. They withdraw to process their feelings. They may start to exhibit antisocial behavior. They feel alien to others and experience themselves as outsiders. They may live in a rich fantasy world and become disengaged and disdainful of practical reality. Self-pity, envy, depression and melancholy are often present. Maintaining a regular routine becomes challenging.

Individualist (4) When Fixated
They experience themselves as a failure and feel shame. They become drained of energy and angry at themselves and others. They have difficulty functioning in normal society and feel increasingly alienated. Full depression may set in. Everything becomes a source of self-

torture and a reminder of their sense of failure. Their sense of reality is lost and replaced with despair and hopelessness. The future seems dark. They drive away anyone who tries to help. Feelings of despair and hopelessness intensify. They feel trapped and may become self-destructive, with mental, emotional or physical breakdowns in the picture. Suicide attempts are possible.

Keys If You Are In A Relationship With An Individualist (4)

 "Don't take it personally when I need time away from you."

Ericha, Individualist (4)

"I have a tendency to withdraw when I am overstimulated or stressed. My partner helps me by not taking this personally. His trust in me helps me to feel relaxed so I can focus on feeling better instead of trying to convince him that I'm going to be ok or that it's not about him."

Margaret, Perfectionist (1) married in a 15-year relationship with Antony, Individualist (4)

"A challenge for me is his tendency to withdraw and how he needs a lot of alone time. We've been together almost 15 years, so we've made great progress, but when we first started dating, I took his tendency to withdraw personally or was impatient if it was getting in the way of plans we had that day. I know that I can sometimes be too focused on the schedule and details. And I think he gets impatient having to advocate to have space for his feelings. We've come a long way, but this continues to be one of our central challenges."

Individualist (4)s have a lot of emotional intensity, and this drains them. They need time alone to process their feelings and to renew their energy. They rejuvenate best with unstructured, solitary downtime. They often can't share their feelings during this time, because they don't always know exactly what they are feeling. They use this alone time to process their emotions. This withdrawal is often followed by a need for attention. This isn't some kind of manic indecisiveness but rather a legitimate need to balance alone time with the need to be understood by others. Finding this balance can be hard, and it often appears to be a push-pull to others. Individualist (4)s report it is more like learning to navigate the dynamic between interior and exterior, between understanding themselves and being understood by others.

This can be confusing and even hurtful to their partners who often take the withdrawal personally and as a sign there is a problem in the relationship.

If you are an Individualist (4):

Understand that your partner can't read your mind, and your withdrawal may feel scary or threatening to them. Try to reassure them the relationship is OK (assuming it is) and try to put parameters around how much time you need alone. Don't just disappear with no explanation as this is hurtful and confusing to other people in your life.

If you are with an Individualist (4):

Understand that your partner needs time alone to process their feelings. This time alone is important for their well-being. Try not to take their withdrawal personally, as your unhappiness with their need may trigger an emotional response which drains them even more. Instead, focus back on yourself and do things that make you feel good, positive and stable. The more you can respect their need to withdraw and still feel balanced and stable, the faster they will be able to return to you and the relationship.

 "Share your flaws and your personal struggles with me."

Margaret, Perfectionist (1) married in a 15-year relationship with Antony, Individualist (4)

"Antony is very in touch with the emotional world and helps me process feelings I might otherwise not fully absorb. Few things make him happier than than when I say, "I'm in a funk," and while I'm not a person who is terribly comfortable talking about my feelings and emotions, he's the complete opposite. He wants to hear both when I'm happy and when I'm unhappy. Neither situation scares him. It's wonderfully nurturing, and it helps me break free from always thinking about how I "should" act."

Philippe, Helper (2) with Crystal, Individualist (4)

"This is the warmest, most passionate and nonjudgmental relationship I have ever been in. We are good medicine for each other. Crystal encourages me to be myself and to be healthy and balanced. With her, I feel relieved when I discuss my problems and concerns about issues in my daily life. She is an amazing listener who offers me wise advice. She helps me focus on my needs – what they are and how to get them met. From time to time, she encourages me to concentrate on my own needs instead of hers, and this can be really helpful for me."

Individualist (4)s place authenticity and keeping it real as top priorities. They deeply appreciate when their partner comes forward with personal struggles and personality quirks and flaws. Individualist (4)s feel these things intensely themselves, and it makes them feel closer to their partner when their faults, foibles and daily challenges are shared.

If you are an Individualist (4):
One of the gifts you offer to the world is your emotional fluency. You are uniquely talented at creating a safe space for people to come forward to heal their emotional wounds. Understand that many other types are less able to share their fears, their shame, their doubts and their frustrations. Try not to get frustrated if you don't get the same amount of sharing as you offer. Your partner may not have the same level of emotional fluency.

If you are with an Individualist (4):
Your Individualist (4) likely feels closer to you when you share your personality quirks and personal challenges. Individualist (4)s are sensitive and empathetic. They have high emotional fluency and can hold the emotional space on a wide range of issues. Your Individualist (4) will appreciate your rawness and candor. It makes you real to them.

 "Please don't try to fix me or tell me how I should be."

Ericha, Individualist (4)

"I find it very easy to slip into a depression. My partner does an amazing job of witnessing those dark feelings without trying to fix me. His ability to allow me just to feel how I'm feeling helps me not to get attached to the way that I'm feeling. He knows that my sadness or my anxiety will pass with time, and he doesn't amplify my feelings by worrying about me or freaking out when I'm depressed.

But he doesn't ignore me or belittle my feelings, either. He takes my emotions seriously by asking how I feel and letting me share openly. He will gently offer to connect with me saying things like "do you want a hug?" or "can I sit with you?" without being pushy or forcing me out of my shell. He respects my boundaries, and if I tell him I need to be alone, he gives me that space. I know the offer to talk is always there and when I am ready, he is willing to listen or even to just hold me without judgment. It's amazing, really. I never thought I'd find someone like him."

Aiden, Individualist (4)

"All these intense feelings of mine are like weather patterns over my heart. They come and go, and they are impermanent. I have to live with them, and I do my best to manage them through meditation, yoga and so forth. But they are still there and can feel very real. As my partner, I am so grateful when you can stay calmly at my side or gently help me to see that it is a false rainy day pattern while sharing our umbrella in the fake storm."

If you are an Individualist (4):
Understand that your emotional storminess can feel threatening and confusing to your partner. Their attempts to give you advice aren't meant to be insensitive. They don't understand your moods and are struggling for a solution to what they see as your unhappiness. Be direct that you want to be heard and not fixed.

If you are with an Individualist (4):
Individualist (4)s desperately want to be understood and accepted for who they are. If that isn't possible for any reason, they want to, at a minimum, be heard. If you are in a relationship with an Individualist (4) learning and practicing active listening is crucial to the success of the relationship. This is a highly sensitive and intuitive person, so you will not be able to fake your way through this. You will need to learn to really listen. Individualist (4)s often report they appreciate humor as a way to help them gain perspective. Laughter can be amazing medicine to bring light into darker emotional spaces.

INDIVIDUALIST (4) 360 DEGREE REVIEW

The next section features the 360 degree review--partnership with an Individualist (4) from the perspective of each of the nine types.

4:1 Individualist (4) with Perfectionist (1)

Ailie, Perfectionist (1) in a 1-year relationship with Laird, Indvidualist (4)

"Laird is compassionate, creative, emotionally supportive and loyal. I love his mind. He sees the world in lines and colors, dark and light, depth and texture, whereas I see it mostly in symbols. He can break the physical world down into tiny pieces and appreciates it for its smallest components, whereas I'm usually zooming far out and around the corners, looking at the big picture but missing the amazing little details until they are pointed out to me.

One of his greatest strengths as a partner is his complete acceptance of me for exactly who I am. He lets me be me without any judgment. This makes me feel safe, loved and secure. I haven't felt this safe with anyone else in my life, and that feeling of unconditional acceptance, of being allowed to be right or wrong, to make mistakes, to look stupid, is worth a lot to someone like me who can be so self-critical. Because he is so accepting, I feel free to be more fun, goofy and spontaneous than my normal calculated self. I love being able to express this part of me.

CHAPTER FOUR INDIVIDUALIST/ARTIST

We were friends for 25 years before we came together as a couple, and we have a wonderful dynamic together. We both notice and appreciate the beauty in our lives, whether it's a perfect hour at the beach with our family, just digging in the sand and enjoying the ocean air or a movie that's so complex and well done that we'll both be thinking about it for days and know we need to watch it again as soon as the end credits are rolling. Laird sees the artistic side of me. As a CFO, I don't consider myself an artist, but I do express creativity through the cakes I make. I'm critical of my cakes, but he is able to point out artistically why things work and what's great about them. He'll focus on how two or three colors blend together or how the texture of the cake makes it more interesting. He focuses on the creative elements instead of being critical. By having someone supportive and less critical of me, I've been less critical of others. I've become a kinder person, more willing to ignore flaws and offer more praise.

While our dynamic is balancing and affirming, we do have our differences. We navigate the practical details of life differently. I'm a planner. I do an annual budget. I keep a calendar. I update both at least weekly. I respect deadlines and the expectations I've set for others. Laird operates under much looser guidelines, not making any concrete plans even when it comes to something big like driving across the country. He'll estimate it should take about 4 days for the trip. I interpret this as 4 days or 5 days at the most. But then it takes 10 days! He doesn't plan even a day into the future, sometimes, realizing at 10:00 pm that he has no clean laundry to wear the next day, much to my dismay.

But we've adapted. I try to be less scheduled, within reason, and I try to help him plan a little better like pointing out the washing machine is free in case he has to do laundry for the next day. He will also say things now like "I know you're a planner, so I want to make sure I know what's expected...." The fact he even bothers to say these words makes me feel like I'm being heard and that the plans we make together are important. It lets me know he's trying, and it reminds me to try harder too.

I wish he could see himself the way I see him – as a valuable, unique and amazing person. I wish he understood his worth as a friend, an employee, a human being, without letting other people take advantage of him. I hope he knows how important he is to me. Before he came into my life and our home, something was missing. It was out of balance. He brings true balance to me and my environment.

I love that we have the bond of music. Music has always brought us together, and it keeps us together. It's something we use to communicate with both when we're having good days and on bad days. We use it when we're hanging out together, having a great time and on the rare occasions when we don't want to be around each other. I think our taste in music, if we graphed it, would be very similar to our relationship as a whole. The majority of the music that I like, he also likes and vice versa. But there are a few songs that I love, and he hates and vice versa. It's like there's just this sliver of ourselves where there's no crossover and no agreement, but it's such a small piece, it doesn't taint the rest of the relationship. It's one of those things that just makes each of us look at the other and say "huh; you're a weirdo," in the most loving, adoring way possible.

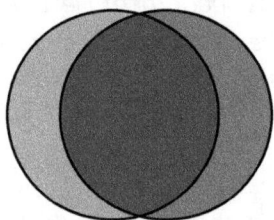

Usually, we walk a common path, and a small portion of the time we are absolutely opposite on our likes, tastes or how we see things. I love this about our relationship – we love and support each other but can also teach each other things, even if the lesson is as simple as tolerance. I'm grateful to have this man as my life partner."

Margaret, Perfectionist (1) married in a 15-year relationship with Antony, Individualist (4)

"Antony is an extraordinary listener and earnestly compassionate in all situations. He's also a keen reader of people and has helped me be less disappointed when others don't live up to my expectations. He's good at understanding why people may act in a way that's unkind or neglectful. We both can be self-critical, but he's encouraged me to be kinder to myself when I make mistakes. I love that he's fiercely protective when others try to take advantage of me."

4:1 The Theory

4:1 When In Balance
The Perfectionist (1) and the Individualist (4) bring many complementary personality traits to the relationship and when self-aware, they balance each other's blind spots and appreciate each other's strengths.

The foundation of this pair is shared core values layered with very different operating styles. Perfectionist (1)s offer efficiency, order, logic, purpose and rational thinking. They can provide a stable, organized environment for the Individualist (4) and model self-discipline, follow through, emotional containment and self-sacrifice for the greater good. They can help the Individualist (4) get out of their fantasy world and ground them back down to the material world. Perfectionist (1)s are action-oriented, and their structured, disciplined approach to life can be balancing for the Individualist (4).

Individualist (4)s offer emotional awareness, sensitivity, creativity and a more intuitive approach to life. They have high emotional fluency and can help their Perfectionist (1) partner access a wider range of emotions. Individualist (4)s can see the deeper subtext of situations and offer wise counsel to their Perfectionist (1), who tends to be more literal in their interpretation of events. They also help the Perfectionist (1) to slow down and not feel guilty just "being." This can be healing and helpful for the Perfectionist (1) who naturally feels driven to stay on the go accomplishing their various tasks.

Together this couple combines intuition and rational thought, efficiency and sensitivity, strategic focus and attention to detail. When approaching life together, they successfully blend intuitive and practical operating styles.

4:1 The Downward Spiral

Like a logician and an empath, these two types see the world from very different vantage points and have very different emotional responses to situations. When fixated, their balancing traits can become trigger points, and intolerance, disappointment and frustration build. This can set the downward spiral into motion.

Both handle their emotions and their emotional reactions differently. Individualist (4)s seek to allow themselves to feel the full spectrum of feelings, and this requires them to have time to process and absorb their experiences. Perfectionist (1)s are driven by efficiency and don't want or require as much time to "feel." If these differences aren't understood and accepted, problems arise. To the Individualist (4), the Perfectionist (1) starts to feel stiflingly rigid and controlling. They resent the never-ending "to do" lists and long for a deeper emotional connection. And to the Perfectionist (1), the Individualist (4) starts to seem wallowing, self-absorbed and in need of copious amounts of unstructured time. They are mystified by their Individualist (4)'s desire to "do nothing" and to relax and hang out. When one or both starts to resent these differences in each other, the downward spiral begins.

As each type starts to get rigid in their interpretation of events, the Individualist (4) may feel unseen and misunderstood. This triggers an intense emotional response and more need for time to process their feelings. The Individualist (4) may start to feel drained and judged by their Perfectionist (1). The Perfectionist (1) may resent or take personally the Individualist (4)'s need for time alone. They interpret this as self-absorbed, wallowing, self-pitying and in extreme cases, pathetic. This triggers the Perfectionist (1) to become more rigid and critical in their reaction. The downward spiral gains momentum.

Both can be spiteful and unforgiving, tracking past grievances and emotional wounds. If the relationship continues its downward trajectory, it ends in bitter frustration, mutual disrespect and nasty arguments until it finally splits apart.

4:1 The Lighthouse
Keeping a strong heart connection and minimizing feelings of disappointment are key to stopping the momentum of the downward spiral in this relationship. Remembering common values and mutual respect can take the sting off the differences. A shared gratitude practice can help bring this couple closer together.

4:1 The Kundalini Yoga Connection
The growth path for the two types in some respects heads in different directions so they can use this to their advantage and balance each other. The Individualist (4) needs to move towards equanimity and to be more neutral in the face of intense emotions. The Perfectionist (1) needs to move towards serenity and tranquility. They need to resist the urge to try and improve things. They must learn stillness.

The Individualist (4) needs to strengthen their nervous system, so they don't feel as overwhelmed by their intense emotional responses. While letting themselves fully feel their emotions is important, managing the energy of emotion is also key to maintaining personal stability and balance. Kundalini Yoga kriyas or meditations that lower anxiety, cultivate self-love and to promote neutral mind and stability are beneficial.

Perfectionist (1)s need to connect to and speak from their heart. They need to wake up to their inner compassion. Expanding their emotional fluency and range can help them connect to the emotional world of the Individualist (4). Kundalini Yoga kriyas and meditations that promote energy awareness, heart-opening and burn out anger can help bring forward their softer feelings.

See the appendix for Perfectionist (1) and Individualist (4) recommended Kundalini Yoga kriyas and meditations.

4:2 Individualist (4) with Helper (2)

Philippe, Helper (2) married in a relationship for one year with Crystal, Individualist (4)

"Crystal is creative, honest, intelligent and adds to my life in so many ways. Simple things like her ideas on how to be more festive for holidays and on fun things to do get me excited. Her honesty allows me to be conscious of the reality of a situation so I can focus on the right issues. Her intelligence provides me with another perspective and means I don't have to explain things in detail – she already gets it. Her sense of humor lights up my life. Her encouragement motivates me and gives me the confidence to be more inner-directed which helps me be more balanced.

Regarding issues within the relationship, we both can be very emotional and require a lot of closeness and intimacy. And while we both feel a lot of emotional intensity, we express it differently.

She holds her emotions in more and doesn't always express what she is feeling directly. I can be anxious in my thinking and can create imaginary problems in the future that don't actually exist in the present moment. With these differences, sometimes things can get unnecessarily dramatic. As a simple example, she was unhappy about how much I was watching football, a sport I love. She didn't want to bring the issue up because she worried I might get mad. When she did finally bring it up, I had to deal with all my own emotions on the subject, which weren't small. It became a big misunderstanding that was probably more about communication than it was about sports. Another challenge we work on is spending enough time together so that she and I feel connected. This is important to both of us.

Overall, I think we want the same things – to have a wonderful deep and intimate relationship. I love being with her and want to connect with her all the time. And I feel truly fortunate because we are best friends in addition to our great romantic relationship."

4:2 The Theory

4:2 When In Balance

The Helper (2) and Individualist (4) make a closely bonded, supportive, caring and loving combination. Both have high emotional fluency, and the world of feelings is center stage in this relationship. They openly share their thoughts, impressions and emotional responses with each other and can spend hours recounting the events of the day, their reactions and so forth. Together they create a safe haven to be real and authentic, and this can be a very healing relationship for both partners.

Helper (2)s are typically outward facing, social and comfortable interacting with a wide range of people. They can give the Individualist (4) confidence and energy to do the same by joining them socially. They are thoughtful, encouraging, patient, kind and considerate. They can make their Individualist (4) feel seen, something that is deeply healing for the Individualist (4).

Individualist (4)s bring emotional fearlessness, creativity, humor and broad picture thinking. They seek emotional honesty, and as they tend to be highly sensitive to arising conflicts, they are often the ones to bring up thorny issues. Individualist (4)s are deeply intuitive and can read the subtle undertones of a situation. They offer wise counsel to their Helper (2). More self-referencing, they give the Helper (2) permission to get in touch with their own needs and make themselves a priority.

Together they create a positive feedback loop, both admiring and appreciative of what the other brings. Both seek deep emotional connection, and they find it in each other. This is a couple known for its closeness.

4:2: The Downward Spiral

When fixated with tightening defenses, the emotional connection and intensity they share polarizes this couple. As both crave intimacy, they can spend a lot of time and energy processing small grievances and minor misunderstandings. Under stress with tightening defenses, this intensifies, and themes of insecurity, shame and blame enter the picture. Without a healthy mechanism to come back into balance, an endless loop of misunderstandings can begin, thus triggering the downward spiral.

The two types express their emotional needs very differently. Individualist (4)s are guided by their feelings, and their feelings are ever-changing. They need a lot of downtime to process their experiences and emotional energy, and this can be frustrating to the Helper (2) who wants a more engaged partner. With time, Helper (2)s can start to feel the Individualist (4) is self-absorbed, temperamental, testy and emotionally unpredictable. They may tire of the Individualist (4)'s negative self-image and difficulty accepting the nurturing the Helper (2) wants to provide.

The Individualist (4) can become suspicious of the Helper (2), as they see through their people-pleasing behavior and question its authenticity. They may feel smothered by the

Helper (2), finding them needy and overly-involved. And because Individualist (4)s can be quite intuitive, they may tire of the often-unspoken need for appreciation coming from the Helper (2).

If the downward spiral gains momentum, the Helper (2) starts to feel increasingly unappreciated, and the Individualist (4) starts to feel increasingly misunderstood and alone. Both find each other emotionally needy and draining. Eventually one or both start to feel they would be better off without the relationship, and the relationship is in danger.

4:2 The Lighthouse

Because both Helper (2)s and Individualist (4)s are so charged with the energy of emotion, energy management is essential to break the momentum of any downward spiral. Both types are very emotionally driven so learning to balance the ever-changing fluctuations of emotional current is key to the health of the relationship. Under stress, they move in opposite directions, the Helper (2) leaning in for connection, and the Individualist (4) pulling back to conserve what little energy they have. To break the momentum of the downward spiral, each partner needs to learn to stay energetically still.

4:2 The Kundalini Yoga Connection

When the downward spiral starts, Helper (2)s need to get in touch with their own needs and place a priority on self-care. They need to resist the urge to lean forward into the energetic space of the Individualist (4) as the Individualist (4) typically wants to withdraw to process their feelings. Kundalini Yoga kriyas to build the nervous system, that center and balance the energy centers and that cultivate self-love and self-acceptance are helpful for Helper (2)s.

Individualist (4)s need to cultivate feelings of trust and self-love. They need to learn to honor their emotions while resisting the urge to withdraw. They grow as they become more balanced. Kundalini Yoga kriyas and meditations that promote a strong nervous system and a consistent breathwork practice to build stability, equanimity and neutral mind are beneficial.

See the appendix for Helper (2) and Individualist (4) recommended Kundalini Yoga kriyas and meditations.

4:3 Individualist (4) with Achiever (3)

Amber, Achiever (3) formerly in a relationship for less than a year with Nigel, Individualist (4)

"Nigel was empathetic, mature and considerate. He was a very caring person, good at his work, a responsible son and a kind father. He was emotionally brave and could hold and honor all different feelings that surfaced. Whereas other people might have shied away from difficult emotions, he did not.

In our relationship, we had interesting, heartfelt talks. He was a good listener, and we shared our deeper feelings, our past experiences and discussed for hours how our respective backgrounds had influenced us. Our times together surfaced memories of my youth, and I could see how these experiences framed my present and my future plans. Our dialogues had no hidden agenda; we just wanted to get to know each other better. In the process, I gained insight into myself. He gave me a safe harbor to park myself that felt authentic, and I felt cherished for who I was and not what I was doing.

While he was emotionally brave, he also had what felt like never-ending emotional needs and became like an energetic vampire. We talked e-n-d-l-e-s-s-l-y about his feelings of inadequacy. We would go to a social event, and his post-mortem afterward would center on how inadequate he felt while the rest of us were catching up. I started to feel like I had to censor my own social sharing to not make him feel overshadowed. I grew tired of the role of filling up his bottomless pit by constantly reassuring him he was fine as he was. The list of issues seemed endless. And after dealing with one issue, another one would pop up.

He seemed trapped in the past. He was not good at handling conflict and wasn't able to create healthy boundaries with his ex-wife. In the end, I got tired of being his booster and not getting boosted in return. The final straw was when he withdrew completely from the relationship for several weeks with no explanation.

The relationship ended, but even the ending became complicated. He wanted to stay on the periphery of my social life. I wanted him to understand that when he broke it off, my friends wanted nothing to do with him. The chapter closed for good when a couple of months after the breakup, he invited me out for dinner. When I arrived, I was shocked. During our relationship, he had presented himself as a clean-cut, conservatively-dressed professional… what turned up at the restaurant was a Hulk Hogan – long straggly hair liberally streaked by grey, bushy beard, wearing a bomber jacket, not someone I would trust with a stethoscope! I left wondering, "Did I even know this guy?"

4:3 The Theory

 ### 4:3 When In Balance
The Achiever (3) and Individualist (4) approach the world from different directions, the Achiever (3) seeking their identity from the outside in, and the Individualist (4) seeking their identify from the inside out. When in higher states of awareness, these fundamental differences can be balancing, intriguing and can offer growth opportunities for one another.

The Achiever (3) models confidence, polish, goal-setting, discipline and a practical focus on achievement. They value efficiency and organization and show the Individualist (4) how to march on in the face of their ever-changing emotional world. Achiever (3)s help the Individualist (4) stay present and grounded in the practical world. More emotionally-contained than their Individualist (4) partner, they use achievement as their guideposts of how to behave and where to put their energy. All of these traits can be helpful and balancing for their Individualist (4) who sees the world from a very different lens.

Individualist (4)s are well-versed in the language of feelings and place a much higher value on the emotional world. They value authenticity, creative expression and originality. They seek to be understood more than they seek approval. They help their Achiever (3) partner pinpoint and discuss their feelings and emotional responses. They can help their partner cultivate empathy, compassion and open-heartedness. The Individualist (4) offers the Achiever (3) a safe container to explore hurts, wounds and past failures, and the Achiever (3) generally feels held and supported as they move this previously uncharted emotional territory.

When self-aware and accepting of their very different ways of relating to the world, this can be a pair who really feel they complete each other and keep each other in balance. When their differences are understood and respected, this has the potential to be a long-lasting and symbiotic match.

 ### 4:3 The Downward Spiral
Because both types approach the world from such different angles, it can be easy for needs to go unmet and for both to feel misunderstood. Both share a sensitive issue of shame, and both can have a fragile sense of themselves. With tightening defenses, Achiever (3)s cut off from their emotions, and Individualist (4)s sink more deeply into their emotions. These reactions can trigger the downward spiral in one another.

Achiever (3)s may grow weary of the Individualist (4)'s focus on their own deficiencies and perceived shortcomings. Achiever (3)s want to focus on practical matters, the positive and the image of success. The low self-esteem of the Individualist (4) can be wearing on the Achiever (3). The more the Individualist (4) laments, the more the Achiever (3) turns their attention away from the Individualist (4).

Feeling unseen, unheard or misunderstood is a huge trigger for the Individualist (4) who responds by either withdrawing or getting angry. Like salt on an open wound, having feelings go unacknowledged can prompt an immediate and intense response in the Individualist (4). These reactions can be mystifying to the less emotionally driven Achiever (3). Both partners start to polarize. The Individualist (4) may vacillate between needing more time alone to process their feelings and wanting more of their Achiever (3)'s attention. The Achiever (3) start to see their Individualist (4) as needy, dramatic and emotionally draining and unstable.

As the downward spiral gains momentum, both partners become a source of irritation to each other. The respect and admiration they both shared evaporates and is replaced by disgust and disdain that is potentially undermining. The relationship may end, leaving both partners bitterly disappointed.

4:3 The Lighthouse
Feelings of inferiority mark the beginning of the downward spiral for this couple. Both types have a sensitivity towards shame, though the Individualist (4) is much more in touch with this emotion. Shame and a lack of self-love is often at the forefront of the Individualist (4) experience. Conversely, Achiever (3)s don't always directly relate to shame. Instead, they under-process this emotion by staying on the go to achieve, with the subconscious belief that enough achievement will prove their worth.

To dissolve shame, both partners need to cultivate self-acceptance and self-love. This balances the dependence on the outside world and external factors. With self-acceptance and self-love, both types can feel stable independently.

4:3 The Kundalini Yoga Connection
Both types need to manage their reactivity and cultivate heart-opening.

Achiever (3)s need to learn to sit still, to listen deeply and to speak from the heart. This requires nervous system work since their natural reaction to stress is to stay active. They are generally uncomfortable remaining in negative emotional spaces for long periods of time, so they need to cultivate a tolerance for discomfort. Kundalini Yoga kriyas and meditations to build the nervous system, open the heart and to balance the head and heart are beneficial.

Individualist (4)s need to learn self-love and to resist the temptation to withdraw when they feel overwhelmed. Nervous system work is helpful to allow them to stay outside their comfort zone. They overidentify with their flaws and undervalue their talents, so Kundalini Yoga kriyas and meditations to cultivate a neutral mind, inner balance and self-acceptance are helpful.

See the appendix for Achiever (3) and Individualist (4) recommended Kundalini Yoga kriyas and meditations.

4:4 Individualist (4) with Individualist (4)

Doran, Individualist (4) formerly in a 2-year relationship with Gala, Individualist (4)

"The relationship lasted less than two years, and I would characterize it as intense, colorful and unpredictable. Gala tried to understand me and when it was emotionally possible for her, was very giving and sensitive. But it was an exhausting and volatile relationship.

Due to her emotional issues, I would not see her for an entire week; then she would show up on my doorstep expecting to be given love and attention and spontaneously take a trip out of town. I was unsure of the relationship from the start. In fact, we both were, but we tried to make it something it was probably never meant to be with the people that we were at the time.

Eventually, she became unconvinced about my love and devotion to her and expected a "grand gesture of love" from me to prove it. I don't think I ever was able to come up with such a thing, but towards the end of the relationship, I finally decided to commit myself to her completely whatever the difficulty. Ironically, by then, she had grown emotionally tired of the relationship and felt numb toward me.

We parted as friends and are still very close, in fact, closer than we were those many years ago trying to be lovers. I credit her with turning my life upside-down in a good way after I had come out of a divorce from an unhappy 9-year marriage. She helped me to understand who I really was and who I wasn't."

Ilaria, Individualist (4) married in a 6-year relationship with John, Individualist (4)

"I love that my husband is funny, non-conformist, passionate, profoundly intelligent, wise and most of all REAL. He is an amazing thinker who doesn't waste his energy worrying about what other people think. He follows his heart and his passions without hesitation. He is incredibly attractive, not just because he is fit and handsome, but also because of his energy. He has a pure heart and is fearlessly in touch with his emotions. He balances masculine and feminine qualities in a wonderful way. He has a unique and fascinating mind, which I really admire.

In all this rare combination of important qualities, he has an even greater strength: his commitment to personal growth. He is dedicated to inner work and continues to grow, so our relationship never gets stuck or stagnant. I love this about him as we both value presence and self-development.

John and I connect on so many levels. When I met him, I felt I was finally understood and seen by somebody. We immediately created a special bond, and that bond continues to grow and deepen.

We share an intense intimacy. Since the beginning of our relationship, we have had a lot of physical and sexual chemistry, and this has only increased over the years. I trust him completely, and beyond the physical connection, we are each other's best friend. I can be totally open and real with him and even after six years together, there is no one I'd rather spend my time with.

In our relationship, he helps me grow and see myself in a real, authentic way. My emotions don't scare him. When I'm upset about something, he is concerned and probes until we get to the deeper feelings and causes.

At the same time, he's easygoing and calms me down using his sense of humor. Laughter and humor for me are a fundamental part of any relationship, and they are also a great strategy to get me to relax my rigidity. He figured this out, and it has helped our dynamic flow.

He is incredibly creative and invites me to be imaginative too. Being an infinite source of originality and ideas, he brings a lot of mental excitement in the relationship. We discuss our inner work, the Enneagram and other things that really matter to us.

As it relates to differences, he is introverted, much more than I am, and this aspect has taught me a lot about myself. Through him, I've learned the value of being alone.

The relationship has gone through many phases. I have trust issues and went through a period of testing him in various ways. John can be avoidant of certain topics which to me feels like a breach of honesty and authenticity. Early in our relationship, John would tell me that I was making him walk on eggshells and that it was difficult for him to respond to my questions because of my emotional reactivity. We both had to work a lot on ourselves to change the way we approach each other on these issues. It's not like that anymore, and I trust him completely now, but it took me years!

We almost never fight, but when we do, we both have an intense need to be heard and seen. Our conflicts can become endless spirals in which we both want to express how we feel and why we were hurt. It is hard for either of us to feel heard or loved by the other person during a conflict. Painful emotions do eventually get resolved, but a conflict between us can last hours, and it takes priority over anything else happening at that moment, even practical stuff.

An issue that I still work on in our dynamic is that I get easily annoyed with people in general, and I'm moody and sometimes passive-aggressive. I have expectations about the relationship and about John understanding what I need without telling him. I can be uncommunicative, and then I get upset when my needs are not met. Improving my communication is something I work on.

We have had to learn how to manage our emotional reactions. I can get angry and be dismissive in the heat of an argument, and John has had to learn to trust that I love him even in these moments.

John is my best friend, my lover and my husband. He's the best man I could have chosen to live my life with. I'm deeply grateful for our relationship. His presence changed the course of my existence in the most beautiful way."

4:4 The Theory

4:4 When In Balance

Emotional intensity is one of the hallmark traits with a double Individualist (4) pairing. Both partners are highly fluent in the language of emotion and deeply connected to the world of feelings. Authenticity is a key value, and this couple will seek to keep it real. Individualist (4)s have a certain fearlessness about the darker side of the emotional world and can share deep, dark personal experience with each other with relative ease. Both have an intense need to be understood and to be seen as a unique individual. They create a safe space for one another to explore their emotional world.

Both partners are highly accepting of each other. Flaws, quirks and imperfections are welcomed, not shunned. Both seek intense emotional connection and a partner who accepts them and sees them clearly. When they experience this with each other, the feeling is almost unmatchable. It is as if they have found their soulmate.

4:4 The Downward Spiral

Lack of emotional balance usually triggers the beginning of the downward spiral in this couple. Individualist (4)s can be self-absorbed and intolerant of each other. When one feels misunderstood by the other, it can trigger deep emotional wounds. Misunderstandings can quickly escalate into long, drawn-out arguments over who hurt who the most, and fights can spiral out of control, taking priority over practical matters.

With tightening defenses, Individualist (4)s often withdraw to heal, process their emotions or for attention. This can be challenging for their partner and may trigger abandonment issues. Trust issues can also be a theme in this relationship with one Individualist (4) testing the other. This can include tests of loyalty, commitment, transparency and so forth. As both partners start to polarize, this same emotional intensity that was the foundation of their connection becomes the foundation for their split. They may start to feel they hate the other or vacillate between love and hate, creating a push-pull dynamic. Eventually one or both partners becomes exhausted and decides they want something else, ending the relationship.

4:4 The Lighthouse

The fact both partners are capable of deep listening and can on some level understand each other's moodiness can help heal this relationship. The ability to understand the other's emotional storms, mood swings, need for attention and an alternating need to withdraw can help break the momentum of the downward spiral. Both partners need to manage their reactivity and cultivate emotional balance, so there is space for them to hear one another.

4:4 The Kundalini Yoga Connection

Intense emotional reactions triggering more intense emotional reactions mark the beginning of the downward spiral for this couple, so cultivating stillness, balance and emotional control are important to break the momentum. Both partners need to learn to manage their emotional storms. Nervous system work helps Individualist (4)s feel less overwhelmed by the energy of emotion. Kundalini Yoga kriyas and meditations for stability, balance, neutral mind and to act, not react are helpful.

See the appendix for Individualist (4) recommended Kundalini Yoga kriyas and meditations.

4:5 Individualist (4) with Investigator (5)

Thomas, Investigator (5) in a 2-year relationship with Ericha, Individualist (4)

"Ericha brings inspiration, understanding, listening, caretaking, humor, sensuality, insightfulness, examples of new ways to live my life and a reflection of myself through her own perspective. She offers chances for both of us to engage with new and interesting activities, for me to explore deeply a human being other than myself and ways to be aware and in touch with my body and emotions. She inspires mutual acceptance to be as weird as we need.

Some of our differences come up in the intensity of her emotional experiences which I see as frustrating or distracting her from focusing on practical solutions. In response to her emotional intensity she might rush into a decision she may change her mind about later. I tend to take my time and analyze the data.

In my life and specifically, in this relationship, it is a challenge for me to keep a balanced perspective regarding rationality and emotions. I'm not sure how well I do, but I am consciously trying to bring them together as my rational side is really well-developed and my emotional side is less so. She really helps me grow this way."

4:5 The Theory

4:5 When In Balance

The Individualist (4) and Investigator (5) bring complementary traits to each other, and this can be a very harmonizing relationship. Both seek depth, albeit in different arenas and coming from different angles. Both are curious, open-minded and private, valuing time alone and giving their partner a great deal of personal freedom.

Individualist (4)s are tuned into the colorful and vivid world of emotion. They bring a lyrical and artistic quality to their experience as well as a sensitivity to their own feelings and the feelings of others. This can be fascinating to their Investigator (5) who tends to have a more monochromatic experience in the world of emotion. Individualist (4)s can be passionate, creative, nurturing and invite their Investigator (5) to get out of their head and more into their body.

Investigator (5)s are logical, rational, methodical and curious. They bring a grounded, focused, comprehensive quality to their experience as well as willingness to live life on their own terms and outside of the mainstream. They help anchor their Individualist (4) who can get swept away by their emotional storms. They accept their Individualist (4) fully and easily which can be healing for their partner.

Together, this couple can share a high level of contextual communication. They may have inside jokes, facial expressions, signals and so forth that serve as a private language shared just between the two of them. Both can be unconventional and irreverent, and they may bond through their shared quirkiness. Neither is easily offended by the other which helps to foster intimacy between the two. In this match, both partners feel they have full permission to be themselves and follow their own drumbeat.

4:5 The Downward Spiral

Different needs for time together and time apart can trigger misunderstandings and an environment for the downward spiral. Individualist (4)s follow the rhythm of the emotional world and as such, are more spontaneous. They operate from instinct and intuition. This can be confusing and off-putting for their Investigator (5), who feels secure when outings and events are carefully planned. With tightening defenses, both partners polarize, the Individualist (4) interpreting the Investigator (5)'s containment as rejection, and the Investigator (5) interpreting the Individualist (4)'s emotional intensity as threatening.

Individualist (4)s may feel analyzed rather than understood, observed rather than treated with empathy. Individualists can feel frustrated at the amount of time it takes for their Investigator (5) to respond when a situation calls for action, and they can take the Investigator (5)'s boundaried approach to life as rejection.

In contrast, Investigator (5)s can begin to see their Individualist (4) partner as draining and demanding. They experience their Individualist (4) as acting irrationally and immaturely. The Investigator (5) may start to question the Individualist (4)'s stability, which can feel threatening to the Investigator and cause them to retreat more.

As the downward spiral gains momentum, the Investigator (5) retreats more into self-containment and hard-managed boundaries, triggering feelings of abandonment, neediness and emotional chaos for the Individualist (4). The cycle continues, and the relationship can get into loop of unmet needs that may ultimately end in a breakup.

CHAPTER FOUR INDIVIDUALIST/ARTIST

 4:5 The Lighthouse
Dramatically different emotional styles and stress response of these two types is the central factor in the deterioration of this relationship. As such, stress and energy management are keys in repairing damage in this relationship. Both partners need tools to deal more effectively with stress, and both need to learn to manage their energy. Investigator (5)s need to resist the urge to withdraw, and Individualist (4)s need to resist the urge to demand a reaction.

 4:5 The Kundalini Yoga Connection
Strengthening the nervous system helps both of these types come into balance.

The Individualist (4) needs to strengthen their nervous system, so they don't feel as overwhelmed by their intense emotional energy. Instead of acting out feelings of rejection, they can start to use internal tools like breathwork to gain feelings of stability. Kundalini Yoga kriyas and meditations to manage energy and balance emotional states like depression, anxiety and anger are helpful.

The Investigator (5) needs to stay engaged and resist the impulse to withdraw for security, as this triggers insecurity and feelings of rejection in their Individualist (4) partner. The stronger the nervous system, the less overwhelmed the Investigator (5) will likely feel. Kundalini Yoga kriyas and meditations to strengthen the nervous system, to move the energy out of the head and into the heart and to build energy are beneficial.

See the appendix for Individualist (4) and Investigator (5) recommended Kundalini Yoga kriyas and meditations.

4:6 Individualist (4) with Loyalist (6)

Sarah, Loyalist (6) formerly in a relationship for less than one year with Gregory, Individualist (4)

"Gregory was very emotionally sensitive, thoughtful and conscientious about how his actions affected other people. He had depth, and no conversation with him was ever boring. He was extremely honest – sometimes painfully so as he would share with me literally every single tiny detail about his life. While he would sometimes say things with me that made me uncomfortable, I found his honesty and eagerness to be open to be a beautiful personality trait that I came to value. He was emotionally bold. When he was telling me how he felt about me, I could see that he was really nervous, but he would continue on

THE NINE KEYS

strongly in the face of that fear, and that's part of what made his expression of his feelings so romantic for me...

From the beginning our connection was intense. We both knew that we wanted to be together just after having seen each other from across the room. It wasn't so much a physical attraction as something more indescribable – an intense energy. When our eyes met for the first time, it felt like this giant warm wave of water came over me. He felt it too. Later, after we had been dating for a few weeks, he had mentioned that the experience was the same for him. As I reflect on that connection, I think that he had this really strong sense of emotion about him as if he carried a sorrow that was palpable. Something about him made me think that he could feel as deeply as I could. I wanted to be with that sort of person because I have never known anyone else like that before. To this day, I still haven't met another man who could meet me on the same emotional level that he could.

In our relationship, he would tell me about all the ways that he wanted to improve as a person, and I would help him come up with practical plans to help him initiate his paths of personal development...And vice-versa...it felt like a great dynamic. He was really low-energy, and that made him easy for me to be around. I could spend eight hours with him and still feel like I had the energy to do other things when we would finally part ways.

He brought a feeling of security into our relationship which helped me to feel safe in expressing my emotions. He was the very first man who made me feel like I would be secure if I let all of my feelings known. And I was. He never judged me. Not once. He never offered advice or told me how to fix things. He never even labeled my feelings as "right" or "wrong," "good," or "bad." He was strong enough to let things be simply as they were.

In our relationship, I felt needed. He was unstable, and we both sensed it. He relied heavily on me for comfort and help, and I loved every second of it. Our relationship became co-dependent, with a sort of mother-son style that required me to take on a bigger role of caregiver than I had ever done before. Interestingly, I didn't mind this, and it really brought me in touch with the way I love and how steadfast my love is. Before him, I hadn't realized how loyal I was.

As it relates to issues, we both have issues with abandonment, and these issues caused toxicity in our relationship. We clung to each other like leeches. Because neither of us had any sense of self, we looked to each other for reassurance of our worth and value as human beings. Eventually, I think he began to feel like I was choking the life out of him. He never said that out loud, but it was this sense I got. Being so enmeshed with each other wound up making the ending of our relationship much more challenging. He was really depressed at that point, and I was completely devastated. I felt like I could not live without him, so when our relationship ended, it felt like my whole world had been ripped away from me.

I learned many lessons from this relationship, particularly around the importance of maintaining a strong sense of self when in an intimate relationship. Ultimately, the co-dependence we created was unhealthy. And I wish he had felt more comfortable telling me when I had hurt him instead of letting things escalate to the point where drastic action felt necessary. I do credit him for helping me understand myself better as he was a powerful mirror."

4:6 The Theory

4:6 When In Balance

Individualist (4)s and Loyalist (6)s share many common traits that make it easy for this couple to understand and support each other. Both take a somewhat defensive position about the world, trusting others reluctantly and easily imagining negative scenarios. Both can be emotionally intense, both have a deep-rooted fear of abandonment and both seek a stable, secure home. With this as the common foundation, this pair also has some striking differences.

Loyalist (6)s bring a focus on stability, security and predictability to the dynamic. They are dependable, loyal, committed, placing a high value on a select few relationships in their life. Their attention is constantly scanning for threats and as such, they help ensure the home front is guarded, protected and safe. These traits can all be soothing to the Individualist (4) who feels they have finally found a safe haven.

Individualist (4)s bring emotional fluency, creativity and inspiration to the dynamic. They help their Loyalist (6) get in touch with their deeper emotions and can bring out the nurturing instinct of the Loyalist (6).

This couple can develop a subconscious dependency on each other, with the Individualist (4) acting as the one in need of rescue and the Loyalist (6) as the rescuer. If the couple is able to maintain balance, this can be healing for both partners as the Individualist (4) finally feels seen and supported, and the Loyalist (6) feels needed and cherished.

4:6 The Downward Spiral

Concerns with abandonment that can help to bring this couple together can also be the trigger for the downward spiral. With tightening defenses, both partners become reactive and trigger a toxic loop of mistrust. A fixated Loyalist (6) reacts by becoming more paranoid, more cautious and projecting more imagined outcomes into seemingly benign situations. They may start to question the motives of their Individualist (4) and try to control their behavior. This leaves the Individualist (4) feeling misunderstood and unseen, triggering their own scenario of emotional abandonment. Consciously or subconsciously, they may start to withhold affection, further threatening the sense of stability of the Loyalist (6).

As the downward spiral gains momentum, both partners start to focus on their complaints with the other. Individualist (4)s see the Loyalist (6) as overly cautious and emotionally shut down. Loyalist (6)s see the Individualist (4) as too impulsive, unreliable and unpredictable. With both types having emotional intensity, arguments can quickly escalate to overreactions and projections. If something doesn't break the downward spiral, the two partners polarize until one decides they have had enough and leaves the relationship.

4:6 The Lighthouse
This couple loses its way because of unaddressed issues around fear of abandonment and anxiety. These fears trigger anxiety that makes the Loyalist (6) feel unstable and insecure and makes the Individualist (4) feel misunderstood and unseen. To break the downward spiral, both partners need to cultivate an inner sense of security, so they don't become overly dependent on the other.

4:6 The Kundalini Yoga Connection
Reactivity triggers the downward spiral for this couple, so learning to manage reactions and the energy of emotion is important to re-establish balance.

Individualist (4)s need to cultivate self-love, so they don't feel forced to seek it in their outside environment. Kundalini Yoga kriyas and meditations to cultivate self-love, release shame and mend a broken heart can be helpful.

Loyalist (6)s need tools to manage their anxiety so they can approach life feeling expansive instead of contracted. Kundalini Yoga kriyas and meditations to lower anxiety, for stability and to cultivate a neutral mind are helpful.

See the appendix for Individualist (4) and Loyalist (6) recommended Kundalini Yoga kriyas and meditations.

4:7 Individualist (4) with Enthusiast (7)

Benjamin, Enthusiast (7) married in an 11-year relationship with Liam, Individualist (4)

"Liam is kind, gentle, generous and extremely empathetic. He understands emotions and the experience of other people in ways that are like whale sounds to me. He feels deeply, and his connection to the emotional world allows him to have experiences on levels that I can't even fathom. He's very tuned in with his circle of family, friends and me.

Liam has a strong commitment to improving not only himself but our dynamic as a couple. He's always looking for ways to improve our communication or the quality of the time we spend together. I love that he brings sensitivity to the relationship and encourages me to have a more empathetic eye to the world around us.

As a couple, our strengths are opposite but complementary. We have an almost yin-yang combination of emotional resilience on my part and the deep understanding of the internal world of feelings on his part. This combination has been fuel for our many shared artistic and life journeys. I often encourage him not to take life so seriously, and he often helps me see my artistic practice and our worldviews more deeply. It's a wonderful combination that makes me feel really anchored and at home. I feel very moored by him.

Our dynamic lets us offer true support to the people in our social circle, especially if one of our friends is in pain or going through a difficult period. Liam is a gifted listener and can truly feel the pain of someone else. With him, they feel seen and heard in a deeply healing way. Then I jump in with actionable items – practical things they could do, a habit they can adopt, books they could read, exhibitions they could attend and so forth. Our dynamic works really well this way, and this has become a finely-honed skill we enjoy sharing with the people we care about.

Like all relationships, we have our challenges. We both can be easily frustrated, sometimes about our careers and sometime about our life paths. Both of us, but Liam in particular, can wallow in self-doubt and melancholy. We have to remind ourselves to take action when this hits – something to soothe our minds, brighten our mood, improve our outlook.

We have a big difference in self-confidence, and his self-doubt can be a challenge for me. My mind is clear about what is good, what is bad and what I should do. Decisiveness comes easily to me, almost like an instinct, and I've made a career based on making quick and confident decisions. Liam rarely sees things in black-and-white, living more in the spectrum of grey and doubt. This makes him very, very slow to make decisions about his life. He spends a tremendous amount of time looking at a situation from all angles and second-guessing his own perception of events, situations, potential outcomes and so forth. This can be difficult and frustrating for me to watch...But I also see this as a growth edge for myself.

Overall, I'm very happy in my relationship. I love the way we balance each other, and I feel like I learn from Liam every day. He makes me a better person, and I'm so grateful to have him as my partner."

Eva, Enthusiast (7) formerly in a 7-year relationships with Nikos, Individualist (4)

"Nikos was an emotional and sophisticated movie director. He fascinated me with his ability to turn even everyday obligations into magical and unforgettable moments.

At the beginning of our relationship, he was sentimental, romantic, sensitive, aesthetic, creative, intuitive and artistic. He put me on a pedestal, and we shared creativity, romance, passion and joy.

However, the relationship changed, and by the end of seven years together, he was in emotional chaos: egocentric, dramatic, moody, fussy, difficult and unbearably jealous with a strong inferiority complex. He made every possible effort to knock me off the pedestal.

He was like an ivy, needing support to grow but at the same time ready at any moment to demolish his own support. Eventually, the relationship collapsed."

4:7 The Theory

 ### 4:7 When In Balance

The Individualist (4) and Enthusiast (7) combination has the classic appearance of opposites attracting. Their strengths offset each other's weaknesses and when in balance, this couple is highly complementary with the Enthusiast (7) leading the way through the external world, and the Individualist (4) leading the way through the internal world.

Individualist (4)s are introspective, emotional, self-doubting and leaning towards a pessimistic and cynical view of the world. They are comfortable with the darker side of the emotional spectrum and are well-versed in the language of emotion. Individualist (4)s help Enthusiast (7)s get in touch with their full range of emotions and help them process negative experiences. They bring depth and richness to the relationship and can help the Enthusiast (7) to be less self-referencing and more empathetic towards the suffering of others.

In contrast, Enthusiast (7)s tend towards the bright side of the emotional spectrum, filled with enthusiasm, self-confidence, joy and optimism. They are more mental, and while they can be emotional, they are also avoidant and have great difficulty staying with negative emotions. Enthusiast (7)s help Individualist (4)s see the bright side, develop confidence, try new experiences and overcome self-consciousness. They help the Individualist (4) advocate for themselves and model self-love instead of self-loathing.

Together, the relationship is one of attraction and intrigue. They think, feel and react so differently that they can gain great insight by dissecting events, situations and emotions trying to understand each other and themselves better.

As it relates to similarities, both are highly verbal and may share an offbeat sense of humor, enjoying rich, deep, entertaining and often hilarious conversations together. As each partner is open-minded, neither is threatened by new ideas their partner might want to introduce. This flexibility is important, as in some respects this couple may not be able to get all of their needs met with each other. This difference can be used as a strength, however, creating an environment of candor and openness. They creatively use this as a problem solving exercise, and it can bring them closer together.

This couple can complement each other well, with each compensating for the other's blind spots and weaknesses. When in balance, this is a committed, enduring partnership.

4:7 The Downward Spiral

While the differences can be points of intrigue when in balance, they can also trigger the downward spiral. Both types can be self-absorbed and self-referencing so if they start to feel their needs aren't being met, they can get testy with each other.

Individualist (4)s can feel exhausted by the relentless pace and energy of the Enthusiast (7). They can find their Enthusiast (7) too shallow, too excitable, too busy and too impulsive. They long for a deep, emotional connection and may feel unseen in the face of their Enthusiast (7)'s multiple plans and activities.

Enthusiast (7)s can see their Individualist (4) as moody, impractical, negative and endlessly self-absorbed with their negative self-image. They can get frustrated with the low energy and tendency to withdraw of their Individualist (4), seeking a more engaged, available partner. The downward spiral begins when either partner starts to lose respect for the other and focus on the negative differences instead of the positives.

If the downward spiral gains momentum, the Individualist (4) may become more hostile, sarcastic and withdrawn. The Enthusiast (7) may try to solve the issue by adding more things to their schedule in an attempt to lower their growing anxiety. The Individualist (4) responds by wanting to discuss every negative element of the relationship in detail. The Enthusiast (7) views this as the rough equivalent to hell on earth and plans more outside activities and distractions to try to keep a positive frame of mind. Both partners polarize, and their emotional connection is threatened.

If the core issues don't get aired and adequately resolved, this relationship starts to collapse. The differences which were once so admired become a source of frustration and irritation until the relationship eventually ends.

4:7 The Lighthouse
A fundamental inability to accept each other's differences is what triggers the downward spiral for this couple. Cultivating tolerance towards each other can help break the momentum. Energetically, these two can be opposites, so it is helpful for Enthusiast (7)s to learn to be still and for Individualist (4)s to resist the urge to withdraw. For both types, strengthening the nervous system helps make these things possible.

4:7 The Kundalini Yoga Connection
Individualist (4)s need to learn to weather their emotional storms without getting frustrated at their Enthusiast (7)'s tendency to try to reframe everything as positive or to be emotionally avoidant of the negative. Kundalini Yoga kriyas and meditations to cultivate neutrality and self-love, burn out anger, release depression and lower anxiety can be helpful.

Enthusiast (7)s need to learn to allow their Individualist (4) to have their full range of emotion and emotional reactions without feeling threatened. They need to resist the impulse to avoid and flee from negative feelings. It can be healing for Enthusiast (7)s to stay with darker emotions. Kundalini Yoga kriyas and meditations to lower anxiety and open the heart can be helpful.

See the appendix for Individualist (4) and Enthusiast (7) recommended Kundalini Yoga kriyas and meditations.

4:8 Individualist (4) with Leader (8)

Joyce, Leader (8) in a 1.5-year relationship with Marissa, Individualist (4)

"Marissa is the most compassionate person I have ever met. She's intuitive, creative, an incredible artist and an amazing mother. She is grounded with a strong work ethic and is financially savvy. Her ability to forgive those who've hurt her and stay flexible in her personal relationships is astounding to me.

In our relationship, we balance each other. She teaches me how to be compassionate and empathic, and I offer her the energy to set strong personal boundaries and to create some space from her emotions.

Our relationship has been an incredible roller coaster ride. From the first moment, our connection has been intense. We met on a crowded dance floor and hadn't exchanged a single word before we were locked in each other's arms. It was like time stood still, and no one else was in the entire bar. There was an energetic charge that was completely unspoken but insanely powerful. Our relationship grew at an alarming rate – we both felt completely swept away.

It has not been an easy relationship. She was in the middle of divorcing her husband, and I was in the midst of a big career change when we met. We were together, and then we broke up, then I moved in with her and her two children, then I moved out. Then I moved back in. We're striving for a more balanced, consistent environment but with us, it seems this intense energy always manifests itself somewhere.

We can trigger each other. When we have conflicts, we both tend to withdraw affection and attention. I withdraw more completely, while she tends to withdraw emotionally and becomes outwardly critical. We both also tend to draw our friends into our disputes in subtle ways. I may reach out to her friends looking for support in helping her through a "stormy" time, while she seeks their support of her when she feels I have done something wrong.

Vulnerability is hard for me, and even with the woman that I love, it is difficult for me to let down my guard. I experience my more vulnerable self only in tiny bursts. I'm probably more open with her than I've been with anyone else, but I continue to work hard to expose myself. I can only do it if I feel she has created an extremely safe space for me.

Overall, I'm extremely grateful to be with Marissa. I have experienced more growth as a person in this 1.5-year relationship than the entire rest of my life. It has its ups and downs, but it is all worth it."

Nicole, Leader (8) married in a 10-year relationship with Pierce, Individualist (4)

"My husband is gifted in the world of emotion, feelings and matters of the heart. He understands his own emotional world and sometimes acts as a translator for me, as I can be less clear about my own feelings. He wears his heart on his sleeve, which is very helpful and healing for me as I can be more guarded. Because he is so willing to share his internal world with me, he creates a very safe space for me to explore my own emotional world.

We are both intense. We can match each other in volume and words when it comes to a disagreement. That said, I like our shared intensity, and when we have a common goal, we are unstoppable.

My biggest challenge in our dynamic has been learning to accommodate his melancholy. It has been hard for me to relate to this feeling because while I can experience depression from time to time, it is usually something I can pull myself out of. I can't do that with my husband. I allow him time, sometimes days, to feel bad but then eventually remind him we can't live our life without some glimmer of hope. I also struggle with his low self-esteem. He doesn't see his accomplishments, like when he is recognized for a job well done, and sometimes has a hard time seeing the good things in life. And I know I can frustrate him with my intensity and bullheadedness. Sometimes he wants me to feel emotions that I want to ignore so I can focus on getting a job done or finding the justice. Justice is a huge theme and value for me. I will always have the back of my family and close friends, and this focus can become a top priority. It can take higher importance than feeling my vulnerable emotions.

Overall, I'm very happy in my relationship. We've been together for over 10 years and have been through many of life's ups and downs. I'm grateful to have my husband as my partner, and we've truly learned to rely on each other's strengths."

4:8 The Theory

4:8 When In Balance
The Individualist (4) and Leader (8) make a powerful, creative, intuitive pairing. Intensity is a key word to describe this coupling and together, they can be a provocative, colorful match. When their intensity is aligned for a common goal, they are almost unstoppable. While they have many similarities, they also have key differences that provide growth edges for each other.

Individualist (4)s bring compassion, creativity, an intuitive understanding of the human condition and a fearlessness of the emotional spectrum. They feel a wide range of emotions on a regular basis and can act as a translator and guide through the emotional world for their Leader (8) partner. They create a safe space for the Leader (8) to be less guarded and more vulnerable. They help the Leader (8) identify and pinpoint their emotions and can also help the Leader (8) cultivate empathy towards others.

Leader (8)s bring a practical orientation and earthiness to the dynamic. They are clear, powerful, bold and decisive which allows them to stay grounded in the face of the Individualist (4)'s emotional storms. With their direct approach, they hold the Individualist (4) accountable for their behavior and responses, which can be highly beneficial for less self-aware Individualist (4)s.

When self-aware, they offer each other balance. Individualist (4)s appreciate their Leader (8)'s pragmatism, focus on the material world, protectiveness and stability in the face of the Individualist (4)'s emotional rollercoaster. The Leader (8) appreciates the Individualist (4)'s sensitivity, attunement to the emotional world and ability to express love. They are attracted to the mysteriousness of the Individualist (4)'s inner world. Together, both partners feel they can be free to express their full intensity, and this is a relief to both. They make each other feel alive, and there is a vitality and an emotional juiciness to this couple that is noteworthy.

4:8 The Downward Spiral
Themes of vulnerability and control can be the trigger for the downward spiral of this couple. Tightening defenses make the Leader (8) more controlling and more domineering while the Individualist (4) becomes more emotionally volatile and reactive. Because both types are so intense and self-referencing, there may not be an easy way to de-escalate fights, and disagreements can spiral out of control. The conflicts aren't always about what they appear to be about. On a deeper level, the Leader (8) is seeking to control their environment as a

way to feel stable and avoid vulnerability. The Individualist (4) seeks stability through being heard and understood. When either partner feels threatened, they turn up the emotional volume. The depth of the downward spiral depends on how much each partner is able to see the deeper issues driving the wedge between them. Without insight, this couple may turn their emotional intensity against each other until the relationship eventually ends.

4:8 The Lighthouse
Emotional reactivity is the trigger for the downward spiral for this couple so learning to manage their emotional responses is important in bringing them back together. Both partners like to feel intensely. They need to learn healthier ways of sharing this emotional intensity.

4:8 The Kundalini Yoga Connection
Both partners need to learn to manage their energy differently so they can have more control over their emotional reactions. Strengthening the nervous system is beneficial for both.

For Individualist (4)s, managing intense emotions, including anger, despair and depression is important. Kundalini Yoga kriyas and meditations that cultivate stability, neutrality, gratitude and self-love are beneficial.

For Leader (8)s, managing an anger response and general reactivity to vulnerable emotions is important. Kundalini Yoga kriyas and meditations to act and not react, to open the heart and to burn out anger are helpful.

See the appendix for Individualist (4) and Leader (8) recommended Kundalini Yoga kriyas and meditations.

4:9 Individualist (4) with Peacemaker (9)

Stephen, Peacemaker (9) married in a 15-year relationship with Nadia, Individualist (4)

"Nadia is resilient, persistent, focused and determined. When she sets her intention, she conquers whatever obstacle she encounters to reach her goal. For example, she applied to graduate school and was rejected. Rather than back down, she applied to the same school the following year and was accepted with a full scholarship. She is creative with an eye for design. Our home is smartly, minimally decorated and consistently praised for being welcoming and comfortable.

In our relationship, we share many values. Having a positive impact in the world is paramount to both of us. I'm a public school music teacher, and Nadia is a mental health counselor. We both seek self-awareness to know ourselves more fully and to have a more meaningful existence. We want to have a comfortable life; a steady paycheck, routine, long-term friends. Neither of us loves change, though I am probably more uncomfortable with it than she is. I have a high tolerance to stick with something despite difficulty or unhappiness.

What I love about her the most and what also drives me the craziest is the same thing – she has a deep desire to be connected with me, to know what I'm thinking and to understand what I want and need. While I want this too, this level of connection doesn't come easily for me. When she is stressed, she ratchets up her desire for communication and time together, whereas my natural tendency under stress is to go that other way and to isolate myself. I'm easygoing, and she is not. With her, things can quickly escalate from small to HUGE.

We've been together for 15 years and work hard on bridging our differences. As the years have passed, I have gotten clearer in my needs and the fact I need her encouragement and space to take risks, and to learn what I want, prefer and need. This doesn't come naturally to me. I easily default to what other people think and prefer. I've learned when she gives me time, space, approval and support, I can come to clarity much faster. And from that space, we can come together to decide how to proceed.

Overall, I am grateful to have Nadia as my partner on this self-discovery journey. There is no chance I can fall asleep at the wheel with her at my side. I'm thankful for that, and I love her deeply."

Roman, Peacemaker (9) formerly in an 8-year relationship with Brigitte, Individualist (4)

"Brigitte had creativity, vision, passion, high integrity, great intellect, determination and an ability to focus and complete tasks. To the relationship, she brought a love of beauty and nature and a desire to connect. I appreciated the beautiful home she created with many natural wood touches.

She helped me grow. I was brought up in an environment where feelings weren't discussed much and was ready to make some growth in that area as I started this relationship. She helped me get in touch with my feelings.

It wasn't always an easy relationship. She was very moody and often exhibited a lot of push-pull behavior, yet she was self-aware and expressed surprise that I wasn't affected by her moods. If she ever initiated sex, it was infrequently, probably due to an abusive childhood and related psychological issues. I could handle all this though, because of my easygoing nature. I would often initiate physical intimacy by asking if she would like a massage.

While she appreciated my nonjudgmental nature, I think eventually she felt I was too unmotivated for her. I became unemployed in the latter part of our relationship, and I believe a big part of the reason she left me was because she didn't see me growing. I wish she could have seen that I was growing, just more slowly than she expected.

The relationship lasted over eight years, and while we are no longer together, it is still easy for me to speak highly of her and to think of the relationship with affection."

4:9 The Theory

4:9 When In Balance
The Individualist (4) and Peacemaker (9) can be an accepting, soothing, healing match who find a deep enjoyment from shared time together. The foundation of the relationship is a combination of support and allowing one another personal freedom to pursue their own goals and interests. Both enjoy the shared harmony they create together.

Peacemaker (9)s are steady, reliable, solid, dependable, inclusive and accepting. They don't get blown off course by the emotional storms of their Individualist (4), and this is very grounding for their partner.

Individualist (4)s bring rich expressiveness and intensity to the dynamic, helping to wake up the Peacemaker (9) and adding color to the dynamic. The Individualist (4) adds emotional electricity to the house ensuring issues gets discussed and important topics aren't swept under the rug. This is very balancing for the more avoidant Peacemaker (9).

This couple can share a deep, intense, intimate connection with each other.

4:9 The Downward Spiral
While their differences can be balancing, they can also be a source of frustration between these two partners. The mellow, easygoing Peacemaker (9) may experience the Individualist (4)'s focus on the emotional world as relentless and extreme, disrupting the harmonious environment the Peacemaker (9) strives hard to create. And the Peacemaker (9)'s tendency to resist change and maintain the status quo can be frustrating to the Individualist (4) who is on a never-ending quest in search of self. As defenses tighten, both partners polarize in opposite directions.

As the Individualist (4) demands more engagement and attention, the Peacemaker (9) begins to stonewall and withdraw. This further triggers the Individualist (4) who turns up the emotional volume and becomes more temperamental and explosive. As the downward spiral gains momentum, the Peacemaker (9) becomes more unresponsive, stubborn, disengaged and distant. Energetically, it is like an unstoppable force meets an immovable object.

Alternatively, the Individualist (4) may become frustrated with the Peacemaker (9)'s avoidant behavior and withdraw either physically or emotionally themselves, further weakening the bond. Unless something breaks the momentum of separation, the relationship may end.

4:9 The Lighthouse
Differing emotional reactions to stress and frustration mark the beginning of the downward spiral for this couple, so learning alternative stress responses can break the downward momentum. They need to recognize the pain in each other. Individualist (4)s feel wounded when they are misunderstood or feel unseen. Peacemaker (9)s become anxious in the face of conflict. Both are trying to alleviate their own pain rather than trigger the other. Both partners need to strengthen their nervous systems to accommodate changes in their own behavior as their resistance is their reactivity.

4:9 The Kundalini Yoga Connection
Individualist (4)s need to learn to manage the energy of their intense emotions. Cultivating energy management and energetic stability are important in the quest to act and not react. Kundalini Yoga kriyas and meditations that strengthen the aura and cultivate stability, neutrality and balance are beneficial.

Peacemaker (9)s need to learn to resist the instinct to shut down in the face of potential conflict. They need to stand their ground and remain engaged and present. Nervous system work as well as Kundalini Yoga kriyas and meditations to strengthen the navel center, stay connected with the energy of emotion and to burn anger are helpful.

See the appendix for Individualist (4) and Peacemaker (9) recommended Kundalini Yoga kriyas and meditations.

This book is a living document. We will be updating it periodically with new information. If you are or were in a relationship with an Individualist (4) and you would like to participate in the related relationship survey, please email me at lynn@lynnroulo.com.

Type Five
INVESTIGATOR/ OBSERVER

(seeks self-sufficiency/avoids external demands)

 ## Overview

Investigators (5)s are typically introverted, curious, analytical and insightful. These are the owls of the Enneagram with a very boundaried and contained approach to life. This person can focus and concentrate deeply. Investigator (5)s are quite observant and curious, but they generally like to observe from a distance, slightly out of the group. They see, often with anxiety, the expectations and the demands of the outside world and have a heightened awareness and concern about personal resources, including time and energy. The central question they focus on is "What is required of me, and do I have what it takes to deliver?" They fear they do not.

Their attention moves towards concerns about scarcity and away from feelings of abundance and adequate resources. Facts and information serve as guides for what is important for Investigator (5)s.

These are the intellectual deep divers of the Enneagram, and when an Investigator (5) is interested in a topic, they want to learn everything about it. They can maintain concentrated focus for long periods of time and may have sparks of genius. Investigator (5)s can leave lasting, original innovations to the world. They tend to be frugal, not just financially, but in the way they share themselves with the world. Many Investigator (5)s only disclose small parts of themselves to others, fearing they will be overwhelmed if they offer too much.

In an intimate relationship, partners generally appreciate that their Investigator (5) is independent, supportive, kind, undemanding, low drama, stable, loyal, an attentive listener, open-minded, rational and a good problem-solver. Partners are challenged by their Investigator (5)'s lack of spontaneity, the slow decision-making, their lack of emotional expression and their secrecy. Interdependence does not come easily to them.

• Attention Bias/Habit Of Attention:
Their attention goes to maintaining self-sufficiency and avoiding demands from the outside world. This often leads to disengagement from others.

• Emotional Style:
Contained, minimal, avoidant, thrifty, thoughtful, controlled, sincere.

• Communication Style:
Reserved, quiet, precise, analytical, factual, informational, shy, observing, robotic.

• Brings To The Relationship:
Rational thinking, practical problem solving, an independent, undemanding nature, stable, loyal, curious, open-minded, kind.

• Unique Strengths:
Amazing ability to focus and hold a point of attention. Genuine curiosity and desire to understand. They are original thinkers and problem solvers. They can have sparks of genius and creative inventions and solutions.

• Challenges:
Investigator (5)s are known for hiding from the world. Isolationism, withholding, secrecy and intense privacy can be challenges. May have difficulty connecting with the emotional world and identifying and understanding what they are feeling.

• Stability And Security:
"I feel secure when I understand exactly what is required of me and when I feel certain I can meet those requirements. I feel stable when I have all the facts and information I need to make a decision and be well-informed. I feel wonderful when I am left alone to pursue my interests."

- **Instability And Insecurity:**
"I feel insecure when I don't understand the exact parameters of a demand, request or desire. I may feel unstable when the subject being discussed is something I am not knowledgeable in. I feel terrible when I'm asked to do something spontaneously."

- **Path Of Growth:**
Non-Attachment
Investigator (5)s grow from moving from avarice to giving, from withholding to sharing. Investigator (5)s must learn to stay engaged in the world and generously offer their gifts.

- **Energy:**
Detached, remote, robotic, cerebral, disengaged.

- **The Kundalini Yoga Connection:**
Investigator (5)s have an exaggerated sense of scarcity and feel easily overwhelmed. Bright lights, loud music, big crowds and so forth can feel threatening. They question if they have enough energy (physical, emotional, mental) to do what is asked of them. Any physical practice to build the immune system, nervous system and energetic field can be helpful in making them feel more stable in their environment. Energetically, they live in their heads more than in their bodies or hearts. Kundalini Yoga kriyas and meditations that bring them into their body are beneficial. A practice that connects them to the energy of emotion is particularly useful.

The Investigator (5) Subtypes

"Castle" Self-Preservation Subtype:
The self-preservation Investigator (5) expresses concerns about resources by having very clearly-drawn boundaries. This is the most guarded, remote and introverted of the Investigators (5)s. This is a person who sometimes describes feeling like they hide. To the outside world, this is someone who may be hermit-like and not overly social. They tend to live very frugally, even if they have plentiful resources. This is the least communicative of the Investigators (5). Internally, this is someone who feels a great awareness and concern about scarcity and an intense drive to live without the trappings of the physical world. They have the title "Castle" because of the way they isolate themselves.

This is the most isolationist Investigator (5), so there generally isn't a high level of socializing outside of the relationship. This Investigator (5) rejuvenates by spending time alone and generally only allows a small group of people into their inner circle.

On the positive side, this person is not needy or intrusive and gives their partner a great deal of independence. This is likely a low maintenance relationship without a lot of drama.

On the less positive side, this person can isolate to the extreme and can have difficulty socializing normally. While they attach strongly to a few people, they don't always enjoy the level of emotional and social support that would be available to them if they were less closed down.

"Totem" Social Subtype:
The social Investigator (5) expresses concerns about resources and boundaries by minimizing the need for emotional connection and in some cases interpersonal relationships in exchange for the pursuit of knowledge. At the core, this is a person who relates more to values represented by certain people than to the people themselves. To the outside world, this Investigator (5)s is more social and engaging than the other Investigators and is someone who can become very idealistic or spiritual. Internally, this person is searching for the meaning of life and ultimate ideals. They can feel disinterested in ordinary, everyday life. They have the title "Totem" because of the way they orient around symbols and representations more than actual people and tangible reality.

Social Investigator (5)s are steady, independent people who give their partners freedom while offering practical support. Social Investigators are not overly emotional, and, in some ways, they prefer not to feel.

On the positive side, this Investigator (5) is more engaged in the practical world and brings new ideas, passions and information to their relationships.

On the less positive side, this is someone who can have difficulty connecting with and expressing their emotions. This can be an engaged, yet simultaneously disengaged partner.

"Confidence" Intimate Subtype:
The intimate Investigator (5) expresses concerns about resources and scarcity through the ongoing search for an ideal partner. All Investigator (5)s are seekers, and this person is seeking the most perfect, safest, idealized union with another. This subtype is a more emotional, romantic and sensitive Investigator (5). Trust is a key issue. To the outside world, this is someone who still appears very contained, reserved, observant and emotionally stoic. However, internally this is someone who has a very intense, vivid and romantic emotional life. They feel and suffer a lot, almost resembling the experience of Individualist (4). They have the title "Confidence" to mean someone who can be confided in. They are given this title because of their search for one ideal partner to bond with completely.

This is a person who is deeply emotional but in a controlled way. Because their standard for an ideal partner is so high, it can be easy for this Investigator (5) to feel disappointed. Feelings can be confusing and overwhelming, particularly the softer emotions like compassion. This person can have a push-pull relationship with their own emotions, both wanting emotional intensity and feeling a need to guard against it.

On the positive side, partners can bond deeply on an emotional level with this Investigator (5), and this can be a very passionate partner.

On the less positive side, this person can feel easily hurt and disappointed when their partner demonstrates regular human flaws. There can be a great deal of internal turmoil for this Investigator (5).

Investigator (5)—Levels of Awareness

Investigator (5) When Self-Aware
Investigator (5)s experience sparks of genius that can lead to original inventions, creative solutions and innovative thinking. They are open-minded about the world while penetrating deeply into subjects of interest, striving not just for rational knowledge but also knowledge of the heart. They develop wisdom. Investigator (5)s are keenly observant, discerning and insightful with a heightened awareness of the world. Nothing misses their attention, and they can use their observation and concentration skills in a productive, beneficial way. They may be reserved but not isolationist, and they can share insights and stay engaged with others. At this level, they can synthesize experience with knowledge. They understand there is value in the emotional world. They become skilled masters of their field of interest as excitement about knowledge increases their pursuit. They develop original thinking, innovative approaches and rare inventions. They are highly independent, quirky and distinctive, and their off-the-beaten-path genuineness often gives them a certain charm.

Investigator (5) With Tightening Defenses
The Investigator (5)'s decision-making slows as the mind tries to solve all elements before acting. Their concerns about scarcity, including resources and energy, intensify. Their planning process can be lengthy to consider and ensure adequate resources from all angles. Their focus remains intense, and in areas of interest, they may develop a specialization. They may challenge the norm with their outside the box thinking. As Investigator (5)s focus on complicated ideas, imagined worlds and abstract scenarios, they become less connected with reality. They are more hypothetical in their thinking and less grounded. They can become highly strung and intense. They often experience unrealistic concerns

about the environment and may feel threatened by seemingly small disturbances. Isolation from the outside world intensifies as a way of guarding against disturbances in their inner world. Investigator (5)s may become provocative and outrageous with extreme views and beliefs. They can be secretive, private, cynical and argumentative. They may have difficulty behaving appropriately in social environments.

Investigator (5) When Fixated

Isolated, eccentric and withdrawn, they start to develop misanthropic tendencies. They become increasingly disconnected from reality and the practical world. Fear and anxiety start to dominate their experience, and feelings of instability and aggression may arise. They distance themselves from all social attachments and become hermit-like. Investigator (5)s become obsessed yet disturbed by their own ideas as the reality distortion grows. They have a tenuous connection to reality, and practical matters become difficult to navigate. They may fall prey to phobias and their own fears and paranoia. They begin to have psychotic breaks with reality as their imaginary world takes over. Barely functioning, they become deranged and self-destructive.

Keys If You Are In A Relationship With An Investigator (5)

"I need to plan things in advance, and I process information and feelings slowly. Please don't expect spontaneity from me."

Ericha, Individualist (4) in a 2-year relationship with Thomas, Investigator (5)

"Thomas finds stability in structuring his time. I'm more spontaneous and enjoy going with my intuition when it comes to plans and scheduling. This can be challenging because I'll wake up some mornings and want to go out together – to a coffee shop to work or to the park for a walk or to meet up with some of our friends for dinner – but if we haven't discussed it the night before, or sometimes even days in advance, it's difficult for him to make the adjustment to going out. In the beginning, I took this personally – I thought his inability to adapt and "act quickly" meant he wasn't interested in spending time with me. But I've come to realize that his ability to stick to a schedule – and work slowly and steadily – makes him more available to me during those times that we do spend together. When he sticks to his schedule, he can be 100% present when we are together. He is not distracted by his to-do list or stressed out that he is not working; he is focused on our time because it is our time."

Edmund, Investigator (5) formerly in relationship for less than one year with Bob, Achiever (3)

TYPE FIVE INVESTIGATOR/OBSERVER

"We had a big "pace" difference. Bob was much faster in almost all arenas. A simple example is how we would take photos. I need time to set up a great composition and so forth while he could take these amazing photos with seemingly no preparation. And energetically, we were quite different. I'm always managing my energy, and vigilant about what I say yes to and commit to doing. In contrast, Bob had seemingly unlimited supplies of energy for socializing, parties, activities and didn't seem to have a point of reference to understand why I need so much downtime."

Investigator (5)s have an exaggerated sense of scarcity and easily feel overwhelmed. When an unplanned outing is sprung on them, their mind jumps into a future in which they are in an overwhelming environment. They need to carefully plan the energetic, emotional and physical requirements before they agree to anything. While it may feel like a personal rejection, it isn't. Investigator (5)s, like all of us, want to feel stable. They also want to plan their actions carefully. Their minds tend to work methodically and in a rational way. Skipping steps, taking shortcuts and so forth is only something Investigator (5)s do with great deliberation.

If you are an Investigator (5):
Understand that your concern is anxiety about the future, not the current moment. Try to use your rational mind to determine how truly threatening an unexpected outing or engagement would be. Stretch your comfort zone. Prioritize experience over data. The more experience you have that you can survive a surprise outing, the more relaxed you will be when unavoidable surprises occur.

If you are with an Investigator (5):
Understand that your partner experiences a different reality than you do and is very sensitive to energy drains. Unknown factors are anxiety provoking. Even if you get your partner to do something spontaneous, they are likely going to be anxious during the outing, worrying about what will come next and so forth. With spontaneous ideas, give your partner a little time to think through the variables and to plan. And don't be disappointed if the answer is no. It isn't personal.

"Despite the fact that I am reserved and not very emotionally expressive, I do care deeply about you and other people."

Sandy, Investigator (5)

"Even though I'm not great at expressing my emotions or showing up for others emotionally,

I do care about other people. My inner life is much messier than anyone can understand. I am emotional, and I have attachments that can get complicated. When I do open up and trust someone, that person becomes a lot of things to me. I can be emotional; I can be inconsistent and murky and confused with them. I may present a front of being put together in daily life, but my partner knows the reality. It's like I can take off my ill-fitting human suit around him."

Emotional expression does not come easily to Investigator (5)s. They prefer to discuss topics that are objective, and they naturally gravitate towards facts, reason and logic. They often don't identify easily with feelings and often don't know what they are feeling themselves. Some Investigator (5)s report they don't actually want to feel their emotions. The world of emotion is an area that can feel confusing and overwhelming to them.

If you are an Investigator (5):
If you do care about someone, try to find ways to express it. While expressing your emotions may feel overwhelming, it is part of the human experience and part of a healthy relationship. A little bit of expression goes a long way.

If you are with an Investigator (5):
Emotional fluency is not always easy for your partner, and emotional expression may be minimal. If you are feeling insecure about the relationship, voice your concerns. You will probably be shocked to learn how content your partner is. If you need more affection, you will need to be clear and specific. Your partner isn't always able to connect the dots in the emotional world.

"Going to social functions is generally uncomfortable and draining for me. Please don't pressure me to socialize a lot."

Sandy, Investigator (5)

"From a young age, I felt at odds with the people around me – my schoolmates, neighbors and so forth. When I was really young, I'd climb up on the counter and push the medicine cabinet mirror towards the main one so they'd reflect each other infinitely, and I could contemplate eternity. When I started talking I'd ask hypothetical question after question until my parents would give up and say they didn't know the answer. While I wouldn't say I'm more intelligent, I think my mind works differently from other people's. At a young age, I started to understand that I was different, and this difference became more apparent in social functions.

Trying to relate to other people wasn't a positive feedback loop, so social interaction became something I would tend to avoid. In contrast, I love learning and spending private time exploring my interests. Because my taste can be obscure, and my drive is to dive deeply into the subjects I study, I often end up having interests that aren't easily shared by others. This sets me apart and enhances the negative feedback loop of socializing. The irony is that part of my drive to learn things deeply is to find a niche where I can be truly needed and useful to others and not always sitting out on the sidelines...

And if all this weren't enough to make social functions difficult, the reality is that for the most part, other people bore me. I don't care about a lot of their customs, their values, their rules or their lives, and not valuing these things has a lot to do with why I didn't learn them. Of course, it is an open question – did I lose interest in social functioning because I didn't fit in, or did I not fit in because I don't have interest in social functioning? Hard to say but probably both are simultaneously true.

Since people aren't interesting to me, and since I do not have much in common with most people, events tend to be draining and boring for me. I mostly stand around and drink or eat or play with the host's pets. I am extremely introverted, so I'm not bound to enjoy this type of thing much to begin with. Small chat is irritating and exhausting. I usually can't dive in deep intellectually with anyone at social events. When I can, it's great. But otherwise, I am left alone, and I'd rather be on my computer or doing some other solitary activity."

Investigator (5)s often don't connect easily with others unless there is some clear, shared activity or interest. Socializing is not comfortable or enjoyable, so asking them to participate in most social events is likely draining and stressful for them. This can be puzzling to others who get a great deal of enjoyment and satisfaction from group connection.

If you are an Investigator (5):
Try to find balance in your tendency to withdraw and stay withdrawn. While isolated in your home may feel the most comfortable, it isn't necessarily the healthiest thing for you to do.

If you are with an Investigator (5):
Offer social events in small doses and at a measured pace. Attending six parties in one weekend is likely not going to work for your Investigator (5). Understand that group activities might be draining and unenjoyable for your partner. They may need to time to rejuvenate and recover after social outings.

INVESTIGATOR/OBSERVER (5) 360 DEGREE REVIEW

The next section features the 360 degree review--partnership with an Investigator (5) from the perspective each of the nine types.

5:1: Investigator (5) with Perfectionist (1)

Claudia, Perfectionist (1) in a 2-year relationship with Simon, Investigator (5)

"I really love Simon's ability to look at a situation, analyze it and come to a valid conclusion without things getting one-sided or overly competitive. We can disagree about something but still laugh about our different views and enjoy each other's company. In our relationship, we never have actual fights or arguments that end with one another truly being upset or offended. I also love his ability to be observant and logical yet still show emotions when warranted.

As a couple, we can be very fact-oriented. When we disagree about even a simple thing, one or the other will immediately go online to find the correct answer.

Our relationship is characterized by respect and giving each other space. Early in our relationship, it was difficult to get my boyfriend to talk about his feelings, and I was afraid to push him because I could tell how uncomfortable he felt. For example, a few months into our relationship he was offered a job in France and was on the fence about taking it. When

I tried to ask him what he wanted or what was most important to him, his response would usually be "I don't know" or just a shrug. When I backed off on the questioning, he finally started to open up a bit more and use me as a sounding board which allowed him to make his decision to stay.

I think because we faced this obstacle early on in our relationship and were able essentially to overcome it, our communication style from that point forward changed, and we were both able to be more open with each other. If this job offer scenario had not come about when it did, I don't know if we would be where we are now. There are still times when he is hesitant to share his feelings on something, but I can sense that and give him the time and space he needs to process everything. When he is ready, he comes back to me to share. I've learned not to overshare with him as this is my natural tendency, and I know he doesn't want to be bombarded with everything I am thinking all of the time.

I knew quite early on that I wanted to be with him, and it was going to get serious. However, his pace was slower than mine. When he was essentially living in my apartment, and I mentioned he could just move out of his place and save the rent money, he clearly stated he wasn't ready for that. Even though I wanted to push the issue, I knew I had to leave it alone and wait until he came to me stating he was ready. I used the same approach when it came to saying "I love you." I was ready and wanting to say it early on but knew it would be better to wait until he said it."

5:1 The Theory

5:1 When In Balance

The Perfectionist (1) and Investigator (5) share many traits and values that make for a steady, satisfying partnership punctuated by mutual respect, independence and shared interests.

Values of personal freedom, respect, integrity and pursuit of knowledge are the foundation of this pair. Both are interested in facts, data and being well-informed and correct. Together they enjoy verbal sparring and lively discussion. They share an attraction to each other's intellect, and this can be a highly cerebral couple. Both partners value objectivity and try to avoid drama. They are highly respectful of personal boundaries and are generally contained with their emotions. They work hard to allow each other personal space and freedom as this is seen as a foundational element to their relationship.

Their differences offer opportunities for growth. Their thirst for knowledge is different, and they can learn a lot by observing each other. Perfectionist (1)s seek fairness, justice and correctness. They tend to have a more rigid perspective, and this absolutism can be intriguing to their Investigator (5). Investigator (5)s are more relative, open-minded and on a never-ending quest for knowledge. When in balance, this open-mindedness can offer a growth edge for the Perfectionist (1), inviting them to be more flexible in their thinking.

Both types tend to manage time differently. Perfectionist (1)s are structured, organized and precise in their time commitments and time management. They are schedule oriented and often have future plans carefully laid out weeks or months in advance. This can be a growth opportunity for Investigator (5)s who resist making concrete long-range plans with others since they have difficulty predicting their energy levels or appetite for social engagements. When these differences are seen as opportunities to cultivate flexibility, compromise and compassion, they can be an asset to the relationship.

Overall, this is a sweetly contained, affectionate and even-keeled couple. Their devotion to each other is evident and inspiring to those around them.

5:1 The Downward Spiral
When in a fixated or unaware state, the same differences that offered growth opportunities can trigger the downward spiral of the relationship. When Perfectionist (1)s tighten their defenses, they become more critical, rigid, harsh and close-minded. When Investigator (5)s tighten their defenses, they withdraw, disengage and shutdown. This polarization triggers the downward spiral.

Perfectionist (1)s may become critical and judgmental about their Investigator (5)'s less structured approach to life and their sometimes radical intellectual ideas. Investigator (5)s may start to see their Perfectionist (1) as rigid, close-minded and focused on the details at the expense of the bigger picture. Criticism, stonewalling and a lack of respect may enter the picture. As both types are highly contained with their emotions and respectful of personal boundaries, open fighting may be rare. However, the warm bond the couple shared weakens, and coolness and isolation set in. Both may craft fairly independent lives for themselves, so while the relationship may appear intact to the outside world, true intimacy is lost. At this stage, an eventual breakup is likely.

5:1 The Lighthouse
As isolation and coldness characterize the path of deterioration in this pairing, connecting on an emotional level is the path to healing. Sharing time and space together and reconnecting around their shared interest and hobbies can help break the momentum of the downward spiral. Moving the energy out of the head and into the heart is the path back to balance.

5:1 The Kundalini Yoga Connection

Both Perfectionist (1)s and Investigator (5)s can relate very much from their intellect and much less from their heart center. Ultimately, a head connection alone may not be enough to maintain a long-term intimate relationship. Both types need to learn to connect and speak from the heart, so heart opening Kundalini Yoga kriyas and meditations are beneficial. Kundalini Yoga kriyas and meditations for strengthening the nervous system help both types relax their habit of attention.

For Investigator (5)s, a powerful and precise physical practice to bring focus to the body can be effective. Strengthening the immune system is helpful as Investigator (5)s can feel overwhelmed easily. And as the emotional world can sometimes feel foreign to Investigator (5)s, energy awareness exercises can be helpful.

Perfectionist (1)s need to burn out anger and irritation so they can become less rigid and more flexible in their thinking. Kundalini Yoga kriyas and meditations to relieve anger, strengthen the nervous system and open the heart are beneficial.

See the appendix for Perfectionist (1) and Investigator (5) recommended Kundalini Yoga kriyas and meditations.

5:2 Investigator (5) with Helper (2)

Constanza, Helper (2) formerly in a 2-year relationship with Matias, Investigator (5)

"Matias was focused, generous and curious. He wanted to know me intensely, and we had meaningful, interesting conversations on a range of topics from spirituality, science, travel, art and so forth. He had undefended eyes, which I loved to look into.

He really appreciated my affection, my attention and my help with decorating. He liked to take me shopping, to share walks in the park, trips to museums and metaphysical discussions. He didn't need to socialize with other people so we could easily have a great time together home alone or going out. He loved to demonstrate his competence, how he could fix or design things or show off any of his talents. Touch was not casual for him, so our physical connection was always great together.

In our relationship, Matias was great at figuring out what I liked and creating plans for us. We both enjoyed hiking and good food, so he would create combined hiking and restaurant adventures that were delightful. We both were raised without television, so we shared a sense of being outside of normal society. This was bonding.

Matias had a hard time distinguishing between his thoughts and reality. For example, if he thought a lot about a new activity such as losing weight, he felt like he had mostly achieved it even if nothing physical had changed yet. His mental construct seems to override reality at times, and this applied to me and our relationship as well. In social conversations, he would describe our relationship based on his mental images more than on how we actually interacted. I found it amusing, and at times puzzling.

As it relates to issues in the relationship, it was hard to find balance. Matias was possessive about wanting to know everything about me and to have me to himself, yet he would be happy spending consecutive whole days on his own. He was unable to consider my side of the experience and imagine how it felt for me. Then he would feel rejected if I didn't provide him the same level of nurturing that I had earlier in the relationship, a level that I had offered based on more sharing of time and space than he seemed able to maintain. He had difficulty handling intense emotions and could become pretty volatile when he was upset. He was more of an individual than a partner, and this was tough. It was like he had a tight wall around his core issues.

Bringing him home to my family was challenging. He had a narrow range of people that he liked to interact with, and my family didn't fall within that range. He also didn't like having to share my attention. He much preferred me to be focused on him, so socializing with others was challenging at times.

A thorny issue in the relationship was when I expressed something I wanted us to work on as a couple, Matias would often ignore it or get defensive. It was hard to penetrate his world, and if I did, it seemed to trigger his insecurities. I learned to become very gentle, affirming and non-reactive when he got triggered, but it only helped the events pass more easily. We made very little movement on the actual issues.

Eventually, the stalemates and differences became too great, and we split up as a couple."

Belinda, Helper (2) married in a 16-year relationship with Moses, Investigator (5)

"I really value my husband's loyalty, both to his friends and to me. I know I can count on him to be at my side through the trials and tribulations of life and to encourage me to get back up when I get knocked down. He is extremely stable which can help to balance my emotional ups and downs.

In our relationship, I provide the outward focused care and attention he craves but might never ask for, and he provides the general stability I need. Our sense of boundaries is really different as I tend to reach out to others quite a bit. He's much more reserved. While this could be a problem, for us it seems to provide balance. He's my rock.

One of the challenges in our dynamic is that he can be so reserved, I sometimes feel insecure in the relationship and worry that maybe he is bored. When I ask him this directly, he usually looks surprised and confused and says "No! That's not at all the case." This, of course, reassures me, but I do wish he'd be more openly expressive and affectionate. However, I also know this just isn't his character.

Overall, I'm very happy in my relationship. I feel like I have a life partner who loves me and gives me balance. We have a deep bond, and I enjoy sharing my journey with him."

5:2 The Theory

5:2 When In Balance

The Helper (2) with the Investigator (5) is a classic example of opposites attracting, the social butterfly with the reserved wallflower. Their differences form not only the initial attraction but the longer-term bond between the two. Together, this couple balances each other.

Helper (2)s are socially adept with high emotional intelligence, charm, warmth and engaging, friendly behavior. They value personal relationships highly and seek deep connection with others. They are at home in the world of feelings, emotions and social connections. In contrast, Investigator (5)s prefer to minimize their connection to others as they seek to preserve what they experience as very limited energy. They value self-sufficiency, limited demands and personal freedom. They are at home in the world of logic, facts, information and reason. Blended, this couple creates a home that values both logic, facts, feelings and relationships.

The Helper (2) offers the Investigator (5) caring, nurturing, concern, attentiveness and an introduction to the soft skills in life: communication, emotional fluency and social graces. Investigator (5)s report their life becomes upgraded with the influence of their Helper (2). Their home is cleaner, they dress better, they eat better, they understand other people more and so forth. In return, the Investigator (5) offers a solid foundation to their Helper (2). Less clouded by emotion, the Investigator (5) brings clear analysis, rational thought and logic to the decision-making of the Helper (2). They help calm emotional storms and are a stable rock for the Helper (2) who can get drawn into interpersonal dramas.

Successful negotiation of time spent together and independently is key in this relationship. Investigator (5)s and Helper (2) set their personal priorities differently, and successful couples report giving each other a lot of personal freedom to pursue things that are important to them.

Together, this is a highly balancing couple who share a deep bond of affection, commitment and loyalty.

5:2 The Downward Spiral
A key difference between Investigator (5) and Helper (2) is their sensitivity to personal boundaries (including time alone) and the different way they express love and affection. Investigator (5)s feel stable and secure when they are isolated and left to their individual pursuits. Helper (2)s feel stable and secure with constant, consistent personal connection. Investigator (5)s express love indirectly, though loyalty, consistency, good listening and problem solving. Helper (2)s are more openly affectionate and verbally expressive. These differences are fundamental and can create conflicts when either partner is fixated.

The Helper (2) may get frustrated and feel rejected by the Investigator (5)'s desire for solitude and lack of emotional expression. This triggers the downward spiral, with the Helper (2) trying harder to connect with their Investigator (5) who now feels their stability threatened. The more the Helper (2) leans in, the more the Investigator (5) shrinks back. The Helper (2) may not understand how their interest is interpreted as intrusion the same way the Investigator (5) may not realize how their isolation is interpreted as rejection.

Or conversely, the Helper (2) may start to withhold care and nurturing as a passive aggressive way of expressing dissatisfaction over the lack of attention they feel from their Investigator (5). This may be confusing to the Investigator (5) who feels their desire for time alone is healthy and acceptable. They feel rejected without cause.

How far the downward cycle goes depends a lot on each person's self-awareness and tolerance for discomfort. If there is awareness of the disconnect, it may be mended. If the fixation continues, both partners polarize, and the relationship may end.

5:2 The Lighthouse
Differences in stress responses characterize the downward spiral of this pair, so both partners need to notice their opposite push-pull response and come into balance. Both partners experience personal boundaries very differently. They each need to gain an awareness and understanding of the other person's experience around these boundaries.

5:2 The Kundalini Yoga Connection
The Helper (2) needs to stand more firmly in their own energetic space and resist the urge

to lean forward into the space of their Investigator (5), who may feel this as intrusive. Self-care, self-acceptance and self-love must be cultivated. Helper (2)s have a strong drive to send their energy outward and to focus on others. Kundalini Yoga kriyas and meditations to develop physical awareness, self-love, self-acceptance and balance are beneficial for Helper (2)s.

The Investigator (5) needs to stay engaged with others and resist the impulse to withdraw for security, as this triggers insecurity and stress in their Helper (2). Kundalini Yoga kriyas and meditations to build the nervous system, to move the energy out of the head and into the heart and to cultivate energy awareness are helpful.

See the appendix for Helper (2) and Investigator (5) recommended Kundalini Yoga kriyas and meditations.

5:3 Investigator (5) with Achiever (3)

Victoria, Achiever (3) in a 3-year relationship with Pablo, Investigator (5)

"I love how Pablo is so effortlessly himself. I try really hard to please others and be what they want, but he is always exactly who he is – without a care about what others think about him. It is really refreshing for me to see his strong sense of himself.

Pablo brings me a sense of protection, security and depth. He is extremely observant and aware of his environment. Whenever we are out in public, he is constantly observing, aware of what is happening around him and who is watching me. In the beginning, I used to think he was looking at other women, and I would get angry and disappointed. But as time has passed, I realize he is actually scanning the whole space, and this awareness makes him feel in control.

In the relationship, he's more practical and always tries to find solutions to make my life easier. I'm bolder, and when he is insecure, I boost his self-confidence. Our relationship is based on respect and giving each other space to pursue our dreams. With him, I don't feel my usual drive to compete. I see us as a team, so there is no need to compete – when he wins, I win.

Pablo is reserved and doesn't speak much, but when he speaks from the heart, he blows my mind with his caring. He knows so much about me in such a short amount of time, and it is all because he practically studies me. This makes me feel loved and seen.

Like all couples, we have our challenges. Our communication styles are really different. We can both be intense, and when we argue there is no stopping until we are done. It's hard to reconnect after a fight because we both withdraw and become super stubborn. We have a bad habit of trying to blame one another.

I am very direct, and this can hurt him. And when he is hurt, he goes into his shell for a while but doesn't tell me what the issue is. He is extremely sensitive and keeps a distance, maybe to protect himself.

Because we are so different, we have to work hard to understand each other. He can be quite secretive, and if he has a personal or work problem that doesn't involve me, he becomes very distant and shut down. I take this personally and try to get him to open him up. It doesn't work, and in the end, I usually end up angry.

I would like him to know I don't mean to hurt him on purpose, but my directness and temper are the way I am. I wish he would tell me when I hurt him, so we don't waste time and energy trying to reconnect.

Our pace is different. I have a lot of energy and am extremely active. He is the slower type who wants to take his time enjoying his space. He likes a lazy morning with coffee and a cigarette. I want action immediately. When I wake up, I'm ready to go for a hike or some other activity. We've had to compromise here. I usually get up and start my things, and he joins me when he is ready. This works and becomes a win-win situation because both of us get our needs met.

Overall, I am very happy in my relationship. I have a loving and supportive partner who I respect and admire in every way. And despite his highly analytical mind, he is much more romantic than I am!"

5:3 The Theory

5:3 When In Balance
The Achiever (3) and Investigator (5) share many core values and interests though their habit of attention is quite different. Both are interested in intellectual pursuits, gaining knowledge and expertise and becoming well-regarded in their chosen fields. Both value discipline and are willing to work hard. They seek to make a positive impact on the world. Both tend to be emotionally contained and while they may feel things deeply, this rarely conflicts with their

pursuit of tangible, concrete goals. Beneath it all, there is a practical, logical undercurrent in both partners.

To the dynamic, the Achiever (3) brings a focus on image, polish and good communication skills. Achiever (3)s tend to be outwardly facing and have a high awareness of the impression they are making on others. This can be a point of learning for Investigator (5)s who generally are less interested in appearances and who tend to prefer written, rather than interpersonal, communication skills. Achiever (3)s are also more spontaneous than the Investigator (5) counterpart. They model for their Investigator (5) how to wing it, go with the flow and work out unexpected issues in real time. This can be helpful and inspiring for the Investigator (5).

Investigator (5)s offer depth of insight, a focus on details and planning and a more methodical, rational approach to situations. They are interested in satisfying their curiosity more than in getting to a specific outcome. This allows them to be more flexible in their thinking and more thorough in their approach. This difference can be balancing for their Achiever (3) who in their drive to succeed may be tempted to cut corners or take a less comprehensive approach.

As a couple, they can be proud of and admire each other. They may feel they have found their perfect match – someone who can keep up with them intellectually, who gives them sufficient personal freedom, who supports their endeavors and who they can show off to the outside world. This can be a successful, enduring match.

5:3 The Downward Spiral

While this couple has many similarities, they also have some key differences that can trigger the downward spiral. Their lifestyle pace is different, with the Achiever (3) on the go like an Energizer Bunny® and the Investigator (5) more like the tortoise with a slow but deliberate pace. Both are interested in being competent and successful in their chosen fields and in a fixated state with tightening defenses, there can be a competitive element in this relationship. And as both types tend to underemphasize the emotional world, important issues can go unaddressed.

In a fixated state, one or both partners may start to get frustrated with the other. The Achiever (3) may feel their Investigator (5)'s lifestyle pace is slow and threatening their ability to achieve their goals. They may mock their partner's careful and deliberate planning for all various scenarios. Likewise, the Investigator (5) may start to lose respect for their Achiever (3), feeling they are overly concerned about image and achievement and all to willing to sacrifice depth for appearance. One danger this couple has is that their connection can be largely mental, professional and pragmatic. If they aren't strongly connected at the heart, the lack of an emotional connection can create distance in the relationship that is hard to recover. As the downward spiral gains momentum, they may become harsh, hard-hearted and arrogant with each other. If this couple can't find a way to get out of their heads and into their hearts, the relationship can drift apart or end abruptly.

5:3 The Lighthouse

A lack of a truly heartfelt connection is ultimately what starts this pair into a downward spiral. Both partners need to find ways to connect more deeply to their emotional world and to communicate from their heart. Both need to learn to place value on interdependence and collaboration.

5:3 The Kundalini Yoga Connection

Achiever (3)s need to slow down, connect with their heart center and stay collaborative. If they put the partnership before self-interest, the deterioration of the relationship may reverse. Kundalini Yoga kriyas and meditations to cultivate stillness and to balance the head and heart are particularly good.

Investigator (5)s need to learn to share more of their feelings with their Achiever (3). While open emotional expressions may not come easily for most Investigator (5)s, a practice to open the heart and move the energy out of the head and into the body can be useful. Kundalini Yoga kriyas and meditations to open the throat chakra and to cultivate gratitude are beneficial.

See the appendix for Achiever (3) and Investigator (5) recommended Kundalini Yoga kriyas and meditations.

5:4 Investigator (5) with Individualist (4)

Emma, Individualist (4) married in a 10-year relationship with Hunter, Investigator (5)

"My husband is very level-headed and has excellent problem-solving skills. I can talk with him about anything, and he helps contain my big frenetic energy. I think he is perfect just as he is, faults and all.

In our relationship, he is my "rock" and holds my space well, and I am his "muse," helping him find his playful side. We have a lot of fun together, especially when we separate ourselves from mundane day-to-day life. When we go on vacation, it's a total blast and a part of our relationship I really treasure.

We both can see the big picture, though we experience it differently. I see the picture from the vantage point of a kite that flies overhead and surveys what's happening like a giant roadmap. My husband is more like Google Earth, seeing everything in a more methodical way and able to zoom into all the details.

He helps bring balance into my life. I don't have a lot of close relationships, and he encourages me to develop friendships and stay in touch with family. I used to change coffee shops if the barista knew my order when I walked in whereas he loves going to places where he knows people. Through him, I'm learning to appreciate the comfort that familiarity can bring.

As it relates to relationship challenges, we definitely process things and live life at a different pace. Mentally, I operate in fifth gear and overdrive. Energetically, he is still pulling out of the driveway when I'm already halfway to where I think we're going. It takes my husband f.o.r.e.v.e.r. to make up his mind to do something. I feel like nothing is ever permanent, so I'm okay jumping in and risking mistakes. He, on the other hand, hates to make mistakes, and this keeps him from trying things that I think he would probably be really good at. Sometimes he will have big dreams, and I can feel the excitement in him, but if he doesn't think he can accomplish his goal, even though he may have planned this goal out for an entire decade, he will let the dream die. He's also more in his head, while I am more kinesthetic and connected to my body.

Overall, I'm very happy in my relationship. I feel like my husband is a great match for me, and I love that he feels comfortable enough with me to show me all of his sides, even the ones the outside world doesn't get much of a glimpse of."

Ericha, Individualist (4) in a 2-year relationship with Thomas, Investigator (5)

"One of the things I truly love about our relationship is the depth – of emotion, of creativity, of intellectual discussion, of sharing. We can comfortably talk for hours! But we both also cherish our alone time, so I never feel pressure to interact with him. We often sit quietly together, thinking or daydreaming privately, but sharing space.

I really appreciate that nothing – no thought, no emotion, no opinion, no idea – is too weird or "out there" for him. I can express myself, my creative impulses and my emotions without the fear of being judged. And I think I offer him the same thing in return.

He has this amazing ability to take me completely seriously but also help me to lighten up. One of the most amazing gifts of our relationship is the humor. We are both totally bizarre; we have endless inside jokes, we make funny faces and use funny voices. This is especially *helpful when I'm feeling overwhelmed by my emotions or in a dark place, as he helps pull me out of my funk without belittling my emotions.*

He is not afraid of his emotions and has done a lot of personal work to stay connected to his feelings, which when combined with his intellect, makes him a fantastic partner and communicator. I often get overwhelmed by my emotions, and he really keeps me anchored, offering me a space to share my feelings or analyze my thoughts, depending on my mood.

Our difference in pace has been a big challenge in our relationship. My boyfriend likes to take his time, to think things through, not to feel rushed. I tend to go on instinct and to act quickly based on my emotions. This can create a lot of friction. I get frustrated that it takes him so long to do tasks or make decisions. This applies whether we are talking about cleaning the dishes or making weekend plans. He guards his time very closely, and he often says "no" to spontaneity in our relationship, especially if he is stressed with work. I interpret this as inflexible, and if I'm feeling particularly insecure or vulnerable, I feel that he is not prioritizing our relationship. He gets frustrated with my insistence on action and that sometimes elicits an even firmer "no" on his part, whereas if he'd been left alone to make the decision himself, he would probably have gladly done it although tomorrow, not today. In this relationship, I'm learning patience, which is not my strong suit, and we try to meet in the middle.

I love that my partner does not feel threatened or shocked by the things I say and do when it comes to my sexuality and my self-expression. For example, my sense of humor can be really raunchy. I'm a pole dancer, I don't shave my body, and I'm really vocal about breaking down the gender binary. Instead of being critical or judgmental, he offers me acceptance and curiosity. Even when he doesn't agree, he is still so open because he is interested in learning – about people and ideas that are so different from him.

I have a tendency to be really hard on myself. I focus on my mistakes and my failures more than my successes. Thomas helps bring perspective and often boosts my self-esteem with praise and support. For example, I'm trying to sell my house right now, and I've never done that before. I'm making a lot of small mistakes, and I disproportionately beat myself up for those missteps. He is really helping me to stay grounded by encouraging experimentation and praising my learning curve saying things like "You've never done this before, how are you supposed to know?" or "Now you know for next time what to do differently, but you did the best you can." or "This is such a great chance to learn something new about yourself!"

But he doesn't coddle me either! He holds me accountable when I am disrespectful and doesn't punish me for my mistakes in our relationship. For example, sometimes we have arguments, and they can be intense. I often let my feelings affect the way I communicate, and I can come across as aggressive or mean. I often make facial expressions or use biting words, before I can stop myself. He calls me out on my immaturity or meanness but also accepts my heartfelt apologies and doesn't hold onto the past. Whenever we "fight," there's always this underlying trust inside of me that we will work through it because he has shown me, again and again, that when we disagree or misunderstand each other, he is always willing to meet me halfway. It's all about communication. I think that's why we do so well as a couple. We talk, and we are BOTH willing to take responsibility for our part in the fight. We trust each other to find the lesson of what we can do better so that it doesn't happen again. That's why it works. We try."

5:4 The Theory

5:4 When In Balance

The Individualist (4) and Investigator (5) bring complementary traits to each other, and this can be a very harmonizing relationship. Both seek depth, albeit in different arenas and coming from different angles. Both are curious, open-minded and private, valuing time alone and giving their partner a great deal of personal freedom.

Individualist (4)s are tuned into the colorful and vivid world of emotion. They bring a lyrical and artistic quality to their experience as well as a sensitivity to their own feelings and the feelings of others. This can be fascinating to their Investigator (5) who tends to have a more monochromatic experience in the world of emotion. Individualist (4)s can be passionate, creative, nurturing and invite their Investigator (5) to get out of their head and more into their body.

Investigator (5)s are logical, rational, methodical and curious. They bring a grounded, focused, comprehensive quality to their experience as well as willingness to live life on their own terms and outside of the mainstream. They help anchor their Individualist (4) who can get swept away by their emotional storms. They accept their Individualist (4) fully and easily which can be healing for their partner.

Together, this couple can share a high level of contextual communication. They may have inside jokes, facial expressions, signals and so forth that serve as a private language shared just between the two of them. Both can be unconventional and irreverent, and they may bond through their shared quirkiness. Neither is easily offended by the other which helps to foster intimacy between the two. In this match, both partners feel they have full permission to be themselves and follow their own drumbeat.

5:4 The Downward Spiral
Different needs for time together and time apart can trigger misunderstandings and an environment for the downward spiral. Individualist (4)s follow the rhythm of the emotional world and as such, are more spontaneous. They operate from instinct and intuition. This can be confusing and off-putting for their Investigator (5), who feels secure when outings and events are carefully planned. With tightening defenses, both partners polarize, the Individualist (4) interpreting the Investigator (5)'s containment as rejection, and the Investigator (5) interpreting the Individualist (4)'s emotional intensity as threatening.

Individualist (4)s may feel analyzed rather than understood, observed rather than treated with empathy. Individualists can feel frustrated at the amount of time it takes for their Investigator (5) to respond when a situation calls for action, and they can take the Investigator (5)'s boundaried approach to life as rejection.

In contrast, Investigator (5)s can begin to see their Individualist (4) partner as draining and demanding. They experience their Individualist (4) as acting irrationally and immaturely. The Investigator (5) may start to question the Individualist (4)'s stability, which can feel threatening to the Investigator and cause them to retreat more.

As the downward spiral gains momentum, the Investigator (5) retreats more into self-containment and hard-managed boundaries, triggering feelings of abandonment, neediness and emotional chaos for the Individualist (4). The cycle continues, and the relationship can get into loop of unmet needs that may ultimately end in a breakup.

 ### 5:4 The Lighthouse
Dramatically different emotional styles and stress, response of these two types is the central factor in the deterioration of this relationship. As such, stress and energy management are keys in repairing damage in this relationship. Both partners need tools to deal more effectively with stress, and both need to learn to manage their energy. Investigator (5)s need to resist the urge to withdraw, and Individualist (4)s need to resist the urge to demand a reaction.

 ### 5:4 The Kundalini Yoga Connection
Strengthening the nervous system helps both of these types come into balance.

The Individualist (4) needs to strengthen their nervous system so they don't feel as overwhelmed by their intense emotional energy. Instead of acting out feelings of rejection, they can start to use internal tools like breathwork to gain feelings of stability. Kundalini

Yoga kriyas and meditations to manage energy and balance emotional states like depression, anxiety and anger are helpful.

The Investigator (5) needs to stay engaged and resist the impulse to withdraw for security, as this triggers insecurity and feelings of rejection in their Individualist (4) partner. The stronger the nervous system, the less overwhelmed the Investigator (5) will likely feel. Kundalini Yoga kriyas and meditations to strengthen the nervous system, to move the energy out of the head and into the heart and to build energy are beneficial.

See the appendix for Individualist (4) and Investigator (5) recommended Kundalini Yoga kriyas and meditations.

5:5 Investigator (5) with Investigator (5)

Sandy, Investigator (5) formerly married in a 6-year relationship with Marco, Investigator (5)

"I really value Marco's intellectual clarity, rational thinking, reason, kindness, compassion, spiritual awareness and his willingness to take others' feelings into consideration. He can connect with the emotions of others and takes people's needs and feelings seriously.

In our relationship, we shared a desire to create a secure home, to talk about our deeper selves and to protect each other's needs. Both of us are extremely sensitive to energy drains, and as such were equally vigilant in protecting our mutual need to escape back to our safe place. We traveled well together because we both understood the need for taking social events in small doses. Mostly, we just looked out for each other and didn't need to explain or defend our needs over and over. For example, despite being together for years, we would never touch each other's laptops or phones. That might seem odd to others, but I would never dream of it and would recoil if anyone ever touched mine. It would be like touching my liver! And I never had to have a conversation about this with Marco. We naturally understood each other. This was and is extremely important to both of us as we are not always the best at communicating our needs and feelings.

We illustrated that even though people might have similar wiring through a shared Enneagram habit of attention, we are all totally unique individuals. We had many differences and actually balanced each other out. I was more emotionally unaware and clumsy whereas he could keep in touch with the needs and feelings of people around him. I relied on this strength of his a lot. I was able to learn from him. Marco brought emotional understanding and compassion to our dynamic. He helped me understand and translate my own feelings when I was unable to. He creates a space for people to have their feelings heard and understood.

As it relates to issues in our relationship, they were as you might expect with two very similar people. It was too easy to fall into patterns based on mutual dysfunction. Both of us wanted to stay in and avoid the world. Both of us wanted to evade social responsibilities and experiences. Both of us wanted to give in to our anxieties. And there was no one to challenge us because we both wanted the same thing. We fell into this pattern of needing not to challenge the other for fear that they would challenge us back, make us face what we weren't ready to face. My partner was all too willing to overlook my mental traps because if he didn't, he would need to challenge his own, and vice versa. While we eventually split up as a couple, we have remained close friends and have a deep understanding and affection for each other."

5:5 The Theory

5:5 When In Balance

Two Investigator (5)s feel a great sense of relief to have found each other. They may share an immediate, intense cerebral connection and as the Investigator (5) experience is generally to feel like an alien or an outsider, they may feel mindblown to have met someone like them. They generally share a deep and profound understanding of each other including the desire to be reclusive, the need for privacy and time alone, the strong sense of personal boundaries and the gravitation towards logical, rational thought.

Each partner gives the other a lot of personal space and makes few demands either individually or on the relationship. Both are independent and self-sufficient. Both are emotionally contained, intellectually curious and interested in a pursuit of knowledge. While familiarity may be established instantly, intimacy is developed more slowly with both partners careful to respect the boundaries of the other. While this relationship may look contained and even robotic to the outside world, Investigator (5)s can get very attached to their partners, and this is no different in a double Investigator (5) couple. Affection may be expressed indirectly and connection may not require physical presence. This is a couple that feels bound to each other almost psychically. When in balance, this can make an intimate and intense match between kindred spirits.

5:5 The Downward Spiral

The very similarities that serve to bind this couple can also be what tears them apart. They can be too reclusive, too private, too independent and too distant from each other. In a fixated state with tightening defenses, Investigator (5)s want more privacy and more time alone. With another Investigator (5), no one is likely to question this or make demands for time together. Without fully knowingly it, this couple can easily drift so far apart, the relationship is almost inexistent or occurs only in their heads.

It can be difficult for this couple to connect at an emotional or heart level. Without this connection, romantic and sexual energy may fizzle, leaving the partnership as one more closely resembling friends or roommates. They become like two unicycles side by side instead of a tandem bicycle. Two Investigator (5)s can also get in the trap of overly identifying with their intellect and becoming arrogant or competitive with each other. This further weakens the fragile bond of intimacy.

As the downward spiral gains momentum, both Investigator (5)s go deeper into their heads and isolation intensifies. This is a logical, rational couple so heated fights are unlikely. This couple may end their relationship in a simple, logical conversation with very little emotional expression.

5:5 The Lighthouse

Managing mutual blind spots and connecting on a deep emotional level is the key to reversing any downward spiral between this pair. Because this pair is so much in their heads, recognizing and honoring the energy of emotion can be difficult. For a healthy relationship, both partners need to push past their comfort zones. Because they share blind spots, they may need to rely on others to point these spots out.

5:5 The Kundalini Yoga Connection

Both Investigators need to strengthen their nervous systems and connect with their energy of emotion. Redirecting energy from the head down to the heart and body is helpful. The Investigator (5) needs to stay engaged and resist the impulse to withdraw for security, particularly as it relates to one another. It is easy to create too much distance. Kundalini Yoga kriyas and meditations to strengthen the nervous system are helpful as are any kriyas or meditations to move the energy out of the head and into the heart.

Because of the tendency to isolate, a shared meditation or spiritual practice can be really helpful. Group classes are also helpful for Investigator (5)s.

See the appendix for Investigator (5) recommended Kundalini Yoga kriyas and meditations.

5:6 Investigator (5) with Loyalist (6)

Sarah, Loyalist (6) formerly in a relationship for less than a year with Fredrick, Investigator (5)

"I was first drawn to Fredrick's intellectual intensity. I used to joke that being with him was like being in a hospital room – no matter what you were doing, there was always that gentle buzz in the background, the noise that the lights make. His energy was like that. It wasn't huge and extroverted. It didn't call attention to itself. But it was always there...humming in the background, and only the quietest and most perceptive of people could pick up on it. I was one of them. That same intellectual energy is what kept our relationship going.

His alertness, his ability to just sit quietly and pay attention to what was going on around him is a large part of what won me over. The night we met, I was having a conversation with someone else at the party about my favorite types of candy. A week later, he came over with all those different types of candy I had mentioned, giving them to me as gifts. I remember being taken slightly aback because I hadn't even known that he was paying attention to my conversation with someone else. I thought it was kind of sexy how he could seem to be so disengaged with what was going on in the room but was, in fact, more in tune with it than the rest of us. It was interesting because he knew so much about me in such a short amount of time, and all of it came through his observing me in my everyday routine and his listening in on my conversations with other people. I never directly told him anything. He never had to ask one question. He just sat and listened everywhere he went. I thought of him like an "intel vault" because he was always gathering information.

His curiosity and his love for learning made our relationship fun and adventurous. I never knew what odd little adventure he was going to have planned for the day. He was very scientific in his approach to life. He enjoyed cause and effect type problems. He was always wondering, "If I do this, I wonder what will happen..." and then he would go and find out. He was investigative and was never afraid to learn. I'm different. New information intimidates me because I know that once I learn something, I can't unlearn it. And if the information that I garner challenges my existing beliefs, I fear that might create an existential life crisis for me. So, I can be a "keep your head in the sand" kind of person. He, on the other hand, seemed stimulated by new information. For him, his identity wasn't attached to the information. He loved to learn and to explore. I joked with him a lot about it. I would tell him, "I know just how you'll die one day. Your last words will be, 'What does this button do?'" Emotional calm described him perfectly. Sometimes it seemed unnatural that he seemed so unscathed by life.

While our intellectual attraction brought us together, it also pulled us apart. We disagreed about almost everything which created a huge feeling of separation for me. He began to see me as stupid and inferior to his intellect. Everything that I said became material for his sarcastic jokes. And I began to see him as an arrogant narcissist who thought he was better than everyone else. By the time our relationship was over, I found him to be mean and uncaring, and even delusional at times because of the really weird theories about life that he ascribed to. While he never said directly, he found me to be too clingy. Initially, my neediness allowed him to play the role of macho protector, and he really got off on that. But a short time later, what was once an eagerness to be my knight in shining armor had morphed into patient tolerance of my "leech-like" relational style. And shortly after that, it was becoming obvious that my presence was annoying him. He took to putting his headphones on whenever we were in the car together so that he wouldn't have to talk to me. Of course, I felt hurt. He never really opened up emotionally to me. By the end of the relationship, I knew practical things about his plans for the future and his opinions, but I knew almost nothing about his fears, his dreams, his most painful memories, what made him happy, what kinds of people he liked and disliked and so forth. I wanted to know him at a deeper level, what made him a human. But I felt like all he was interested in showing me was what made him a robot. He tried to build our relationship on intellectual sparring and mind games. I tried to build our relationship on romance and sentimentalism. In the end, we were both miserable.

While I wasn't sure if it was a strength or a weakness, I was impressed with how Fredrick could assess all of life with almost complete emotional detachment. He was so good at this that it was actually the reason our relationship ended. He called me one day and very calmly and simply said, "I've decided to end our relationship." When I asked him why, his response was, "Because I was thinking about it yesterday, and I realized that you're not someone that I could see myself spending the rest of my life with, and if I know that I'm not going to spend the rest of my life with you, then I'm wasting my time with you. If we end our relationship now, before we get too attached, then we both will have the opportunity to find people that we know we could live with forever. It just makes sense." After the fact, I realized he was right, although at the moment I was quite in shock.

With time and distance, I appreciate that he was able to see that we just didn't fit well together. Deep down, I saw it too, but at the time, I was not able to allow myself to accept that reality. I think that our relationship would have become really toxic, really fast, if he had not been able to see himself as separate from me."

5:6 The Theory

 ### 5:6 When In Balance

The Investigator (5) and the Loyalist (6) share an intellectual attraction, and mutual respect and admiration are at the foundation of this pair.

The Investigator (5) appreciates the patience, kindness, devotion and tenacity of their Loyalist (6). The more outwardly facing Loyalist (6) helps ensure their Investigator (5) doesn't get too isolated both socially and in the context of their relationship. This is healthy and helpful for the Investigator (5) who may start to place a higher value on personal relationships as a result of the influence of their partner.

The Loyalist (6) appreciates the intellectual intensity, the curiosity, creativity and the adventurous nature of their Investigator (5). The Investigator (5) mind is always at work solving problems, posing questions and experimenting. This is fascinating to the Loyalist (6) and can help widen their worldview. They also appreciate and admire the emotional calm of their Investigator (5) who seems unscathed by the ups and downs of life.

They function well as a team because their minds work so differently. The Loyalist (6) tends to think more narrowly, dedicated to tested and established methods. The Investigator (5) is more experimental and more creative in their approach. Together, they are well balanced to tackle life's challenges.

When they both truly believe their hearts and minds are in the same place, the trust between this pair is powerful, and they can share a lasting, fulfilling bond.

 ### 5:6 The Downward Spiral

The intellectual intensity that draws this couple together can also be what pulls this couple apart. They come at the world from very different perspectives, with the Investigator (5) on a continuous pursuit of new information and ideas and the Loyalist (6) more interested following and maintaining the agreed upon paradigms. This can be a source of frustration for both partners and may trigger the downward spiral.

With tightening defenses, both become more extreme. As the Investigator (5) explores new horizons, they may lose respect for their Loyalist (6), finding them close-minded, fearful and believing them to be intellectually inferior. Loyalist (6)s feel threatened by their Investigator (5)'s drive to question their fundamental worldviews. New information can feel destabilizing to the Loyalist (6), triggering an anxiety response. As the Loyalist (6) clings harder to their beliefs, the Investigator (5) pushes harder to question the status quo. Trust erodes, and the belief that both have their hearts and minds in the same place may fall into question. Unless the momentum of the downward spiral can be broken, the relationship may end.

5:6 The Lighthouse

Intensifying anxiety and radically different interpretations of stability are the roots of the downward spiral for this couple. To heal, both types need to learn to manage their anxiety and accept core differences in each other. Investigator (5)s need to accommodate their Loyalist (6)'s potential discomfort with threats to their established way of thinking and living. And Loyalist (6)s need to accommodate their Investigator (5)'s quest for knowledge and their tendency to question the status quo.

5:6 The Kundalini Yoga Connection

The Investigator (5) needs to relate more from the heart and less from the head, particularly when their Loyalist (6) is feeling insecure. Recognizing and honoring the energy of emotion can be a good initial practice. Kundalini Yoga kriyas and meditations to open the heart, strengthen the immune system and tune into the energy of emotion are beneficial. Strengthening the nervous system is also helpful to make their own anxiety feel less overwhelming and oppressive.

The Loyalist (6) benefits from strengthening their nervous system, so they don't feel as threatened by new information, particularly as this is a source of security for their Investigator (5). Loyalist (6)s also need to become more self-reliant in their quest for security. Kundalini Yoga kriyas and meditations to lower anxiety, cultivate self-reliance and quiet the mind are beneficial.

See the appendix for Investigator (5) and Loyalist (6) recommended Kundalini Yoga kriyas and meditations.

5:7 Investigator (5) with Enthusiast (7)

Eva, Enthusiast (7) married in a 26-year relationship with Demis, Investigator (5)

"I am 56 years old and have been married for 26 years to Demis who is 70 years old. At the time, the wedding was a big surprise for my friends and family as we had only been dating for six months. During this period, I was a journalist – extroverted, full of interests in many different areas, with a wide social circle.

THE NINE KEYS

Before Demis, my taste in men had been the artistic, bohemian, aesthetic and sophisticated types. We would share creativity, romance, passion, joy and some magical and unforgettable moments. All of this we would share until they began showing their emotional chaos... Then I would learn they were egocentric, dramatic, moody, fussy, difficult, antagonistic and jealous, with a huge inferiority complex. So, these relationships kept ending, leaving me deeply disappointed.

Being tired of this repeating cycle, I was open to another type of relationship – something stable, grounded, secure and supported and not necessarily as romantic and passionate. From the first time Demis and I went out together, we realized that we shared common values and a common vision, although we respond to life in different ways. We became close friends, and after six months, we decided to get married. I left journalism, and we started an interesting business which became successful and profitable.

At the beginning of our relationship, we were totally different characters: I didn't care about details – I was looking for the forest, and I was missing all the trees. Just one glance was enough for me to come to conclusions – simplified, superficial, without depth. Demis, on the other hand, was looking deeply at the leaf, but he was missing the tree, not even to mention the forest – although his persistence with details has proved invaluable many times for our business. Eventually, I also started looking at the trees – although my bigger picture view has proved valuable for our everyday life.

Because he was so intellectual and introverted, he didn't really like the social gatherings early on. He tried his best to follow my social life, but it was obvious he was just compromising. So, separate from him, I continued traveling a lot and having my own social activities, while he was engaged in his projects. From time to time, he would participate in my social life, and this balance worked for a while. Over the years, surprisingly, things have changed. I've turned inward more, and I am enjoying it, and he has become more social. A lot of times, he asks me to organize travel and gatherings with friends – not for my sake, but for his own because he really enjoys it himself.

The challenges in our relationship center around our differences — he is more cerebral and distant. He can be secretive about his activities and his feelings, he isolates himself, and he thinks and acts slowly. I am the opposite of these traits.

He filters everything through his mind, and he analyzes a lot. I try to help him connect with his feelings by insisting for an emotional answer to my questions, instead of his intellectual and distant ones. For example, when I ask him "how do you like the food?" he answers "the lentils have a lot of vitamins." OK... but he has not answered how the food tasted. So, I insist, without pressing him, "Is it too spicy for your taste?" He says that it is OK. I continue, "Spicier, would it be tastier for you?" And so on...

Because he doesn't have a strong connection to his feelings, he needs a long time to figure out how he feels and an even longer time to express his feelings. Unfortunately, many times when he is ready to say how he feels finally, the moment has passed, and it is meaningless to say anything. The best thing I can do is to help him connect with his feelings and draw the energy from his head into his heart. I'm affectionate with him – I kiss him a lot, I give him big hugs, I tickle him, and I pat him on the chest and on the back, behind the heart. It really works! This affection triggers him, and eventually, he starts talking about his feelings.

He can be quite secretive...He works on his projects without saying anything about them, and one day he presents me a very comprehensive thing which obviously he has spent a lot of time on. I respect his privacy, imagining it has to do with lack of self-confidence. I try to encourage him to continue doing whatever he is doing, saying something like, "you have a shine in your eyes, your movements are electric, and you seem very creative. Keep doing whatever you do!" But, when I see him stuck inside a cloud of his thoughts, I try to help him to connect with his body, by walking, exercising, dancing and singing, despite the excuses he is giving me for not doing it. As his energy spreads through his body, the shine in his eyes returns, he goes to his project very energetically, and very soon he is ready to present me his finished work.

The more serious issue about his secretiveness is that sometimes he tells me about major difficulties that he has faced a long time after the fact. He says he doesn't want to worry me. I've let him know I would prefer to be at his side so that he wouldn't be dealing with his problems alone, and he agrees to involve me, but then the next time the cycle continues. I have come to accept this is who he is, and I will never have the full picture of his activities and feelings.

I'm very verbal and emotionally expressive so from the beginning of our relationship my husband has seen how I share my thoughts and feelings with my friends and family. That was something new for him, as in his upbringing they didn't share thoughts and feelings openly. Over the years, he has started becoming more verbal and emotionally expressive – first with me, then with my family, then he started developing his own friends, which he didn't have before, and now sometimes he shares a bit with strangers. He still prefers to be alone, but he gives time and space for social life as well.

His pace is slower than mine in everything, but in fairness, I'm extremely speedy. This was a huge challenge early in our relationship, and when we would go out together, I would feel trapped like a lion in a cage. I had to be patient, and it was so difficult for me! "Are you ready to go?" "Yes, let's go!" And then, I would be waiting at least 30 minutes in front of the open door for him! After I learned the lesson of patience, I understood his rhythm, and instead of waiting, I now do a lot of things in between: I cook (1 hour), I clean the house (30 minutes), I do my nails (45 minutes) and so on...

Some of my close friends misunderstand my husband. He can be so filled with enthusiasm, and they congratulate me for my influence. The reality is that he becomes enthusiastic when he is under stress, and his mind starts running at extremely high speed. Very soon he becomes spasmodic and goes from one idea to another, without completing anything and without being satisfied by anything. When this happens, I encourage him to leave behind the narrow image in which he has framed himself. This helps him settle down, focus and apply his knowledge and skills for a good outcome.

Relating to me, there is another common misunderstanding among our friends…When I repeatedly avoid participating in social events, because I am working on a creative project, they accuse Demis saying he has made me anti-social and withdrawn. The reality is that I am not scattered, I am saving my energy. I strengthen my creativity, productivity and depth, and I feel more and more complete. And every day there is at least one thing that fascinates me that I am involved in.

I am very happy to live with an accommodating, quiet, low-profile, creative, helpful, kind, grounded, stable and supportive husband. He is a blessing, and I am grateful for him."

5:7 The Theory

5:7 When In Balance

The Investigator (5) and Enthusiast (7) share a strong mental connection, an insatiable curiosity and a strong desire for personal freedom and independence. These values form the foundation upon which their differences are energizing and balancing.

Investigator (5)s bring depth, focus, perseverance, discernment, self-reliance and an original, often eccentric sense of humor. They have sharp minds, insightful observations and curiosity, all things Enthusiast (7)s enjoy and appreciate. Rational and logical, they can be highly grounding for their Enthusiast (7). They model perseverance and show the Enthusiast (7) how to stick things out even in the face of obstacles.

Enthusiast (7)s offer positive thinking, spontaneity, boldness, a thirst for the new and a drive for fun that manifests in all different ways. Enthusiast (7)s seek adventure, and their minds are constantly on the hunt for the next new thing: windsurfing, travel to Malta, sewing classes, the latest issue of Home Design, an adventure race and so forth. They encourage their Investigator (5) to try new things, to be more social and to open up more. With a lively Enthusiast (7) at their side, social settings seem less daunting and because Investigator (5)s are naturally curious, they are often willing partners in their Enthusiast (7)'s quest for the new.

This dynamic is one in which frugality balances gluttony, and where both partners have permission to independently explore their interests. When in balance, this is a highly supportive, symbiotic and loving match.

5:7 The Downward Spiral

Both types deal with issues of anxiety, but they respond in different, and almost opposite ways. This threatens their connection and can create conflict. When Investigator (5)s start feeling anxious, they retreat and work hard to conserve their resources, including energy, time, money and so forth. To gain a feeling of stability, they cut ties with the outside world becoming more isolated, reclusive, irritable, cynical and private. This can be hard on their Enthusiast (7) who finds their partner shutdown, cold and hard to reach.

In contrast, Enthusiast (7)s head in the opposite direction in times of stress. To minimize anxiety and gain feelings of stability, Enthusiast (7)s become more energized and manic looking to their external environment to help quell their anxiety. They want distraction and can seek it in a variety of forms — parties, socializing, frenetic activity and so forth. They fill their schedule and stay on the go. Stillness and isolation feel threatening. With both partners heading in opposite directions, the downward spiral is triggered.

Investigator (5)s may feel threatened by the Enthusiast (7)'s stress response. They see their partner as out of control, unpredictable, escapist and juvenile. This lack of support triggers the Enthusiast (7) even more, and they become frustrated with their Investigator (5), wanting them to be more engaged, less reserved, less negative and more exciting. Both partners start to polarize, the Enthusiast (7) becoming more demanding and domineering, driving the Investigator (5) further into retreat. As anxiety grows, trust erodes making it difficult to find common ground from which to repair. The positions may become more polarized until there is little keeping this couple together, and the relationship collapses.

5:7 The Lighthouse
These two types head in opposite directions energetically when they are feeling anxious. Enthusiast (7)s engage more with their outside environment to lower their anxiety. Distraction is soothing to them. Investigator (5)s cut off from their outside environment to lower their anxiety. Isolation soothes them. Anxiety can feel overwhelming for both, so managing their anxiety and their reaction to anxiety is key to reversing any downward spiral that starts.

5:7 The Kundalini Yoga Connection
The Enthusiast (7) needs to strengthen their nervous system, so they don't act out their anxiety quite as manically. Anxious Enthusiast (7)s can be very demanding, and this can feel threatening to their Investigator (5) partner. Instead of relying on their external environment to feel stable, they can start to use internal tools like breathwork to gain feelings of stability. Kundalini Yoga kriyas and meditations to lower anxiety and to cultivate focus and stillness are helpful.

The Investigator (5) needs to stay engaged and share more of themselves, resisting the desire to cut off to feel stable. Strengthening the nervous system is key to staying engaged and resisting the urge to withdraw. Part of sharing themselves more includes becoming more verbal, particularly about the world of emotion. Kundalini Yoga kriyas and meditations to open the throat chakra, to lower anxiety and to cultivate feelings of abundance are helpful.

See the appendix for Investigator (5) and Enthusiast (7) recommended Kundalini Yoga kriyas and meditations.

5:8 Investigator (5) with Leader (8)

Ruby, Leader (8) married in a 14-year relationship with Abel, Investigator (5)

"I love that my husband is so deeply caring and affectionate. He has a creative soul that is not afraid to love deeply. He is extremely thoughtful and a great listener. He loves to help and support me. He makes me feel like a queen. My husband is very in touch with his emotions and emotionally mature. I remember the first time I got jealous that he was talking at length to an attractive woman – a woman who I could tell was interested in him. I said I was feeling jealous, and he calmly replied: "What can I do to make you feel better?" He didn't get defensive and instead focused on addressing the impact his interaction had on me, not his intention, which of course was innocent. What I also really appreciate is that he can set very clear boundaries and agrees to do something only if he really wants to do it.

TYPE FIVE INVESTIGATOR/OBSERVER

He doesn't have a mean bone in his body, and his sensitivity makes him very empathetic to understand where others are coming from.

I love the balance we have in our relationship and how well we complement each other. I'm in touch with my body and feel very powerful and in command of my physical presence. I love to use this power energetically in a protective role with my husband. He isn't intimidated by my anger and force and in fact, finds it attractive. I remember the first time I really unleashed my temper at someone else in front of him. Afterward, I asked if he thought it was sexy when I was assertive and aggressive. He smiled and nodded a definite yes. I don't scare him. He knows that I was a punk rocker and still have attitude and even though he was a self-proclaimed geek growing up, he appreciates and admires my rebelliousness. I can be rash and sometimes extreme. He calms me down and encourages me to consider a spectrum of options.

As it relates to challenges, we both have a sensitivity to rejection. I have seen when he feels rejected by friends and how much that hurts him, as he is always trying to be a very good friend to others. Between us, we have a deep bond and an intimate connection so fortunately, we haven't experienced the feeling of rejection between each other. If I do need more space, which I sometimes do, I'm able to ask for it in a way that does not offend him personally. He may be disappointed, but he understands that I have always been very independent and sometimes need time alone.

Because we're are a close, supportive team, the biggest life challenges, like wanting children but being unable to have them have actually brought us closer together. We have also been able to be there fully for each other during life crises such as the loss of a parent. He understands that I just need some space when I am sometimes stressed. He gives me that and sometimes a day or two away exploring new things by myself is the reboot I need. We are a team in the game of life, and we support each other to be our best."

5:8 The Theory

5:8 When In Balance

Investigator (5)s and Leader (8)s bring balancing but opposite traits to the relationship and can compensate for each other's blind spots. They protect each other, albeit in different ways, and as a team, they are more powerful than they are individually.

Leader (8)s have a big, direct, powerful energy. They are assertive, earthy and in touch with their own body. They can step easily into their power, and engagement in the world isn't something they shy away from. These traits are all on the growth path for Investigator (5)s, and they can learn a lot from observing their Leader (8) in action. The Leader (8) makes the Investigator (5) feel safe, secure and supported, all necessarily elements to allow Investigator (5)s to share more of themselves.

Conversely, Investigator (5)s are contained in their energy and calculated in their actions. They think deeply before they speak and act and naturally model self-restraint, control and moderation. They act as the wise sage, helping to reign in their Leader (8)'s more impulsive and at times destructive behavior. They demonstrate emotional calm and control and help their Leader (8) think more strategically about the impact of their actions.

This relationship is a blend of autonomy, respect, trust and deep bonding. Both partners are highly independent with a strong sense of personal boundaries. Their home serves as a shared foundation and in partnership, this can be a powerful, deep, effective and thoughtful pair with a dash of brilliance and a dash of brashness. When aligned, they make a powerful combination and an almost unbeatable team.

5:8 The Downward Spiral
This couple can run into trouble due to issues around trust, rejection and a natural tendency to isolate. With tightening defenses, both struggle with vulnerability choosing instead to disengage and become self-protective. This triggers the downward spiral.

In times of stress, the Investigator (5) withdraws to restore themselves. This can feel like rejection to the Leader (8) who responds by either withdrawing or confronting. If the Leader (8) confronts, the Investigator (5) retreats more, creating an ugly loop of increasing threats and increasing withdrawal. If the Leader (8) withdraws, communication breaks down. As both types are capable of denying pain and isolating, it can be difficult for this couple to repair.

5:8 The Lighthouse
Energetic differences can be the trigger for a downward spiral in this couple, so energy management and the ability to act, not react, are key. Leader (8) can access big, aggressive energy easily, and this intensifies an Investigator (5)'s sense of being overwhelmed. Both types need to strengthen their nervous system to relate to each other better.

5:8 The Kundalini Yoga Connection
Energetic balance and energy management are the keys to healing this relationship. The Leader (8) needs to manage their energy, so it doesn't feel as angry and aggressive to

others. They must learn to act and not to react. Kundalini Yoga kriyas and meditations to open the heart, to manage anger and to cultivate stillness are helpful.

Investigator (5)s need to stay engaged and resist the impulse to withdraw for security, as this triggers the Leader (8) even more, creating more aggressive energy. Strengthening the nervous system is helpful, as is any work to build the energetic field surrounding the body, the aura.

See the appendix for Investigator (5) and Leader (8) recommended Kundalini Yoga kriyas and meditations.

5:9 Investigator (5) with Peacemaker (9)

Anastasyia, Peacemaker (9) married in a 14-year relationship with Vladimir, Investigator (5)

"I really value my husband's open-mindedness, sharp-mindedness and resourcefulness. He is kind, trustworthy and willing to try hard for whatever seems worthy to him. I also love how he combines a breadth of knowledge with an acute ability to process information. And I admire his ability to inspire others and broaden their horizons.

A foundational element of our relationship is freedom for each of us to pursue our own interests independently, without feeling guilty or bitter towards each other. For example, one of my husband's main hobbies is caving, an activity that requires a lot of time away – sometimes up to a week away from home – often without the possibility of communication. We both know that we will miss each other, but we also know how good it is for him and that's what we focus on. When he comes back from these trips, he is really refreshed, and that is something that we can both benefit from. For me, it is very important to see my friends on my own from time to time, and my husband is very supportive and does whatever he can so that I can have this precious time with my friends. He is happy to see me happy, and that makes me even happier!

We view our time apart as an opportunity to do things that we wouldn't normally do if we were together, like dealing with items from our huge personal to-do lists or watching a movie that only one of us is interested in watching or ordering food from places that the other avoids and so on. Likewise, the common free time we have together is devoted to our common interests, which are quite many, many of which I've developed as a result of my husband's interests.

Like all couples, we have our challenges, though I feel fortunate that from my perspective, ours are relatively minor. We are both procrastinators, something that can make things quite difficult, especially when the quality of our everyday life is affected. Along with the accumulation of things to be done and decisions to be made, tension emanating from this procrastination and the accompanying unresolved issues builds, making us both edgy when we finally get to the point in which we must deal with the issues.

Initiative can be another sensitive spot. Even though my husband is very responsive whenever I ask something from him, it would be a relief to me if he took the initiative more often to do things on his own in the household or regarding the children's routine, without him expecting me to ask for his contribution each time. From his side, I know my wandering attention can be a challenge. It is very easy for my husband to tell when my attention is truly with him or not, even the times I might not realize that it isn't there. Our communication is good, so this hasn't ever threatened our relationship. We know that it can happen, we talk about it, and if I have overdone it to the point that he feels neglected, which sometimes does happen, I will set it as my priority to make it up to him.

Before meeting my husband, I idealized the men I fell in love with to the point that I lived almost the whole relationship in my imagination. After my husband and I became a couple, it was a turning point in my life, because it was the first time I entered a relationship with my eyes open, gradually falling in love with him for what he really was and not for what I imagined him to be. My heart and mind were in unison for the first time, whereas before logic seemed to be blocked out from the process. For the first time, I could also cope with the intensity of feelings I had. There was enthusiasm without the violent feelings, the suffering and all the craziness I had experienced before – emotions that in retrospect seem like I was thrown into them and enslaved by them – and that had exhausted me. There was a sense of calmness, progression and stability that worked on me therapeutically; it allowed me to realize what was going on inside of me, to appreciate it, enjoy it, welcome it and finally nurture it because I was into something that I really wanted and was good for me.

I feel very happy in my relationship and enjoy the certainty that our relationship is the most important thing in our lives. It is a mutual source of strength and joy, and we both have a strong will to tend and protect it."

5:9 The Theory

5:9 When In Balance

Freedom and independence to pursue their personal goals are foundational elements of the Investigator (5) and Peacemaker (9) partnership. Both are committed to each other's

TYPE FIVE **INVESTIGATOR/OBSERVER**

happiness and dedicated to the relationship itself. From this base, this couple has a mix of balancing and similar traits.

Investigator (5)s are insightful, observant, resourceful, calm, objective and trustworthy. Their thinking is rational, logical and methodical, and these traits are useful to their Peacemaker (9) whose thinking can be more circular and emotionally-clouded. Their ability to focus and stay present is balancing for the Peacemaker (9) whose attention is more distractible and prone to wandering. All these traits make the Investigator (5) very grounding for their Peacemaker (9).

Peacemaker (9)s are undemanding, understanding, accepting and nonjudgmental. They accept their partner's desire for independence and time alone without taking it personally. They bring a warmer touch and a greater focus on human connection, and this is very balancing for the Investigator (5) who tends to isolate and relate more from the world of facts and data. Peacemaker (9)s offer easy companionship and nurturing, traits that can be deeply healing to their Investigator (5).

5:9 The Downward Spiral

Issues around too much space, feelings of neglect and relationship inertia can trigger the downward spiral in this couple. Both types can operate independently, both can be distracted by their own pursuits and neither is overly eager to bring up thorny issues in the relationship. In this environment, interdependence suffers, and this couple can drift far apart without fully realizing it. Another potential trigger is if either partner puts their needs above the needs of the partnership. As both types are independent, it is important that they stay aligned with shared priorities.

A gradual awareness that their deeper needs are not being met may be the trigger for the downward spiral. With tightening defenses, Investigator (5)s isolate and Peacemaker (9)s withdraw and stonewall. As both raise their defensive gates, problems can go unaddressed, emotional wounds fester and tensions build, albeit a low simmering build rather than explosive expressions of frustration. The relationship may continue on this path for some time with more and more distance growing between the couple. Eventually, an outside event or an emotional outburst force the gap between this couple to be addressed.

5:9 The Lighthouse

The lack of a deep emotional connection and an emotional coolness are the roots of the downward spiral for this pair, so connecting from the heart is key to repairing the relationship. Both types can be avoidant about dealing with hard issues so finding a safe way to air grievances is important. In addition, finding ways to enjoy shared time is critical for this couple.

5:9 The Kundalini Yoga Connection

Staying present is important for both partners in this dynamic. Peacemaker (9)s must resist the urge to withdraw and avoid real issues. Investigator (5)s need to recognize and balance their drive to isolate. They need to work hard to stay connected.

Investigator (5)s need to connect with their heart and get their emotional energy moving. Engaging more deeply is easier with a strong nervous system. Kundalini Yoga kriyas and meditations for energy awareness, heart opening and to strengthen the nervous system are beneficial.

Peacemaker (9)s needs to connect with suppressed anger and burn it out. They need to stay actively engaged and actively present. Kundalini Yoga kriyas and meditations that bring them into their body are helpful, as well as practices that burn anger and open the heart.

See the appendix for Investigator (5) and Peacemaker (9) recommended Kundalini Yoga kriyas and meditations.

This book is a living document. We will be updating it periodically with new information. If you are or were in a relationship with an Investigator (5) and you would like to participate in the related relationship survey, please email me at lynn@lynnroulo.com.

Type Six
LOYALIST/ DOUBTER/SKEPTIC

(seeks security/avoids danger)

 ## Overview

Loyalist (6)s are typically responsible, reliable, trustworthy and value security and loyalty. The Loyalist (6) is the African gazelle of the Enneagram—scanning and on high alert for danger at all times. This person can quickly and easily identify what could be dangerous or problematic in a situation. They start preparing for that outcome. Loyalist (6)s align with the values of duty and loyalty and often feel responsible to step in during challenging situations. It can be difficult for the Loyalist (6) to believe in positive outcomes and more moderate scenarios.

Loyalist (6)s are gifted at identifying risks and dangers, particularly to anything that threatens their security. They can have an exaggerated sense of danger that makes it difficult for them to trust. In relationships, Loyalist (6)s seek security, stability and predictability. Partners typically value their Loyalist (6)'s loyalty, devotion, reliability, safety awareness, thoroughness and sense of honor and duty. Many partners also say their Loyalist (6) has a wonderful sense of humor and is playful. Their partners are challenged by their Loyalist (6)'s mistrust, suspicion, anxiety, indecision and overly-cautious behavior.

- **Attention Bias/Habit Of Attention:**

Their attention goes to potential danger and threats to security. They see hazards, pitfalls, risks and experience worst-case scenario thinking. They experience this thinking as vividly as a high-definition motion picture with the worst-case scenario unfolding before their eyes. Their attention moves away from more moderate potential outcomes or what could go right in a situation.

- **Emotional Style:**

Warm, engaging, guarded, cautious.

- **Communication Style:**

Friendly, polite, cautious, reserved, alert, precise, prepared.

- **Brings To The Relationship:**

Rational thinking, practical problem solving, an independent, undemanding nature, stable, loyal, curious, open-minded, kind.

- **Unique Strengths:**

Able to identify danger and risks, good at foreseeing and taking steps to avoid negative outcomes, highly loyal, highly dutiful.

- **Challenges:**

Hypervigilance, overly cautious, overly suspicious, negative, mistrusting, paranoid.

- **Stability And Security:**

"I feel stable when I have thoroughly addressed every potential risk and danger I see. I feel secure when you spend time helping me think through negative outcomes and when you reassure me about our relationship and other things that I worry about."

- **Instability And Insecurity:**

"I feel unstable when something I see as risky isn't addressed. I feel insecure when I don't know what to expect in the future."

- **Path Of Growth:**

Courage

Loyalist (6)s grow when they connect with and trust their inner guidance. They must stop looking for stability and security outside themselves.

- **Energy:**

Vigilant, anxious, warm, contained, penetrating, solid.

• **The Kundalini Yoga Connection:**
Loyalist (6)s have a strong connection with worst-case scenario thinking and can experience stress and anxiety as a result of these catastrophic thoughts. Projected future scenarios can feel as real as though the projected events are unfolding before their eyes. Because their thinking can be so anxious, Kundalini Yoga kriyas and meditations to bring them back to the present moment and to lower anxiety can be helpful.

The Loyalist (6) Subtypes

"Warmth" Self-Preservation Subtype:
The self-preservation Loyalist (6) expresses the drive for security through forming friendships and warm relationships. This is a person who strives to have no enemies and who wants to feel the warmth of a supportive environment. They seek a protective force, someone whom they can rely on for safety, stability and decision-making. To the outside world, this person looks very friendly, warm and pleasant. They are typically in an environment where someone else is making the decisions for them or acting as their protector. Internally, this person feels a great deal of doubt, insecurity and fear. The dependence on an outside "protector" can present almost like separation anxiety, and it can be challenging for this person to connect with their own inner guidance. They have the title "Warmth" because of their cultivation of warm relationships.

This is the Loyalist (6) who most seeks outside support and appears the most in need of protection. They can develop a deep dependency on their partner.

On the positive side, they are warm, loyal, supportive partners who tend to be in a good mood with a pleasant disposition.

On the less positive side, they struggle with self-doubt. They have a difficult time making independent decisions.

"Duty" Social Subtype:
The social Loyalist (6) expresses the drive for security by aligning with systems and guidelines of conduct. This is a person who finds safety in authority figures and systems (political, religious, family) and often has an underlying fear of disappointing the authority figure. This person often has a philosophical or intellectual way of thinking. They rely less on intuition and feelings and more on their mind. To the outside world, this is someone who is highly reliable, precise in their action and committed to doing the "right" thing. Unlike the

self-preservation Loyalist (6) who can look very insecure, the social Loyalist (6) can look almost too sure. Internally, this person is feeling a great deal of anxiety and insecurity. They feel most secure when things are in clear categories and can have a very hard time with ambiguity. They have the title "Duty" because of their sense of obligation and commitment and their feelings of duty and responsibility. Whereas the self-preservation Loyalist (6) seems warm to the outside world, this Loyalist (6) seems cool.

This is a person with a lot of anticipatory anxiety – they believe that things will go wrong. They often have an internal set of rules about how to stay safe, and they can get frustrated when the people in their intimate circle don't follow these rules.

On the positive side, these Loyalist (6)s are loyal, dutiful and gifted at anticipating and avoiding danger.

On the less positive side, they can become alarmist and ungrounded in reality due to projecting negative scenarios.

"Strength/Beauty" Intimate Subtype:
The intimate Loyalist (6) expresses the drive for security through cultivating an inner sense of strength. This Loyalist (6) wants to come at their fear from a position of power. They go against their fear by rushing at it. They are constantly on the lookout for danger, feeling like it is a dangerous world out there, and anyone could become a threat at any time. To the outside world, this person can look strong, powerful and intimidating. In women, this person looks polished and composed. However, this person is also usually inconsistent and can seem to change their mind and direction frequently. They can be strong, yet weak, decisive, yet indecisive, secure, yet insecure. They have the title "Strength/Beauty" because of their focus on using their power to diffuse their anxiety. Whereas the self-preservation Loyalist (6) is warm and the social Loyalist (6) is cool, the intimate Loyalist (6) is hot. These Loyalist (6)s are often highly protective of their intimate circle. They may appear reserved, stoic, critical and watchful, but internally, they may feel paranoid, as if ready to spring into defensive action at a moment's notice. On the positive side, these Loyalist (6)s are less openly anxious or self-doubting. They appear confident and in control. On the less positive side, their inner world is often quite different than their presentation, and they can struggle with anxiety and a great deal of inner conflict.

Loyalist (6)—Levels of Awareness

Loyalist (6) When Self-Aware
Loyalist (6)s trust their inner guidance and have faith and confidence in others. They successfully balance interdependence and independence. They exhibit strong leadership skills and are fair and courageous. They are balanced and assess risk thoroughly and accurately. Their genuineness and caring touches others. Loving, affectionate, endearing and appealing, they have trust, duty and reliability as core traits. Honest bonding and long-term relationships are essential. The Loyalist (6) is deeply supportive and dedicated to issues and people with which they are aligned. They are hard-working, self-sacrificing, cooperative and idealistic in their pursuit of creating a safer and more secure world.

Loyalist (6) With Tightening Defenses
The mental focus is very much on safety, security and stability. Vigilant and anticipatory of problems, they look outside themselves to alliances and systems to keep them safe. In the face of mounting anxiety, they become indecisive, suspicious, cautious, evasive and contradictory. They experience a lot of internal confusion, becoming highly reactive. Alternatively, they may become passive-aggressive as a way to avoid direct confrontation. Their actions become unpredictable, even to themselves. Blame enters the picture as a way of compensating for their own insecurities. The line between "us" and "them" may be drawn more clearly and more harshly. Their mind constantly scans for threats while their relationship with authority may take on a push-pull nature.

Loyalist (6) When Fixated
Anxious, erratic behavior is peppered with angry outbursts or deeply evasive strategies. Fearing they have jeopardized their security, they may become harshly self-critical with acute feelings of inferiority. Their thinking becomes extremely clouded as nothing feels safe and secure. They seek outside parties or systems to help them clarify their thinking and make decisions. They feel attacked by everyone and begin lashing out violently. Their extreme behavior begins to bring what they fear in terms of abandonment and a loss of security. They become deeply suspicious, even of their own inner circle. They become hysterical, self-destructive and hyper-anxious.

Keys If You Are In A Relationship With A Loyalist (6)

"New information can feel threatening to me so sometimes I'm not open to your new ideas."

Sarah, Loyalist (6)

"New information intimidates me because I know that once I learn something, I can't unlearn it. And if the information that I garner challenges my existing beliefs, I fear that might create an existential life crisis for me. So, I can be a "keep your head in the sand" kind of person."

Simon, Investigator (5) about his wife Mary, Loyalist (6)

"Mary has always been Anglican, and my explorations of other spiritual pathways like Eastern Orthodoxy and Buddhism are things she understands in me but places she would never dream of going herself. She finds my interest in the dark side of life difficult to comprehend. She doesn't understand my desire to watch TV shows with a lot of violence or the sex and violence I included in the novel I wrote. For me, I don't experience an exploration of the dark as problematic in and of itself. I overcome my fears by facing them. This is my healing. Running and avoiding doesn't work for me.

Some of my energy in writing comes from 'the dark side,' and I view this as healthy. I think there is always a fundamental optimism in my writing and in my worldview that might be bland and facile without the shadow element."

Loyalist (6)s feel stable when they have a set of beliefs they can rely on. Security is their top goal, and anything that may threaten their security may make them anxious. As such, they are not always eager to get new information that might create internal conflicts with the beliefs they rely on. Others might experience this as rigid thinking or a lack of curiosity, but it is more deeply rooted in anxiety.

If you are a Loyalist (6):
Become aware of your somatic reaction to new information. Does your body tense? Do you feel yourself contract? Notice when anxious thinking begins and start to address the root cause, your anxiety, rather than the surface cause of new information.

If you are with a Loyalist (6):
Understand that your partner might not be as open to new ideas and new information as you are. Respect this difference and don't try to force them to be exposed to all the things you want to explore.

 "If I don't fully trust you, don't take it personally."

Amelia, Enthusiast (7) about her husband Jan, Loyalist (6)

"After over 25 years together, despite the fact it isn't logical, he doesn't fully trust me. In earlier years, this used to make me really sad, but I have learned it isn't personal. Being in a relationship for such a long time is a great way to learn unconditional love. I love him irrespective of how much he is able to trust me."

Loyalist (6)s have a reality distortion around anything that they perceive as threatening to their security. For things that are important to them, this reality distortion is even more intense. Many Loyalist (6)s have trust issues with their partners that are not based on the behavior or character of their partner. The trust issues are based on the Loyalist (6)'s fear that a very important relationship might be at risk. This causes the Loyalist (6)'s mind to scan for danger and threats, even if objectively there is no basis for this distrust.

If you are a Loyalist (6):
Understand you have a blind spot here. Your mind may be interpreting information incorrectly. Try to balance your suspicious thinking with actual history with your partner. Try to allow for multiple scenarios of what could be happening instead of jumping to worst-case scenario assumptions.

If you are with a Loyalist (6):
Understand your partner has a blind spot and may not be interpreting the data correctly. Try to exercise patience and work with them to process through all potential areas of mistrust. Understand that this mistrust isn't personal, even if it feels like it is.

 "Please reassure me often."

Paulina, Loyalist (6)

"My mind is super anxious, and I think about the worst-case scenario a lot. Reassurance makes me feel relieved, calm and optimistic. It reminds me that what I think is not objective and helps me put my crazy-thinking mind to rest a bit, even if it is only for a bit, as this is a non-stop process.

When I'm in a relationship, I continually ask my partner to reassure me that everything will go well or that the worst-case scenario that is large in my mind will not materialize.

For example, when I leave the house, I am thinking "Have I left any electrical appliances on? Did my boyfriend check as well? The dogs are not in danger, are they?" I ask this while I have already left the balcony doors open for the dogs to jump – to eternity most probably – just in case my kitchen – where the last time I cooked was two years ago – takes the initiative to switch on by itself. In my mind, a huge fire will start from the hotplate that will destroy my house and, of course, kill my beloved dogs. With this in my mind, reassurance is what I need from my partner. I know my thinking is extreme, but it is my thinking nonetheless. When a calm voice reassures me the house is fine, the dogs are safe and the kitchen is secure, I feel better. In many cases, I also seek reassurance to ease my guilty conscience for something I did. My mind asks "Was this the best I could do? Could I have helped her more?" The same goes for the relationship itself of course, but this time I do not ask for reassurance. I need to have it without asking and in a practical way. So when my partner lets me know he thinks about me, expresses his love and interest by considering my needs, values my opinion and so forth, I feel reassured. If I don't get enough reassurance, I would most probably leave the relationship."

Loyalist (6)s spend a lot of mental energy focusing on what could go wrong. From that perspective, they then begin to look for matches to support their imagined negative outcomes. This tires them out and makes them anxious. In particular, they need reassurance around the relationship, and anything they are doing that is important and involves risk.

If you are a Loyalist (6):
Understand you need a lot of reassurance, and don't be afraid to ask for it. Since your mind naturally creates the worst-case scenario, you feel more balanced when outsiders give you positive messages. Try to recognize your reality distortion around risk and threats.

If you are with a Loyalist (6):
Reassurance from you goes a long way. Reminding them that the relationship is stable and committed helps them to be less anxious. Reassuring them that the risks they are taking in life are worthwhile is also very soothing to them. And helping them see the bigger picture can give them perspective, as they often get focused on potential negative outcomes for small details.

LOYALIST (6)
360 DEGREE REVIEW

The next section features the 360 degree review--partnership with a Loyalist (6) from the perspective of each of the nine types.

6:1 Loyalist (6) with Perfectionist (1)

Gabriela, Perfectionist (1) married in a 32-year relationship with Heinrich, Loyalist (6)

"Heinrich is reliable, a great listener and a gifted problem solver when he's engaged. He is ahead of his time and original in his thinking. He would have made a great inventor, but his self-doubt and risk aversion have held him back. When he creates a habit, it sticks. While it may take him a long time to change a habit, he doesn't go back once he does. He thinks rationally and is usually unswayed by his emotions. This provides a helpful balance for me as I tend to be more emotional.

In our relationship, we are both steadfast, faithful, loyal and have worked hard to build a solid foundation together. I may look more like the leader, as I am more decisive since I get to mental clarity quicker. And while I am more willing to make changes, we often return to my husband's plan when mine falls over... My husband is more deliberate and risk-averse, so collaborative decision making takes a long time, but we end up with solid results. Over the years, we've found ways to come together to use our differences as strengths.

While he's more social in casual environments, I'm the one who cultivates relationships with our adult children. We both work hard in different ways and struggle to relax in a deep and restorative way.

As it relates to issues, I am interested in outcomes, solving the problem, making progress and getting on to the next issue. This can be overwhelming and wearing on my husband who sees my list as never-ending. When we were younger, I felt my husband reacted to my drive for efficiency and perfection by spending long hours at work to avoid the situation. I now believe he was less avoidant of me than loyal to work requirements and providing for his growing family. He's at home more now, but he has great difficulty expressing or even identifying his feelings, so many difficult conversations never get off the ground.

I have to watch my judgmental drive. I can be condescending and feel superior to him because I am putting a lot of effort into my inner work, whereas he doesn't follow this path much. I also sometimes feel frustrated that much of the basic household maintenance, gardening, weeding and so forth, falls to me. Finding balance can be challenging.

We are at an interesting moment in our relationship. We see aging very differently. He is depressed about the physical changes taking place in his body. For me, that's just life and gives me an opportunity to go deeper to enjoy things so much more in later life. To him, it's as though youth has passed him by and left him unfulfilled.

I'm on a self-discovery journey that has been crucial to my mid-life path. He is not, nor does he have the same interest in this pursuit. He thinks doing what he has always done should work just fine. I see mid-life as an opportunity to do things differently. This difference between us is deeply disappointing to me. I feel as though I'm in the middle of a physical, emotional and spiritual housecleaning project, and he wants the house untouched.

That said, we've built a stable life together for 32 years. I'm deeply grateful for that and have significant hope for the future together."

6:1 The Theory

 ### 6:1 When In Balance
The Perfectionist (1) and Loyalist (6) have a blend of shared qualities and balancing differences. In a self-aware state, this can be a steadfast, stable, loyal and committed pair.

Both types have a strong work ethic and sense of duty and responsibility. This is a couple where work comes before play, decision-making is thorough and methodical, and practical

TYPE SIX LOYALIST/DOUBTER/SKEPTIC

issues may dominate the shared landscape. Foundational elements of trust, respect, fairness, reliability and stability are at the core of this relationship.

To the dynamic, the Perfectionist (1) brings precise thinking, decisiveness, order, logic, clear thought and efficiency. They are action-oriented and don't like to stay frozen in indecision. They have a mental framework to follow that gives them guidance, self-confidence and the ability to act with assurance. Their internal compass is strong, and when they act, they act with conviction.

Loyalist (6)s are more doubtful, insecure and indecisive. These qualities make them relatable and bring warmth, approachability, vulnerability and a more human touch to the dynamic. The Loyalist (6) brings an eye for potential pitfalls to the relationship and helps ensure security and safety. As they spend a lot of time considering all possible risks, their decision-making tends to be slow but reliable. This is something their Perfectionist (1) comes to value.

When self-aware and aligned, this is a committed, grounded, loving team.

6:1 The Downward Spiral

When in a fixated or unaware state, the stability and security that were hallmark of this couple become threatened. When Perfectionist (1)s tighten their defenses, they become more critical, rigid, harsh and close-minded. As Loyalist (6)s tighten their defenses, they become more negative, indecisive, insecure and frozen in worst-case scenario thinking. The Perfectionist (1) leans forward with criticism, and the Loyalist (6) pulls back to try to avoid their Perfectionist (1)'s attack.

Perfectionist (1)s have a keen sense of fairness and efficiency and when fixated, their thinking narrows. They may become critical of their Loyalist (6) or the relationship itself on any variety of topics ranging from household chores, life decisions, personal growth and so forth. This criticism, either direct or indirect, is very anxiety-provoking for the Loyalist (6) who begins to project a worst-case scenario. Contempt and criticism from the Perfectionist (1) and stonewalling and avoidance by the Loyalist (6) enter the picture. What the Loyalist (6) needs is reassurance, but if neither partner can break the momentum, reactivity intensifies with the Perfectionist (1) becoming increasingly critical, and the Loyalist (6) becoming increasingly insecure and indecisive. Stability erodes, and without of reversal of the momentum, the relationship becomes increasingly distant and may eventually end.

6:1 The Lighthouse

Opposite stress responses of the two types are at the base of the downward spiral, so learning to manage stress is a key to healing for this hard-working couple. Taking time out to relax, reconnect and feel expansive is important to help mend the relationship. Reconnecting at the heart level is also important as both types can be overwhelmed with anger and anxiety.

6:1 The Kundalini Yoga Connection

This couple needs to work hard to stay in balance. Loyalist (6)s experience more self-doubt, and Perfectionist (1)s can assume a leadership role in a way that stifles the development of their Loyalist (6) partner. The Perfectionist (1) must learn to leave things as they are. The Loyalist (6) must learn to find their own inner guidance.

For the Loyalist (6), Kundalini Yoga kriyas and meditations, particularly breathwork, to help manage anxiety are beneficial. Kundalini Yoga kriyas and meditations to strengthen the nervous system are also helpful, so they don't feel as overpowered by worst-case scenario thinking and as fearful of the future.

The Perfectionist (1) needs to burn out anger and irritation so they can drop some of their harshness and rigidity. Kundalini Yoga kriyas and meditations to burn anger are helpful. They should also strengthen their nervous system to help them resist the urge to correct things. They must learn stillness.

See the appendix for Perfectionist (1) and Loyalist (6) recommended Kundalini Yoga kriyas and meditations.

6:2 Loyalist (6) with Helper (2)

Sophia, Helper (2) married in a 12-year relationship with Frank, Loyalist (6)

"Some of the things I value the most are Frank's loyalty, dependability and emotional honesty. When I say dependable, I don't mean that he will show up to appointments on time, but more that I know he will be there for me through thick and thin. In my past relationships, I often had a fear that my partner might leave, but with Frank, I never have this concern. He is steadfastly loyal, and I can depend on him to be there always. Regarding emotional honesty, he never manipulates, and this too lets me relax.

Frank brings a light spirit and joy to my life. He knows how to tell a story, he is great with jokes, and he can always make me laugh and lighten me up when I'm getting too intense for my own good.

Like all couples, we have our difficult moments. Frank reacts poorly under pressure and can become paralyzed by it. And when he's stressed, he becomes very negative, his thinking gets cloudy, and he can't see solutions that are right in front of him. Early in our relationship, I would overreach with my attempts to help him, to solve the problems for him or to intervene in the situation. He'd become angry and resentful towards me, and I'd withdraw with my feelings hurt. It wasn't effective at all.

Over the 12 years we have been together, I've learned to offer suggestions and let him process the information on his own and at his own pace. We discuss the details as often as needed until he is ready to make a decision. Getting him to voice his concerns, keeping him from unraveling under pressure and waiting for him to make a decision have been some of my challenges in the relationship but with patience and communication, we've found our rhythm. I'm very happy with our relationship and feel positive about our future."

6:2 The Theory

6:2 When In Balance

The Helper (2) with the Loyalist (6) have foundational values of mutual support, dependability and deep caring. This is a kind, nurturing couple in which both partners know they can rely on each other. Stability, both at home, at work and in their community is important to them and something they actively cultivate. With this as the base, they have some balancing differences.

Helper (2)s seek positive human connections and are warm, generous and kind. Protective and observant of those they love, they offer their sometimes anxious and reactive Loyalist (6) sage advice and a more rational, objective perspective. Because of their high emotional intelligence, they can often understand the subtle undercurrents of a situation, and this is balancing for the Loyalist (6) who has more narrow, worst-case scenario thinking. They work hard to create a nurturing, loving, supportive environment, and this effort is noticed and appreciated by the Loyalist (6).

Loyalist (6)s are hardworking, diligent, reliable, responsible and committed. They have an eye for danger and work hard to make sure threats to the home and the relationship itself are minimized. Helper (2)s appreciate this is someone who they can depend on through thick and thin, and this helps relax the Helper (2)'s fear of abandonment. The Loyalist (6)s can be affectionate, playful, and humor may be an important element in this couple's dynamic.

Together this can be a sweet, steady, straightforward pair. They respect each other's values and share an easy enjoyment of each other's company. This relationship grows and deepens over time. Dependability and commitment are at the core of this couple, and they can share an enduring, enjoyable partnership.

6:2: The Downward Spiral

The anxiety response of these partners can be the trigger for the downward spiral. With tightening defenses, Loyalist (6)s freeze or become erratic, and Helper (2)s lean in to help. This creates an environment of confusion, resentment and misunderstanding. In times of stress, Loyalist (6)s become highly anxious, worried, panicky, suspicious and confused. Their thinking becomes circular and clouded leaving them unable to make clear, firm decisions.

As the Loyalist (6) freezes, the Helper (2) pushes to assist. Under stress with tightening defenses, they may become overly involved and domineering without realizing it. The Loyalist (6), prone to suspicion and anxiety, doesn't appreciate this behavior and the feeling they are being controlled. Resentment and confusion on both sides builds. The more the Helper (2) tries to get involved, the more the Loyalist (6) gets resentful. As the downward spiral gains momentum, there can be cycles of anxiety, anxious decision-making, resentment, apology, forgiveness and more anxiety.

The line between how much or how little the Helper (2) should get involved can be blurry and ever moving. Helper (2)s don't always understand that their efforts aren't appreciated, and with tightening defenses, Helper (2)s can become needy and demanding. The self-confidence of the Loyalist (6) can wax and wane with cycles of independence followed by neediness. The Loyalist (6)'s fears of being controlled are interwoven with the Helper (2)'s fears of rejection. Continuing downward, the Helper (2) can enter into a power struggle, threatening withdrawal if their partner doesn't change. With each cycle, the Helper (2) tries to come closer, and the Loyalist (6) tries to pull further away. If left unchecked, the downward momentum continues to build with exhausting cycles of dependency and rejection. Without a mechanism to break the momentum, the relationship suffers and may split.

6:2 The Lighthouse

Different responses to anxiety and fears of rejection are at the core of this couple's downward spiral. Loyalist (6)s worry about an uncertain future. Helper (2)s lean too far forward to try to become indispensable. To heal and break the downward momentum, both partners need to learn to become still and stay present in the face of anxiety and discomfort.

6:2 The Kundalini Yoga Connection

Helper (2)s need to manage their impulse to be overly involved in the lives of others and to get more in touch with their own needs. Kundalini Yoga kriyas that increase body awareness are helpful for Helper (2)s. Doing a yoga or meditation practice independently can be very beneficial to keep them focused on their own experience.

Loyalist (6)s need to manage their anxiety so their thinking becomes clear. Breathwork to change the body's response to stress and meditations to connect with inner guidance are a good first step. Kundalini Yoga kriyas and meditations to address anxiety and self-authority are beneficial.

See the appendix for Helper (2) and Loyalist (6) recommended Kundalini Yoga kriyas and meditations.

6:3 Loyalist (6) with the Achiever (3)

Raj, Achiever (3) in a 39-year relationship with Sangita, Loyalist (6)

"I love my wife's thoughtfulness, loyalty, diligence, care and her gift of helping to make things successful by anticipating the possible downside in a situation.

In our relationship, my wife teaches me about loyalty and diligence, and she extends my focus beyond our home and relationship. She reminds me of the importance of family, social causes and outside events.

One challenge we have is that she tends to place responsibility and duty over spontaneity and fun. I can get very enthusiastic about ideas of things we can experience together only to have her remind me of other commitments. This can take the wind out of my sails and be wearing.

That said, we've been together for over 39 years and have built a rich and full life together. I appreciate how she balances my strengths and brings care, thoughtfulness and family connection into my life."

Anita, Achiever (3) formerly in a relationship for less than a year with Coenraad, Loyalist (6)

"I admired Coenraad's gravitas, and I felt like with him, there was no need to show off. He went to the heart of the matter and the inner person. He was perceptive and could be very

discerning. He was an example of getting things done in a low-key way, working in a team of equally low-key people. He didn't need or want flash. Slow and steady was more his motto.

He was a good listener and offered me valuable input that went beyond the normal "work harder" or "be more sensitive" feedback. He read people well and could understand group dynamics in an insightful way. With him, I could slow down, drop my guard and just be in the present moment. I appreciated this tremendously.

While many things worked in the relationship, there were also many that didn't. We had basic lifestyle differences. He found it puzzling that I always had many things on my plate, with many friends and contacts in a variety of areas of life. He had a very small circle, and he preferred it that way. He found it exhausting that he would carefully select a place out of the way for dinner and suddenly, I would unexpectedly bump into someone I knew. When this happened, I would politely acknowledge the person since I was sensitive to the fact Coenraad and I were on a date. Still, I could tell this bothered him. He found these moments of interruption somewhat intrusive, irritating and inconvenient. His needs were more basic. He liked participating in team sports with the guys, something that held no interest for me. In the end, it felt as if we liked and respected each other, but our foundation lacked more than that. And those silos alone weren't enough for a healthy, sustainable relationship.

A major challenge for me was when he would go silent or disconnected in public. I was often left wondering if I did something wrong, but I rarely got a straight answer. He was selective in his answers to my direct questions. He considered some things very private and shared on a "need to know basis."

In the end, I learned that he had unresolved feelings towards an ex-girlfriend of his who he had seen over the summer when he went back to his country, South Africa, for a visit. This trip happened while he and I were together exclusively, so it stung to get this news. But I think deep down I knew he wasn't the love of my life and while it was a painful ending, the pain for me was mercifully brief. I have to admire his courage in throwing it all in with the ex-girlfriend, who he believed to be the love of his life. He eventually went on to try to commit to her, moving back to South Africa, despite some significant obstacles like the fact she was over 20 years older than him. I don't know that I have the guts to give it all up for love so, in the end, I raise a glass to him."

6:3 The Theory

 ### 6:3 When In Balance
This couple shares the values of hard work, discipline, determination and a drive for comfort and security. Both are willing to put in effort, energy and sacrifice to reach their targets. They share many fundamental values and have a high degree of respect and admiration for each other.

Achiever (3)s bring optimism, a can-do attitude and a sense of expansion and possibility. They present confidently to the outside world and communicate positively and easily with others. They give the relationship polish and a drive to be the best. With their relentless focus on success, their efforts go a long way in establishing practical comforts in this couple's shared life.

Loyalist (6)s offer reliability, caution, a strong sense of duty and responsibility and an eye for potential pitfalls. They remind their Achiever (3) to be more cautious and realistic and of the value of human relationships and connection with other people. With their collaborative, interpersonal approach, they can take the edge off their Achiever (3)'s competitive drive.

When in balance and connecting at the heart, this is a stable, supportive partnership. Both can be each other's best cheerleader, and they highly value the life they have built together.

 ### 6:3 The Downward Spiral
In the lower levels of awareness, these types can bring out the worst in each other.

Both partners share a competitive nature and when under stress, this may be directed towards each other. Both have the potential to be workaholics and to look outside themselves to feel secure and valuable. It is easy for them to lose their own internal compass and to get lost in the opinions and impressions of others. Both may avoid deep introspection, making it difficult for true motivations and desires to be discussed or even acknowledged.

Each type has a different stress response and can become irritated watching the other, thus triggering the downward spiral. Achiever (3)s see their Loyalist (6) as anxious, over-reactive and unnecessarily negative. They feel their Loyalist (6) is taking the wind from their sails, bringing them down and creating an unnecessarily pessimistic environment. The Loyalist (6) may grow weary at the relentless orientation towards goals of their Achiever (3). They may feel their partner is missing out on the truly important things in life and can grow frustrated with the Achiever (3)'s need to constantly achieve. They can also get irritated at their Achiever (3)'s desire to put a positive spin on everything, feeling this is disingenuous.

With tightening defenses, each feels their stability slip, and the downward spiral gains momentum. They may begin to lose respect for each other and become evasive and withdrawn. The relationship takes on a lifeless flavor as deeper, more meaningful issues are avoided, and both partners craft independent lives for themselves. Because both value security so highly, the relationship may continue, with the Achiever (3) presenting a mask to the world and the Loyalist (6) keeping quiet, afraid to rock the boat. The relationship may coast along in a stable yet zombie-like state until eventually some outside force enters the picture and exposes the truth. At that point, the partners are either forced to deal with previously repressed issues, or the relationship splits.

6:3 The Lighthouse
Differing responses to stress are usually the trigger for the downward spiral, and the fact the heart connection gets broken helps the downward spiral gain momentum. To break the momentum and begin to mend the relationship, both partners need to learn healthy ways to handle stress and anxiety. And to come back together, both partners need to learn to become still and speak from their heart.

6:3 The Kundalini Yoga Connection
Because both partners need to break their patterned reactions, Kundalini Yoga kriyas and meditations to strengthen the nervous system are beneficial to both.

Achiever (3)s need to get in touch with their deeper feelings and to learn to cultivate stillness. The drive to constantly achieve has a negative impact on their intimate relationships. Kundalini Yoga kriyas and meditations to cultivate stillness, to move from the head to the heart and a deepen the heart connection are helpful. Cultivating self-love is also important to help relax the drive for achievement.

Loyalist (6)s need to manage their anxiety and the accompanying worst-case scenario thinking. They need to relax their tendency to project into situations and quiet their overactive mind. Kundalini Yoga kriyas and meditations to lower anxiety, to manage stress and to cultivate a neutral mind are helpful.

See the appendix for Achiever (3) and Loyalist (6) recommended Kundalini Yoga kriyas and meditations.

6:4 Loyalist (6) with Individualist (4)

Emma, Individualist (4) in a 10-year relationship with Victor, Loyalist (6)

"I value that Victor is committed, responsible, a good provider and insightful. He makes sure our basic needs are met and sees things beneath the surface even though sometimes he can't express himself directly to me. He is dependable, and I trust he will always be there, though I sometimes question whether it is out of convenience or because of the kids.

Our relationship is a complicated one in that we have very different communications styles and different tolerances for change. In many ways, we trigger each other's insecurities.

I like to communicate a lot about my emotional world, but Victor doesn't share his vulnerabilities. Instead, he acts as if everything is fine and keeps stress hidden and repressed. Then his expressions come as random blowups and a loss of connection between us where I want to meet him on a deeper level. I am very sensitive to his energy. I get frustrated easily which turns into an angry tone and if provoked can go from anger to rage. When I try a different, calmer technique of communicating, he shuts down and communicates like everything I observe in our relationship is not true. So, our communication can be extremely challenging.

As it relates to the relationship dynamic, he falls more into the role of caretaker. I can be very needy because at home I get stressed and feel overwhelmed easily. He has had to step up as the decision-maker and guardian, and I worry that this has caused him to lose respect for me. It is hard for me to stand in my own power, to make decisions and to take the lead to help him feel reassured in his own role. At the same time, I feel like I am being held back due to so much responsibility that is expected of me and his need to keep me close. He doesn't like how I am growing professionally and really doesn't like that I have begun to travel. He uses passive-aggressiveness in a way that looks like I am the one holding myself back.

The topic of security and change is complicated in our relationship. Victor gives me security, but I feel like he's also holding me back with his insinuations every time I try to do something different to better myself or our situation. He is less comfortable with change than I am and, in fact, change triggers insecurities within him. He begins to guilt and shame me for wanting something new or different. Or, worse, he plays this passive-aggressive game where he plants seeds of doubt. As a recent example, I want to join the gym to help heal my back. He doesn't suggest I can't join the gym, but instead says I can stay home and do the exercises here and gives me suggestions on items I can use. It's true he doesn't directly tell me not to do things, but I can feel the energy behind every rejection of my ideas and attempts towards self-growth.

Another example of our complicated relationship with security is an issue he has with me traveling for work. He "reminds" me that anything could happen in the future which could cause me to regret taking this trip and to think about the consequences of going and how it will affect my relationship with the kids. He doesn't directly tell me I cannot go but instead tries to guilt me into not going. I can see how my leaving triggers all his fears. And as a further complication, his family questions my motives which causes him to be aloof with them and then rescind the initial support he gave me. It becomes a very thorny issue, and he becomes critical of what I am doing.

We're at a difficult period in the relationship, and these are the issues we are facing."

6:4 The Theory

6:4 When In Balance
Individualist (4)s and Loyalist (6)s share many common traits that make it easy for this couple to understand and support each other. Both take a somewhat defensive position about the world, trusting others reluctantly and easily imagining negative scenarios. Both can be emotionally intense, both have a deep-rooted fear of abandonment and both seek a stable, secure home. With this as the common foundation, this pair also has some striking differences.

Loyalist (6)s bring a focus on stability, security and predictability to the dynamic. They are dependable, loyal, committed, placing a high value on a select few relationships in their life. Their attention is constantly scanning for threats and as such, they help ensure the home front is guarded, protected and safe. These traits can all be soothing to the Individualist (4) who feels they have finally found a safe haven.

Individualist (4)s bring emotional fluency, creativity and inspiration to the dynamic. They help their Loyalist (6) get in touch with their deeper emotions and can bring out the nurturing instinct of the Loyalist (6).

This couple can develop a subconscious dependency on each other, with the Individualist (4) acting as the one in need of rescue and the Loyalist (6) as the rescuer. If the couple is able to maintain balance, this can be healing for both partners as the Individualist (4) finally feels seen and supported, and the Loyalist (6) feels needed and cherished.

TYPE SIX LOYALIST/DOUBTER/SKEPTIC

6:4 The Downward Spiral
Concerns with abandonment that can help to bring this couple together can also be the trigger for the downward spiral. With tightening defenses, both partners become reactive and trigger a toxic loop of mistrust. A fixated Loyalist (6) reacts by becoming more paranoid, more cautious and projecting more imagined outcomes into seemingly benign situations. They may start to question the motives of their Individualist (4) and try to control their behavior. This leaves the Individualist (4) feeling misunderstood and unseen, triggering their own scenario of emotional abandonment. Consciously or subconsciously, they may start to withhold affection, further threatening the sense of stability of the Loyalist (6).

As the downward spiral gains momentum, both partners start to focus on their complaints with the other. Individualist (4)s see the Loyalist (6) as overly cautious and emotionally shut down. Loyalist (6)s see the Individualist (4) as too impulsive, unreliable and unpredictable. With both types having emotional intensity, arguments can quickly escalate to overreactions and projections. If something doesn't break the downward spiral, the two partners polarize until one decides they have had enough and leaves the relationship.

6:4 The Lighthouse
This couple loses its way because of unaddressed issues around fear of abandonment and anxiety. These fears trigger anxiety that makes the Loyalist (6) feel unstable and insecure and make the Individualist (4) feel misunderstood and unseen. To break the downward spiral, both partners need to cultivate an inner sense of security, so they don't become overly dependent on the other.

6:4 The Kundalini Yoga Connection
Reactivity triggers the downward spiral for this couple, so learning to manage reactions and the energy of emotion is important to re-establish balance.

Individualist (4)s need to cultivate self-love, so they don't feel forced to seek it in their outside environment. Kundalini Yoga kriyas and meditations to cultivate self-love, release shame and mend a broken heart can be helpful.

Loyalist (6)s need tools to manage their anxiety so they can approach life feeling expansive instead of contracted. Kundalini Yoga kriyas and meditations to lower anxiety, for stability and to cultivate a neutral mind are helpful.

See the appendix for Individualist (4) and Loyalist (6) recommended Kundalini Yoga kriyas and meditations.

6:5 Loyalist (6) with the Investigator (5)

Margaret, Investigator (5) married in a 46-year relationship with Albert, Loyalist (6)

"I appreciate my husband's intuitive nature, his patience, kindness, his giftedness as a doctor, his tenacity and his single-mindedness. He is devoted, caring and loving towards me, and his attention keeps me from becoming too isolated, specifically in relationship to him. We trust each other and truly believe that our hearts and minds are in the same place. Part of the glue in our 46-year relationship is our commonly held belief in God and the underlying confidence that all will be well.

Mutual respect and admiration characterize our relationship. I appreciate his ability and talent as a doctor, and he appreciates my penetrating curiosity, my "out of the box" thinking and ability as a jack-of-all-trades.

We function well together as a team because our minds work so differently. His thinking is more narrow – he is an excellent problem solver in the medical field, but that ability seems to be locked up safely behind closed doors to be applied only to medical solutions. Albert relies on textbook answers to stave off his emotional responses and particularly his anxiety. I stay more emotionally detached and am less likely to bring emotional strings into a decision. This keeps my mind freer and allows me to be more openly curious and creative in my approach.

As it relates to differences, he relies on outside guidance much more than I do. This works well for him when there is a precedent, but he flounders in more ambiguous situations. A practical example is our son's struggles with addiction. There are no instruction books on how to be or what to do in such a deeply personal, emotionally charged situation. In fact, the successful strategies we have used in other situations are the exact opposite of what is effective with our son. We only know what doesn't work, not what does. I'm more willing to look at more unconventional methods of treatment, but this is a bigger stretch for Albert. Fortunately, he is receptive to my approach and doesn't think my ideas are useless or strange. He even steps up to handle the group work elements, which I appreciate as these are a total nightmare for me.

As it relates to our perspectives, he has a much greater sense of darkness and catastrophe than I do, calling himself a realist when I see him as more as a pessimist. He exercises worst-case scenario thinking. For example, we'll get to the airport hours before a flight to accommodate his anxious concerns. Interestingly, despite his focus on external calamity, he can be unable to talk about or even know his deep desires and the dark corners of his thoughts. This can be challenging for me, as I am clearer about these issues. And despite our long relationship, he still sometimes gets hurt by my deep need for time alone each day. He takes it personally when of course, it is not. This is just how I'm wired.

Learning the Enneagram has helped a lot in this regard, as it explains so much of our individual and combined behavior and helps to show we all have pre-programmed responses and reactions. This tool has also given me great hope, illustrating that we are not trapped in our personalities. Rather, we have a choice to be healthy or unhealthy within ourselves.

Overall, I'm very happy in my relationship. I love our shared values, our shared history and our shared life journey."

Corinna, Investigator (5) formerly in a 1-year relationship with Kenneth, Loyalist (6)

"I admire Kenneth for his caring and concern for others, his intuition and his tender heart. He could pay great attention to detail, focus and master a task when he wanted to. He is highly intelligent and understands complex ideas and complicated situations quickly. I appreciated his warmth, his outgoing personality and his engagement with the world. He is patient and a good listener so I felt heard in the relationship.

I admired all these traits but also saw the things that held him back. He would become trapped in his own fear and indecision. He was moody and a bit unpredictable – he could be super excited one hour and depressed the next. In the beginning, his mood swings left me feeling a bit uncertain and almost unsafe, but as I realized the moods passed quickly, I learned to be patient with his ups and downs. His pessimism could be intense, and he had an attitude that nothing was ever going to work out right. This was tiring. I too can be a pessimist, but he was much more extreme.

While our dynamic worked in many ways, we triggered each other too. My communication style can be harsh and blunt, and I would inadvertently hurt his feelings. I needed him to respond with equal strength, but his response was to withdraw. This made it hard for us to heal. I struggled to have patience with his unpredictable moods. His world is constantly shifting, and he doesn't know himself well. I'm even-keeled, so I didn't get swept into his emotional ups and downs, but I think he wanted someone who would feel along with him more, be glad with him in his joy and sad in the sorrow.

Ultimately, the relationship ended. He left because he said he wasn't happy without giving me further explanation. To me, happy is a feeling, not something I would base big decisions on, and I wish I had more closure.

In the balance, I can't say if we were a good pair or not, but I have deep respect for him as a person and appreciated many things about the relationship."

Simon, Investigator (5) married in a 40-year relationship with Mary, Loyalist (6)

"Mary is compassionate, caring and forgiving. She has a strong sense of ethics and dedication to overcoming injustice and helping the vulnerable, along with a wonderful sense of humor. She takes her Christian faith seriously in all its demands. She connects with nature and has a love of the earth, growing plants and exploring wild places and different countries.

In our relationship, I provide calm and detachment to balance Mary's occasional despair and exhaustion, while her intense idealism gets me motivated and shakes me out of my inertia or detachment. Our relationship began romantically and expanded into a relationship between colleagues, rather than the other way around. Luckily, we work well as a partnership, in the ministry together and also in life in general. Support and acceptance are foundational elements in our dynamic. She accepts all of me, even the parts that must seem strange or off-putting to her. We work as a team, and when life presents its challenges, we collaborate to overcome them.

We balance each other. There is often a point when Mary feels we're bound to fail, but I'll stay firm with my decisions, and my optimism is usually vindicated in the end. She helps ground me in the real world around practical matters with her sense of time and organization.

Our minds work differently. In practical matters, like planning services, holidays, finances and so forth, I tend to do the high-level overview - where we'll go on a holiday or a walk for example – while Mary attends to the smaller details of timing, what we need to take, who we need to ask to do what and so forth.

On more complex issues, Mary often feels tempted to give up earlier than I would. If we have a malfunctioning computer or some other item not working, I stay determined to explore options and stay focused on finding a practical solution. Usually, this thinking prevails, and we are able to solve the problem.

We've been together for 40 years so of course along the way, our way of relating to each other has grown and changed. There have been times when we have wanted different things in regards to intimacy. I am extremely curious and explorative, so my search for experimentation and my imagination for darkness have at times clashed with Mary's more orthodox needs. Her respect for authority has sometimes clashed with my tendency to rebel. But we have always found our way through these issues.

The times when my need to explore has gotten out of hand have been difficult on the relationship. Sometimes, especially in ministry, I have been frustrated by the moral and intellectual conventionality of the church, something Mary at times has seemed to embody. Generally, we reach a compromise between my angry urge to provoke, which I have learned can be counterproductive, and Mary's more peaceful approach. The reality is her desire to please authority is often superficial and conceals the fact that she often feels angrier with leaders than I am, but she sees no point in fighting. Knowing this has helped me calm down to a more cautious approach myself.

We've learned to respect our differences. Mary's expectation of catastrophe and sense of being overwhelmed by duties has often clashed with my optimism and 'it'll be all right' approach. I have learned to stay with her in her negative feelings rather than leaping in with solutions or condemning her confusion and 'lack of faith' – and sometimes I still forget.

Overall, I am very happy in my relationship. I have a compassionate, accepting partner at my side with whom I've shared a very big portion of this life's journey. And I feel immensely grateful for this."

6:5 The Theory

6:5 When In Balance

The Investigator (5) and the Loyalist (6) share an intellectual attraction, and mutual respect and admiration are at the foundation of this pair.

The Investigator (5) appreciates the patience, kindness, devotion and tenacity of their Loyalist (6). The more outwardly facing Loyalist (6) helps ensure their Investigator (5) doesn't get too isolated both socially and in the context of their relationship. This is healthy and helpful for the Investigator (5) who may start to place a higher value on personal relationships as a result of the influence of their partner.

The Loyalist (6) appreciates the intellectual intensity, the curiosity, creativity and the adventurous nature of their Investigator (5). The Investigator (5) mind is always at work solving problems, posing questions and experimenting. This is fascinating to the Loyalist (6) and can help widen their worldview. They also appreciate and admire the emotional calm of their Investigator (5) who seems unscathed by the ups and downs of life.

They function well as a team because their minds work so differently. The Loyalist (6) tends to think more narrowly, dedicated to tested and established methods. The Investigator (5) is more experimental and more creative in their approach. Together, they are well balanced to tackle life's challenges.

When they both truly believe their hearts and minds are in the same place, the trust between this pair is powerful, and they can share a lasting, fulfilling bond.

6:5 The Downward Spiral
The intellectual intensity that draws this couple together can also be what pulls this couple apart. They come at the world from very different perspectives, with the Investigator (5) on a continuous pursuit of new information and ideas and the Loyalist (6) more interested following and maintaining the agreed upon paradigms. This can be a source of frustration for both partners and may trigger the downward spiral.

With tightening defenses, both become more extreme. As the Investigator (5) explores new horizons, they may lose respect for their Loyalist (6), finding them close-minded, fearful and believing them to be intellectually inferior. Loyalist (6)s feel threatened by their Investigator (5)'s drive to question their fundamental worldviews. New information can feel destabilizing to the Loyalist (6), triggering an anxiety response. As the Loyalist (6) clings harder to their beliefs, the Investigator (5) pushes harder to question the status quo. Trust erodes and the belief that both have their hearts and minds in the same place may fall into question. Unless the momentum of the downward spiral can be broken, the relationship may end.

6:5 The Lighthouse
Intensifying anxiety and radically different interpretations of stability are the roots of the downward spiral for this couple. To heal, both types need to learn to manage their anxiety and accept core differences in each other. Investigator (5)s need to accommodate their Loyalist (6)'s potential discomfort with threats to their established way of thinking and living. And Loyalist (6)s need to accommodate their Investigator (5)'s quest for knowledge and their tendency to question the status quo.

6:5 The Kundalini Yoga Connection
The Investigator (5) needs to relate more from the heart and less from the head,

particularly when their Loyalist (6) is feeling insecure. Recognizing and honoring the energy of emotion can be a good initial practice. Kundalini Yoga kriyas and meditations to open the heart, strengthen the immune system and tune into the energy of emotion are beneficial. Strengthening the nervous system is also helpful to make their own anxiety feel less overwhelming and oppressive.

The Loyalist (6) benefits from strengthening their nervous system, so they don't feel as threatened by new information, particularly as this is a source of security for their Investigator (5). Loyalist (6)s also need to become more self-reliant in their quest for security. Kundalini Yoga kriyas and meditations to lower anxiety, cultivate self-reliance and quiet the mind are beneficial.

See the appendix for Investigator (5) and Loyalist (6) recommended Kundalini Yoga kriyas and meditations.

6:6 Loyalist (6) with Loyalist (6)

Monica, Loyalist (6) in a relationship for less than a year with Xavier, Loyalist (6)

"Xavier prided himself on being a good friend who would drop everything to help a friend in need. These were his strengths and ultimately made him a better friend than partner.

In our relationship, we had great communication – greater than in any relationship I have ever had. He was the person who seemed most interested in getting to know me and asking the most questions about who I was and why. I appreciated this about him.

While we had great communication, he was very reactive and would project imagined concerns into situations. He had commitment issues that got brought into our relationship. He would react to things that he imagined based on feeling suffocated, a bias that related to his past. I did not react well to these issues and would also blow up. Towards the end of the relationship, and ultimately even our friendship, it got to the point of him fluctuating between calling me names then telling me he was in love with me. He was confused and conflicted, unable to think clearly and separate reality from delusion."

6:6 The Theory

6:6 When In Balance
Two Loyalist (6)s share a unique bond as they both take a very defensive position about the

world and may feel like they have finally found someone who understands them. Because they feel understood, they drop some of their defenses faster than usual allowing them to share more of themselves with each other.

Both value trust, loyalty, commitment and dependability. When relaxed and expansive, both can be humorous, playful and affectionate. Both want to eliminate risks and uncertainty to create a stable foundation. They may strive to deeply understand each other, uncovering more and more layers of nuance and detail about each other's lives, motivations, psyche and so forth. Both naturally scan for danger and threats to their security, and much of this couple's focus can be in building together a safe fortress against an unpredictable outside world.

When trust is established and this couple is committed, there can be an intense loyalty that is almost unshakeable.

6:6 The Downward Spiral
While this relationship can be characterized by loyalty and trust, with tightening defenses it can also feature reactivity, projection, paranoia and suspicion. When fixated, the Loyalist (6) mind naturally gravitates to projected worst-case scenarios. One or both partners may have difficulty distinguishing reality from projection, and this triggers the downward spiral.

As thinking gets clouded, accusations and paranoia enter the picture. Both partners become more anxious and more reactive. Emotional confusion is added to the mix and this partnership's once loving container becomes a cauldron of anxiety, volatility, accusation, apology, suspicion and blame. As the downward spiral gains momentum, one or both partners lose their emotional stability. It can be hard to break the momentum of the downward spiral as so much of the core fear is based on imagined future events. Unless there is a mechanism to firmly root this relationship in the present moment, the downward spiral gains momentum. Once trust is lost, it is hard to keep this relationship together.

6:6 The Lighthouse
Fear of an uncertain future is what ultimately causes this relationship to unravel. For the relationship to repair, partners must become very present, manage their anxiety and connect again from the heart.

6:6 The Kundalini Yoga Connection
Because anxiety, doubt and projection undo this couple, trust, stillness and presence may bring them back together. Both partners must develop tools to manage their own

escalating anxiety and projection. With these tools, the tendency to assign blame and feel like a victim can be decreased. Kundalini Yoga kriyas and meditations to strengthen the nervous system, to lower anxiety and to cultivate self-reliance and trust are beneficial.

See the appendix for Loyalist (6) recommended Kundalini Yoga kriyas and meditations.

6:7 Loyalist (6) with Enthusiast (7)

Amelia, Enthusiast (7) married in a 26-year relationship with Jan, Loyalist (6)

"My husband is hilarious and playful with a razor-sharp and millisecond-quick wit. I love that he makes me laugh almost every day and that he is a good and solid man. He is extremely loyal, dependable and thoughtful. He brings wisdom; I can come to him with a problem, and his insights are wonderful. He models hospitality and generosity, which are not effortless or easy for me. He helps keep me grounded and reigns me in when I start getting too scattered with my many activities and projects.

In our relationship, we enjoy verbal sparring and do it all the time! We have silly or clever things we came up with years ago that we still use with each other. I feel secure in the relationship because he is wonderfully loyal. I never have to worry about him being unfaithful to me – I know in my bones it isn't in his character to cheat.

We've had to work on balancing his negative thinking and my unbridled enthusiasm. He is keenly aware of limitations and why things cannot be done whereas I'm more likely to believe all things are possible. I have an entrepreneurial spirit, I don't like limitations, and I have a higher risk tolerance, so we occasionally have uncomfortable moments... Every time I hand him the tax information for my fledgling business, which always shows losses, he freaks out a bit. This is despite the fact I'm using seed investment from an outside supporter.

His pessimistic side can seem extreme. He tends to catastrophize, so if our cat doesn't act quite right one day, she must have feline AIDS. A mysterious bug bite leads him to strip and disinfect all bedding and the mattress with bed bug spray. Before I knew the Enneagram, I would be insensitive about his worrying, telling him he's over-reacting and trying to talk him out of it or even expressing open disdain. Now that I understand that he can't help where his attention goes, and his experience is different from mine, I just schedule the vet appointment or help wash linens and don't say much. I try to be supportive because that's what he needs most at these times.

I've had to adjust to some of his ways. He can have low self-esteem which at times triggers depression, a situation that is really hard on both of us. He doesn't forgive easily and holds grudges a long time, and despite the fact it isn't logical, he doesn't fully trust me. In earlier years, this used to make me really sad, but I have learned it isn't personal. Being in a relationship for such a long time is a great way to learn unconditional love. I love him irrespective of how much he is able to trust me.

One of our quirks as a couple is that we almost never have resolution to an argument. We rarely argue, but when we do, we never get to "I'm sorry"' or "Oh, I can see your point of view." We just eventually come to a stalemate and move on.

While we understand each other well, I do wish he felt that some of my new projects and ideas are valid. He can be dismissive of them without really discerning that some are good ideas. And I wish he knew how sad it makes me when he takes it for granted that I'm resilient. He sometimes assumes he can be callous with me because, as he says, "You'll get over it."

Despite our normal relationship issues, my husband is precious to me. Ninety percent of our relationship is sweet, easy and life-giving. He is my greatest joy; I can't wait to get home from work to see his face and ask how his day went. And that's after more than a quarter-century of marriage! Through him, I've learned we all have flaws that we're trying to work out. It's been a non-stop lesson in letting go of ego and loving without cause. With him, I've found an amazing partner for this journey, and I'm extremely grateful he's my husband."

Isabella, Enthusiast (7) divorced, formerly in a relationship for 20-years with Carlos, Loyalist (6)

"Carlos is very dependable, hardworking, reliable and loyal. I appreciated his discipline, loyalty, intelligence, humor and fun. He balanced my tendency to be impulsive, and he kept me grounded. I knew he would never cheat on me or intentionally hurt me. I always trusted him and still trust him – it is his character to be trustworthy.

He was very good about preparing for a secure financial future. Because of his foresight and careful planning, we started college accounts for our four children when each was born; we made great investments, we have two homes and contributed annually to our IRAs.

While our marriage worked for many years, eventually our differences started to deepen. Carlos is very mental, spending a lot of time in his head and speaking from logic and reason *almost exclusively. He seems unable to speak from his heart, and I can count on one hand the number of times he was emotional, or we had a meaningful, heartfelt conversation. With his parents and me, he avoids difficult topics, stating simply "I don't want to talk about it." This stonewalling meant many important issues had no way to get aired and addressed. He is impatient with neediness and emotion.*

We socialize very differently. He has a core group of longtime friends and doesn't feel the need to expand his circle. He has developed very few meaningful relationships as an adult. I have an active social life, and I had the sense he felt threatened by that. His position was that any free time on weekends should be available to him. He would become irritated if I went out to do something independently.

In the last ten years, Carlos became more and more focused on work and less on me and our marriage. Apart from work, watching professional sports became his priority. He felt burdened if I asked him to help with household chores. He became irritated and easily frustrated if the kids and house were not in order when he came home from work.

Our home wasn't as loving as it could have been because he often assumes that others are not truthful or forthcoming. For example, he always thinks our teenage son is trying to dupe me and that I am a fool for believing what our son tells me. He can be critical when he doesn't agree with certain behavior or views. As this intensified, I felt bossed around and criticized, and the kids felt frustrated and angry, which was sad for me to watch.

As time passed, we continued to grow apart. He wasn't supportive of, and in fact seemed threatened by, my interest in yoga, spirituality, astrology and so forth. He didn't like that I was interested in things that he didn't trust or believe in. We stopped working as a team. He felt he worked harder, and his job was more important than mine, and therefore I should be responsible for all household chores, childcare and activities. If I had a conflict between kids and work, I had to figure it out on my own – he would rarely help me balance the two. I became resentful of the fact he was neither helpful nor supportive.

I began to feel more isolated and trapped. I often would not go out on the weekends or do things that I wanted to do because he asked me not to. I ended up staying at home a lot of the time to make him happy and then getting resentful and angry because I never had an opportunity to escape the family dynamic which I felt was imbalanced. Upon reflection, I should have advocated for myself harder, but I didn't. I was trying to make things work and keep the peace.

THE NINE KEYS

The relationship continued to deteriorate. From the very beginning of our relationship, he confessed his fear that I would cheat on him. Ironically this is what ended up happening and the reason our marriage ultimately ended. I felt trapped, ignored, judged and unliked in our marriage, and I went outside the marriage to feel loved again. When he found out I had cheated, he made certain demands, one of which was to give up a best friend who knew about the affair, and the other was to take a periodic lie detector test. I refused to agree to either, and he decided there was no way to save the relationship.

All of the building negative energy had really started to wear on the kids and me. When we separated, it was like we all took a sigh of relief. Now that he has his own place, he seems to be much more balanced and happier."

Emma, Enthusiast (7) married in a 19-year relationship with Frank, Loyalist (6)

"Frank is reliable with a practical perspective and a great sense of humor. He commits and sticks with things even when they are at their hardest. I appreciate that he is logical and willing to stretch outside his comfort zone. He can face his fears, and he takes leaps of faith.

He is patient with me and my never-ending ideas, knowing that most won't come to fruition. And when I actually do decide to follow through on something, he is fully supportive of that as well. He'll say, "I know you might die out there on the mountain, but if you do, you'll die happy. I trust you to make smart decisions when you're out there."

Our relationship is fun! We love to verbally spar and entertain ourselves through conversation. We balance each other. I usually generate the ideas, though he has some of his own. He is the more practical one, aware of all the requirements, needs and potential pitfalls we might face as we move forward with the plan. Because I don't tend to focus on the risks, I think he becomes even more nervous and alert to potential problems. He's the detail person while I am the big picture thinker. I'm grateful for this because if it weren't for him and his focus on the finer points, a lot might get forgotten or figured out at the last minute. His loyalty and reliability to take care of practical things have enhanced my life and my pushing him past his comfort zone has enhanced his.

As it relates to issues, like any couple we have our challenges. We can polarize around his fears and my aversion to his negativity. If I start to feel trapped by his worst-case scenario thinking, I pull away, which makes him more anxious and angry. Another trigger for me stems from his need for constant, ongoing reassurance from me that I love him. While I do love him deeply, this need can provoke my aversion to feeling controlled, like I have to say or do something against my will. I am very sensitive to feeling trapped or limited in any way.

Overall, I'm very happy in my relationship. Over 20 years, we've found ways to bridge our differences, and I appreciate having a loving, supportive spouse who sees many of the things that are blind spots for me."

6:7 The Theory

6:7 When In Balance
When understanding and accepting of their differences, the Loyalist (6) and the Enthusiast (7) can make a charming, successful and balancing couple. Both types are future-oriented, verbal and enjoy entertaining each other with colorful stories and lively debate. Their habit of attention points in opposite ways and when self-aware, they use this difference as an asset. The unbridled enthusiasm of the Enthusiast (7) and the cautious discernment of the Loyalist (6) balance each other with the Enthusiast (7)'s eyes looking up at the stars and the Loyalist (6)'s feet planted firmly on the ground.

The Loyalist (6) brings a cautious, methodical approach to life. They carefully plan and analyze potential future outcomes always with an eye for danger and pitfalls. They model commitment, discipline, reliability, loyalty, duty, realistic thinking and danger awareness. The Enthusiast (7) may come to rely on these traits and may feel even more emboldened to try new things with their Loyalist (6) at their side.

The Enthusiast (7) offers enthusiasm, expansive thinking, high spirits, a positive outlook, adventure and a constant source of new ideas. They can be decisive and action-oriented. As they aren't encumbered by a fear of failure, they model resilience and boldness, traits which are refreshing for the Loyalist (6) to witness.

This couple genuinely enjoys each other's company. They find their differences as points of intrigue and balance and offer steady, loyal support to each other. Their affection towards each other is observable, and this can be a sweet, charming and successful match.

6:7 The Downward Spiral
The radically different habits of attention of these two types can become a weakness in lower states of self-awareness. When unaccepting of their different worldviews, this couple starts to polarize, and the downward spiral is triggered.

Loyalist (6)s are focused on security and seek a safe, predictable future. Anxiety is often part of their daily experience and to reduce their anxiety, they take proactive steps to eliminate or minimize perceived threats to their security. They seek to keep their feet firmly grounded on the earth and their eyes scanning for what could go wrong.

Enthusiast (7)s look at the world differently. Their focus goes to trying new things, exploring the unknown and keeping an upbeat, positive attitude. They believe all things are possible and are not particularly interested in hearing about problems or limitations with their ideas and plans. They can be impatient, impulsive and avoidant. This avoidance triggers stress in the Loyalist (6), making them ratchet up their caution and concern about what could go wrong. The downward spiral gains momentum as the Enthusiast (7) sees their Loyalist (6) as negative, fearful and overly cautious. And in turn the Loyalist (6) sees their Enthusiast (7) as avoidant, escapist and dangerously unrealistic. Each polarizes further into their corner, triggering the other even more. Both may begin to doubt a happy future with the other as the relationship falters. Without a break in the downward momentum, the relationship may end.

6:7 The Lighthouse
The trigger for the downward spiral is anxiety, which both Enthusiast (7)s and Loyalist (6)s experience but react to differently. The Loyalist (6) tries to remove risk, and the Enthusiast (7) tries to remove limitations. Thus, to break the momentum of the downward spiral, both partners need to develop healthier coping mechanisms to manage their anxiety. Risk and limitations are both unavoidable aspects of life. Developing a healthy balance to risk and limitation by both partners helps this relationship.

6:7 The Kundalini Yoga Connection
The Loyalist (6) typically has a more direct relationship with their anxiety and can sometimes be so anxious that they need a powerful physical practice to quiet their mind. Kundalini Yoga kriyas and meditations to bring them out of their head and into their body are beneficial. Kundalini Yoga kriyas and meditations that incorporate breathwork to lower anxiety, to cultivate self-reliance and to develop trust are also helpful.

Enthusiast (7)s need to resist the urge to avoid the negative. They need to develop the ability to feel the full spectrum of human emotion. Kundalini Yoga kriyas and meditations to build the nervous system, enhance focus and lower anxiety are helpful.

See the appendix for Loyalist (6) and Enthusiast (7) recommended Kundalini Yoga kriyas and meditations.

6:8 Loyalist (6) with Leader (8)

Sophia, Leader (8) married in a 10-year relationship with Philip, Loyalist (6)

"I value my husband's devotion, loyalty, rational, clear thinking and his tenderness. He's not complicated, but complicated enough to be interesting and is always ready to talk about issues. I admire his spirit of protectiveness and the way he will fight for the underdog. He brings playfulness to the relationship which helps to balance my seriousness. Above all, he brings me love.

Our relationship felt solid from the very beginning, and I think this is because, at a fundamental level, there were no trust issues between us. We have a strong, deep and, thus far, long-lasting bond. We both feel the world is a highly unpredictable place and that we need to take care of each other and of our little family in the best possible way.

In our dynamic, he is more rational, cool-headed and analytical whereas my thinking can get clouded by emotion. Most of the time, he's the rock in our partnership. He is seldom overwhelmed by problems – even serious problems – so on the rare occasions he is overwhelmed, it worries me a lot. I value his steadiness.

We've had to learn to balance our different emotional styles – I'm more emotional, direct and don't hide my feelings as much. My husband is tougher to read. He is sensitive, caring and compassionate but doesn't show much of it except to a small circle of people to with whom he is close.

Deciding who is in charge has also been a challenge. We both lead, depending on the topic. But my natural tendency is to want to be the one in control, to set the tone and to make decisions. Philip doesn't necessarily let me do this and pushes back, sometimes in a very decisive way, which can drive me crazy – especially when I feel that he does that only to defy me, which happens from time to time. I have had to learn to back off and sometimes let him win just for the sake of peace. This can be frustrating sometimes, and in the past, this frustration has led me to question the relationship. Philip seems aware of this dynamic, and we work hard to keep it balanced. I sometimes wonder if he realizes the extent to which I compromise. That said, I admire and love the fact he has a strong personality. I wouldn't like to be with a weak, fearful person. I need to know we are both equal.

Energetically, we are a good match. Philip sometimes seems less active than me, but when he is into a project he loves, he won't stop unless he finishes it and finishes it perfectly.

He can be very focused and zealous, whereas I am generally more active but in a less passionate way.

Overall, I'm very happy in my relationship. I have a loyal, committed, stable husband who loves me and brings me joy."

Gail, Leader (8) (widowed) previously married for 54 years of a 57-year relationship with Tim, Loyalist (6)

We were together for 57 years, and we were a great team. Tim and I could achieve miracles when we were in sync. Our finest moment was probably the time we prevented a stadium fire and saved hundreds of lives. I was the one who noticed the burning above the stage. I alerted Tim and suggested we leave, giving management at the door notice on our way out. Tim would have none of it. His blue eyes flashed yellow, and then he strode off to find workers and directed them on how to extinguish the fire. By the time management discovered the issue, the fire was extinguished. They tried to thank my husband, but he didn't care about credit. He preferred to go quietly back to his seat to enjoy the show."

6:8 The Theory

6:8 When In Balance

The Loyalist (6) with the Leader (8) share a solid, enduring, supportive, loving partnership with a foundation built on trust, protectiveness and loyalty. Both can have a suspicious, skeptical view of the world and with each other, they can have an "us against the world" attitude. In partnership, they share many similar traits and a few key differences. High trust is a key attribute in this relationship, mainly because both partners have trust issues. Once trust between these two is established, they bond deeply. Both share the values of commitment, responsibility, duty and a willingness to work hard.

Loyalist (6)s bring playfulness, warmth, a sensitivity to the emotional world and an eye for danger. They are more deliberate and thoughtful in their actions offering helpful insights about potential consequences and pitfalls to their Leader (8).

Leader (8)s bring decisiveness, resilience, willpower, resourcefulness and determination. This can be inspiring to their Loyalist (6) who is more emboldened to leave their comfort zone with their Leader (8) at their side.

Together, this is a genuinely affectionate couple with strong chemistry and emotional

TYPE SIX LOYALIST/DOUBTER/SKEPTIC

intensity. With their base of trust, the connection between them has the potential to gradually grow and deepen.

6:8 The Downward Spiral
As trust is at the foundation of this couple, any fissures in trust can trigger the downward spiral for this couple. Both types are ready to believe the worst in others, and both can become extremely reactive. Because of the deep sensitivity to betrayal, fissures in trust may be real or imagined.

With tightening defenses, the phobic Loyalist (6) and Leader (8) head in different directions. The Leader (8) pushes and confronts to get to the bottom of the issue and to establish where they stand. This direct and powerful approach can trigger reactivity in the Loyalist (6) who projects a worst-case scenario outcome. As a protective measure, they retreat, further provoking the Leader (8). This cycle of attack and retreat can continue with increasing intensity until a truce is drawn or a line is crossed.

In the case of counterphobic Loyalist (6)s who behave like Leader (8)s when stressed, this cycle looks different. This couple may get into open conflict with both pushing the other to back down. The more the Leader (8) pushes, the more the counterphobic Loyalist (6) meets the attack. This cycle ends the same way, with increasing intensity until a truce is drawn or a line is crossed.

6:8 The Lighthouse
Power struggles and trust issues are what ultimately undo this couple, so reconnecting at the heart to allow for surrender and to rebuild trust are required to bring this couple back together. Both have powerful issues around control, trust and abandonment. These shared issues manifest very differently. Leader (8)s want control, so they aren't left feeling surprised and vulnerable. A breach of trust or a lack of control might trigger vulnerability for a Leader (8) which can feel almost on par with annihilation. Loyalist (6)s have an equally intense reaction to an unknown future. They want control so they can avoid risk. An unaddressed risk is extremely anxiety provoking for Loyalist (6)s.

6:8 The Kundalini Yoga Connection
Reactions due to anxiety and anger start the downward spiral in this pair so managing reactivity is key to reversing the momentum. Strengthening the nervous system for both partners is important in slowing down reactions.

Loyalist (6)s project negative thinking into an uncertain future. This causes an expectation for a worst-case scenario outcome. To counter this thinking, Loyalist (6)s need to actively cultivate an ability to stay present. Kundalini Yoga kriyas and meditations to lower anxiety, release fear and cultivate self-reliance are beneficial.

Leader (8)s quickly move from vulnerability to anger so managing the anger response is important. Leader (8)s grow when they understand the power of their vulnerability. Kundalini Yoga kriyas and meditations to burn out anger and to manage reactivity are helpful. Kundalini Yoga kriyas and meditations to connect with and open the heart are also beneficial.

See the appendix for Loyalist (6) and Leader (8) recommended Kundalini Yoga kriyas and meditations.

6:9 Loyalist (6) with Peacemaker (9)

Cynthia, Peacemaker (9) divorced, formerly in a 25-year relationship with Douglas, Loyalist (6)

"Douglas was tremendously supportive and was great at identifying risks, mulling over details and steering us away from potential pitfalls. Much of our 25-year relationship was characterized by stability and a balance of autonomy and teamwork. For example, Douglas insisted on separate bank accounts, and he kept a running ledger to balance who owed whom until we had children, and I stopped working. We did a lot of home renovations throughout our relationship, and when it came to making decisions, it was very much a team effort. In general, we didn't purchase anything without a deliberate discussion – he was always the devil's advocate. I appreciated his input as I usually didn't delve too deeply into details and potential risks when making a decision. I think his analysis slowed us down a bit, but we ultimately made good decisions. We built a pretty conventional life together with two kids in a suburban neighborhood with our stable 9 to 5 jobs. At the same time, we both had an entrepreneurial bent that, aside from a number of home renovations, didn't become realized until I took over the family business.

While we are conventional in most respects, every now and then we'd do something a little out of the mainstream. When we rebuilt our last house, we created a very modern structure that looked starkly different from the other houses in the neighborhood. I was quite nervous about taking such a daring step, but it actually turned out really well.

Our marriage worked smoothly for many years, but things changed when I took on the role

TYPE SIX LOYALIST/DOUBTER/SKEPTIC

of Chairman of the Board of my family business when my parents passed away. I tend to be a leader, but I need someone to have my back and to reassure me that I'm on the right track. Douglas acted in this capacity, and in my first few months in this role, he was supportive as he coached me on how to behave, where to draw boundaries, who I could trust and so forth. He knew a lot about the company culture, had strong opinions about what was and was not working in the company and in the early stage of my role, he gave good insight. And because I had a need to please him, I would generally follow his advice. He had a great fear of assuming any responsibility, so this power dynamic worked well.

As time wore on, his anxiety around the business grew. Douglas was terrified of the responsibility I had taken on, and he would keep me up at night with his paranoia. He imagined that my perfectly healthy company was going to go bankrupt at any moment. He would obsess for hours on end, driving me crazy with his lecturing on all the possible worst-case scenarios. It was extreme. I wish he had understood I really wanted constructive criticism, but the relentless stream of negative feedback was counterproductive. At a certain point, I just stopped listening...Like any company, there were issues, but I felt I had things under control and just wanted to shut him out and go to sleep. At one point, I got so frustrated that I threw the alarm clock across the room – breaking it – because I couldn't turn him off.

It was hard to separate work from family life, and he would constantly bring up business issues during family time. And for my part, I felt conflicted because, as Chairman, I thought I should be taking the input whenever and wherever I got it.

Eventually, during my job as Chairman, his worst fears started to come true. The company took an operational dive, headed in the wrong direction, and it became clear we had the wrong person managing it. At this point Douglas really became unhinged and became so paranoid and unstable, he couldn't function properly. In an effort to keep things together, I listened too much to his advice and even took some rather irrational actions myself that didn't help the situation. I spent a lot of energy managing his moods and trying to keep Douglas happy. As the relationship continued to deteriorate, Douglas started to drink quite heavily and became verbally abusive. As a final straw, he then decided to retire based on my earnings. I came to realize that I was shouldering the burden of responsibility for the kids, the house, the business, our lives – in short, everything. I held on far too long, trying to keep the marriage, the company and the family together. In the end, it was not possible.

During our divorce, it was extremely challenging to deal with Douglas as he would not take any responsibility for anything. Indeed, he made it very clear that I had a "responsibility" to support him for the rest of his life although he was never able to come up with a reasonable argument for this as there was none.

Coming to terms with the fact that we needed to divorce was one of the hardest things I've ever done. But I began to see that the alternative would be enormously detrimental to my health on top of everything else. This was 15 years ago, and I now see the situation much more clearly."

David, Peacemaker (9) married in an 8-year relationship with Monique, Loyalist (6)

"I value my wife's constant drive to make our marriage, our home and our lives better. To her, better means safer, more secure and more confident. She's action-oriented with energy and drive and just the pursuit of this security seems to make her more confident and assured. And I enjoy getting swept along for the ride.

I love the balance we have together. Our relationship is like a kite tied to an anchor. I'm the anchor – I would never move without energy and input from the kite. She's the kite, and without an anchor, she might drift away into the wide-open sky. I offer her support and total acceptance, both of which come easily to me. When we were discussing getting married, she was concerned that she might grow into a person I wouldn't like, drifting away from me or becoming too rebellious for me. My promise to her was that I would always accept who she was and who she would become. This was an easy promise for me as it is my character to be nonjudgemental and accepting. It is who I am and probably the best gift I can offer my wife – a safe haven.

I've learned she needs a lot of reassurance. Eight years later, she continues to look to me for approval that what she's doing, saying things like "What if you don't like who I become? I don't want us to grow apart. I'm scared you'll just wake up and realize that you don't like me anymore."

In our relationship, we have to stay alert for inertia. We both have a big capacity to get comfortable. For me, it is a type of lethargy, and for her, it is not wanting to stray from the safety of the known. We've gotten into ruts in the past, almost living just as roommates and not really being truly connected. One particular time, she got fed up with the emotional distance and confronted me. Our relationship must have gotten to the point where she no longer felt safe and that I had drifted too far. I am very susceptible to drift, and her confrontation was enough to jostle me out of my own funk and refocus on our relationship. She brings balance this way.

My biggest struggle in our relationship isn't actually about her at all but about me getting the time I need to decompress. I am naturally an introvert, and with my personality, I focus on the needs of the group when I'm in one. This leaves me drained, and I need time to recharge. My wife feels a strong connection to her family who lives very close to us. She spends a lot of time with her mom and siblings, maintaining her relationships and cultivating the extended family. I have trouble being around her family for long periods of time. For me, they're loud and frequently chaotic, and it drains me. We've had to work on how to balance out my need for personal time and her need for community. Our solution has been to change the expectation, so no one expects me to be at all family events. Her family knows and understands that I am the quietest, and they accept me doing my own thing. They just carry on.

Overall, I am very happy in our relationship. I love the way my wife pushes me and brings new ideas and perspectives to my life. And I am happy I can provide her the safe haven she seeks."

6:9 The Theory

6:9 When In Balance

The Loyalist (6) with the Peacemaker (9) build a relationship based on stability and a healthy mix of autonomy and teamwork. Both share a desire for a predictable, secure life centered on a committed relationship. Family, work life and routine take priority over adventure and risk-taking, and this couple share a fairly conventional life together.

The Loyalist (6) brings loyalty, curiosity, energy, and a drive to guard, protect and improve their environment and the relationship itself. Mentally active and vigilant, Loyalist (6)s can be endearing in their insecurity. They bring a warmth and a playfulness to the dynamic. Because they can be insecure and unsure of themselves, they make the Peacemaker (9) feel needed. Peacemaker (9)s readily step into this role, feeling they can offer their Loyalist (6) the unconditional acceptance they crave.

The Peacemaker (9) brings steadiness, commitment, nonjudgment, tolerance and a drive for peace and harmony. These traits are stabilizing and deeply healing for the Loyalist (6) who tends towards anxious thinking and who fears abandonment. Peacemaker (9)s are calm, grounded and collaborative but with a need for independence. This couple might be very tightly enmeshed in certain area of their lives but also have a great deal of autonomy in others.

Together, this is a balancing pair with the Peacemaker (9) offering the solid foundation and the Loyalist (6) bringing energy and vitality to the mix. This is a caring, committed couple who have a great deal of admiration for each other.

6:9 The Downward Spiral

There are several potential triggers for the downward spiral in this relationship. Inertia can be a factor as both partners are reluctant to question the status quo. The relationship can get rote and routine to the point where emotional connection suffers, and true intimacy is lost. Unfulfilling jobs may be maintained, dysfunctional financial situations continue and thorny problems go unaddressed far longer than they would with other couples. The relationship may march along but neither partner is truly happy, and there is a lack of alignment on future goals. Stalemates and unaired issues litter the environment threatening the core of the relationship.

Alternatively, differing stress responses can be a trigger. With tightening defenses, Loyalist (6)s become more anxious and more catastrophic in their thinking. If this is directed at their partner, the Peacemaker (9) reacts by withdrawing, shutting down or stonewalling. This further triggers the Loyalist (6) who becomes more reactive, demanding and hysterical. As the downward spiral gains momentum, both partners polarize into their corners without a clear path to reconciliation or healing. Without a break in the momentum, the relationship is at risk.

6:9 The Lighthouse

Issue avoidance, at a very deep level, and resistance to change can be the beginning of the downward spiral for this couple. Contrary to their nature, both partners need to work hard to stay alert to inertia and from the tendency to retreat from important issues. As this can be anxiety provoking for both, tools and techniques to lower anxiety are helpful. This couple also needs to periodically take time out to reconnect and reestablish life priorities. It can be easy for this couple to drift and not realize they are off course until they are very far off course.

6:9 The Kundalini Yoga Connection

Strengthening the nervous system helps both partners stay present and connected even in the face of uncomfortable conversations or situations. Connecting deeply to their body helps both partners get back in touch with their intuition and their sense of themselves.

Loyalist (6)s need to learn to manage their anxious thinking, which ultimately clouds their judgment. Anxious thinking leads to contraction so they cut off from the somatic information that would otherwise be useful. Loyalist (6)s have strong, useful instincts, but these can get lost in the face of anxiety. At an energetic level, they may lose touch with their inner guide and the voice of their soul as their mind and ego take over. Kundalini Yoga kriyas and meditations to release fear, to lower anxiety, to cultivate self-reliance and to develop trust are helpful.

Peacemaker (9)s energetically numb out as a strategy to avoid conflict. Despite the fact Peacemaker (9)s can be extremely powerful, they subconsciously cut off from their power as a mechanism to avoid the discomfort it would involve to step into it. Peacemakers (9)s need to wake up to their anger and discontent and learn healthier ways to engage in conflict. They need to get clear about their own ambitions, dreams and desires. Kundalini Yoga kriyas and meditations to build the navel center (third chakra), to help them energetically wake up and to burn anger are helpful. Kundalini Yoga kriyas and meditations to build inner fire and resolve are also helpful.

See Appendix for for Loyalist (6) and Peacemaker (9) recomended Kundalini Yoga kriyas and meditations.

This book is a living document. We will be updating it periodically with new information. If you are or were in a relationship with a Loyalist (6) and you would like to participate in the related relationship survey, please email me at lynn@lynnroulo.com

Type Seven
ENTHUSIAST/ ADVENTURER

(seeks positive/avoids negative)

 Overview

Enthusiast (7)s are typically energetic, lively, adventurous and optimistic. These are the experience junkies of the Enneagram – curious, positive and often bold, they are drawn to try almost anything they haven't done before. This person has a very easy time imagining what could go right and what could be amazing. They may have a very difficult time imagining what could go wrong. They frequently underestimate danger and sometimes get themselves into difficult situations because of this attention bias. Lack of focus and discernment are often themes for Enthusiast (7)s. Their attention moves away from negative emotions. Enthusiast (7)s typically don't like rules and limitations. Personal freedom is a big priority. They have a mental fixation around planning.

In intimate relationships, Enthusiast (7)s can be slow to commit, but once they do, they are typically quite committed. Partners appreciate that their Enthusiast (7) is upbeat, high-energy, positive, adventurous and resilient. Their mind naturally gravitates to the positive, and their cheerful energy can be uplifting for others.

Partners report they are challenged by their Enthusiast (7)'s relentless pace, their scattered attention, their lack of attention to detail, their avoidance of negative emotions and difficult situations and their compulsive reframe to the positive.

- **Attention Bias/Habit Of Attention:**

Their attention goes to what is positive, what is new and what could be fun. They seek uplifting, enjoyable experiences, freedom and multiple options. Their attention moves away from the negative, and they have a strong resistance to rules and limitations. Their fear is to be trapped in pain. They have a mental fixation around planning and imagining a better future.

- **Emotional Style:**

Positive, happy, grateful, demanding, avoidant.

- **Communication Style:**

Playful, rapid, positive, joyous, spontaneous, scattered, gregarious, talkative, imaginary, associative, exaggerated.

- **Brings To The Relationship:**

Fun, joy, new experiences, adventure, gratitude, positive attitude, resilience.

- **Unique Strengths:**

Gratitude and joy. Enthusiasts (7) can feel and share a deep, genuine gratitude for life and everything in it. Positive thinking comes naturally to them.

- **Challenges:**

Enthusiast (7)s often flee from difficulty. They can be self-referencing, scattered, hedonistic and impatient. Enthusiast (7)s can be avoidant without being fully conscious of their avoidance.

- **Stability And Security:**

"I feel stable when I have a lot of options, flexibility and personal freedom to pursue my interests. I feel secure when I have a full schedule of enjoyable activities."

- **Instability And Insecurity:**

"I feel unstable when I am trapped, limited in my options and when I don't have personal freedom. I feel insecure when I need to sit with and experience negative emotions. My instability and insecurity often manifest as anxiety and a drive to stay on the go."

- **Path Of Growth:**

Discernment/Sobriety

Enthusiasts (7) grow when they learn to distinguish what really makes them happy and fulfilled and what is just new and novel. They also must learn to process pain and negative emotions. They grow when they moderate their drive for more.

- **Energy:**
High, restless, scattered, buoyant, zany.

- **The Kundalini Yoga Connection:**
Enthusiast (7)s have high amounts of energy, and energy containment can be an issue for them. Their energy gets diffused and unfocused as their attention scans for the new and the positive. They can have classic "monkey mind" with their thoughts quickly moving from topic to topic like a monkey swinging from branch to branch. Kundalini Yoga kriyas and meditations that require full focus and that promote energy containment can be beneficial.

The Enthusiast (7) Subtypes

"Keeper of the Castle" Self-Preservation Subtype:
The self-preservation Enthusiast (7) expresses gluttony and a drive for new experiences by finding opportunities to leverage and expand their network. This is a person who typically has a large circle of friends and contacts and acts as a connector or influencer to leverage this circle. Earthy, practical, driven and sometimes self-interested, this Enthusiast (7) is often professionally accomplished and successful. This person has the title "Keeper of the Castle" because of their cultivation of a gang or self-created family, within which they occupy a key role.

This is the least commitment-phobic of the Enthusiast (7)s. They view close relationships and committed participation in groups as an investment, giving them access to resources, social capital and so forth should the need arise. While emotional, they can be disconnected from their true emotions and tend to be more practical, materialistic, transactional and rebellious than the other two Enthusiast (7) subtypes.

On the positive side, these are Enthusiast (7)s who may commit to a partner with relative ease. They are gregarious, popular people with a talent for getting things done, knowing the right people and making things happen. They may become indispensable in their social circle. This is the person whom others go to for help, and the self-preservation Enthusiast (7) may like that others depend on them.

On the less positive side, there is an element of self-interest to most of these transactions that may be subconscious to the Enthusiast (7)s themselves. Their mind automatically seeks and measures opportunities, and they may use people without being consciously aware of it.

"Sacrifice" Social Subtype:

The social Enthusiast (7) counters gluttony and a drive for new experiences by consciously trying to control their urge for more. This is a person who often puts the needs of others ahead of their own needs and may focus their energy into a social cause or support of the family. Generous, idealistic, active and often naive, this type has the title "Sacrifice" because of their tendency to subvert their own desires for the greater good.

Idealism is a foundational trait of the social Enthusiast (7). This idealism manifests in relationships as a quest for pure, true romantic love, and there can be an air of innocence around this Enthusiast (7). They seek admiration from others more than the other two Enthusiast (7)s, and they tend to be very active, taking their idealism and manifesting it in a way that is practical, useful and often beneficial to others. They can resemble the Helper (2) in their sacrifice and focus on benefiting outsiders, but unlike the Helper (2), the social Enthusiast (7) is self-referencing and remains in touch with their own needs, even if they choose to sacrifice them for the greater good.

On the positive side, these are inspiring Enthusiast (7)s who can imagine a better, healthier, more peaceful world in a visionary way. They inspire through enthusiasm and are typically gifted with good social skills. There can be a certain purity about them.

On the less positive side, this Enthusiast (7) can have an intense need for admiration and recognition. They can be idealistic in their intimate relationships and may subconsciously create a hierarchy of virtue with them at the top.

"Fascination" Intimate Subtype:

The intimate Enthusiast (7) expresses gluttony and a drive for new experiences by embellishing reality to see it as much more positive and vivid than it actually is. Their mind overemphasizes the positive data leaving this Enthusiast (7) "trapped in sunshine." This is a person who genuinely experiences the world as an amazing place filled with endless potential for positive experiences and encounters. Less grounded than the other Enthusiast (7)s, this person is more interested in things of a higher world, the metaphysical, intellectual or philosophical. They have the title "Fascination" because they experience the world with intense fascination and enthusiasm.

This Enthusiast (7) can have issues around idealizing their partner and significant people in their lives. They may have blind spots around the negative traits of those close to them and can stay in unhealthy relationships longer than expected for a person who values feeling good and avoiding pain. It can be as though they try to stay above dark, thorny issues as a way of escaping pain. This thinking extends beyond relationships. This Enthusiast (7) may have a feeling that they can do everything and that the world is their oyster. The strategy works fine until that unfortunate intersection with reality which can be extremely shocking and confusing for the intimate Enthusiast (7).

On the positive side, the intimate Enthusiast (7) experiences the world as a beautiful and amazing place, filled with positive experiences just waiting to unfold. They naturally and easily see the best in others, including their intimate relationships. Their suggestibility can influence and inspire others in positive ways.

On the less positive side, the reality distortion of this Enthusiast (7) can be extreme. They can miss red flags in their relationships. They live more in their minds than on the earthly plane and can have an unrealistically idealized vision of love.

Enthusiast (7)—Levels of Awareness

Enthusiast (7) When Self-Aware
Enthusiast (7)s experience and express deep gratitude for life and what life offers them. They feel profound appreciation, awe and delight in simple things and share this positive energy easily with others. These Enthusiast (7)s are naturally uplifting in a deep and sustainable way. Their gratitude is rooted in the full spectrum of experience. They can be deeply healing. They are enthusiastic, high energy and both stimulated and stimulating. They find everything invigorating. They are cheerful, lively and vivacious. At the same time, they don't feel driven to avoid negative feelings or situations. Accomplished in many fields and areas, they are multi-talented as they use their boundary-free mind to cross-fertilize their areas of interest. Practical and productive, they can maintain focus and determination long enough to achieve their goals.

Enthusiast (7) With Tightening Defenses
Anxiety, masked as restlessness, intensifies the drive to have more choices and options. The person is adventurous and worldly but has difficulty staying focused and committing to anything long-term. There is a high drive for new things. They become indiscriminate, engaging in activities in an unfocused way to compensate for the fact they are unable to remain still. They become manic, hyperactive, uninhibited and unfiltered. Their ideas are overflowing, but their follow-through is weak. The behavior takes on a self-interested edge, and they can be greedy, demanding, self-centered and filled with gluttony for new experiences, food, alcohol, parties or other forms of distraction. Nothing feels like enough as they are unable to get relief from their anxiety.

Enthusiast (7) When Fixated

Their behavior starts to exhibit a desperate quality as they become impulsive, infantile and excessive. Healthy limits disappear, and extreme behavior including addictions may enter the picture as a form of escapism. The Enthusiast (7) becomes unpredictable and out of control, their moods become erratic and volatile, and there can be an element of mania to the person. This Enthusiast (7) is unable to slow down long enough to process any negative emotions. Despair kicks in as this person is exhausted, disillusioned and broken. Their energy is depleted, their health destroyed, and they may fall into a deep depression, feeling despair about their life. Self-destructive behavior, including impulsive suicide attempts, can occur as a reaction to avoid being trapped in pain.

Keys If You Are In A Relationship With An Enthusiast (7)

"My avoidance of negative feelings is so compulsive, I don't even realize I am doing it."

Evi, Enthusiast (7)

"At one point I went to therapy because I was having problems with my anxiety, and I thought talking to someone might help. During the course of therapy, I was asked to describe my childhood. In my mind, I had a happy childhood growing up in a stable home, so that's what I talked about. When we dug a little deeper, and it surfaced that I had suffered from serious health issues as child and had grown up with an emotionally distant mother and an alcoholic father, I remember being surprised that the therapist seemed shocked. Her eyes started to well up with tears on my behalf which made me very uncomfortable. In my mind, my childhood had been happy, or at least happy enough, and there wasn't anything to feel bad about. It took her a full year to convince me there had been a problem..."

Enthusiast (7)s are often described as "trapped in sunshine" and avoidant when it comes to negative emotions or experiences. The reality is much deeper. The internal wiring of an Enthusiast (7) blocks out painful emotions, and difficult memories dissolve away. The chronic focus on the bright side isn't a choice; it is actually the way the Enthusiast (7) brain works. It takes a great deal of self-observation and self-awareness for an Enthusiast (7) to break out of this habit of attention and feel the full spectrum of emotion.

If you are an Enthusiast (7):
Understand that you have a reality distortion and probably aren't taking in full information.

Try to slow down and get in touch with the emotional energy in your body to help you have a more accurate reading of an event or situation. Trust that there is value in feeling the full range of emotion, including the darker feelings like sadness, despair, loneliness and melancholy.

If you are with an Enthusiast (7):
Try not to take your Enthusiast (7)'s denial of negative emotions personally. Their brain moves away from dark emotions as they feel these emotions too threatening to process. An Enthusiast (7)'s subconscious fear is that if they start feeling bad, they may never stop. Try to allow space for your Enthusiast (7) to feel bad on their own timetable.

"My schedule of activities is important, and unstructured time often makes me uncomfortable."

Anders, Peacemaker (9) about Anette, Enthusiast (7)

"I've noticed Anette needs me to headline everything we do, otherwise she takes no pleasure in it. It's different to have no plans and end up watching a movie than to have the plan be a "Movie Night." Staying at home and cleaning is not the same as when I say to her "We are going to wake up, have breakfast, listen to some music and clean up the apartment." She needs some time to think about what we are going to do, process it and enjoy it before we do it. After that, she will most likely enjoy when it actually happens. She doesn't like to schedule things at the last moment as she does not have time to take enjoyment as she thinks about it in advance.

This, of course, is not easy for me as I do not like to overthink something because I fear the actual thing will let me down. I like to keep low expectations so I will be positively surprised instead of let down about something."

Elsa, Perfectionist (1) about Lars, Enthusiast (7)

"I used to draw the parallel that you should never make a man choose between his wife and his mother because no matter the choice, you will lose. It is the same with my husband and his schedule. I never made my husband choose between his schedule and me. Lars and I worked out the balance of time commitments, finances, parenting and then some time together."

At a very basic level, Enthusiast (7)s stay on the go to ensure anxiety doesn't surface. This is largely subconscious, so most Enthusiast (7)s don't know they are doing it. What they do know is that unstructured time feels uncomfortable and unenjoyable. This is also why they have a burning drive to schedule things, even things they may ultimately not do. A full schedule makes them feel relaxed.

If you are an Enthusiast (7):
Notice your drive to maintain a full schedule. Why is unscheduled time so uncomfortable? Also, notice how defensive you become if someone makes requests or demands on your personal time. Try to notice if there is some link between your anxiety and your relationship with time.

If you are with an Enthusiast (7):
Making your Enthusiast (7) choose between you and their schedule is potentially a no-win situation. Find ways to compromise, so you both are left feeling ok. Understand that your Enthusiast (7)'s schedule is a tool they use to deal with their anxiety.

 "It hurts me when you are dismissive or negative about my new ideas."

Emma, Enthusiast (7) married in a 19-year relationship with Frank, Loyalist (6)

"While Frank usually supports my numerous ideas, when he doesn't, it gets under my skin. I can get very excited about a new idea, and when I hear the dreaded "Uh oh" from him, I cringe inside. I wish he could understand that freedom for me is a mental construct. It isn't as though I need to actually do all the things I think about. I just need the freedom to say them and explore the idea without feeling limited in any way. I get a lot of pleasure from the mental exercise of imagining."

Isabella, Enthusiast (7) divorced, formerly in a relationship for 20-years with Carlos, Loyalist (6)

"Carlos always says no first to whatever I ask. It doesn't matter if it's a request to take out the trash or to plan a vacation. He always pushes back with an immediate "no," and must think before he will respond without this impulse. Eventually, he may agree after given time to think and reflect upon the request. I began to feel angry and resentful of this impulse of his."

Enthusiast (7)s are a mental type and gain a lot of pleasure from the act of imagining positive scenarios. It is part of their magical reality. They don't expect to follow through on all their plans, ideas and schemes, but they want the freedom to mentally explore them. This exploration is a big source of enjoyment for them. Partners of Enthusiast (7)s often get tense at their Enthusiast (7)'s ideas, understanding they will be involved, at least peripherally, if the idea comes to fruition. In the idea stage, any negative feedback about their potential future plans feels like a limitation.

If you are an Enthusiast (7):
Understand that people close to you may take your ideas more seriously than you do. They may be reacting negatively from a place of concern about the feasibility or actual execution of an idea that for you is just a thought exercise. When you are sharing your new ideas, consider framing the discussion by making it clear that this is just brainstorming or imagining so your partner doesn't start to stress out about all the details.

If you are with an Enthusiast (7):
Understand that your Enthusiast (7) loves the act of imagining. Many of their ideas are just thought exercises. And some of their ideas are actually valid and good. The Enthusiast (7) mind works differently than most, and they are capable of making seemingly random connections that can inspire original creations. Your Enthusiast (7) will be happiest if you imagine along with them and only get serious if it seems like the plan will actually be implemented.

ENTHUSIAST (7)
360 DEGREE REVIEW

The next section features the 360 degree review--partnership with an Enthusiast (7) from the perspective of each of the nine types.

7:1 Enthusiast (7) with Perfectionist (1)

Elsa, Perfectionist (1) married in an 18-year relationship with Lars, Enthusiast (7)

"I was with my husband for 18 years – married 15 years and 2 days – before he died suddenly of a massive heart attack. We were both 44 years old. I still miss him beyond words just over 5 years later. We had both been in active recovery from addiction for a couple of years before we got together as a couple, so we had the advantage of being in a very conscious relationship.

There are so many things I loved about my husband…He was quick on the uptake, brilliant but never realized how much smarter he was than so much of the crowd. One of his greatest gifts was that he could step into a conflict and defuse the situation without letting either party lose face or feel embarrassed. He could be incredibly gentle, firm but kind, yet still sometimes wickedly sarcastic. I felt safe with him. I knew he would always back me up, no matter what. He did this with the doctors when we had children, with my own mother when she got pushy with me, even with the kids when they didn't listen to me. He was incredibly resilient and good at landing on his feet – I knew I could trust in his ability even if at times he didn't trust his ability himself.

Early on in our relationship, our roles were set: it was his job to make sure I had fun, and I made sure we didn't go bankrupt. For example, about three months into our engagement I took a job that required us to move to a new city. Before we did anything I had to be satisfied we could afford the upcoming changes given we both had bills and debt, some with serious emotional strings. None of these topics was his idea of a good time, but I knew we needed to lay all the cards on the table and come up with a plan. The Saturday morning between the job offer and my accepting it, I walked up to him and very matter-of-factly blurted out, "Tonight after dinner we have to see where our collective finances stand to make our decision. If you would please gather all of your monthly bills and debts, as will I, we can sit down and take a look. There will be no judgment, no blaming, nothing but assessment and strategic planning to eliminate as much debt as possible before our move." As I turned to leave, I caught the flash of pure panic in his eyes. We did, however, sit down and do exactly as I said we would at about 7:00 that night, strategy and all. This was how it went with us.

Things were not always easy in our marriage. There was a time when our children were young, I was home full-time with them and struggled with loneliness. I found myself getting disproportionately angry at my husband for being away, even if the reason he was away was something like he was fixing my car! After getting advice from a friend and reading a book she recommended, my husband and I sat together one night and did a reflective inventory of what was working well in our marriage and what wasn't. Owning our own parts, willing to do what we needed to support the other, we focused together on supporting the marriage rather than attempting to get our own needs met. We found that by doing just that, we pulled ourselves out of a needy space and back into a loving, supportive one. Basically, we needed to have more play time together. Children can suck that out of a marriage rather fast; thankfully we were able to restore it.

He loved me like no one else ever has, imperfections and all and was willing to work through whatever we came up against. He wasn't afraid to face the hard issues, to deal with unpleasant topics, but he never got stuck there and could always see an opportunity to be of service to the greater good, whether it be our family, friends or addiction recovery. Spending the best part of 20 years with this generous and loving husband gave me the ability to be bold and visionary in ways I would never have dared before.

Being married to my husband has been the absolute best part of my life. The most tedious tasks, the most boring life events, were never so bad if I was doing them with him. I appreciated that he could handle my energy when I let it all come to the surface. When I would get hesitant, stuck in the planning phase, he helped me to see that there's no such thing as failure, only feedback, and more information to gain wisdom from moving forward. He took me to places in life and inside myself I wouldn't think to go or bother to indulge in. He could shine his inner light on things that looked dull beforehand. He brought new perspectives to things I thought I already knew. And when he committed, I knew it was complete. I never once doubted till death do us part.

As a further note, I had been a student of the Enneagram for several years before meeting Lars. The insights about our Enneagram types, where our attention goes, how this attention shines as well as distorts reality made a difference in our relationship. Much of what would otherwise have been serious conflict became complementary with that insight. If I had expected him to see things as I did as a Perfectionist (1), I don't know that we would have lasted very long, especially if he had turned his sarcasm on me as criticism — that could have gone very badly...

Our success as a couple went beyond our love for each other. It was also based on a deeper understanding and ability to comprehend each other. We gave each other space for these differences without being threatened. I could back up and observe, he's an Enthusiast (7), he wants to see fun, the possibility, the big picture... And he knew, she's a Perfectionist (1), she wants it organized, planned out, methodical, rational... And we could enjoy the differences instead of feeling frustrated. And I think that made all the difference."

Dietrich, Perfectionist (1) married in a 12-year relationship with Marta, Enthusiast (7)

"Marta brings excitement and new ideas to the relationship. She is the initiator. I love her positive thinking and all the excitement and euphoria that come with her fresh ideas and planning.

In our relationship, Marta comes up with the new projects, and I help us execute them and set priorities. In many ways we are opposites, but it works well because we take the positive characteristics of each other. She's the big picture thinker, and I'm the detail guy.

For example, when we moved into our new apartment, she wanted to renovate the kitchen. I agreed but insisted we create a thorough plan with all the details – where the cupboards will be placed, what color will we paint the cupboard doors, where we will put the refrigerator, how do we create a spot to sit and eat breakfast, where will the oven go, how we do it all to ensure we don't overload the electricity and so on. We have a really tiny flat, so we needed to make a very clear, precise plan. I also kept us on track, because very often she was very close to quitting the renovation. But I said no! I would tell her, "just take a breath, sit down, relax for a while, I will continue. But it is necessary to finish properly."

It is true we are opposites in many ways. But we take the positive characteristics of each other in a very complementary way. We are like a pot and lid. Of course, we have our arguments, but those moments are really rare. We communicate well, which is important because we are very different, but in the end, we are one team.

As it relates to challenges in our relationship, I am pretty sure I sometimes criticize her too much. I love to have things done perfectly – even very mundane or trivial things. It's just how my mind works, and it is important to me. But I know she sometimes gets frustrated about the criticism.

And I sometimes get frustrated that she gets distracted or loses interest in accomplishing our goals. And sometimes, we just have different priorities, like the night before our wedding when I was working on the light bulbs in the wedding space, and she was drinking wine with her sister, mother and grandmother.

At the end of the day, the differences don't matter because I love her, with all her strengths and weaknesses. She is still perfect, or at least we both learned to be perfect together. We help each other to achieve new growth. We have a very close relationship with great communication. I think this is key and if I couldn't tell her my thoughts, I wouldn't feel happy with our dynamic. Honesty and frankness is an important part of our relationship - it helps us overcome our weaknesses. That's cool."

7:1 The Theory

7:1 When In Balance

The detail-oriented, practically-minded Perfectionist (1) and brainstorming, big picture Enthusiast (7) enjoy a symbiotic, balancing relationship with both offering valuable traits the other generally lacks. When self-aware and in balance, they complete each other. This can be a highly complementary pairing. Perfectionist (1)s bring order, efficiency, tactical thinking, practicality, follow-through and commitment to high standards. Enthusiast (7)s offer high energy, a positive outlook, resilience, strategic thinking and an orientation towards fun and adventure.

Perfectionist (1)s help Enthusiast (7)s stay the course and remain focused in the face of difficulties and obstacles. The Perfectionist (1)'s attention to detail and practical thinking means projects and initiatives get done well with favorable results. They are methodical, thorough and more contained with their energy, and this can be helpful for the excitable Enthusiast (7).

Enthusiast (7)s bring joy and playfulness to the relationship and can help make sure things don't get too heavy, balancing the seriousness of the Perfectionist (1). They remind the Perfectionist (1) to have fun, to relax and to enjoy life. With their insatiable belief in a brighter future where all things are possible, the Enthusiast (7) inspires new projects, new trips and new adventures for the couple.

Both types can admire each other. Enthusiast (7)s appreciate the Perfectionist (1)'s methodical and systematic approach to life as well as their reliability. They are happy to have a detail-oriented person at their side as most Enthusiast (7)s are aware that attention to detail is not their forte. Perfectionist (1)s admire the Enthusiast (7)'s high spirits, joy and sense of fun and adventure. Enthusiast (7)s charge enthusiastically forward in life, and this can be balancing for Perfectionist (1)s who sometimes hold back and get overly involved in the details.

When aligned and in balance, this can be a mutually satisfying, fulfilling relationship.

 ### 7:1 The Downward Spiral
When fixated or in low stages of awareness, this can be a frustrating and difficult match riddled with misunderstanding and misaligned goals.

Under stress with tightening defenses, Perfectionist (1)s become more rigid, judgmental, irritated and blaming. They start to resent the playful, high-spirited Enthusiast (7) who is rarely interested in details or a methodical approach to situations. Perfectionist (1)s see the Enthusiast (7) as pleasure seeking, unfocused, impractical and with a lack of commitment to high standards. It may feel as though a social contract has been broken, and the Perfectionist (1) may start to take this behavior personally, as though it were directed at them.

Enthusiast (7)s, on the other hand, get frustrated with the rigidity and seriousness of the Perfectionist (1). They start to feel penned in and trapped by what feels like a relentless "work before play" attitude. They can see the Perfectionist (1) as a strict schoolmarm who brings them down, limits them and drains their enthusiasm.

Conflicts between the two usually stem from their different approaches—Enthusiast (7)s have an immediacy of wanting to enjoy life to its fullest, and Perfectionist (1)s want to make sure all practical responsibilities are met before they allow themselves to relax and enjoy life. Enthusiast (7) start to feel like the Perfectionist "just doesn't get it" while Perfectionist (1)s see the Enthusiast (7) as irresponsible and immature. If the downward spiral gains momentum, the differences they share start to polarize the couple. The Enthusiast (7) may feel worn down and frustrated by the Perfectionist (1)'s continual criticism and dissatisfaction. They look for pleasant distractions to make themselves feel better. The Perfectionist (1) gets even more frustrated with the Enthusiast (7)'s way of dealing with the situation. Their Enthusiast (7) partner begins to seem unreliable, scattered and hedonistic, someone with whom it is very difficult to imagine a positive future. The Perfectionist (1) might start developing feelings of contempt for the Enthusiast (7). With a panicking and frustrated Enthusiast (7) and a disillusioned, contemptuous Perfectionist (1), the connection falters, and the relationship is in trouble.

7:1 The Lighthouse
Tightening defenses move in the opposite directions in this couple, so coming back to the center is key to stopping the downward spiral. The Enthusiast (7) needs to resist the urge to flee in the face of rising anxiety and stress. The Perfectionist (1) needs to resist the urge to lean in and try to control too much of the environment. And for both partners to change directions, they need to strengthen their nervous systems.

7:1 The Kundalini Yoga Connection
The Enthusiast (7)'s underlying anxiety can benefit a lot from Kundalini Yoga kriyas and meditations that incorporate breathwork. Practices that require grit and determination and that lower anxiety are particularly helpful.

The Perfectionist (1)'s frustration can be released with Kundalini Yoga kriyas and meditations to burn inner anger and to open the heart. Any practice that connects the Perfectionist (1) with their softer emotions is beneficial.

See the appendix for Perfectionist (1) and Enthusiast (7) recommended Kundalini Yoga kriyas and meditations.

7:2 Enthusiast (7) with Helper (2)

Winter, Helper (2) married in a 12-year relationship with Justin, Enthusiast (7)

THE NINE KEYS

"I have a long list of things I love about my husband, but some of them are that he's emotionally open, fun and always willing to try new things and experiences even if it might not be "his" thing. For example, when we were first dating, he agreed to take the Green Tortoise – a hippy bus – with strangers to Death Valley for a camping trip. He knew it was a dream of mine and even though he had no actual interest in the trip himself, he was game for it.

He really makes me feel appreciated and heard. He is very loving in words and deeds and is quick to apologize and admit his part in a conflict.

In the relationship, he pushes me to expand my point of view and to advocate more for myself. I have a hard time saying no to other people, but he doesn't have this issue at all, so he is quick to remind me to make myself a priority. I offer hospitality more readily than he does, but then I also exhaust myself doing things for others. Since my overcommitments impact him, I've learned to try to control "offering" my help to friends more now because of his influence.

One of our challenges is our differences in communication. I'm more sensitive and not good at expressing my feelings in the moment. Feelings usually marinate inside me for a while before I'm ready to express them. Justin has a much more direct communication style. If something upsets him, he blows up quickly – swearing or shouting – and after it's out, it's over for him. Over the years, he's gotten better in tune with my moods and feelings, and he knows if I'm too quiet it means something is upsetting me.

Our social calendars are also pretty different. Oftentimes I'm spread thinly, having lots of social commitments and events. I know it exhausts my husband. But unlike many couples, we are very comfortable doing things independently. I usually plan things months in advance, and once I commit to something, I honor it. My husband's style is more fluid, and he doesn't always feel comfortable committing to things way in advance. The hedging is frustrating to me at times, but then again, I don't want to be his social planner, so I usually try to be clear with him about events that are important for me to attend with him.

Our relationship started when I was 41, and he was 51. We had known each other casually for over 15 years before, so we had seen each other through various phases of life. I think one thing that has really helped our relationship was the amount of internal work we had both done leading up to our relationship through life lessons, failed relationships, challenges and triumphs. If we had tried to date earlier, I don't know that it would have worked, but by the time our relationship did start, we both understood ourselves pretty well. I feel so grateful and lucky to have him as my husband."

7:2 The Theory

7:2 When In Balance
The Helper (2) and the Enthusiast (7) are a high energy, social, engaging and outgoing couple who enjoy creating a positive environment to share with those around them. Both share a lust for life and a natural curiosity about the world and other people.

While their external behavior can look similar, their habit of attention and internal world are very different. Helper (2)s are more other-oriented with a sensitivity to the feelings and conditions of others. They offer emotional depth to the relationship and are genuinely concerned about other people. This is inspiring to their partner and can help awaken the sometimes-latent capacity for compassion in their Enthusiast (7).

Enthusiast (7)s bring positive energy, a thirst for adventure, a bold "can-do" attitude and a sense of endless possibilities. Enthusiast (7)s generate excitement in their environment and uplift others with their joy, humor and storytelling. Helper (2)s admire this and appreciate the happiness their Enthusiast (7) brings to them and those around them. Enthusiast (7)s are self-referencing, and they can help their Helper (2) establish clearer personal boundaries. By example, they show the Helper (2) how to advocate for themselves and make their own desires a priority.

Both types can be idealistic and get pleasure sharing their abundance with others. This can be a highly altruistic, generous and inspiring pair. They make others feel warm, welcomed, loved and included.

7:2 The Downward Spiral
Their different habits of attention can become a source of conflict under stress with tightening defenses. Helper (2)s seek a deep, intimate connection to feel stable whereas Enthusiast (7)s seek personal freedom and an absence of limitations for their sense of stability. Under stress or in an unaware state, the Helper (2)'s fear of rejection may trigger clingy and dependent behavior. They lean forward towards their Enthusiast (7) wanting more connection and more assurance that the relationship is stable. The Enthusiast (7) may sense their personal freedom is at risk and begin to turn their attention to new possibilities. The degree to which the Helper (2) can manage their urge to lean in and the degree to which the Enthusiast (7) can resist their urge to flee determines how much momentum the downward spiral gains.

The Helper (2) can also become disillusioned with the self-referencing nature of the

Enthusiast (7). The Helper (2) longs for a deep, stable emotional connection and as they start to understand the degree that their Enthusiast (7) focuses on themselves, they may start to doubt the chance of a happy future together. When fixated, Enthusiast (7)s adopt a "me first" attitude, and this can be disappointing to their Helper (2). The downward spiral can be triggered through themes of rejection and limitation. Once this couple starts to polarize, it can be hard to break the momentum.

7:2 The Lighthouse
Differences around core fears and core desires are what starts the downward spiral for this couple. Helper (2)s fear rejection, and Enthusiast (7)s fear limitations on their freedom. As fears get triggered, they begin to move in opposite directions energetically – Helper (2)s moving towards the Enthusiast (7), and Enthusiast (7)s running away from the Helper (2). To break the downward momentum, both types need to learn to stay still.

7:2 The Kundalini Yoga Connection
A strong nervous system will help both the Helper (2) and Enthusiast (7) cultivate stillness to act, not react.

Helper (2)s need to stay centered and turn their attention back to themselves when they start to get triggered by fears of rejection. Self-care is important, and Kundalini Yoga kriyas and meditations that cultivate self-love, self-acceptance and raise body and energy awareness are beneficial for Helper (2)s. It is beneficial for Helper (2)s to do their practice independently so they can fully focus their attention on themselves.

Enthusiast (7)s need to connect with their heart and to lower their anxiety around perceived limitations. Enthusiast (7)s can have a physical response to limitation, a contraction, that triggers stress and anxiety. Kundalini Yoga kriyas and meditations for heart opening, anxiety management and decreasing stress are helpful. Breath management exercises, particularly long deep breathing, can be helpful for Enthusiast (7)s.

See the appendix for Helper (2) and Enthusiast (7) recommended Kundalini Yoga kriyas and meditations.

7:3 Enthusiast (7) with Achiever (3)

Anita, Achiever (3) married in a 19-year relationship with Harold, Enthusiast (7)

"My husband brings laughter, fun and joy into my life and has helped me to have a less

regimented and more spontaneous attitude. He is not afraid to try new things and has a can-do attitude. If he encounters a problem, he has the patience and persistence to work on it until it is solved. I know he has my back and will support me. He is not a quitter and can be quite committed. When his first wife was diagnosed with Huntington's Disease, he stayed with her until the end and fought that battle at her side.

He is a partner in the truest sense of the word. No matter what crazy idea I come up with, he is there to help me accomplish it. Harold is quite adventurous and participates in all types of activities – ballroom dancing, whitewater rafting, line dancing, skiing, snowshoeing, photography, hiking, traveling, reading, ziplining, writing classes, cooking classes and so on. I enjoy that I have a partner who is active and willing to explore new vistas.

In our relationship, we are both optimists, seeing the glass as half full – and sometimes more than half full! Gratitude comes easily to both of us. We both have LOTS of energy, despite being in our 70s and 80s. Our friends call us Energizer Bunnies®. We like to stay busy and are very active in our community. Together we spearheaded a group of local residents to make, paint and hang wooden Christmas decorations for all the storefronts on the Main Street of our small California town. We love the holidays and are Santa and Mrs. Claus for our town's Holiday Parade of Lights. We are also active in our local church community and organize lots of events and initiatives there. We are energized doing these types of activities and enjoy doing them together. They give us a chance to give back to the community and all we are grateful for.

We met and married later in life, and we often speculate what our lives would have been like if we had married earlier. However, we've concluded we would probably have burned each other out – we both enjoy a very full schedule and a breakneck pace.

Regarding issues in our relationship, we both had long-term, first marriages that left their impressions on us. We've had to recalibrate that the prior issues are not part of our existing relationship with each other. Overall, together we are a good match and enjoy a happy relationship."

7:3 The Theory

7:3 When In Balance
The Achiever (3) with the Enthusiast (7) make an extremely high energy couple, and this can be a complementary match as both have ample energy to keep up with each other. Both

are extroverted, positive, social, lively, outgoing with full schedules and multiple activities. They share a can-do attitude and a belief in a brighter future that can be uplifting to those around them.

To the dynamic, the Achiever (3) brings a practical orientation, a sense of priority and a concern about appearances. They have a heightened concern about what others might think and spend time and energy to make sure the couple is appropriate, accomplished and well-regarded in the community.

Enthusiast (7)s are driven by a sense of adventure, a desire for fun and an appetite for the new, and thus they are less concerned about the opinions of others. Resilient and not overly concerned about failure, they can be spontaneous and outrageous, traits that are both balancing and sometimes healing for the Achiever (3).

The two complement each other with the Achiever (3) bringing a focus on goal achievement and practicality, and the Enthusiast (7) bringing a sense of fun and adventure, boldness and good cheer. They work as a team with the Enthusiast (7) generating the ideas and plans and the Achiever (3) stepping in to make sure the plans are well executed. This couple can be almost legendary in its energy level with others marveling at how they keep it up.

7:3 The Downward Spiral

Both Achiever (3)s and Enthusiast (7) are likely to stay on the go and instinctively turn their attention to the positive. With so much energy focused outward, it can be challenging for this couple to slow down enough to look at deeper issues and examine real problems. There can also be an air of superficiality to this relationship. The couple may look great together but lack true intimacy. Without the ability to drop the masks, slow down and share weaknesses and vulnerabilities, the emotional connection may be lost. In this environment, the downward spiral can be triggered in a variety of ways.

Avoidant behavior can inadvertently trigger the downward spiral if the partners hurt each other without realizing it. Enthusiast (7)s reframe negative situations into positive ones. The defense mechanism of the Achiever (3) is to work harder in negative situations. Since neither is particularly skilled in directly dealing with negative issues, problems can pile up with minor resentments growing, frustrations building and concerns going unaddressed. Without learning to slow down, to sit quietly together and to honestly discuss real issues and the relationship itself, the intimacy the couple once shared becomes eroded.

Alternatively, competing agendas can be an issue. Both Achiever (3)s and Enthusiast (7)s are self-interested and when their personal goals fall out of alignment, it can be difficult to reach compromise. With tightening defenses, both dig in their heels, the Achiever (3) focusing more on their goals and the Enthusiast (7) focusing more on their freedom. Both partners may have the instinct to run, feeling their life priorities are at risk. Without a mechanism to put the relationship first and break the momentum, this couple may put individual interests ahead of the partnership, leading to a split.

7:3 The Lighthouse

Difficulty facing negative emotions can be the start of the downward spiral for this pair so learning to hold the full spectrum of emotions can help to break the momentum. Both types have drive and energy and stay on the go as a subconscious strategy to avoid deeper feeling. Achiever (3)s avoid shame. Enthusiast (7)s run from anxiety. Both types need to cultivate stillness and to learn to slow down so the full range of emotions can be processed. To break their ingrained pattern, strengthening the nervous system is a critical first step.

7:3 The Kundalini Yoga Connection

Achiever (3)s need to relax the drive for constant achievement and face shame, feelings of inadequacy and low self-worth. They must cultivate self-love and self-acceptance so their identity is felt internally, and they aren't as reliant on the opinion of outsiders. The goal is to cultivate a strong sense of self that includes self-acceptance and compassion. Kundalini Yoga kriyas and meditations to get out of the head, to connect with the heart and to cultivate self-love are helpful.

Enthusiast (7)s need to face pain and the darker emotions like sadness, despair and melancholy. They need to sit still, let all their feeling arise and manage their avoidant tendency. They grow when they learn they can tolerate negative emotions, and in fact, see the benefit of feeling and processing these emotions. Kundalini Yoga kriyas and meditations to lower anxiety, cultivate stillness, open the heart and quiet the mind are helpful.

See the appendix for Achiever (3) and Enthusiast (7) recommended Kundalini Yoga kriyas and meditations.

7:4 Enthusiast (7) with Individualist (4)

Simon, Individualist (4) married in a 36-year relationship with Kate, Enthusiast (7)

THE NINE KEYS

"Even after 36 years of being together, Kate and I are still intrigued by each other. I really value her pragmatic, practical intelligence, imaginative vision, optimistic outlook, genuine care for friends and family and of course, her zany energy. One other important thing she brings is a clear analysis of situations without emotional interference or overload. Because I'm so emotionally driven, this is much harder for me, so I really value her perspective and input.

We have a morning ritual in which we go through accounts of the previous day together – in the context of describing what we feel grateful for and what we found difficult on the previous day. This ritual is one of the foundational elements of our relationship.

What anchors us is a deep love for each other since we do have some pretty fundamental differences. I do sometimes feel worn down by my wife's relentless pace and high energy, and she sometimes feels worn down by my emotional moodiness. When we are both stressed or overtired at the same time, it's a recipe for disaster.

We both need real space from each other and also a close togetherness. Over 36 years, the ups and downs have happened so many times that I've learned the trick for me is not to attach any importance or significance to it. Things will pass, things will change. And underneath the deep love remains.

One of the biggest challenges in our relationships is that we aren't able to get all of our needs met with each other. For example, I need more emotional support than Kate is able to provide. With some couples, these issues might drive them apart. Interestingly, however, with us, the differences actually hold us together. We both understand we need people outside our relationship to get some of our needs met. And we both understand we need real space away from each other at times. But we also know that doesn't mean we don't enjoy spending time together.

While it isn't always obvious to other people, we don't have a conventional relationship, but we have one that works well for us. I think our relationship is based on honesty and connection. In that sense, the daily reflection on the previous day's events is very key to keeping us connected.

I often think that knowledge of the Enneagram is what has saved our relationship and helped it to flourish. It has given us a powerful tool for understanding very profoundly just why we keep misfiring or not understanding each other. It gives us a framework for understanding the need to deepen compassion and acceptance of the misunderstanding.

We are both very well blessed."

7:4 The Theory

7:4 When In Balance

The Individualist (4) and Enthusiast (7) combination has the classic appearance of opposites attracting. Their strengths offset each other's weaknesses and when in balance, this couple is highly complementary with the Enthusiast (7) leading the way through the external world, and the Individualist (4) leading the way through the internal world.

Individualist (4)s are introspective, emotional, self-doubting and leaning towards a pessimistic and cynical view of the world. They are comfortable with the darker side of the emotional spectrum and are well-versed in the language of emotion. Individualist (4)s help Enthusiast (7)s get in touch with their full range of emotions and help them process negative experiences. They bring depth and richness to the relationship and can help the Enthusiast (7) to be less self-referencing and more empathetic towards the suffering of others.

In contrast, Enthusiast (7)s tend towards the bright side of the emotional spectrum, filled with enthusiasm, self-confidence, joy and optimism. They are more mental, and while they can be emotional, they are also avoidant and have great difficulty staying with negative emotions. Enthusiast (7)s help Individualist (4)s see the bright side, develop confidence, try new experiences and overcome self-consciousness. They help the Individualist (4) advocate for themselves and model self-love instead of self-loathing.

Together, the relationship is one of attraction and intrigue. They think, feel and react so differently that they can gain great insight by dissecting events, situations and emotions trying to understand each other and themselves better.

As it relates to similarities, both are highly verbal and may share an offbeat sense of humor, enjoying rich, deep, entertaining and often hilarious conversations together. As each partner is open-minded, neither is threatened by new ideas their partner might want to introduce. This flexibility is important, as in some respects this couple may not be able to get all of their needs met with each other. This difference can be used as a strength, however, creating an environment of candor and openness. They creatively use this as a problem solving exercise, and it can bring them closer together.

This couple can complement each other well, with each compensating for the other's blind spots and weaknesses. When in balance, this is a committed, enduring partnership.

7:4 The Downward Spiral

While the differences can be points of intrigue when in balance, they can also trigger the downward spiral. Both types can be self-absorbed and self-referencing so if they start to feel their needs aren't being met, they can get testy with each other.

Individualist (4)s can feel exhausted by the relentless pace and energy of the Enthusiast (7). They can find their Enthusiast (7) too shallow, too excitable, too busy and too impulsive. They long for a deep, emotional connection and may feel unseen in the face of their Enthusiast (7)'s multiple plans and activities.

Enthusiast (7)s can see their Individualist (4) as moody, impractical, negative and endlessly self-absorbed with their negative self-image. They can get frustrated with the low energy and tendency to withdraw of their Individualist (4), seeking a more engaged, available partner. The downward spiral begins when either partner starts to lose respect for the other and focus on the negative differences instead of the positives.

If the downward spiral gains momentum, the Individualist (4) may become more hostile, sarcastic and withdrawn. The Enthusiast (7) may try to solve the issue by adding more things to their schedule in an attempt to lower their growing anxiety. The Individualist (4) responds by wanting to discuss every negative element of the relationship in detail. The Enthusiast (7) views this as the rough equivalent to hell on earth and plans more outside activities and distractions to try to keep a positive frame of mind. Both partners polarize, and their emotional connection is threatened.

If the core issues don't get aired and adequately resolved, this relationship starts to collapse. The differences which were once so admired become a source of frustration and irritation until the relationship eventually ends.

7:4 The Lighthouse
A fundamental inability to accept each other's differences is what triggers the downward spiral for this couple. Cultivating tolerance towards each other can help break the momentum. Energetically, these two can be opposites, so it is helpful for Enthusiast (7)s to learn to be still and for Individualist (4)s to resist the urge to withdraw. For both types, strengthening the nervous system helps make these things possible.

7:4 The Kundalini Yoga Connection
Individualist (4)s need to learn to weather their emotional storms without getting frustrated at their Enthusiast (7)'s tendency to try to reframe everything as positive or to be emotionally avoidant of the negative. Kundalini Yoga kriyas and meditations to

cultivate neutrality and self-love, burn out anger, release depression and lower anxiety can be helpful.

Enthusiast (7)s need to learn to allow their Individualist (4) to have their full range of emotion and emotional reactions without feeling threatened. They need to resist the impulse to avoid and flee from negative feelings. It can be healing for Enthusiast (7)s to stay with darker emotions. Kundalini Yoga kriyas and meditations to lower anxiety and open the heart can be helpful.

See the appendix for Individualist (4) and Enthusiast (7) recommended Kundalini Yoga kriyas and meditations.

7:5 Enthusiast (7) with Investigator (5)

Ian, Investigator (5) married in a 14-year relationship with Claire, Enthusiast (7)

"My wife is clever, enthusiastic, compassionate and a huge animal lover. I admire her ability to feel and express her emotions. I also admire her competence – she has an amazing ability to very quickly work out how to do new things based on her past experience and maybe a Google search. I love her enthusiasm, her excitement and her endless energy. She gets me out and about doing things I might not do without her influence – travel, photography at the zoo and so on. Early in our relationship, this even translated to practical things I had avoided doing for years, like getting a mobile phone and learning to drive.

In our relationship, we maintain a good, reciprocal balance as she provides the excitement and drive for new experiences, and I provide a calming, stabilizing influence. We have lots of overlapping interests such as fantasy novels, movies, Dungeons and Dragons as well as generally common opinions regarding politics and religion. Our spending habits are different but not so different that it creates problems in our relationship. I appreciate that she tolerates my absorption in my own interests, and I appreciate her intelligence. It is rare for me to find "a girl I can talk to," and I've found it in her.

We've been together 14 years and married for 11 of them, so we've also experienced various challenges along the way. Anxiety is something we both deal with and that can create distance between us. For example, she sometimes retreats into her video games as a way to deal with her anxiety. And while communication style isn't a central problem for us, she occasionally complains, not unjustifiably, that I'm being too cold or remote. Neither of us focuses a lot on basic maintenance types of things like bill paying or house cleaning so dividing those tasks up can be challenging. And as we both can be a bit avoidant about issues, it can be hard to bring up things that need addressing in the relationship.

That said, overall, we're a great balance and complement each other immensely."

7:5 The Theory

7:5 When In Balance
The Investigator (5) and Enthusiast (7) share a strong mental connection, an insatiable curiosity and a strong desire for personal freedom and independence. These values form the foundation upon which their differences are energizing and balancing.

Investigator (5)s bring depth, focus, perseverance, discernment, self-reliance and an original, often eccentric sense of humor. They have sharp minds, insightful observations and curiosity, all things Enthusiast (7)s enjoy and appreciate. Rational and logical, they can be highly grounding for their Enthusiast (7). They model perseverance and show the Enthusiast (7) how to stick things out even in the face of obstacles.

Enthusiast (7)s offer positive thinking, spontaneity, boldness, a thirst for the new and a drive for fun that manifests in all different ways. Enthusiast (7)s seek adventure, and their minds are constantly on the hunt for the next new thing: windsurfing, travel to Malta, sewing classes, the latest issue of Home Design, an adventure race and so forth. They encourage their Investigator (5) to try new things, to be more social and to open up more. With a lively Enthusiast (7) at their side, social settings seem less daunting and because Investigator (5)s are naturally curious, they are often willing partners in their Enthusiast (7)'s quest for the new.

This dynamic is one in which frugality balances gluttony, and where both partners have permission to independently explore their interests. When in balance, this is a highly supportive, symbiotic and loving match.

7:5 The Downward Spiral
Both types deal with issues of anxiety, but they respond in different, and almost opposite ways. This threatens their connection and can create conflict. When Investigator (5)s start feeling anxious, they retreat and work hard to conserve their resources, including energy, time, money and so forth. To gain a feeling of stability, they cut ties with the outside world

becoming more isolated, reclusive, irritable, cynical and private. This can be hard on their Enthusiast (7) who finds their partner shutdown, cold and hard to reach.

In contrast, Enthusiast (7)s head in the opposite direction in times of stress. To minimize anxiety and gain feelings of stability, Enthusiast (7)s become more energized and manic looking to their external environment to help quell their anxiety. They want distraction and can seek it in a variety of forms — parties, socializing, frenetic activity and so forth. They fill their schedule and stay on the go. Stillness and isolation feel threatening. With both partners heading in opposite directions, the downward spiral is triggered.

Investigator (5)s may feel threatened by the Enthusiast (7)'s stress response. They see their partner as out of control, unpredictable, escapist and juvenile. This lack of support triggers the Enthusiast (7) even more, and they become frustrated with their Investigator (5), wanting them to be more engaged, less reserved, less negative and more exciting. Both partners start to polarize, the Enthusiast (7) becoming more demanding and domineering, driving the Investigator (5) further into retreat. As anxiety grows, trust erodes making it difficult to find common ground from which to repair. The positions may become more polarized until there is little keeping this couple together, and the relationship collapses.

7:5 The Lighthouse
These two types head in opposite directions energetically when they are feeling anxious. Enthusiast (7)s engage more with their outside environment to lower their anxiety. Distraction is soothing to them. Investigator (5)s cut off from their outside environment to lower their anxiety. Isolation soothes them. Anxiety can feel overwhelming for both, so managing their anxiety and their reaction to anxiety is key to reversing any downward spiral that starts.

7:5 The Kundalini Yoga Connection
The Enthusiast (7) needs to strengthen their nervous system, so they don't act out their anxiety quite as manically. Anxious Enthusiast (7)s can be very demanding, and this can feel threatening to their Investigator (5) partner. Instead of relying on their external environment to feel stable, they can start to use internal tools like breathwork, to gain feelings of stability. Kundalini Yoga kriyas and meditations to lower anxiety and to cultivate focus and stillness are helpful.

The Investigator (5) needs to stay engaged and share more of themselves, resisting the desire to cut off to feel stable. Strengthening the nervous system is key to staying engaged and resisting the urge to withdraw. Part of sharing themselves more includes becoming more verbal, particularly about the world of emotion. Kundalini Yoga kriyas and meditations to open the throat chakra, to lower anxiety and to cultivate feelings of abundance are helpful.

See the appendix for Investigator (5) and Enthusiast (7) recommended Kundalini Yoga kriyas and meditations.

7:6 Enthusiast (7) with Loyalist (6)

Maya, Loyalist (6) in a 2-year relationship with Peter, Enthusiast (7)

"Peter is a friend to all, and everyone loves him. He enjoys life – if he gets a $100 bill from his grandfather for his birthday, he doesn't put it in savings. Instead, he uses that gift for something fun. He is balanced. Peter takes his work very seriously, but in his free time, he is playful and fun. He has a childlike innocence and hopefulness that I adore.

In our relationship, he makes me feel safe. He really listens to me and is delicate about my fears and anxieties. He's very stable. He helps put my fears and anxious thinking into perspective. As a simple example, recently we were out on a hike. During the hike, I kept thinking about these cheese fries I love and how much I was craving them! I shared this with Peter, and he agreed that after the hike we HAD to go get some. As we were on the return leg of the walk, a million anxieties about the cheese fries began to flood my mind: "I wonder how much they will cost?" "How much will I have to tip the waiter?" "Will this count as dinner or will I have to plan to eat something else later?" "Do I really need these cheese fries?" "I'm going into the city this weekend with my friends, and I'm going to be spending a lot of money then" "I could just eat something I have at home and save my money for something more important." When we finally got to the car, I suggested we just make something at home. He refused. He said, "If you don't get these cheese fries right now, you're just going to be thinking about them all night. Plus, now I want them." He drove us to the restaurant. We ordered cheese fries. As we sat there and ate the cheese fries, he looked at me and "You need to indulge yourself more. You deserve it."

Peter acts as a mirror, and I see how my anxiety impacts our dynamic. I have ruined many nice evenings by raising questions that stem from my fears. He has a very big dream – he wants to be a famous writer – and he feels he cannot be truly happy if he doesn't achieve that goal. He says that he will do just about anything to achieve his dream, and that makes me worry that I could become irrelevant to him overnight. I worry that he is an idealist and will be crushed by the reality of the world. Also, I am religious, and he is not. I don't like to talk to him about this part of my life because I don't want him to judge it. He had negative experiences in the past regarding religion and is clear in his decision to stay away from it. I worry that in the future, when push comes to shove, our values will not align, and we won't be able to understand or properly support each other. I recognize these concerns are all about an uncertain future and that in the present moment, he is stable and supportive. But I still feel these fears.

I hope he understands that I don't play devil's advocate to try to destroy our relationship. I poke around for the holes and weaknesses so that we can strengthen those parts. I am never sure about my decisions, and I am terrified of making the wrong choice. I need the chance to explore the different outcomes before I can decide.

We've been together for two years, and part of me feels that we will break up soon. That same part of me feels that we will find each other again once we have both grown up a bit. I guess this is how my mind sees the worst-case scenario but also tries to leave me hope."

7:6 The Theory

7:6 When In Balance

When understanding and accepting of their differences, the Loyalist (6) and the Enthusiast (7) can make a charming, successful and balancing couple. Both types are future-oriented, verbal and enjoy entertaining each other with colorful stories and lively debate. Their habit of attention points in opposite ways and when self-aware, they use this difference as an asset. The unbridled enthusiasm of the Enthusiast (7) and the cautious discernment of the Loyalist (6) balance each other with the Enthusiast (7)'s eyes looking up at the stars and the Loyalist (6)'s feet planted firmly on the ground.

The Loyalist (6) brings a cautious, methodical approach to life. They carefully plan and analyze potential future outcomes always with an eye for danger and pitfalls. They model commitment, discipline, reliability, loyalty, duty, realistic thinking and danger awareness. The Enthusiast (7) may come to rely on these traits and may feel even more emboldened to try new things with their Loyalist (6) at their side.

The Enthusiast (7) offers enthusiasm, expansive thinking, high spirits, a positive outlook, adventure and a constant source of new ideas. They can be decisive and action-oriented. As they aren't encumbered by a fear of failure, they model resilience and boldness, traits which are refreshing for the Loyalist (6) to witness.

This couple genuinely enjoys each other's company. They find their differences as points of intrigue and balance and offer steady, loyal support to each other. Their affection towards each other is observable, and this can be a sweet, charming and successful match.

7:6 The Downward Spiral
The radically different habits of attention of these two types can become a weakness in lower states of self-awareness. When unaccepting of their different worldviews, this couple starts to polarize, and the downward spiral is triggered.

Loyalist (6)s are focused on security and seek a safe, predictable future. Anxiety is often part of their daily experience and to reduce their anxiety, they take proactive steps to eliminate or minimize perceived threats to their security. They seek to keep their feet firmly grounded on the earth and their eyes scanning for what could go wrong.

Enthusiast (7)s look at the world differently. Their focus goes to trying new things, exploring the unknown and keeping an upbeat, positive attitude. They believe all things are possible and are not particularly interested in hearing about problems or limitations with their ideas and plans. They can be impatient, impulsive and avoidant. This avoidance triggers stress in the Loyalist (6), making them ratchet up their caution and concern about what could go wrong. The downward spiral gains momentum as the Enthusiast (7) sees their Loyalist (6) as negative, fearful and overly cautious. And in turn the Loyalist (6) sees their Enthusiast (7) as avoidant, escapist and dangerously unrealistic. Each polarizes further into their corner, triggering the other even more. Both may begin to doubt a happy future with the other as the relationship falters. Without a break in the downward momentum, the relationship may end.

7:6 The Lighthouse
The trigger for the downward spiral is anxiety, which both Enthusiast (7)s and Loyalist (6)s experience but react to differently. The Loyalist (6) tries to remove risk, and the Enthusiast (7) tries to remove limitations. Thus, to break the momentum of the downward spiral, both partners need to develop healthier coping mechanisms to manage their anxiety. Risk and limitations are both unavoidable aspects of life. Developing a healthy balance to risk and limitation by both partners helps this relationship.

7:6 The Kundalini Yoga Connection
The Loyalist (6) typically has a more direct relationship with their anxiety and can sometimes be so anxious that they need a powerful physical practice to quiet their mind. Kundalini Yoga kriyas and meditations to bring them out of their head and into their body are beneficial. Kundalini Yoga kriyas and meditations that incorporate breathwork to lower

anxiety, to cultivate self-reliance and to develop trust are also helpful.

Enthusiast (7)s need to resist the urge to avoid the negative. They need to develop the ability to feel the full spectrum of human emotion. Kundalini Yoga kriyas and meditations to build the nervous system, enhance focus and lower anxiety are helpful.

See the appendix for Loyalist (6) and Enthusiast (7) recommended Kundalini Yoga kriyas and meditations.

7:7 Enthusiast (7) with Enthusiast (7)

Stella, Enthusiast (7) in a relationship for less than a year with Diego, Enthusiast (7)

"I love Diego's approach to life. He's an incredibly social person, a huge jokester, a lighthearted lover of life with the motto "I work to live!" He plays. He lifts the mood wherever he goes. He makes me laugh until I cry and usually at the moment when I need it the most. I literally have no words for how much I love this quality about him. His smile lights up the room.

There is no comparison to the general happiness that I experience when I am with Diego. One of the things I love about our relationship is that we both thrive on spontaneity. We can be sitting together on a Thursday night watching TV when one will turn to the other and say "Let's go out and do something!" We're in agreement so we'll jump in the car, drive around with windows down, music blaring, on our way to our favorite hangout to see who else might be there...In other relationships, my partner would have no interest in leaving the house, but Diego is on the same wavelength - maybe it was even his idea – so off we go. For me, this is pure heaven.

In our relationship, freedom is a guiding principle. He is nothing but supportive of my life, my independence and my need for the freedom to make choices for myself that do not always include him. In return, I feel the same way and am not threatened or sad that he wants to pursue his own interests and life, sometimes without me. We both understand this need for freedom doesn't mean that we don't want our relationship to be an essential part of our lives.

In past relationships, my need for freedom has hurt my partner's feelings and led to incredibly difficult arguments that left me feeling untrusted, unloved, insecure about my choices and sad. In this relationship, I'm with someone who is not only unoffended by this need of mine but who in fact shares it. This similarity creates a loop of support instead of disagreement. We both feel incredibly loved, supported and happy.

While we are very similar in many ways, like any two human beings, we have our differences. Our communication styles are different. Diego, with his strong Leader (8) wing, has no problems expressing himself when he gets frustrated. He's direct and can come across as insensitive. I understand that he's trying to resolve the issue quickly so we can get back to a good time, but others don't experience it this way. I, on the other hand, with my strong Loyalist (6) wing, rarely voice critical thoughts and am pretty uncomfortable with confrontation. Instead, I'll work hard to keep the mood high and make people feel at ease, sometimes causing my own suffering. So, while our desires may be the same, they can manifest really differently.

On a deeper level, I worry that Diego may grow bored of a committed relationship. We were friends for four years before getting together, so I've seen him single, and I also understand that underlying drive for freedom. Since I share this drive, I understand how intense it can be. And like all insecurities, I worry that I will stop being my true self in response to my fears. I am working really hard to live in the moment and to truly trust in myself and in him. Meditation, journaling and focusing on my inner world has worked wonders here!

My hope for our relationship is that we are special because before we chose to be together, we chose to be great friends. Now that we are together, it is hard to describe how much gratitude I feel – Diego makes me want to fall to my knees and thank God for helping us to find each other. I believe we will find ways to make it work for the long haul, but if we decide at some point not stay together, I will always be thankful for experiencing the world with him. Diego is my happy place; he always has been."

Courtney, Enthusiast (7) married in a 6-year relationship with Martin, Enthusiast (7)

"Martin is exuberant, action-oriented, extremely genuine and charmingly funny at times. It is amazing the number of things he can get done in a day. He is a high school biology teacher and has chosen a profession that enables and encourages lifelong learning. This suits him well, as even outside of work he is constantly trying new projects and learning new things.

He is a very motivating partner. He is always pushing me forward to try something new, see things from a different perspective, try something in a different way. He balances me and helps me reorient myself when I am distracted by the needs of others. And while he is a very exciting partner, he is also very devoted and puts a lot of effort into my happiness, which, unfortunately, seems to be more complicated than his.

TYPE SEVEN ENTHUSIAST/ADVENTURER

Our relationship is based on spontaneity, personal freedom and making fun a priority. We both love traveling and met abroad in Peace Corps. We make it a priority to take at least one trip a year, more if we can afford it, and usually have only very loose plans for the time we're away. Our first trip together was during the holidays when we were in Peace Corps, during which we backpacked and hitchhiked around East Africa.

We prioritize positive experiences over things. For our wedding, we spent over half of our wedding budget to rent a house on the beach for our close friends to stay in for the week leading up to the wedding. Within the relationship, we don't have a lot of rules, spoken or implied. Personal freedom guides our dynamic and most expectations we have of each other have been articulated and agreed on casually.

We have one other relationship quirk that we share – and it is good we both have it. We tend to prefer doing things "the hard way" because we find that more interesting. For example, we have two cars, but I prefer to walk the two-plus miles to school every day while my husband usually bikes the five miles to his job.

As it relates to challenges, the general lack of rules occasionally backfires. In a moment of stress, one of us might artificially mandate a rule, which causes confusion, astonishment and sometimes resentment from the other. When we're stressed, we both can become brittle and unforgiving.

For him, some social situations can be stressful, and he prefers more support from me. But I'm very comfortable in a social setting and in fact, more focused on the group in that moment. A perfect example of this was at one of my best friend's wedding last year. Throughout the night, I would talk to Martin and then to other friends. I was moving around and catching up with all of these people from my past that I don't get to see much. But he didn't know many people. At first, we were standing with each other, but I walked away to say hello to someone and didn't bring him with me. Later, I noticed he was sitting alone. When I asked him what was wrong, he said he felt left out, like I didn't even notice he was gone. In the moment, he wanted me to be more attentive and wanted to be with me in my happiness but sort of didn't know how to behave in a strange social setting. His way of coping was to pout. And in the end, I felt constrained having to "take care of him," and not just being free to catch up with others.

It is interesting because although we share the same "wiring," we have a lot of differences. He doesn't always think things through before starting which leads to time lost fixing mistakes. He is a bit more full-on than I am. He'll push himself until he passes out while I'm more likely to pace myself. And he doesn't always understand that me asking for space isn't a form of rejection; it just means I need space.

Overall, I'm very happy in my relationship. We are both generally good at putting stress aside and prioritizing new, fun activities. A few winters ago, we took a Garth Fagan style dance class. Neither of us are dancers, and it was SO fun."

7:7 The Theory

7:7 When In Balance
A double Enthusiast (7) couple share a desire for a relationship free from expectations and limitations where freedom, fun and spontaneity are guiding principles. With each other, finally they have found someone who not only is unoffended by their desire for personal freedom but who in fact shares this same desire. They can be almost giddy to have found a kindred spirit.

Both share positive thinking, a drive for new adventures and experiences, as well as curiosity, resilience and a future orientation. Gratitude comes easily to this couple as their minds naturally orient to the positive things in their lives. Both positively reframe even difficult situations, and this couple focuses on the exuberance borne of overcoming challenges and the thrill of new experiences. Together they radiate happiness, hospitality, good cheer and good vibes. This can be a popular couple sought after by many for their uplifting, positive energy. This energy is contagious.

7:7 The Downward Spiral
The shared blind spot of the Enthusiast (7) can be what triggers the downward spiral of this pair – a deep avoidance of the negative.

Enthusiast (7)s have difficulty staying with negative, challenging emotions. They tend to idealize life and filter in only the positive. Negative emotions are buried and may manifest in judgment or selfishness. With a double Enthusiast (7) couple, this situation is multiplied so the reality distortion can become extreme. Enthusiast (7)s can have a childlike quality about them, and in the less self-aware stages, this manifests as immaturity and an inability to manage their underlying anxiety. With tightening defenses, Enthusiast (7)s grow bored, impatient and turn their attention away from the issue to look for more positive stimulation. Anxiety, masked as boredom and impatience, can be the beginning of the downward spiral for this couple. As one starts to lose interest in the relationship, anxiety from the Enthusiast (7) other grows.

If the downward spiral gains momentum, either or both Enthusiasts may lash out at the other, saying things impulsively, making demands and offering unfiltered, righteous criticism of the other. Enthusiast (7)s are self-referencing so sensitivity towards the feelings of their partner evaporates in the face of stress. In lower stages of awareness, one or both can become self-centered, mean and unreliable.

If the couple can't manage their anxiety enough to tolerate some level of discomfort, this couple can drift away from each other or break dramatically apart, ending the once joyous partnership.

7:7 The Lighthouse

The ability to tolerate discomfort and manage anxiety often masked as boredom determines the long-term prospect for this partnership. Enthusiast (7)s must trust that there is value in experiencing and processing negative emotions. While they may never enjoy the negative, they need to not feel threatened by it. Both partners need to learn techniques to manage anxiety so they can face negative issues, stay still and really sink into the present moment. This allows them to establish a truly heart-based, emotionally rich connection instead of being merely each other's playmates.

7:7 The Kundalini Yoga Connection

Enthusiast (7)s need to strengthen their nervous system to allow them space to stay still in the face of painful and negative emotions. Resisting the intense urge to leave or avoid is difficult particularly when the Enthusiast (7) wiring says "why feel bad?" Kundalini Yoga kriyas and meditations to strengthen the nervous system, to lower anxiety, to improve focus and to open the heart are helpful.

See the appendix for Enthusiast (7) recommended Kundalini Yoga kriyas and meditations.

7:8 Enthusiast (7) with Leader (8)

Allison, Leader (8) in a 17-year relationship with Melinda, Enthusiast (7)

"Melinda is a seeker, pursuing the creative side of life and finding great pleasure and universal truths in the simplest of things such as nature. I appreciate that she is fiercely independent and yet can also shift to interdependence as well. We share a wacky, albeit sometimes dark, sense of humor. Melinda is meticulous about her environment: clean, tidy, sparing in her possessions...which I love. She brings me a practical perspective and can be very grounded when offering assistance to others. She has a deep spiritual life, and I gain a big picture perspective from her insights and thoughts.

As a couple, we are super creative and really supportive of each other. This ranges from creative and spiritual endeavors to more practical projects like home design, furniture-moving, trimming bonsais and caring for our dogs. We both enjoy planning meals, especially for entertaining. We can be an unstoppable team.

We are both strong-willed and independent, and interestingly, this can create challenges in our relationship. Melinda's independence is extreme, and sometimes I feel too separated from her. We both hate feeling controlled, so compromise is a delicate balancing act.

We share emotions differently. While we are both basically optimistic, I'm more emotionally open, more brooding and more comfortable talking about my darker feelings. She's more closed about her emotions, and while she tries to make space for my brooding side, it is a big challenge for her, and something she doesn't really understand. She, at times, experiences it as me harping on and on...Melinda sometimes avoids difficult emotional issues by keeping busy with projects, and this has been painful for me. At times, I have felt she was not connecting with me for a deeper discussion because she felt fearful of the emotional content. This has been my biggest challenge, particularly since I can experience it as rejection.

We've had quite a journey together. We were together for 17 years, then separated for 5 years and are now dating again. It is the most creative partnership I have ever experienced. We have a deep understanding of spiritual pathways; an alliance, a partnership in perspective. This connection is deeper than any of my other relationships."

7:8 The Theory

7:8 When In Balance

The Enthusiast (7) and the Leader (8) make a high energy, adventurous, bold and colorful couple. Fundamentally, both believe they are responsible for their own happiness and fulfillment, giving both a self-referencing, self-interested approach to life. Conversely, they can be magnanimous, generous and giving, particularly with their inner circle of family and friends. Both can be unfiltered, brash and outspoken in their communication, saying out loud what others would only think. They vociferously advocate for themselves and their needs.

This is an energetic pair that enjoys entertaining, exploring, having adventures and living life to its fullest. Both partners individually are a force to be reckoned with, and when united and aligned, this team can be powerful, effective and resourceful. Their accomplishments energize them so the more they achieve, the more they pursue. There can be a lust for life and a taste for wild excitement in this couple.

Enthusiast (7)s bring joy, gratitude, sparkle and a sense of adventure to the dynamic. They are more interested in fun and novelty, bringing ideas for new adventures, plans and celebrations to the pairing. Freshness is stimulating to them, so they are constantly on the hunt for things they haven't tried before.

Leader (8)s tend to be more grounded, focused and determined in the pursuit of their goals, many of which are material. Their communication style is direct and intense. They are generally more interested in material success than their Enthusiast (7).

As a couple, this can be a high energy and engaging team that stimulate those around them. There can be a larger than life element to this pair, and their entertaining can be legendary. When they want the same goals, it is as though they have each found the perfect partner in crime.

7:8 The Downward Spiral

When aligned, this is a highly effective, strong-willed team, but when their interests are out of sync, this strong will can be a recipe for disaster. Forceful and independent, both feel it is extremely important to get what they want. A reality distortion around control and limitations can begin, and it is difficult for either to back down, even around seemingly mundane issues. Leader (8)s want control over their situations, and the Enthusiast (7)'s independence can run counter to this desire. Concerns about power and dominance arise, marking the beginning of the downward spiral. The downward spiral manifests either as a fight for control or an implicit agreement to operate independently to get their needs met, thus eroding intimacy.

Leader (8)s can become dictatorial, harsh and bullying in their attempts to rein in the Enthusiast (7) and to establish control. Enthusiast (7)s can become pushy, demanding and petulant about getting their way. Leader (8)s are more sensitive to power dynamics and may start to look for signs of dissent. Enthusiast (7)s are less interested in power but are extremely sensitive to feeling trapped, limited or controlled in any way. They have an exaggerated sense of limitations and may start acting out as a way to prove they are free to do what they want. Both partners can dig in their heels, becoming insulting, hard-hearted, self-centered and unreasonable. Compassion evaporates as conflict increases.

Because both partners have the energy for it, conflicts can spin out of control becoming emotionally exhausting and externally dramatic. Whereas other couples might have a mechanism to de-escalate the situation, this pair charges forward into conflict time and time again, resulting in screaming and yelling with insults hurled back and forth. If the downward spiral gains momentum, this intensity might start to feel like the norm until this couple decides to call it quits.

Alternatively, this couple may implicitly agree to stay together but operate independently with a lack of true emotional connection. Both isolate into their independently crafted lives with the occasional overlapping touch point. Though this might carry on for some period of time, the relationship eventually ends when one partner decides they want more.

7:8 The Lighthouse
Issues of control and feeling controlled can trigger the downward spiral in this pairing. Both partners feel a reality distortion around control, sparking an anxiety response in the Enthusiast (7) and an anger response in the Leader (8). The Enthusiast (7) suspects their greatest fear, being trapped in pain, may come true. The Leader (8) suspects their greatest concern, being vulnerable, may come to fruition. Both must recognize the reality distortion they are experiencing. Self-soothing, doing a reality check and returning to a heart connection when these triggers occur can help break the momentum of the downward spiral.

Both partners need to come forward and connect at the heart. Both are deeply independent, but there can be too much space created in the relationship, and intimacy can be lost. Establishing and maintaining a strong heart connection is key in this couple.

7:8 The Kundalini Yoga Connection
Because the reality distortion is so great, it is hard for either partner not to feel threatened. Strengthening the nervous system will help both partners decrease their overreaction to their feelings around control. Kundalini Yoga kriyas and meditations that open the heart and cultivate heart energy are helpful. Both partners are capable of great love and compassion, but they can cut off from this energy in an attempt to maintain freedom or assert control.

Enthusiast (7)s need to learn to manage their anxiety and to cultivate a stronger heart-centered way of dealing with others. Kundalini Yoga kriyas and meditations to lower anxiety, open the heart, connect with the energy of emotion and release negative emotions can be helpful. Because Enthusiast (7)s tend to under process negative emotions, these emotions can get lodged energetically in the body. They need to be released.

Leader (8)s need to shed their emotional armor around their heart so they can connect in a more direct, loving, interdependent way. Leader (8)s have a tremendous pool of compassion, kindness and innocence within them, but they cut off from this in an attempt to deny vulnerability. Kundalini Yoga kriyas and meditations to burn out anger, to open the heart and to access compassion are helpful.

See the appendix for Enthusiast (7) and Leader (8) recommended Kundalini Yoga kriyas and meditations.

7:9 Enthusiast (7) with Peacemaker (9)

Anders, Peacemaker (9) married in a 3-year relationship Anette, Enthusiast (7)

"Anette has huge energy and wants to do lots of things. She keeps our schedule filled and loves to socialize. The more she does, the more energy she seems to gain.

She has what I call "the lighthouse effect." Everyone is drawn to her and feeds off her brightness and joy. She is naturally uplifting and positive, and it seems to take little or no effort for her happiness to fill the room. She is a genuinely kind person who feels good when she helps others.

In our relationship, we balance each other. On my own, I sometimes feel insecure and unsure of myself which makes me reluctant to try new things and to put myself out there. Anette is the opposite. She seems to have no fear of failure or the unknown and charges cheerfully forward. I love this about her, and I feed off it. And in our dynamic, I provide a stable base as she sometimes overcommits or doesn't think things through very carefully. I'm more deliberate in my thoughts and actions, and she knows she can rely on my stability and judgment.

Anette is very emotional and expressive which can be both positive and negative. When things are going well, she fills the house with love, joy and happiness. When things are difficult, she can be explosive and temperamental. Either way, the house is always filled with emotion. I'm more stoic – I feel a lot but often don't express myself openly. Being with her is a nice fit because with Anette, everything eventually gets expressed. It is too dramatic to have things go unresolved. Her psychology can't tolerate it.

I really appreciate how committed she is to the relationship and how hard she works to constantly make it better. She also does a good job of accepting me as I am. Sometimes I am lazy and unmotivated. Sometimes I don't want to talk about my feelings. Sometimes I want to avoid difficult situations. She understands and accepts all of this. She's sensitive and knows when she can push me and when it is better to leave me alone.

Her anxiety can be a challenge. She gets very anxious if she feels left out or if she can't do something she wants. Negative thoughts seem to take over her mind, and she can get really worked up. It is hard for me to watch her suffer. And I worry as we enter a period of our lives with more responsibilities that this issue will come up more and more.

Overall, I'm very happy in my relationship. I love Anette and feel like I've found my life partner."

7:9 The Theory

7:9 When In Balance
The Enthusiast (7) with the Peacemaker (9) can make a loving, effective partnership helping to balance each other's nearly opposite energetic tendencies and compensating for each other's blind spots and weaknesses. The Enthusiast (7) helps to energize and wake up the Peacemaker (9). The Peacemaker (9) helps to ground and focus the Enthusiast (7). Foundational values of this partnership are mutual acceptance, the belief in a positive future and supportive, balancing companionship.

Enthusiast (7)s offer high energy, a positive outlook, curiosity and a nearly insatiable drive to try new things. Their extroverted drive for fun and their busy schedule help shake the Peacemaker (9) into action. Enthusiast (7)s are action-oriented without much fear of failure. This allows them to cheerfully charge into new environments and experiences without a lot of hesitation or deliberation. Any actual failure is reframed as positive, and they tend to be quite resilient. All of these characteristics are helpful and inspiring for the Peacemaker (9) whose approach to life is more slow-paced, hesitant and deliberate.

Peacemaker (9)s share a positive outlook about life but tend to be more grounded, calm, steady and reliable. They are considerate, good listeners focused on the needs of others and gifted at making outsiders feel welcomed and accepted. They model dependability, accommodation and a more relaxed laid-back approach to life that is very useful for the Enthusiast (7) to observe and mirror. They provide the Enthusiast (7) with easy companionship for the Enthusiast (7)'s wide range of adventures.

When in balance, this couple can be a wonderful balance of yin and yang energy, of high spirits and mellow acceptance.

TYPE SEVEN ENTHUSIAST/ADVENTURER

 ### 7:9 The Downward Spiral
The downward spiral is usually triggered by the avoidance of negative topics or an imbalance of control.

Both types instinctively gravitate away from thorny issues and painful discussions. When fixated with tightening defenses, Enthusiast (7)s reframe negative events, focusing almost relentlessly on the positive. Processing negative emotions is extremely anxiety-provoking for most Enthusiast (7)s, and their attention instinctively moves to more positive topics. Likewise, addressing negative issues is challenging and anxiety-provoking for Peacemaker (9)s. Difficult discussions feel like a threat to the harmony Peacemaker (9)s seek to feel stable. Major issues may go unaddressed, but the anxiety surrounding the issues remains and in a fixated state, the partners may begin blaming each other, acting out or becoming directly or indirectly critical and frustrated with one another. Thus begins the downward spiral.

An imbalance of control can also be a trigger in this relationship. Enthusiast (7)s are self-referencing, and Peacemaker (9)s are other-referencing so it can be easy for the Enthusiast (7) to make demands, not realizing their Peacemaker (9) partner has different priorities and desires. The less verbal Peacemaker (9) may become passive-aggressive or start to numb out as an indirect strategy to stand their ground. The downward spiral is triggered and without fully realizing it, this couple can start to drift apart and may not consciously realize there is an issue until they have become quite distant.

The depth of the downward spiral has a lot to do with the partnership's level of awareness. In extreme cases, the Enthusiast (7) gets frustrated and anxious and begins attacking the Peacemaker (9), triggering more passive resistance and stonewalling. If the momentum isn't broken, this once joyous and balancing couple can polarize into respective corners of resentment, contempt, criticism and stonewalling until the relationship eventually ends.

 ### 7:9 The Lighthouse
Excessive avoidance of the negative and denial of reality mark the beginning of the downward spiral in this couple so learning to stay present and to address painful topics and issues directly is the key to breaking the downward momentum. The self-referencing Enthusiast (7) and the other-referencing Peacemaker (9) need to find a healthy balance of needs and priorities. Peacemaker (9)s need time and a receptive space to figure out what they really want. Enthusiast (7)s need to cultivate discernment and to learn that they will be ok even if they don't get everything they want.

7:9 The Kundalini Yoga Connection
Both partners will benefit from strengthening their nervous systems as they learn to address difficult topics.

Enthusiast (7)s need to identify and manage their anxiety instead of staying on the go and staying distracted. They need to learn to sit still, let feelings arise and stay present and focused in the face of discomfort. Kundalini Yoga kriyas and meditations to lower anxiety and to quiet the mind are beneficial. Because Enthusiast (7)s have such an active mind, a powerful physical practice can be helpful in slowing their noisy, anxious thoughts.

Peacemaker (9)s need to get in touch with their feelings and particularly their repressed anger. They need to change their relationship with conflict and learn to see it as part of a healthy relationship. Kundalini Yoga kriyas and meditations to burn anger, to get energy flowing in the body and to strengthen the navel center are all beneficial.

See Appendix for Enthusiast (7) and Peacemaker (9) recommended Kundalini Yoga kriyas and meditations.

This book is a living document. We will be updating it periodically with new information. If you are or were in a relationship with an Enthusiast (7) and you would like to participate in the related relationship survey, please email me at lynn@lynnroulo.com.

Type Eight
LEADER/ CHALLENGER/ PROTECTOR

(seeks power/avoids being vulnerable)

 ## Overview

The Leader (8) has a keen awareness of power dynamics: who is in control, who might need protection, who needs to be challenged and so forth. Leader (8)s are usually blunt, direct, "what you see is what you get" people with forceful, big personalities. Sometimes described as a bull in a china shop, Leader (8)s often get feedback at some point in their life that they are just "too much" for people or that their communication style is overwhelming others: "your co-workers are afraid of you," "do you realize you are yelling at the children?" "why are you so angry?" This feedback usually comes as a huge shock to the Leader (8)s who don't feel they are expressing themselves this way at all. Sharing vulnerable, softer emotions can be challenging for Leaders (8)s who are typically not comfortable expressing anything that feels like weakness.

Leader (8)s tend to undervalue the emotional world and express love indirectly, through acts of devotion like working hard to provide for their family, defending their loved ones against others, paving the way for a brighter future for their intimate partners and so forth.

Partners of Leader (8)s appreciate the fact they are protective, good providers, resourceful, determined, strong-willed, independent, tough and resilient.

Partners are challenged by the fact they can be angry, direct, harsh, heavy-handed, controlling and aggressive.

• Attention Bias/Habit Of Attention:
Their attention goes to power. They see hierarchy and power dynamics easily and immediately: who is in control, who is vulnerable and might need protection and so on. They are comfortable challenging power and authority and will often step forward to protect the underdog. Their attention moves away from personal feelings of vulnerability and the softer emotions.

• Emotional Style:
Stoic, sincere, curt, genuine, brief, armored.

• Communication Style:
Direct, clear, assertive, may be loud and abrasive, harsh.

• Brings To The Relationship:
Leadership, protection, determination, resourcefulness, grit, a strong internal code of ethics.

• Unique Strengths:
Protection, justice, guardians of the underdog, extremely strong-willed, resilient, resourceful.

• Challenges:
Controlling, aggressive, angry, confrontational, difficulty expressing softer emotions.

• Stability And Security:
"I feel stable when I am in control of my environment. I feel secure when I am in a leadership position, and I can make the decisions."

• Instability And Insecurity:
"I feel unstable when I am vulnerable and not in control of my environment. I feel insecure when I believe others might have power over me."

• Path Of Growth:
Vulnerability
Leader (8)s grow when they learn the power of vulnerability and how to share their softer feelings and emotions with others.

- **Energy:**
Big, powerful, hot, clear, bright.

- **The Kundalini Yoga Connection:**
Leader (8)s have a lot of energetic armor around their heart center. They have big hearts, but these hearts are strongly guarded. Pure innocence, like children and animals, pierces it. To guard softer, vulnerable emotions, they access anger. Kundalini Yoga kriyas and meditations to manage the anger response, burn out anger and open the heart center are helpful.

The Leader (8) Subtypes

"Satisfaction" Self-Preservation Subtype:
The self-preservation Leader (8) expresses emotional intensity on the most basic level. Strong, powerful, direct and productive, this is a person who likes material comfort, good food and drink and good company. To the outside world, this looks like a no-nonsense personality who dislikes pretense and who pursues what they want without much, if any, hesitation. Internally, there is an instinct that they must act to fulfill their needs. They have the title "Satisfaction" because of their direct drive for personal satisfaction of their desires. They may focus on creating a secure home and "providing" as an expression of love and affection.

Self-preservation Leader (8)s know how to do business and get things done. Because they are so effective in a practical way, they may inadvertently generate dependencies in others, particularly intimate partners, who come to rely on their decision-making and protection. This can be a challenge for the self-preservation Leader (8). On the one hand, they enjoy the feeling of being in control and being important. On the other hand, they believe everyone needs to learn self-sufficiency, and this applies even more to the people they love. They can feel an inner conflict about the dependency their loved ones have on them.

On the positive side, these are powerful people who have a talent for going after what they want. They can be fiercely loyal and protective of their inner circle or anyone who falls under their care.

On the less positive side, their need to be strong can be so great that kindness, good intentions and the world of feelings may get lost. They often don't understand the negative impact this has on their relationships.

"Solidarity" Social Subtype:

The social Leader (8) expresses emotional intensity on a more muted level than the other two subtypes. The least angry of the Leader (8)s, this person tends to align with groups and can have a more difficult time with individualized relationships. To the outside world, this is a person who is nurturing, protective, loyal, friendly and highly concerned with injustices that happen to the weak or underprivileged. Internally, this is someone who has a hard time nurturing their own needs and moves towards the power of the group to have their needs met. They have the title "Solidarity" because of their alignment around groups and their quest for loyalty.

The social Leader (8) can have a complicated relationship with commitment and loyalty. They seek loyalty and value it extremely highly in their personal relationships. At the same time, they are very guarded against rejection, often believing it is almost unavoidable in their intimate relationships. Their fear of rejection can sometimes look like a lack of commitment. However, when they finally find someone they believe will truly never leave them, their bond of trust is strong, and their commitment can be unshakeable.

On the positive side, this Leader (8) is less quick to anger and is caring and protective of others in their lives. They may appear softer and calmer than the other Leader (8) subtypes.

On the less positive side, they can have a blind spot regarding their own needs for love and protection. They often subconsciously give up their own need for love in exchange for power and pleasure.

"Possession" Intimate Subtype:

The intimate Leader (8) expresses emotional intensity through open rebellion. The most emotional and least conventional of the Leader (8)s, this person feels things deeply and tends to be more action-oriented than contemplative. To the outside world, this is a highly magnetic, charismatic person who energetically takes over their environment. Internally, this person has a sense that the world starts when they enter the room. They have the title "Possession" because of their tendency to have possessive relationships with lovers, friends, places, objects and situations.

These Leader (8)s are less focused on the material world and more interested in power over others through their words and influence. They can be magnetic and seductive, with an almost irresistible quality and colorful personality. They seek adventure, risk and challenges. Intimate Leader (8)s can be particularly impatient with weakness, incompetence and dependence. They want to dominate their environment completely, but they often seek strong intimate partners. This adds to the passion of the relationship.

On the positive side, these are fascinating, charismatic people who leave an impression on others. They can be bold. They feel deeply, and when their relationships are going well, the depth of their feelings is a positive thing.

On the less positive side, they can be highly intolerant of others, particularly weak, slow or dependent people. They can be possessive of their lovers and friends. And because they feel so deeply, when their relationships aren't going well, they suffer intensely.

Leader (8)—Levels of Awareness

Leader (8) When Self-Aware
Leader (8)s become generous, magnanimous, restrained, wise and courageous. They connect with a power higher than themselves, allowing them to be discerning and fair in their actions. They can access vulnerability and share it when appropriate. They can leave a significant mark on the world. Assertive, strong, bold and self-confident, they fiercely advocate for themselves and any group they are aligned with or have elected to protect. Tough, resourceful, energized and focused, they aggressively go after what they want with gusto. Decisive and commanding, the Leader (8) shows strong leadership skills and takes the initiative to make things happen. Honorable and protective, other people seek to be under the care and concern of self-aware Leader (8)s.

Leader (8) With Tightening Defenses
Independence and self-reliance become dominating themes and the drive to control their environment intensifies. There are concerns about adequate resources (financial, material and so forth). Earthy, practical and resourceful, the Leader (8) may be pioneering and risk-taking, looking for opportunities to amass personal fortunes. Workaholism may be present as emotional needs are pushed to the side, minimized or ignored. The Leader (8) wants control over their environment and the people in it. Questions of trust and loyalty become central as relationships narrow to friends or foes. Egocentric behavior may be present including bragging, cutting others down and setting themselves at the top of the hierarchy in an arrogant manner. They become argumentative, combative, confrontational and intimidating as a way to manage feelings of insecurity and vulnerability.

Leader (8) When Fixated
The Leader (8) becomes ruthless, tunnel-visioned and dictatorial. They become extremely controlling and hard-hearted. They feel whoever has the most control is the winner, and

they may have delusional ideas about their own power, feeling invincible and omnipotent. Megalomaniacal, they overreach, overextend and power grab, using their environment indiscriminately. Feeling their power may be at risk, they may brutally annihilate everything that doesn't conform to their desires. Surrender is off the table as it feels like self-destruction. They may become filled with revenge and rage, exhibiting irrational and violent behavior.

Keys If You Are In A Relationship With A Leader (8)

"I don't express tenderness like everyone else."

Daphne, Leader (8) married in a 12-year relationship with Antonio, Perfectionist (1)

"We've been together 12 years, and I think he's finally learning that underneath my tough exterior I am incredibly tender. Tenderness looks different in me than it does in other people, especially other women. When I ask for help, that's tenderness; when I share something difficult that I had to process emotionally during the day, even if I don't cry or get emotionally expressive, that's tenderness. And he's learning that when I feel insecure in the relationship, what I really crave is appreciation and reassurance. Each year, we understand each other better, and I think we are both enjoying the journey."

Sydney, Peacemaker (9) in a 2-year relationship with Richard, Leader (8)

"Richard does not gush, he is not effusive, and his expressions of love and tenderness are not plentiful. But when they do occur, they touch me deeply because I imagine that for him, loving me feels like giving away a piece of his heart, and it must be terrifying to fear that I might not treat that piece of his heart with care.

My experience of his expressions of love or tenderness is that they are spontaneous and heartfelt but do not occur often, and the same one usually does not occur twice. This means that if he says something like, "I wish we had met when we were younger, we would have been great parents together," "You are such a gentle soul, I love that," or if he reveals anything private about his feelings or his past, I should remain calm, savor the moment, not make a big deal out of it and hold it close to my heart because he is not likely to say or do the same thing any time in the near future.

I imagine that many women would not be satisfied with his sporadic expressions of love; many of them would not even recognize that allowing your girlfriend to sit at your bedside in the hospital or trusting her to communicate with your kids in an emergency situation could be acts of love, but I know him well enough now to know that they are tremendous expressions of love, tenderness and trust. I treasure these gifts because I know how difficult it is for him to be helpless and rely on someone else. I'm sure that if he were a less evolved person, there would have been grumpiness and perhaps lashing out and conflict when he was in the hospital, but there was not any of that.

I've also learned that trying to pull expressions of love out of him is never a good idea. If he feels like anyone is attempting to control him in any way, he will do the opposite thing just to make sure he remains in charge. I file his expressions of love away in my mind, and if I find myself in need of reassurance, I reach into my own mind and touch those, rather than trying to get him to perform on command."

Leader (8)s are extremely sensitive to being in positions of vulnerability so open expressions of love and affection can feel risky and uncomfortable to them. It can be a negative experience for them to share their vulnerable emotions directly. That said, they still feel deeply and have the normal human need to express these feelings. They solve this conflict by expressing themselves through acts of service and devotion more than through verbal expression.

If you are a Leader (8):
Understand your partner may need more verbal expressions of love than you would naturally give. This is a good growth opportunity as expressing vulnerable emotions helps Leader (8)s develop and evolve. You grow when you move outside your comfort zone and are a little more verbally direct about your softer feelings towards your partner and other people you love.

If you are in a relationship with a Leader (8):
Understand that your Leader (8) may not feel comfortable with direct verbal expressions of love and affection. Look for other expressions of these feelings. Leader (8)s typically work hard to be good providers, to maintain a safe, secure homefront and will powerfully defend those they love. Their expressions of love exist, they may just look different.

 "It is important that I feel in control of my environment. When I don't feel in control, I get angry because I feel vulnerable."

Sydney, Peacemaker (9) about her partner of 2 years Richard, Leader (8)

"Being vulnerable is hard for him, and I've come to recognize small things are really big things. For example, last week, we went to the emergency room to deal with a health issue of his, and when registering, he spontaneously requested that I be added as his emergency contact and next of kin. I realize that for someone else, this would have been a matter of course, but I know that for him it is not. When he had surgery last year, I had to remind him to tell the staff that I was in the waiting room so that they could update me. This time, he ended up being admitted to the hospital with a lung abscess, and I sat at his bedside and held his hand every day until he was discharged. Because I know him so well now, I know that this was not easy for him. His wish to be in control and to maintain his own space had to be at war with his wish to have me there and to be comforted. However, not only did he not once ask me to leave, but he also expressed appreciation and told me I was a "lifesaver," even though all I had done was stay with him. He also trusted me to convey updates to his grown daughters who live in other states, which is huge, because ordinarily, he would want to control that too, but he was just too sick."

Ravi, Leader (8) married in a 9-year relationship with Sangita, Helper (2)

"I have a strong desire, almost a need, to control my environment. It bothers me tremendously to not know 'the plan.' For instance, I don't want to just plan to go to a birthday party; I want to know where it is, when we'll get there and leave, who will be there, what activities are planned and so forth. Recently my wife, my kids and I went to a friend's child's birthday party in our city. I expected it to be at their house and to last for two hours. Instead, we arrived at the address, and it was a roller skating rink. My mind internally screamed "A ROLLER SKATING RINK???" For me, it's completely different preparation if we're going to an outside venue or a friend's house. I had to specifically calm myself down because it was probably going to be fine, and I couldn't do anything about it at that point. Fortunately, we had dressed appropriately, and the afternoon went smoothly. But how hard could it have been for my wife to relay the who/what/when/where of a bloody party? In the moment, I felt angry."

Leader (8)s work hard to avoid feeling vulnerable. They like to control their environment as a way to ensure they stay in a position of power. Surprises can trigger an intensely negative backlash. They can have a strong reaction to a seemingly small miscommunication because of their fear of being trapped in a defenseless position. Defenselessness and vulnerability can feel like annihilation.

If you are a Leader (8):
Understand you have a reality distortion around control that is confusing to others. Your mind is hypervigilant for anything that you feel could put you in a position of weakness. When you feel your body start to tense and when you feel anger start to rise as a result of changes or surprises in your environment, consciously try to exercise long, deep breathing as a tool to manage your reactivity.

If you are with a Leader (8):
Understand your partner has a reality distortion that feels very real to them. Control helps them to relax, and surprises make them tense. Trying to talk them out of this reality distortion is likely ineffective and frustrating to you both. A better strategy might be to try to keep them as informed as possible about small details and to work with them about their concerns when inevitable surprises present themselves.

 "I am extremely sensitive to rejection."

Anna, Leader (8)

"I remember being at a weekend-long conference where we had lots of breaks between workshops. At the breaks, I would quickly head out to my hotel room, or I'd disappear someplace where I could be alone. Towards the end of the workshop, the facilitator asked me why I kept disappearing. Normally I would have taken a "none of your business" attitude, but since it was an environment where we were encouraged to share our thoughts, I answered. I said, "Honestly, I assume no one really wants to be around me." To my horror, the facilitator then asked the group to raise their hand if they would have preferred me to stay engaged with the group. Everyone raised their hands. This would normally raise my suspicion, but a few people even mentioned specific things they liked about me. This was a huge shock. It had never occurred to me I would be wanted as part of the group. I felt like I had to reassess many of my beliefs around rejection."

Juliette, Enthusiast (7) about Anthon, Leader (8)

"I was hosting a party at my apartment with a large group of guests, including my boyfriend. At one point, the kitchen got really full, and I was having trouble serving the food and drinks. I gently nudged my boyfriend to move to the other room, and he freaked out completely. He felt I was pushing him out of the kitchen and that I was making a statement that he wasn't welcome at the party. He abruptly stormed out of my apartment and drove home,

much to my shock. It wasn't until later we got to the bottom of the misunderstanding. But in the meantime, the whole incident ruined my night."

Because Leader (8)s often have an aggressive and direct communication style, over the course of their lives, they get negative feedback about how they interact with others. If they hear this often enough they may begin to believe everyone would be better off if they keep to themselves. They can develop a hypersensitivity to rejection. They may imagine rejection where none was intended. And in some instances, they choose isolation as a way to protect themselves. Their isolation further adds to their emotional armor, and many Leader (8)s report feeling lonely.

If you are a Leader (8):
Understand that you are sensitive to rejection and sometimes imagine messages of rejection where none was intended. If you are unsure, ask clarifying questions. When you become reactive, you create the very environment you are trying to avoid.

If you are with a Leader (8):
You may already realize your partner is sensitive to feelings of rejection so try to reassure them often. Remind them of their positive traits and emphasize the positive aspects of who they are, including how they socialize.

TYPE EIGHT LEADER/CHALLENGER/PROTECTOR

LEADER (8)
360 DEGREE REVIEW

The next section features the 360 degree review--partnership with a Leader (8) from the perspective of each of the nine types.

8:1 Leader (8) with Perfectionist (1)

John, Perfectionist (1) married in an 18-year relationship with Anne, Leader (8)

"I admire my wife's passion and determination, her grit, her honesty and integrity and the way she can focus on something wholeheartedly until she reaches her goal. She is honest to the point of bluntness and will speak the truth, even in situations when it might hurt. This can be refreshing for me, as my concern about offending others prevents me from being so direct.

When we unite for a common goal, we can be quite a formidable and determined pair. During some missionary work in our past, we tolerated living conditions with pit latrines, irregular electricity and water supplies and sub-zero winters without any of it having a negative impact on the relationship. While others might have complained, we stayed focused on the goal and just got on with it! In many ways, we function together more practically and less romantically, more as friends and less as lovers. We work together on tasks very well, but in the busyness of life, our intimacy gets lost.

My wife can have a blunt and sometimes aggressive communication style, and in the early years of our relationship, her aggressive nature would sometimes drive me away. Over the years, she has become more aware and toned down her language, and I've become less sensitive to her manner.

While it's probably fair to say that we'd both appreciate greater intimacy in our relationship, we have a great partnership, enjoy one another's company and relate at a very deep emotional level. We've shared our deepest hurts and woundedness with one another and have a huge amount of love and respect for each other."

8:1 The Theory

8:1 When In Balance
This pair shares many fundamental values while adopting very different approaches. When self-aware and aligned in their goals, the common values serve as a solid foundation and the stylistic and energetic differences keep the partnership interesting and vibrant.

Shared values include a determination, grit and a willingness to work hard to overcome adversity for a higher cause. Both can be fierce, tough, focused, self-sacrificing and unswayed by the opinions of others. Truth, justice and a strong moral compass are key traits and values of both partners.

Energetically the two types are quite different, and this can be balancing, with the Leader (8) bringing a passionate and powerful presence contrasted against the Perfectionist (1)'s more contained, reserved and rigid manner. The Perfectionist (1) appreciates the presence, the big energy and the directness of the Leader (8). The Leader (8) admires the values, convictions and the uncompromising nature of the Perfectionist (1). Like a Mafia boss and a head nun, both embody their beliefs. When balanced and respectful of their differences, this is a powerful and impactful couple.

8:1 The Downward Spiral
Fundamental philosophical and energetic differences can be the trigger for the downward spiral of this couple. Their temperaments and approach to life are different and, in some ways, opposite. When fixated on their habit of attention, the differences can cause challenges. Perfectionist (1)s are methodical, rational, cool-headed and restrained. Work comes before play and self-denial lines up neatly with their values. This is a sharp contrast with the Leader (8) who uses their energetic presence to their advantage to get what they want and further their cause.

Leader (8)s are self-referencing and feel no shame or restraint in their pursuit of what they want. This can offend the Perfectionist (1) who values model behavior as part of their idealized world. The Perfectionist (1) starts to see the Leader (8)'s boldness as crude, unpredictable and untrustworthy. The initial attraction of the powerful, assertive Leader (8) descends into criticism, disdain and contempt.

Conversely, Leader (8)s don't appreciate feeling judged and begin to view the Perfectionist (1) as rigid, nitpicking, delusionally idealistic and hypocritical. Rather than feel controlled by the Perfectionist (1) in any way, the Leader (8) may start to act out, becoming more outrageous, rebellious and irreverent. As the downward spiral picks up momentum, anger, either open or convert, enters the picture. Without a mechanism to stop the momentum, the partners polarize and may eventually split.

8:1 The Lighthouse

Ironically, one of the core areas of work between these two energetically different types is the same: to open the heart. Both of these types have a lot of emotional armor, particularly in the heart center. When the downward spiral begins, the heart connection is lost. To reconnect, they need to dissolve their emotional armor and reconnect from the heart.

8:1 The Kundalini Yoga Connection

Both partners can have issues with control, and both have a strong internal compass and sense of themselves. To bridge their distance, they need to rediscover their common ground and shared values.

The Leader (8) needs to manage their anger response and their drive to control. This helps them reconnect with their heart. Long deep breathing and Kundalini Yoga kriyas and meditations that require energy and breath control are beneficial. Heart opening practices are also important.

The Perfectionist (1) need to burn out anger and frustration so they can access their heart once again. They need to learn stillness and acceptance. Kundalini Yoga kriyas for relaxation, releasing anger, opening the heart and cultivating compassion are beneficial and help them drop some of their rigidity.

See the appendix for Perfectionist (1) and Leader (8) recommended Kundalini Yoga kriyas and meditations.

8:2: Leader (8) with the Helper (2)

Sangita, Helper (2) married in a 9-year relationship with Ravi, Leader (8)

"My husband has been a strong independent person his whole life, and protector is a key word I might use to describe him. He has a protective instinct for the people he loves that amazes me. He can be really aggressive to outside forces that he sees as threats to the happiness of his family. At the same time, he can be nurturing and caring, especially with our kids. I admire how hard he works to pursue his goals, and I also appreciate how much he will compromise to make sure I'm happy. For example, even though it was disruptive to his professional life, he agreed to move across the country so I could be closer to my family when our first child was born.

One key difference between us is that I'm more people oriented – I spend a lot of time and energy worrying about the thoughts and feelings of other people. My husband doesn't have this orientation, and in fact, it can be hard to get him to consider the thoughts and feelings of others. When we're in a good place, we can use this difference to bring each other into balance. But when we're both stressed, it can be a big source of conflict.

One of our challenges is our communication styles are so different. Ravi can be really direct, confrontational and almost hard-hearted and hostile at times. He can be tunnel visioned about being right when we are in an argument, and it can take me several days to get over a really big fight. I don't think he fully understands the impact his confrontational style has on the people around him. This is one thing I wish I could communicate to him, so he understood – just how hard it is on other people when he's so confrontational."

8:2 The Theory

8:2 When In Balance
The Helper (2) and the Leader (8) combination can have an archetypical flavor to it with the Leader (8) embodying many of the traditional masculine or yang traits and the Helper (2) embodying the more feminine or yin traits. This can be a successful and enduring couple in which responsibilities are clearly delineated, and both partners complement and support each other.

Helper (2)s are more interested in the welfare of others while Leader (8)s tend to be more self-interested. Helper (2)s are more directly connected to the emotional world.

They value emotions highly and can identify, discuss and process their feelings and the feelings of others. They can reach even emotionally remote people. This is an important trait in breaking through the Leader (8)'s tough emotional armor. Leader (8)s can be very vulnerable and sensitive on the inside, but this is rarely presented to the outside world, and it takes someone with great empathy and an open heart to reach them. Helper (2)s are affectionate and adoring, and Leader (8)s enjoy basking in their care.

Leader (8)s are tough, practical and results-oriented. They balance out the Helper (2)'s softness and make sure concrete priorities get done. They have few or no issues with personal boundaries, and Helper (2)s can learn a lot from watching their Leader (8) partner. Leader (8)s are hard-working, resourceful, resilient and make sure the couple's concrete needs are met. Helper (2)s notice this and appreciate and admire their Leader (8)'s hard work and sacrifice.

Together, this can be a strong-willed, effective, supportive couple who accommodate each other's blind spots and accentuate each other's strengths.

8:2: The Downward Spiral

Helper (2)s and Leader (8)s value the emotional world very differently and have very different communication styles. With tightening defenses, these differences can trigger the downward spiral.

Helper (2)s place importance on feelings, relationships and emotional responses. Leader (8)s value the tangible, practical world more highly, and in average-to-lower levels of awareness can have a casual disregard for the emotional world. This difference manifests as dramatically different interpersonal styles. Leader (8)s are direct and independent with a potentially harsher way of dealing with people and situations. In average levels of awareness, they fall back on logic and reason, often stripping emotion out of decision-making. They can take pride in this approach. In contrast, average Helper (2)s become highly attached to people. Situations are loaded with emotion. Helper (2)s are more other-oriented in their thinking and feel they can't be at ease if they know someone close to them is suffering. Leader (8)s feel they can't relax if those close to them can't learn to take care of themselves.

Both types can polarize about their approach to interpersonal problems. Helper (2)s want to be overly involved whereas Leader (8)s demand independence. Helper (2)s see their Leader (8) as hard-hearted, confrontational, cold and self-centered. Leader (8)s lose respect for their Helper (2) seeing them as weak, manipulative and creating unnecessary dependencies with others. Fights around value differences can pepper the relationship, with neither side feeling they can move too much into the middle without a loss of their core values. They can be mutually confused by the other's position.

The cycle continues with the Leader (8) losing respect for the Helper (2), finding them people-pleasing and manipulative, and the Helper (2) feeling their Leader (8) is hard-hearted and controlling. Without a break in the momentum, the relationship is at risk, and the partners may split.

8:2 The Lighthouse
Different values around human connection and different communication styles start the downward spiral of this couple so coming back into the center is the way to stop the downward momentum. Helper (2)s need to try to connect with their Leader (8)'s fear of being vulnerable and the accompanying aggression to hide vulnerability. Leader (8)s need to respect their Helper (2)'s orientation towards feelings and emotions.

8:2 The Kundalini Yoga Connection
Both types need to strengthen their nervous system, so the communication style differences don't feel as threatening.

Helper (2)s need to manage their impulse to be so involved in the lives of others and to get more in touch with their own needs. Kundalini Yoga kriyas that increase body awareness, that cultivate self-love, self-acceptance and balance are helpful for Helper (2)s. Doing a yoga or meditation practice independently can be very beneficial to keep them focused on their own experience.

Leader (8)s need to connect with their heart and to learn the value of the emotional world, both their own emotions and the emotions of others. They need to learn to contain the energy of anger and to manage their aggressive communication style. This aggressive style is likely damaging their relationships. And they need to learn the power of vulnerability. Kundalini Yoga kriyas and meditations with heart opening and breath management exercises can be helpful for Leader (8)s.

See the appendix for Helper (2) and Leader (8) recommended Kundalini Yoga kriyas and meditations.

TYPE EIGHT LEADER/CHALLENGER/PROTECTOR

8:3 Leader (8) with Achiever (3)

Hans, Achiever (3) married in a 43-year relationship with Lara, Leader (8)

"Lara is decisive, clear and fast in her thinking. She is powerful – she knows what she wants and goes after it. She has a big energy, but at the same time, she is open to her feelings and encourages me to share mine.

Together we are a dynamic, effective team, and when we are aligned, we are almost unstoppable. My wife and I have been working together in our own business since 2001 and together, we divide and conquer. She knocks down the barriers, and I do a lot of practical tasks. We understand each other's strengths, we communicate well, and generally, we have great trust in each other.

While to outsiders, she looks domineering, I don't experience her this way, and we both know that she can't control me. Our friends think she is the decision-maker in the family, but my wife, our children and I know fully well this isn't the case. Lara has said she would lose respect for me if she controlled everything in our life. We're actually quite balanced, but my way of control is just much subtler than hers.

When we are aligned, we are great, but when we can't find agreement, it is really challenging. As a couple, we've had periods when we didn't have enough money to do all we wanted. Usually, we've been able to agree on priorities. But the times when we could not come to a compromise, it was extremely difficult as neither of us wants to back down or give up our position. Loyalty is another trigger point. My wife is very sensitive to any act she construes as disloyal. We've had issues arise between us when we lose trust in each other or if we interpret situations differently. There was a specific incident in which my wife interpreted the event very differently than I did. She still refers to it to this day, which is puzzling to me since it didn't register as anything worth discussing.

I do wish my wife would understand that sometimes it is difficult for me to share my experiences – especially those where my feelings are involved. It isn't that I don't want to share with her, but it is very difficult for me to start the conversation. I worry that she is not willing to really understand me and to listen with an open heart. I also know this isn't a reasonable concern, as when I do share, she is a good listener. I think opening up is just hard for me.

Overall, I feel very happy and lucky in my relationship. We support each other, we are a good team, and we enjoy our life together. We make each other stronger – not that it is important to be strong towards others, but it is important to be strong internally. We share important values, appreciate each other's company and love each other."

8:3 The Theory

8:3 When In Balance
The Achiever (3) and the Leader (8) make an effective, formidable couple who achieve their shared goals while sharing a deep emotional connection. Both are action-oriented, intense, assertive and practical — they see what they want and go after it. Both are high energy, competitive, disciplined and willing to work hard to further their cause. They can clearly and effectively divide up the duties of running a household or a company, both understanding the other's strengths and weaknesses. And both types are able to put their emotions to the side to stay focused on practical outcomes. With these shared traits, they also have some balancing differences.

Achiever (3)s bring a focus on image, a more diplomatic approach, balanced communication and a greater sensitivity to the way things are being perceived. Practical with a focus on their goals, they bring polish and tact to the dynamic. They strive to be the best in their field, and success is important to them. The Leader (8) finds it easy to admire their Achiever (3) partner, and this admiration brings the couple closer together.

Leader (8)s bring directness, decisiveness, grit, fearlessness and a strong internal compass. They are largely unswayed by the opinion of others and are less image-conscious than their Achiever (3). Honor, honestly, determination and integrity are hallmark Leader (8) traits, and these can be balancing for Achiever (3)s who can be swayed by concerns over image and failure. Leader (8)s have almost legendary willpower and stamina and don't flee in the face of failure. This can offer a growth opportunity for the Achiever (3) who is more inclined to remove themselves if they sense failure on the horizon.

Together this is an impressive, capable, influential couple. Outsiders see them as confident and bold. Once trust is established, this couple is almost unstoppable.

8:3 The Downward Spiral
Both Achiever (3)s and Leader (8)s are focused on practical goals and success so this couple can have a tendency towards workaholism. While this workaholic tendency doesn't usually trigger the downward spiral, it weakens their emotional connection and creates an environment of reactivity.

Tightening defenses cause the Achiever (3) to become more insecure and image-conscious. Situations that would have felt like setbacks start to feel like failures, and the Achiever (3) starts to look for areas where they can score a clear success. Authenticity may be sacrificed as the Achiever (3) becomes fixated about appearances and maintaining a positive external image. This may trigger a breach of trust for the Leader (8) who pushes for authenticity. If authenticity proves evasive, the Leader (8) responds by becoming more controlling and domineering. The downward spiral gains momentum. As both partners polarize, the Achiever (3) becomes more evasive, slippery and avoidant. This prompts an intense reaction in the Leader (8) who seeks to control their environment and wants answers now.

With trust, a common vision and shared goals gone, this couple has lost its way. Intense fights over control and personal agendas may erupt. Without a dramatic change in momentum, the relationship ends, sometimes very bitterly.

8:3 The Lighthouse

Reactions to stress trigger trust issues which mark the beginning of the downward spiral in this team. Trust is a foundational element in this pairing, and any fissures in trust can quickly escalate. As such, rebuilding trust is key to repairing this relationship. To do this, both partners need to go outside their comfort zone and manage their stress reaction differently. Leader (8)s need to learn vulnerability and how to share the full spectrum of emotions, including fear, sadness, melancholy, loneliness and so forth. Achiever (3)s need to speak from their heart, not from their head. They also need to learn self-love so they can dissolve shame and their intense fear of failure.

8:3 The Kundalini Yoga Connection

Both types need to strengthen their nervous system so that going outside their comfort zone feels less threatening. Achiever (3)s need to resist the urge to walk away from what feels like a potential failure. Leader (8)s need to resist the urge to press for immediate resolution.

Achiever (3)s must energetically balance their head with their heart and learn self-acceptance and self-love. With true self-acceptance, the threat of failure feels less intense. Kundalini Yoga kriyas and meditations to cultivate self-acceptance, to connect with feelings of love and gratitude and to strengthen the nervous system are helpful.

Leader (8)s need to learn to share their vulnerability in a heartfelt and raw way. They need to experience the power of their vulnerability. Kundalini Yoga kriyas and meditations to manage anger, to open the heart and to connect with gratitude are helpful.

See the appendix for Achiever (3) and Leader (8) recommended Kundalini Yoga kriyas and meditations.

8:4 Leader (8) with the Individualist (4)

Melyssa, Individualist (4), married in a 11-year relationship Benjamin, Leader (8)

"My husband is hardworking, determined, earthy, grounded and practical. He brings clear communication, social adeptness and is focused on being the best partner he can be. He constantly asks for feedback about how he can be a better husband to me and proactively makes changes based on what I say.

He calls me out on my issues and doesn't let me get away with bad behavior or emotional manipulation. In the long term, I love and appreciate this, but in the moment, it can be difficult. I love that we always react to each other.

In our relationship, we both have a lot of energetic intensity, and together, we go through many emotional highs and lows. We react and re-react to the other's emotional state. Our fights can be intense, though never threatening or scary.

As it relates to issues, my husband can be very dominant and assertive, sometimes without realizing it. It is hard for me, at times, to hold my space and be my own person. Our power dynamics are interesting – we both feel like the other holds the most control in the relationship. The reality is we probably balance each other in a dynamic dance. Benjamin tends to dominate our social life – who we see, how we will socialize and so forth. I control our emotional dynamic more – what we will discuss, where our emotional energy goes and so on.

Overall, I've very happy in my relationship. I like having a strong, vibrant partner, and while we constantly renegotiate control, I like that our relationship is intense. It leaves me feeling alive."

8:4 The Theory

8:4 When In Balance
The Individualist (4) and Leader (8) make a powerful, creative, intuitive pairing. Intensity is a key word to describe this coupling and together, they can be a provocative, colorful match. When their intensity is aligned for a common goal, they are almost unstoppable. While

they have many similarities, they also have key differences that provide growth edges for each other.

Individualist (4)s bring compassion, creativity, an intuitive understanding of the human condition and a fearlessness of the emotional spectrum. They feel a wide range of emotions on a regular basis and can act as a translator and guide through the emotional world for their Leader (8) partner. They create a safe space for the Leader (8) to be less guarded and more vulnerable. They help the Leader (8) identify and pinpoint their emotions and can also help the Leader (8) cultivate empathy towards others.

Leader (8)s bring a practical orientation and earthiness to the dynamic. They are clear, powerful, bold and decisive which allows them to stay grounded in the face of the Individualist (4)'s emotional storms. With their direct approach, they hold the Individualist (4) accountable for their behavior and responses, which can be highly beneficial for less self-aware Individualist (4)s.

When self-aware, they offer each other balance. Individualist (4)s appreciate their Leader (8)'s pragmatism, focus on the material world, protectiveness and stability in the face of the Individualist (4)'s emotional rollercoaster. The Leader (8) appreciates the Individualist (4)'s sensitivity, attunement to the emotional world and ability to express love. They are attracted to the mysteriousness of the Individualist (4)'s inner world. Together, both partners feel they can be free to express their full intensity, and this is a relief to both. They make each other feel alive, and there is a vitality and an emotional juiciness to this couple that is noteworthy.

8:4 The Downward Spiral

Themes of vulnerability and control can be the trigger for the downward spiral of this couple. Tightening defenses make the Leader (8) more controlling and more domineering while the Individualist (4) becomes more emotionally volatile and reactive. Because both types are so intense and self-referencing, there may not be an easy way to de-escalate fights, and disagreements can spiral out of control. The conflicts aren't always about what they appear to be about. On a deeper level, the Leader (8) is seeking to control their environment as a way to feel stable and avoid vulnerability. The Individualist (4) seeks stability through being heard and understood. When either partner feels threatened, they turn up the emotional volume. The depth of the downward spiral depends on how much each partner is able to see the deeper issues driving the wedge between them. Without insight, this couple may turn their emotional intensity against each other until the relationship eventually ends.

8:4 The Lighthouse
Emotional reactivity is the trigger for the downward spiral for this couple, so learning to manage their emotional responses is important in bringing them back together. Both partners like to feel intensely. They need to learn healthier ways of sharing this emotional intensity.

8:4 The Kundalini Yoga Connection
Both partners need to learn to manage their energy differently so they can have more control over their emotional reactions. Strengthening the nervous system is beneficial for them both.

For Individualist (4)s, managing intense emotions, including anger, despair and depression is important. Kundalini Yoga kriyas and meditations that cultivate stability, neutrality, gratitude and self-love are beneficial.

For Leader (8)s, managing an anger response and general reactivity to vulnerable emotions is important. Kundalini Yoga kriyas and meditations to act and not react, to open the heart and to burn out anger are helpful.

See the appendix for Individualist (4) and Leader (8) recommended Kundalini Yoga kriyas and meditations.

8:5 Leader (8) with Investigator (5)

Elisabet, Investigator (5) in a 4-year relationship with Ivar, Leader (8)

"Ivar is capable, creative, self-actualized, an entrepreneur, his own boss, practical, curious, intense – in a way that works for me – and very real. I don't have to worry about inadvertently hurting him as I feel he is naturally strong and resilient.

He has the capacity to move mountains and when he decides on something he carries it through to completion. He offers me an almost psychic level of connection at times, and I feel relaxed and safe to nurture and love him. At the same time, he supports me in areas that are difficult for me without making me feel weak. It's like he gives me an energetic boost of willpower in just the right way. I also appreciate that he's not especially judgmental or perfectionistic.

TYPE EIGHT LEADER/CHALLENGER/PROTECTOR

Our relationship is a blend of autonomy, respect, trust and deep bonding. Although we live together, we each have our separate spaces in our home in addition to our shared space. We spend time in all of our spaces, but the energy and things in our home reflect our personalities and the ways we use our areas. For example, I have a healing room and library as one of my spaces, and he has a woodworking area and office as one of his.

I feel tremendous gratitude for his ability to provide something I cherish and value highly – a secure sense of home and place where I can feel safe in the world. I haven't always had this feeling. Having a safe haven reduces a more neurotic need that I have felt in the past to keep the world out. With our home serving as a shared foundation, we have built a business together that draws on our different strengths and skills.

Our dynamic is balanced in that we respect each other as full, separate people including our limitations. We support each other's growth and actualization. As we're naturally intense, serious and focused, we frequently use humor to shake things up and sometimes defuse tension. We value being an effective team and share an appreciation for the preciousness of our life together though of course, we have our issues.

As it relates to challenges in the relationship, some natural capacities and coping mechanisms that we each bring inadvertently devalues being in a relationship. In stress, I can detach from needs including the need for companionship and connection. I withdraw to restore myself. He is also very independent, capable of denying pain and, under stress, can be self-protective about being manipulated by love and affection. We both share a tendency to be stoic and trusting another person to be there for us has not come easy.

As we have gotten older, we have become more capable of being in touch with our vulnerability, speak simple truths, reassure each other and relax into the natural ups and downs of our relationship. It has taken many years to outgrow some of the childhood survival patterns that we brought to our relationship including a basic mistrust of people and relationships. Growing in our capacity to trust and rely on each other not just in our home but also in our work life has been key to our relationship thriving.

I've very grateful for my relationship. Ivar is a huge inspiration to me in the way he goes about getting things done in the world, showing up as an adult and being creative. I appreciate all he does to create our life together, and I feel extremely fortunate to be his partner."

8:5 The Theory

 ### 8:5 When In Balance

Investigator (5)s and Leader (8)s bring balancing but opposite traits to the relationship and can compensate for each other's blind spots. They protect each other, albeit in different ways, and as a team, they are more powerful than they are individually.

Leader (8)s have a big, direct, powerful energy. They are assertive, earthy and in touch with their own body. They can step easily into their power, and engagement in the world isn't something they shy away from. These traits are all on the growth path for Investigator (5)s, and they can learn a lot from observing their Leader (8) in action. The Leader (8) makes the Investigator (5) feel safe, secure and supported, all necessarily elements to allow Investigator (5)s to share more of themselves.

Conversely, Investigator (5)s are contained in their energy and calculated in their actions. They think deeply before they speak and act and naturally model self-restraint, control and moderation. They act as the wise sage, helping to reign in their Leader (8)'s more impulsive and at times destructive behavior. They demonstrate emotional calm and control and help their Leader (8) think more strategically about the impact of their actions.

This relationship is a blend of autonomy, respect, trust and deep bonding. Both partners are highly independent with a strong sense of personal boundaries. Their home serves as a shared foundation and in partnership, this can be a powerful, deep, effective and thoughtful pair with a dash of brilliance and a dash of brashness. When aligned, they make a powerful combination and an almost unbeatable team.

 ### 8:5 The Downward Spiral

This couple can run into trouble due to issues around trust, rejection and a natural tendency to isolate. With tightening defenses, both struggle with vulnerability choosing instead to disengage and become self-protective. This triggers the downward spiral.

In times of stress, the Investigator (5) withdraws to restore themselves. This can feel like rejection to the Leader (8) who responds by either withdrawing or confronting. If the Leader (8) confronts, the Investigator (5) retreats more, creating an ugly loop of increasing threats and increasing withdrawal. If the Leader (8) withdraws, communication breaks down. As both types are capable of denying pain and isolating, it can be difficult for this couple to repair.

8:5 The Lighthouse

Energetic differences can be the trigger for a downward spiral in this couple, so energy management and the ability to act, not react are key. Leader (8)s can access big, aggressive energy easily, and this intensifies an Investigator (5)'s sense of being overwhelmed. Both types need to strengthen their nervous system to relate to each other better.

8:5 The Kundalini Yoga Connection

Energetic balance and energy management are the keys to healing this relationship. The Leader (8) needs to manage their energy, so it doesn't feel as angry and aggressive to others. They must learn to act and not to react. Kundalini Yoga kriyas and meditations to open the heart, to manage anger and to cultivate stillness are helpful.

Investigator (5)s need to stay engaged and resist the impulse to withdraw for security, as this triggers the Leader (8) even more, creating more aggressive energy. Strengthening the nervous system is helpful, as is any work to build the energetic field surrounding the body, the aura.

See the appendix for Investigator (5) and Leader (8) recommended Kundalini Yoga kriyas and meditations.

8:6 Leader (8) with the Loyalist (6)

Philip, Loyalist (6) married in a 10-year relationship with Sophia, Leader (8)

"I love my wife's independence, her drive, her directness and the fact she takes complete ownership of tasks and duties. I admire the way she has absolutely no fear of responsibility. She brings love, companionship, trust and peace of mind. With her, there is no intrigue, no double talk, no conspiracies. I don't have to wonder what she is thinking – she speaks her mind!

In our relationship, we have a shared worldview believing most people are selfish and untrustworthy, so our bond is a bit "us against the world." While we have a wide social network, we have a precious few, well-scrutinized people that we truly call "friends."

Early in our relationship, it was definitely a test of wills, especially when we moved in together. She was the established authority, and I was the subversive challenger undermining the rigid foundation of her view of how thing should be in the household. There were a lot of discussions, some arguments and a few open fights. Eventually, we reached an equilibrium that feels good to both of us. We tested each other's limits, made our compromises, and we now basically function as one.

We've had to learn our communication differences. There was a period when she didn't recognize when I was anxious or stressed. I tend to analyze everything to the point of exhaustion. She's decisive so she wants to move everything forward. Now she's learned to pause a minute and ask me about my thoughts. But that wasn't always the case, especially in the beginning.

Overall, I love our relationship. I know I'm with someone I can count on 100%, and I really value our deep bond."

8:6 The Theory

8:6 When In Balance

The Loyalist (6) with the Leader (8) share a solid, enduring, supportive, loving partnership with a foundation built on trust, protectiveness and loyalty. Both can have a suspicious, skeptical view of the world and with each other, they can have an "us against the world" attitude. In partnership, they share many similar traits and a few key differences. High trust is a key attribute in this relationship, mainly because both partners have trust issues. Once trust between these two is established, they bond deeply. Both share the values of commitment, responsibility, duty and a willingness to work hard.

Loyalist (6)s bring playfulness, warmth, a sensitivity to the emotional world and an eye for danger. They are more deliberate and thoughtful in their actions offering helpful insights about potential consequences and pitfalls to their Leader (8).

Leader (8)s bring decisiveness, resilience, willpower, resourcefulness and determination. This can be inspiring to their Loyalist (6) who is more emboldened to leave their comfort zone with their Leader (8) at their side.

Together, this is a genuinely affectionate couple with strong chemistry and emotional intensity. With their base of trust, the connection between them has the potential to gradually grow and deepen.

8:6 The Downward Spiral

As trust is at the foundation of this couple, any fissures in trust can trigger the downward spiral for this couple. Both types are ready to believe the worst in others, and both can become extremely reactive. Because of the deep sensitivity to betrayal, fissures in trust may be real or imagined.

With tightening defenses, the phobic Loyalist (6) and Leader (8) head in different directions. The Leader (8) pushes and confronts to get to the bottom of the issue and to establish where they stand. This direct and powerful approach can trigger reactivity in the Loyalist (6) who projects a worst-case scenario outcome. As a protective measure, they retreat, further provoking the Leader (8). This cycle of attack and retreat can continue with increasing intensity until a truce is drawn or a line is crossed.

In the case of counterphobic Loyalist (6)s who behave like Leader (8)s when stressed, this cycle looks different. This couple may get into open conflict with both pushing the other to back down. The more the Leader (8) pushes, the more the counterphobic Loyalist (6) meets the attack. This cycle ends the same way, with increasing intensity until a truce is drawn or a line is crossed.

8:6 The Lighthouse
Power struggles and trust issues are what ultimately undo this couple, so reconnecting at the heart to allow for surrender and to rebuild trust are required to bring this couple back together. Both have powerful issues around control, trust and abandonment. These shared issues manifest very differently. Leader (8)s want control, so they aren't left feeling surprised and vulnerable. A breach of trust or a lack of control might trigger vulnerability for a Leader (8) which can feel almost on par with annihilation. Loyalist (6)s have an equally intense reaction to an unknown future. They want control so they can avoid risk. An unaddressed risk is extremely anxiety provoking for Loyalist (6)s.

8:6 The Kundalini Yoga Connection
Reactions due to anxiety and anger start the downward spiral in this pair so managing reactivity is key to reversing the momentum. Strengthening the nervous system for both partners is important in slowing down reactions.

Loyalist (6)s project negative thinking into an uncertain future. This causes an expectation for a worst-case scenario outcome. To counter this thinking, Loyalist (6)s need to actively cultivate an ability to stay present. Kundalini Yoga kriyas and meditations to lower anxiety, release fear and cultivate self-reliance are beneficial.

Leader (8)s quickly move from vulnerability to anger so managing the anger response is important. Leader (8)s grow when they understand the power of their vulnerability.

Kundalini Yoga kriyas and meditations to burn out anger and to manage reactivity are beneficial. Kundalini Yoga kriyas and meditations to connect with and open the heart are also helpful.

See the appendix for Loyalist (6) and Leader (8) recommended Kundalini Yoga kriyas and meditations.

8:7 Leader (8) with Enthusiast (7)

Stephanie, Enthusiast (7) divorced, formerly in a 25-year relationship with Frank, Leader (8)

"Frank is an amazing individual. He is bold, intelligent and fearlessly pursues his goals. He can be brash and unfiltered, often saying what others are thinking in a way that can be funny and endearing. He is intense. When he decides on a goal, he achieves it. He exudes strength, power and charisma. When he was CEO of his company, he could easily get others to follow his lead, not through his words, but through his magnetic energy. People felt they would succeed just by being around him. He is practical and a good provider. Financial success is important to him, and he knows how to generate money.

I was seduced by his intensity, strength and power. We met when we were both 33 years old, and I had no doubts about him. The attraction was instant, intense and mutual – we knew we were going to get married within five minutes of meeting each other. In the beginning, all his intensity was focused on me. He would buy me airplane tickets to visit him, send me flowers and take me to wonderful places while still keeping his feet on the ground. His solidness and direct way of connecting were irresistible.

Frank and I were bold and adventurous together. We took trips to exciting places and enjoyed biking, scuba, golf and skiing. We entertained with fun parties, free-flowing alcohol, dancing, games and good company. We both had a lust for life.

As a married couple, we divided and conquered. We followed traditional roles, he as a provider, me as a homemaker and both of us serving on various boards. We operated very independently, rarely going to each other for advice or even just to share experiences. Our approach was efficient, practical and relatively conflict-free, but ultimately it lacked intimacy.

Issues of control and independence would pop up now and then. We had two children with learning challenges, and he was so disengaged from the situation, it was hard to give weight to his opinions. If we had to decide whether they should go on ADD medication, he would initially object but would ultimately defer to whatever I decided since he didn't want the involvement required to override me.

Frank loves to golf, and without really consulting me, he decided to buy a vacation home on a golf course in another state. It was a complicated and lengthy process to purchase this house. Without any interest or encouragement from my side, he continued down the acquisition path until I finally told him I wasn't planning to visit or spend time there if he went through with the purchase. That seemed to finally get his attention and, in the end, he decided to forgo buying the house.

This is how it went with us – we kept our lives fairly compartmentalized and separated. My approach was to not involve him in the things that I was doing independently, and he did not share anything that was happening professionally. When he was home, he wanted to leave the office behind; despite the fact, I was curious to hear about his workday.

When we tried to address our issues, we could not have conversations. They always escalated to arguments. I wanted him to share more of himself, and he didn't want to. He wanted me to be happy and was supportive of anything I wanted to do but did not want to focus on me or our relationship.

I later reflected on how we lived in different realities. For him, I was the wife that completed his picture, coming from the right family with the right connections – the ideal spouse for an upstart CEO. Our relationship started out so strong that I spent more time creating my own world and then hoping that our relationship would return again to what it was in the beginning. I thought we could do that. I never faced the reality that you never go back; you only go forward. I avoided confrontation and tried to make everyone happy – and I lost myself in the process. We were ships in the night.

I later learned why. Eventually, it came out that he had been unfaithful for 22 of the 25 years we were together. Typical of my overly positive thinking, I totally missed all the signs of his cheating; I never saw it. He admitted at the end why he never wanted to go to a marriage counselor although I had requested we go many times. He knew successful counseling would require that he told the truth, and if he told the truth, I would divorce him.

Despite the way our relationship ended, I still find it easy to say many positive things about him. I could see the child in him that felt he had to be strong and hide his vulnerability. He wants to be loved, just like everyone else, but his emotional armor makes it hard to reach his heart."

8:7 The Theory

8:7 When In Balance

The Enthusiast (7) and the Leader (8) make a high energy, adventurous, bold and colorful couple. Fundamentally, both believe they are responsible for their own happiness and fulfillment, giving both a self-referencing, self-interested approach to life. Conversely, they can be magnanimous, generous and giving, particularly with their inner circle of family and friends. Both can be unfiltered, brash and outspoken in their communication, saying out loud what others would only think. They vociferously advocate for themselves and their needs.

This is an energetic pair that enjoys entertaining, exploring, having adventures and living life to its fullest. Both partners individually are a force to be reckoned with, and when united and aligned, this team can be powerful, effective and resourceful. Their accomplishments energize them so the more they achieve, the more they pursue. There can be a lust for life and a taste for wild excitement in this couple.

Enthusiast (7)s bring joy, gratitude, sparkle and a sense of adventure to the dynamic. They are more interested in fun and novelty, bringing ideas for new adventures, plans and celebrations to the pairing. Freshness is stimulating to them, so they are constantly on the hunt for things they haven't tried before.

Leader (8)s tend to be more grounded, focused and determined in the pursuit of their goals, many of which are material. Their communication style is direct and intense. They are generally more interested in material success than their Enthusiast (7).

As a couple, this can be a high energy and engaging team that stimulate those around them. There can be a larger than life element to this pair, and their entertaining can be legendary. When they want the same goals, it is as though they have each found the perfect partner in crime.

8:7 The Downward Spiral

When aligned, this is a highly effective, strong-willed team, but when their interests are out of sync, this strong will can be a recipe for disaster. Forceful and independent, both feel it is extremely important to get what they want. A reality distortion around control and limitations can begin, and it is difficult for either to back down, even around seemingly mundane issues. Leader (8)s want control over their situations, and the Enthusiast (7)'s independence can run counter to this desire. Concerns about power and dominance arise, marking the beginning of the downward spiral. The downward spiral manifests either as a fight for control or an implicit agreement to operate independently to get their needs met, thus eroding intimacy.

Leader (8)s can become dictatorial, harsh and bullying in their attempts to rein in the Enthusiast (7) and to establish control. Enthusiast (7)s can become pushy, demanding and petulant about getting their way. Leader (8)s are more sensitive to power dynamics and may start to look for signs of dissent. Enthusiast (7)s are less interested in power but are extremely sensitive to feeling trapped, limited or controlled in any way. They have an exaggerated sense of limitations and may start acting out as a way to prove they are free to do what they want. Both partners can dig in their heels, becoming insulting, hard-hearted, self-centered and unreasonable. Compassion evaporates as conflict increases.

Because both partners have the energy for it, conflicts can spin out of control becoming emotionally exhausting and externally dramatic. Whereas other couples might have a mechanism to de-escalate the situation, this pair charges forward into conflict time and time again, resulting in screaming and yelling with insults hurled back and forth. If the downward spiral gains momentum, this intensity might start to feel like the norm until this couple decides to call it quits.

Alternatively, this couple may implicitly agree to stay together but operate independently with a lack of true emotional connection. Both isolate into their independently crafted lives with the occasional overlapping touch point. Though this might carry on for some period of time, the relationship eventually ends when one partner decides they want more.

8:7 The Lighthouse
Issues of control and feeling controlled can trigger the downward spiral in this pairing. Both partners feel a reality distortion around control, sparking an anxiety response in the Enthusiast (7) and an anger response in the Leader (8). The Enthusiast (7) suspects their greatest fear, being trapped in pain, may come true. The Leader (8) suspects their greatest concern, being vulnerable, may come to fruition. Both must recognize the reality distortion they are experiencing. Self-soothing, doing a reality check and returning to a heart connection when these triggers occur can help break the momentum of the downward spiral.

Both partners need to come forward and connect at the heart. Both are deeply independent, but there can be too much space created in the relationship, and intimacy can be lost. Establishing and maintaining a strong heart connection is key in this couple.

8:7 The Kundalini Yoga Connection

Because the reality distortion is so great, it is hard for either partner not to feel threatened. Strengthening the nervous system will help both partners decrease their overreaction to their feelings around control. Kundalini Yoga kriyas and meditations that open the heart and cultivate heart energy are helpful. Both partners are capable of great love and compassion, but they can cut off from this energy in an attempt to maintain freedom or assert control.

Enthusiast (7)s need to learn to manage their anxiety and to cultivate a stronger heart-centered way of dealing with others. Kundalini Yoga kriyas and meditations to lower anxiety, open the heart, connect with the energy of emotion and release negative emotions can be helpful. Because Enthusiast (7)s tend to under process negative emotions, these emotions can get lodged energetically in the body. They need to be released.

Leader (8)s need to shed their emotional armor around their heart so they can connect in a more direct, loving, interdependent way. Leader (8)s have a tremendous pool of compassion, kindness and innocence within them, but they cut off from this in an attempt to deny vulnerability. Kundalini Yoga kriyas and meditations to burn out anger, to open the heart and to access compassion are helpful.

See the appendix for Enthusiast (7) and Leader (8) recommended Kundalini Yoga kriyas and meditations.

8:8 Leader (8) with Leader (8)

Mia, Leader (8) formerly in a 4-year relationship with Ethan, Leader (8)

"Ethan and I were friends for several years before we were involved romantically. When we first met, I think we both sensed a directness in each other that felt familiar and comforting in a way. Ethan was an ex-Marine and extremely tough. He was resourceful, resilient and had no problem going into a situation and shaking things up. Confrontation didn't scare him, and I think in many ways, he actually enjoyed it. And I understood this completely.

Our relationship took many twists and turns. Because we had such a high level of trust in each other, he asked me to move across the country to help him with a technology company he had been brought in to turn around, and I agreed. This was before we were romantically involved, but shortly after I arrived, we became a couple.

TYPE EIGHT LEADER/CHALLENGER/PROTECTOR

In the beginning, it was exciting. This was New York in the 1990s when the internet boom was happening, and we worked well as a couple. I had his back, and he knew it. I handled many of the administrative parts of the company, and he was free to aggressively pursue growth for the company. The relationship felt solid and secure, and while I was sacrificing a lot, it felt like it was in the name of a shared, stable future.

When the company eventually got a large round of outside investment, the level of stress on the company and the relationship increased tremendously. With this round of financing came a new set of sophisticated investors and suddenly, Ethan's insecurities started to surface. He became paranoid, dividing the company into friends and foes. He was worried about how his relationship with me would look, so he made sure my pay was the lowest. Not only did I get no special allowances, but in fact, I was expected to work harder and earn less. The stock options he gave to new hires were more than mine, even though I had been at his side the entire time. This felt unfair, but I still saw us as a united team, so once again, I was willing to live with it. As the stress grew, he saw I was unhappy and tried to make it up to me. He got me a dog, so I'd have company and protection when he was traveling for work. We tried to go out and socialize a bit more. But even when he was home, our lives were completely dominated by the company, hitting the right milestones, getting the next tranche of investment capital and so forth. Fun, caring, adventure, true intimacy all disappeared to be replaced by stress and workaholism. There seemed no end because we were always waiting for the next round of financing, trying to grow faster than our competitors, trying to increase profits. It was relentless. In the face of all this, I grew disillusioned and started thinking about my own happiness. While we talked about a more balanced future, I started to have my doubts it was ever going to materialize.

The romantic relationship started cooling, although I'm loyal by nature and didn't want to leave him in a lurch professionally. We continued living together, we continued working together, but we were growing more distant by the week. I eventually told him I wanted to separate. At this point, being in a relationship with him was the loneliest I'd ever felt. I knew it would take me a little time to find my own place so we agreed that I would stay in the house we shared until I could find a new home.

The meltdown happened one day when the phone rang early in the morning, and I picked it up. It was another woman. This is how I learned he had brought someone else into the picture. He happened to be traveling during this time. I didn't wait for him to return, I packed everything I owned, including my dog, and I left. I went to stay with a friend until I got my own place. Little did I know, leaving him was like opening the gates of hell.

When I left, despite the fact he started a relationship with another woman before ours had completely ended, he was angry with me for having left so abruptly and while he was traveling. It was as though I was the one who had broken the bond of trust. Suddenly, I became the enemy. It was extreme. He was vindictive, angry and cruel. The lowest point was when he sued me for custody of my dog, the dog he had bought for me as a gift! Because we worked for the same company, I had to leave because it just wasn't working. He couldn't remain professional.

He was angry about the way I left. I was hurt and angry about the failure of the relationship – his lack of participation and the way he behaved after I left.

When I moved out I took all of our photos with me. They included some rare and precious family photos of Ethan's. I wasn't aware initially that I took them, but as I packed and unpacked my way through the next several years, I would come across those photos. What I did or didn't do with them was a barometer as to how I was feeling emotionally. Initially, I felt satisfied that he no longer had them. Many times I would imagine marking or scratching them and mailing them to him. I knew if I did that I would have crossed a dark line within myself that I didn't want to cross so each time I packed them up and forgot about them. Years later as I was packing to leave New York I came across those photos again. I finally knew what I needed to do with them, so I reached out to Ethan to let him know that I had the photos. I asked for his mailing address so that I could send them to him. He was extremely grateful and asked if we could meet. I reluctantly agreed. We met for drinks, I gave him the photos, and we spoke about the past. During our conversation, I discovered that his deplorable behavior was a result of being hurt himself and also being unfamiliar with those types of emotions. He handled it badly and acknowledged that. I was in a good place and took comfort in the fact that seeing him didn't make me feel much at all in any direction.

This relationship was many years ago, and I'm in a great place now with a wonderful partner. When I look back on those years – and I rarely do – I feel a mix of healthy emotions. Every step or misstep I've taken has led me to where I am, and I wouldn't change that. I am grateful for the lessons, the friends I met along the way and the experiences I had."

8:8 The Theory

 ### 8:8 When In Balance
Two Leader (8)s bring energy, passion, directness, intensity and resourcefulness to the relationship. There is an unstoppable quality to this pair.

TYPE EIGHT LEADER/CHALLENGER/PROTECTOR

Both partners are strong-willed, independent, decisive and resilient. Like a veteran team going into combat, they are inspired by each other and also feel a sense of safety and security. They correctly sense the other has their back which frees them up to focus on external goals and achievement. They have high trust and confidence in each other, something Leader (8)s offer to a precious few. This allows them to come together with more vulnerability, strengthening the bond they already share. Communication between two Leader (8)s is generally direct and clear with no hidden meaning or subterfuge. At their best, this is a powerful, passionate, loving couple.

8:8 The Downward Spiral
The intensity that makes two Leader (8)s a powerful couple can also be what tears this pair apart. Issues of trust and control usually mark the beginning of the downward spiral and once breaches of trust enter the relationship, it can be hard to repair.

With tightening defenses, Leader (8)s become more controlling, more demanding and more uncompromising. Rational thought is clouded by intense emotion, and Leader (8)s who feel threatened typically go on the offense. Because both partners have an aggressive stress response, it can be difficult to de-escalate disputes. Fights can spiral out of control as backing down feels like defeat. Issues stop being about the issue itself as fear of vulnerability governs the picture. In this environment, behavior can become vindictive and threatening. Unless there is some mechanism for de-escalation, this partnership may end in fiery flames.

8:8 The Lighthouse
Managing stress reactions and rebuilding trust is the key to healing between two Leader (8)s. Stress triggers anger and paranoia as a defense against feeling vulnerable. The more Leader (8)s can learn the true power of vulnerability, the better the likelihood this relationship can mend once feelings of mistrust have entered the picture. Both Leader (8)s need to reconnect with their innocence.

8:8 The Kundalini Yoga Connection
Leader (8)s have a tendency to react rather than to act. When they feel threatened, they attack. Standing still or pausing in the face of conflict is a huge growth step for Leader (8)s.

Since vulnerability triggers anger, Leader (8)s need tools to manage their anger response. They need to learn to slow down. They literally need to learn to "take a deep breath." Kundalini Yoga kriyas and meditations to manage anger, to open the heart and to strengthen the nervous system are beneficial.

See the appendix for Leader (8) recommended Kundalini Yoga kriyas and meditations.

8:9 Leader (8) with the Peacemaker (9)

Sydney, Peacemaker (9) in a 2-year relationship with Richard, Leader (8)

"I value Richard's strength, decisiveness, great conversation, shared sense of humor and the much laughter we share together. He is fiercely and uncompromisingly principled. I can count on him to do the right thing. He came from a very painful childhood in which even his basic survival was threatened, but he came out not only strong and independent but also surprisingly tender at times. His tenderness is made all the more sweet because it is occasional and not smothering. He is a rock to lean on, as long as I don't become clingy, and he offers total acceptance of who I am.

He was a captain in the U.S. Marine Corps and can be trusted to take charge and to persevere until he succeeds. His drive to succeed is so great that all those under his leadership – in the military, in his family or professionally – end up benefiting, and everyone loves him for it.

I find his decisiveness and innate authoritativeness to be very attractive and fascinating, and as someone who can be accommodating and indecisive, it is a relief to be with someone who knows and says what he wants. He is straightforward about what he wants or when he has a problem, so I don't have to guess what he means.

Sexually the combination of his forthrightness and strong desires with my drive to please and be receptive is an endlessly repeating positive loop. This dynamic has created the most physically satisfying relationship either of us has ever had.

I appreciate that he is happy to be with me and expresses it. He has repeatedly said that I am "so easy to be with" and that I make him feel wonderful. Before our relationship, he was in a 25-year marriage with someone with whom he had a more difficult dynamic. He has expressed that he is delighted to be with someone who doesn't make demands, who doesn't compete with him and who is kind to him. I think he has always had so much conflict in his family of origin and previous relationship that my easygoing acceptance is a new experience for him.

Like all relationships, we've had our challenges. He is so fiercely self-protective that he sometimes has difficulty trusting me despite our 2-year history of me being trustworthy to him. He manages his anger, but he does still get angry, and it takes the form of shutting himself off and ending a conversation abruptly so that he will not lose his temper.

Trying to control him in any way backfires. I am actually grateful for this because I have now met my match – a person I cannot manipulate. It forces me to be responsible for meeting my own needs and standing on my own two feet. I learned this because early in our relationship I was guilty of some passive-aggressive behavior. However, my passive-aggressive reactions only either confused him, caused him to shut himself off or he missed it completely and did what he wanted to do. The bottom line was that the passive-aggressive strategy was so pointless, I stopped doing it.

I've also had to learn he expresses love in his own way and on his own timetable. I am learning to value those expressions when they come and to remember them during times when he is less expressive.

Overall, I'm very satisfied in my relationship. I never before in my life have felt so totally accepted by another human being as I feel with Richard."

8:9 The Theory

8:9 When In Balance

This pairing can be extremely balancing, inspiring and healing for one another. The Leader (8) shows the Peacemaker (9) how to behave with confidence and assertion, and the Peacemaker (9) shows the Leader (8) how to behave with acceptance, accommodation and receptivity to create a soothing, harmonious environment. Together, this pair can have a very supportive, satisfying and fulfilling relationship.

Leader (8)s bring directness, leadership, decisiveness and a bold "take charge" mentality to the dynamic. They can be brash, fierce and confident with big energy and a powerful life force. The more easygoing Peacemaker (9)s admire and are fascinated by these traits, finding the Leader (8) magnetic, attractive and alluring. They appreciate the Leader (8)'s spirit and vitality and can be energized by their Leader (8)'s presence. The Peacemaker (9) enjoys having someone to look up to, and the Leader (8) enjoys the admiration.

Peacemaker (9)s bring calm, stability, acceptance and a soothing, healing manner to the dynamic. They accept and appreciate the Leader (8) which gives the Leader (8) even more strength and encouragement to tackle life's challenges. Their peaceful, quiet energy balances the brashness of the Leader (8), and they offer a secure home, a safe harbor, a tranquil sanctuary for the Leader (8) to retreat to after life's daily battles.

When these two types are aligned in their goals and appreciative of their differences, they can be a dynamic, effective pair: a powerful mast and a durable sail.

8:9 The Downward Spiral

Under stress with tightening defenses, this couple polarizes. The Leader (8) seeks resolution of issues by adopting a strategy of direct confrontation. The Peacemaker (9) heads in the other direction, adopting an avoidant strategy of stonewalling and shutting down. These opposite strategies prompt a more intense reaction in the other, and the downward spiral is triggered.

The Leader (8)s almost can't relax until they understand where they stand so it can be hard to de-escalate a conflict with a Peacemaker (9) in retreat. As the Leader (8) becomes more direct and more aggressive, the Peacemaker (9) shuts down, stonewalls and numbs out even more to avoid conflict. The Leader (8) may interpret this withdrawal as rejection, triggering more anger and more intensity. The downward spiral gains momentum as the Leader (8)'s aggression prompts more withdrawal from the Peacemaker (9). The environment can get heated with verbal aggression, anger and threats.

From the Peacemaker (9)'s perspective, the Leader (8) has become too controlling, harsh and domineering. What before felt like leadership now feels like dictatorship. The depth and power of a Peacemaker (9)'s stubbornness are often miscalculated, and conflicts can continue in a simmering state with no path to resolution on the horizon. Eventually the Leader (8) may turn away in disgust, but at this point contempt has entered the picture, and the stability of the relationship is threatened.

8:9 The Lighthouse

Different stress responses trigger the downward spiral in this couple so learning to be energetically still under stress is important. Both Leader (8)s and Peacemaker (9)s are powerful people. When they move in opposite directions, they stubbornly polarize. To break the reactivity, both types need to strengthen their nervous system to allow for stillness.

8:9 The Kundalini Yoga Connection

Both need to change their relationship with their own power. Leader (8)s need to control their power, and Peacemaker (9)s need to activate their power.

Leader (8)s need to learn to act, not react and to manage the intense energy of their anger response. Their desire for direct confrontation triggers a response to shut down in the Peacemaker (9). Kundalini Yoga kriyas and meditations to burn out anger and to slow the anger response are helpful.

Peacemaker (9)s need to resist the urge to withdraw in the face of stress and potential conflict. They need to stand their ground and voice their feelings instead of withdrawing and relying on stubborn, passive-aggressive behavior. Kundalini Yoga kriyas and meditations to strengthen the aura, activate the throat (fifth) chakra and strengthen the core are beneficial.

See Appendix for Leader (8) and Peacemaker (9) recommended Kundalini Yoga kriyas and meditations.

This book is a living document. We will be updating it periodically with new information. If you are or were in a relationship with a Leader (8) and you would like to participate in the related relationship survey, please email me at lynn@lynnroulo.com.

Type Nine
PEACEMAKER/ MEDIATOR

(seeks harmony/avoids conflict)

 ## Overview

Peacemaker (9)s are typically receptive, good-natured, supportive and soothing. They are great listeners and are gifted at understanding the viewpoints of others. They have a tendency to lose their sense of themselves. This is a person for whom tranquility, harmony and peace is the main focus. They tend to be very conflict avoidant. Indecision, procrastination and stubbornness can be issues for Peacemaker (9)s. They can be prone to low self-esteem.

Peacemaker (9)s have a mellow presence and are easy to be around. Many Peacemaker (9)s report that they enjoy that they can move with relative ease into a wide variety of environments and get along in a conflict-free way. In an intimate relationship, partners appreciate that their Peacemaker (9) is accepting, soothing, welcoming, generous, a good listener, patient, loving, nonjudgemental and easygoing. Partners often say they feel totally accepted exactly as they are by their Peacemaker (9)s. Peacemaker (9)s typically have intimate relationships with little direct conflict.

Partners report they are challenged by their Peacemaker (9)'s lack of initiative, laziness, stonewalling and refusal to discuss thorny issues. Passive-aggressive, stubborn, indirect, checked out and emotionally unavailable are the most common complaints from partners. Peacemaker (9)s don't feel stable in the face of direct anger, and they will often tune out.

- **Attention Bias/Habit Of Attention:**
Attention goes to harmony. Peacemaker (9)s see what it takes to maintain a smooth, peaceful environment and act to ensure harmony is maintained. Their attention moves away from creating a conflict of any type as conflict can be extremely anxiety-provoking for them. They want everyone to get along and for their environment to be happy and relaxed.

- **Emotional Style:**
Congenial, pleasant, diffused, mellow, calm, even-keeled, even-tempered.

- **Communication Style:**
Friendly, harmonious, reserved, attentive, focused on others and the needs of others, slow, cooperative.

- **Brings To The Relationship:**
Support, kindness, understanding, compassion, easy companionship, receptivity.

- **Unique Strengths:**
Peace, understanding, mediation, harmony, unconditional acceptance of others. Peacemaker (9)s can be brought into very acrimonious disagreements and broker peace. They are gifted at finding common ground and compromise. They make others feel accepted and supported.

- **Challenges:**
Peacemaker (9)s numb out. They disconnect and repress true feelings. They can be conflict avoidant to the extreme, passive-aggressive, indecisive, lethargic and self-forgetting.

- **Stability And Security:**
"I feel stable when there is harmony, and I am in a smooth, peaceful environment. I feel secure when everyone is getting along, and there is an absence of conflict."

- **Instability And Insecurity:**
"Conflict, the threat of conflict, discord and personality clashes make me feel insecure. I become very anxious at the prospect of conflict. I feel like I vanish."

- **Path Of Growth:**
Right Action
Peacemaker (9)s need to step into their power. They must stand up and advocate for themselves, vocalize their grievances, become engaged in their own lives and resist detachment as a strategy for harmony.

- **Energy:**
Mellow, grounded yet spacey, open, sleepy.

- **The Kundalini Yoga Connection:**

Peacemaker (9)s have a subconscious tendency to cut off from their own power and to give this power away to others in the form of accommodation and self-forgetting. This looks like sloth, inertia and an inability to decisively pursue their own agenda. Kundalini Yoga kriyas and meditations to help the Peacemaker (9) feel their own power and wake up to their own priorities are helpful. Exercises that fire up the body and bring the Peacemaker (9) into a state of alertness are beneficial.

The Peacemaker (9) Subtypes

"Appetite" Self-Preservation Subtype:

The self-preservation Peacemaker (9) expresses a drive for harmony and merging through physical comfort. This is a person who enjoys food, drink, a comfortable environment and regular routine activities. Self-preservation Peacemaker (9)s direct their attention away from their deeper needs and to a more basic, survival level. They tend to be concrete people more interested in the physical world than in abstract or metaphysical concepts. These are people who live life in a simple, direct way. This is the most introverted of the three Peacemaker (9)s. They have the title "Appetite" because of the way they merge their identity with the fulfillment of these simple needs.

This is a person who gains satisfaction from basic, comfortable things: watching television, reading, sleeping or even working if working feels comfortable. Eating is often a source of great pleasure for these Peacemaker (9)s, and their relationship with a partner may include cooking and preparing meals, dining out together and so forth as a central shared and important part of the relationship.

On the positive side, these are loving people with a joy and zest for fun. They have a stronger presence than the other Peacemaker (9)s and can be highly protective of their inner circle.

On the less positive side, this is someone who has often subconsciously chosen to abnegate their own desires, believing they won't get what they want anyway.

"Participation" Social Subtype:

The social Peacemaker (9) expresses a desire for harmony and a drive to merge through groups and group participation. To the outside world, this is a person who is friendly, talkative, sociable and who often devotes considerable time and energy into supporting their chosen group. Internally, this person often has a feeling of being different or not fitting in, so they feel a need to work harder and to be more supportive, almost as the price of admission. They have the title "Participation" because of a tendency to prioritize the needs of the group over their own needs and because of their drive to participate in their chosen group.

This is a person who is more outgoing and energetic than the other Peacemaker (9)s. Their focus is on the group, whichever group they belong to, and they tend towards workaholism, giving so much of themselves for the group, they often have little left for their personal life.

On the positive side, this is someone who makes a good leader and is gifted at seeing and meeting the needs of others.

On the less positive side, this is someone who can be detached from their emotions but still have a persistent feeling of not belonging.

"Fusion" Intimate Subtype:
The intimate Peacemaker (9) expresses a desire for harmony and a drive to merge through connection with a few intimate others. This is a person who uses relationships to get a sense of being or belonging. For this Peacemaker (9), it can feel threatening to be alone. To the outside world, this is a very kind, tender, sweet and unassertive person. They tend to be very tuned into the needs, concerns and emotions of the people close to them. Internally, these Peacemaker (9)s can have a lot of inner confusion and a sort of melancholy. They struggle to find their own internal compass and can have a special sensitivity to the moods and emotions of important people in their lives. They have the title "Fusion" because of their tendency to fuse to important people in their lives.

These Peacemaker (9)s have their center of gravity in others and live in acute awareness of the wishes, moods and emotional state of other people in their lives. Their sense of security comes from their connection with their intimate partner or "special person." They can have a deep, subconscious fear that if they try to connect deeply with themselves, they will find that nothing is there.

On the positive side, these are people who are very supportive and available in their intimate relationships. They try to provide a lot and ask for little.

On the less positive side, because they don't have a strong sense of themselves, they can develop unbalanced and unhealthy dependencies on others. They may have a subconscious tendency to copy the important people in their lives.

TYPE NINE PEACEMAKER/MEDIATOR

Peacemaker (9)—Levels of Awareness

Peacemaker (9) When Self-Aware
Peacemaker (9)s become autonomous, present to themselves, directed, clear and fulfilled. They become balanced in their relationships with others and are able to set clear boundaries. They are accepting, stable, calm, deeply receptive and caring. They are relaxed and expansive with an openness and curiosity that feels innocent and simple. They are able to hold multiple conflicting perspectives in their minds without judgment or criticism. Their presence can be healing and harmonizing. They are easy and enjoyable to be around.

Peacemaker (9) With Tightening Defenses
Conflict avoidance colors their behavior as they become accommodating and passive, agreeing to things they don't really want to do. They may become indirect and vague, finding it difficult to take a clear stance, although externally, they seem easygoing and relaxed. Action replaces right action, and the Peacemaker (9) fills their days with time-consuming but ultimately unimportant tasks. Stubbornness and avoidance are present as problems are deflected, and important priorities are put off. Their energy drops, and lethargy and sloth enter the picture. Their thinking becomes hazy, and self-medication in its various forms may begin. Indifference and inertia characterize the Peacemaker (9) as they become frozen in their resignation. They try to convince themselves and others that nothing is wrong. A fatalistic stance is taken as change seems unattainable as an option.

Peacemaker (9) When Fixated
Their energy is drained, and they have great difficulty pursuing, or even knowing, their goals. They may fall into depression. Their ability to function in a healthy way is compromised as they disassociate from themselves and become obstinate in their dealings with others. They begin to check out of their life and from reality. They continue in a numb, almost zombie-like manner. Neglect of themselves and others may become apparent. They become almost catatonic and severely dissociated from themselves and reality. They have lost their sense of themselves and have lost their way out of their confusion.

Keys If You Are In A Relationship With A Peacemaker (9)

"Just because I don't react, doesn't mean I didn't notice."

Tom, Peacemaker (9)

"I would describe myself as mellow and easygoing, but I shouldn't be mistaken as naive

or unaware. I notice if you were fair with me, if we went to your movie or mine, if you dominate the conversation or ask me about my day too, all types of things. It is like there is an internal scorecard in my head. I will tolerate and actually feel like I am fine with almost everything but only up to a point. At that point, the line is crossed, and I will open and share my scorecard bringing up everything that I can recall.

Selfishly enough, at that point, I have convinced myself that I am right, that I deserve to be right, and I will not back down. At that point, if you don't back down, I will go to the furthest possible extent and walk out of the relationship. I know that I could be wrong this time, but I cannot be wrong for the things that I have in my scorecard. I know I may be overreacting, but it's OK because I have "under-reacted" all the other times. I know I am selfish in this moment, but I do not care, I deserve for once to be selfish myself. I am really bad, and I do not care..."

One of the hallmark relationship issues with Peacemakers (9)s is that "everything seemed ok, and then one day, he wanted a divorce..." Because Peacemaker (9)s value harmony so highly, they often don't express things that are bothering them. They can do a lot of mental gymnastics convincing themselves that the situation that bothers them is not really a big deal. But they do notice. And they are storing away these slights, hurts and wounds. Eventually, the "scorecard" is full, and a conflict abruptly arises, often including things from the distant past. For many Peacemaker (9)s, by the time they are ready to engage in conflict, they have already decided to leave the relationship. This can be shocking for their partner, who didn't realize there was a problem.

If you are a Peacemaker (9):
Consider the idea that bringing up an issue that is bothering you might be the path to true harmony. Conflict doesn't necessarily mean separation, and many times, people are brought closer by expressing their true feelings in the moment. If you can't tell how seriously an issue is bothering you, check in with your body. The energy of emotion is experienced in your body, and even if you "think" something isn't important, your body might be giving you other signals.

If you with a Peacemaker (9):
Understand that you will have to work extra hard to uncover the grievances your partner might be carrying. Asking "is everything OK?" will not be enough. You may need to frame questions like "if you could change one thing in our relationship, what would it be?" and wait for a genuine response. Your Peacemaker (9) feels unstable in the face of conflict and will

naturally want to avoid anything near conflict. Successful partners usually come up with creative solutions to draw out unexpressed issues. Your Peacemaker (9) might not even be consciously aware they are unhappy. For partners of Peacemaker (9)s, it is important to notice early warning signals. Is your partner tired a lot? Do they seem depressed? These can be signals of unaddressed issues.

 "Maintaining harmony takes a lot of my energy. This tires me out and makes it hard for me to pursue the things that are important to me."

Nancy, Peacemaker (9) married in an 18-year relationship with Roger, Perfectionist (1)

"In our relationship, striking a balance of give and take requires effort and can be a challenge given my drive for harmony and Roger's sometimes rigid views. For our last move, I wanted to go back to New England, but I knew that my husband's more conservative outlook would not be a good match with churches there and that he would have a hard time, even though I might be happier. He was willing to follow my church call this time, and I had several interviews. However, in the end, my energy petered out, and I became frustrated with the dysfunction in some of the search committees with whom I interviewed. It began to seem like moving for my call would be too overwhelming and require too much energy on my part.

I decided the stress of my husband's possible unhappiness was too much for me to handle, and so I told him to start interviewing instead. We ended up moving south to Ohio for his call, as we always have, instead of west to New England for my call.

From time to time over the past few decades, I've resolved to be more outgoing and social, to meet more people and get more involved in the community. I'll tell my husband about my plans, and then inevitably I don't follow through. He says, "Well, you've never done that since I've known you." I feel that he thinks I don't do much, while I wake up in the morning with my important tasks in my head, all are very internally oriented, like going to the gym, walking in the woods with the dog, reading, working and so forth. My husband writes his sermon on Saturday night, although he says he's got it all in his head already, while I spend much more time at the computer writing mine. I feel he doesn't really get how much my interior world influences the way I spend my days."

We often experience Peacemaker (9)s as mellow, easygoing and low energy. What we fail to realize is how much energy it takes them to maintain harmony. A Peacemaker (9) is drained from both sides, constantly weighing the pros and cons of voicing their desires, considering the impact on others and also on themselves. It takes energy to suppress what they want. And it takes energy to consider what others want. In the face of conflict, they very often decide "it just isn't worth it" to bring something up or "it was stressing me out so much to think about how hard it was going to be on my wife…" that they maintain the status quo or give away decision making to someone else…It takes a tremendous amount of energy to consider all possible outcomes and then to consider how they will need to react to maintain harmony. In the wiring of a Peacemaker (9), harmony is the top priority.

If you are a Peacemaker (9):
Spend time each day focusing on yourself and do things that are rejuvenating and healing for you. You give away a lot of your energy trying to maintain harmony with others in your environment. Try to get clear on what your actual priorities are. When you get clear about them, share them with others. While you might not advocate well for yourself, supportive people in your life might help you follow through on your dreams and desires.

If you are with a Peacemaker (9):
Try to help your Peacemaker (9) find their priorities and then advocate for those priorities. Your partner gets confused about what they want, and unless they are clear, they will probably just go along with you and your ideas. This isn't necessarily what is best for them in the long run.

"It is extremely hard for me to bring up something that's bothering me."

Meadow, Peacemaker (9)

"I think my biggest challenge was to be really honest with my boyfriend about what I truly wanted out of the relationship. We were too comfortable with each other, and with the lack of pressure we ended up in a long relationship where neither of us was unhappy, but we also weren't truly happy. The relationship ended because I eventually became very clear in my mind that I wasn't getting what I wanted."

Peacemaker (9)s have an exaggerated sense of conflict and can be very sensitive to anything that disrupts harmony. They may experience an argument where other types might feel the exchange was just a candid discussion. And they have a much more intense reaction to conflict as it fills them with anxiety. Peacemaker (9)s sometimes report they feel like they disappear in the face of a conflict. Because of this, they are extremely reluctant to approach an issue that might feel to them like conflict. This can be conscious (they are aware they are being avoidant) or subconscious (they avoid conflict by convincing themselves the issue is not really a problem).

If you are a Peacemaker (9):
Understand you have a reality distortion around conflict. Conflict doesn't mean the relationship will end and voicing your desires is, in fact, healthy and necessary to maintain true harmony in your relationships. Because repressing your feelings drains you, you may also find an increase in your energy when you start advocating for yourself.

If you are with a Peacemaker (9):
Listen carefully to your partner. While being direct may be difficult, they are probably giving you subtle clues about what they would like. Help them think through their desires and make sure they voice their opinion. They have a voice; it just may be very soft.

THE NINE KEYS

PEACEMAKER (9)
360 DEGREE REVIEW

The next section features the 360 degree review--partnership with a Peacemaker (9) from the perspective of each of the nine types.

9:1 Peacemaker (9) with Perfectionist (1)

Amina, Perfectionist (1) married in a 10-year relationship with Rahim, Peacemaker (9)

"My husband is patient, nonjudgmental, bone-deep kind to children, animals and seniors and is very personable. He is uncomplicated – what you see is what you get. I feel that he loves me unconditionally and that I can truly be my good and "bad" selves with him without losing his love. At the same time, when my actions disappoint him, it pushes me to be better, to try harder and to act with more sensitivity and understanding.

I would characterize our relationship as one of balance and support. My husband supports me in pursuing my mission-oriented work by not being demanding on a daily basis or passing judgment on my professional choices. He tolerates my absences as I frequently travel for long periods of time for work – several of my international projects have required me to be away from home for months at a time. I know he doesn't like my absences, but I also know he understands it is important to me and will never truly stop me if I want to go.

He softens my edges. I tend to let judgments about people seep into my relationships with them whereas my husband is much more nonjudgmental and truly accepts people as they are. It's a quality I admire and aspire towards, but it is something I need to work on all the time. My judgmental nature has been a core factor in my tumultuous relationship with my sister. With the influence of my husband, this relationship improved significantly after my marriage. Rahim is a buffer between us and a calming, neutral yet supportive presence. He has helped make my relationship with my sister more manageable.

Like all relationships, we have our differences and challenges. Our communication styles are different. My husband hates conflict, and when it seems we are about to start an argument, he shuts down or physically removes himself. He is not willing to confront me on any behavior he may not agree with unless I probe and probe and pull it out of him. On my side, I get frustrated that he is so passive. Despite being in Canada for over nine years, he refuses to really learn to write in English which means I need to be his "voice," and I end up handling all of the administrative things in our shared lives. Sometimes this tires me out, and I wish I had more practical support.

In the balance, I'm very satisfied in my relationship. I think I need someone as mellow and accepting as my husband to balance out my more opinionated qualities, and I admire him deeply. He is one of the best human beings I know and a good example for me on how I can be a better person."

9:1 The Theory

9:1 When In Balance

Perfectionist (1)s and Peacemaker (9)s offer each other a blend of shared and compensating personality traits. Both can be altruistic, working in the service of others and subjugating their own needs for the greater good. Both can be committed to improvement and growth, albeit with large energetic differences. Neither type need the spotlight, and both can stay focused on the task at hand, leaving their ego to the side to focus on concrete goals. And with these foundational shared values, they also have many balancing differences.

Peacemaker (9)s bring an accepting, nonjudgmental nature, steadiness and a human focus to their interactions. They are kind-hearted, good listeners with a soothing, easy presence. They easily and naturally accommodate multiple viewpoints and perspectives making others feel unconditionally accepted.

Perfectionist (1)s bring clarity, rational thought, an action-oriented approach, and precise and critical thinking. They are ethical, fair and driven to improve themselves and their environment.

In the relationship, the Peacemaker (9) softens the rigidity of the Perfectionist (1) and helps mute the Perfectionist (1)'s drive to be right. They can broker compromise and help maintain harmony. Perfectionist (1)s give inspiration to the Peacemaker (9). They may push their Peacemaker (9) outside their comfortable zone, helping them to achieve more of their full potential.

This can be a highly idealistic, hospitable, altruistic couple who create good in the world and bring out the best in each other.

9:1 The Downward Spiral

The downward spiral of the relationship begins because of the opposite way the two types behave when fixated, with Perfectionist (1)s expressing criticism and contempt and Peacemaker (9)s stonewalling and becoming stubbornly avoidant. With tightening defenses, Perfectionist (1)s become more openly critical, frustrated, prickly and dissatisfied. This can be directed at themselves, their partner, their other relationships and their environment. They become fixated on finding fault and determining who is to blame. They become increasingly rigid in their views and disconnected from their hearts. Isolationism can occur with no one meeting the harsh standards strictly set by the Perfectionist (1). Compassion is usually nowhere in the picture.

In this environment, Peacemaker (9)s head in the opposite direction and become more shut down, withdrawn, internally confused and uncomfortable. They numb out as a strategy to deflect the criticism and dissatisfaction of the Perfectionist (1). Internally, they try to convince themselves that nothing is wrong or it is a phase the couple is going through.

This further triggers the Perfectionist (1) who feels the Peacemaker (9) isn't addressing the issue. The two partners polarize with the Peacemaker (9) resisting the situation even more, becoming more passive and more withdrawn. The Perfectionist (1) interprets this as passive defiance. The Perfectionist (1) starts to lose respect for the Peacemaker (9), and the Peacemaker (9) starts to lose confidence and trust in the Perfectionist (1).

If the downward spiral continues, the Perfectionist (1) becomes even more condemning, disdainful and critical of the Peacemaker (9). The Peacemaker (9) reacts by becoming more unresponsive, passive, resigned and withdrawn. To the Perfectionist (1), they feel they are merely living up to their own internal high standards. To the Peacemaker (9), they feel they are accommodating their very frustrated partner in the best way they know how. To the outside world, this couple may be hard to be around because of the barely suppressed anger seething from the Perfectionist (1) and the unresponsive passive energy of the Peacemaker (9).

Once the couple reaches this stage, any heart connection is lost. Because of the Peacemaker (9)'s resistance to change, the relationship may continue for long periods in this state before it ends.

9:1 The Lighthouse

The downward spiral starts because of the different and opposite way both partners deal with conflict. Peacemaker (9)s withdraw and shut down. Perfectionist (1)s become more harsh and rigid in their thinking. If both people can break their patterned responses, there can be real healing between these two. Strengthening the nervous system to accommodate alternate reactions to conflict is beneficial.

9:1 The Kundalini Yoga Connection

Both types must shift their energetic patterns to bridge their gap. Peacemaker (9)s need to resist the urge to withdraw and hope that time passing will fix their problems. This inertia is a response to the discomfort of conflict. They must confront this discomfort. Perfectionist (1)s need to break free of their tendency to judge harshly and to polarize in their opinions. They need to move to less rigid, more flexible thinking.

Because the Perfectionist (1) type structure can become so rigid, maintaining a strong heart connection, both to self and others, is vital. In an unhealthy state of awareness, the attention becomes completely focused on improvement and criticism of others allowing no space for compassion. Kundalini Yoga kriyas and meditations to burn out anger and connect to and open the heart can help create this space.

Peacemaker (9)s energetically numb out as a strategy to avoid conflict. For Peacemakers (9)s, conflict is extremely anxiety-provoking and can feel like annihilation. Peacemaker (9)s need to wake up to their anger and discontent. They need to risk conflict. Kundalini Yoga kriyas and meditations to build the navel center (third chakra) and to burn anger are helpful.

See the appendix for Perfectionist (1) and Peacemaker (9) recommended Kundalini Yoga kriyas and meditations.

9:2: Peacemaker (9) with Helper (2)

Emma, Helper (2), married in a 15-year relationship with David, Peacemaker (9)

"David is warm, loving, reliable and offers me stable ground when I feel like I'm falling. He is supportive when I struggle with depression and knows how to be there for me without me asking – sometimes it's just laying next to me and putting on my favorite show to drown out my sadness. He always knows when I'm upset, and he'll never ask what's wrong – instead, he'll wash the dishes, take care of the dogs, watch my favorite show with me or order from my favorite takeout places.

He is truly the peacekeeper in my family. He is an exceptionally loving uncle to our two nephews and spoils them rotten with love, adventures and knowledge.

Our friends think of us as "the chill couple" and "the effortlessly in love couple." We enjoy having people over for games, holidays and so forth but we also appreciate our privacy. While we are both introverts, welcoming people into our home has always been the natural thing for us to do. We have five rescue dogs because we both love animals and feel like if we have space, the time and the money we should give a homeless animal a home.

During our 15 years together, our roles have changed and even reversed. When we were younger, David was unemployed, and I supported him. Now, years later, he helps run my brother's business, and he works nonstop. He works harder than anyone I have ever known.

In our relationship, we don't really fight. I think we're both too lazy to hold a grudge or to be angry for very long. We might argue, but it's over in minutes.

However, this means issues don't always get fully aired, and at the moment we have a very unbalanced power dynamic that we basically treat as an unspoken agreement. Money is always an issue with us, but it is never a sore subject. I left my very high-paying job in Toronto to move to Montreal to be with David after he moved here to help my brother run the business. He wants the status of having a "housewife," but I feel very uncomfortable being financially dependent and without a steady paycheck. He works nonstop, and when he comes home, he drinks to numb out from all the stress. I end up feeling alone, unwanted and unloved. This happens in waves but always gets worse around tax time. We never really talk about it in depth, but we both know it's there, and it's like this omnipresent black cloud that follows us.

He runs our family business with my brother, and I think he is always trying to prove that he is good enough or that he is valuable. I wish he understood he has nothing to prove, and we'd both be happier if time together was a bigger priority than work.

Despite this issue, in the balance, I feel grateful and lucky. David has provided me with a very comfortable life and is supportive of everything I do, of our life, our family, our dogs and our home. He is generous and kind, and though he has become jaded and hardened over these last few years, he still has a tender heart and a loving soul."

Anna, Helper (2) in a 4-year relationship with Moses, Peacemaker (9)

"Moses is very accepting, warm and genuinely interested in other people. He makes our relationship a priority and loves connecting and sharing spiritual exploration with me. We bond in many ways, by making morning walks together a priority, eating dinner together, having cuddle time at night and even eye gazing from time to time. Moses is affectionate, very present in his body and very intentional with his touch, so we enjoy a deep physical connection.

I really admire how he makes requests with absolutely no attachment. He is completely open, whether the answer is yes or no, and I love this about him. Having learned from him that I don't have to feel guilty if I say no, his invitations are a great way for us to reconnect if life has gotten too busy. He pursues personal growth, takes responsibility for his own feelings and doesn't become reactive when I get upset.

Learning to relax and let things be as they are has been key in our relationship. Early in the relationship, I would feel doubtful and anxious when he seemed preoccupied and distracted. I would get angry, acting out my insecurities in a push-pull way that he patiently tolerated. He dealt with his insecurities more directly by asking me for reassurance and then waiting to see how things progressed. As we've both relaxed, things have gotten better and better. I have learned the less pressure I give him, the more he steps into action both with planning activities and helping around the house. The more I have tapped into staying present, the happier and more loving we both have become. I have learned to value his intention at least as much as his actions because I can see his love for me in how he thinks about his life.

I've had to recalibrate my ideas of how much time we would spend together and how many joint projects we would have. Moses needs time to organize himself and just to putter independently. I started to move ahead on projects on my own, and my self-reliance in that regard helped our relationship a lot. This balance is so important that we've actually divided up the house to support it. In our two-bedroom apartment, we each use one of the bedrooms as our own office. We sleep together in the living room which we've made quite comfortable. Each having our own independent space is really helpful.

Understanding each other is a constant learning process. Moses doesn't always know what he likes and dislikes, so I've learned to listen carefully and watch closely for little clues. I've taken him to events that he didn't end up enjoying and then felt guilty about it afterward, even if we agreed together to go. I try to forgive myself and just do the best I can as he learns, explores and discovers more about himself. He is also less specific about who he wants to socialize with and how he wants to spend his time. I try to ask probing questions, and we've both learned he ends up enjoying himself more with people who are introspective and engaged with their lives.

Overall, I'm very happy in my relationship. Moses and I are an amazing match in terms of preferences and lifestyle such as intimacy, nature, socializing, health, spirituality and daily routines. And even things that look like weaknesses, like his distractibility, always mirror to his strengths, like his easygoing acceptance. If he didn't have his "weaknesses," then he would have different strengths that wouldn't provide the amazing fit that we have."

9:2 The Theory

9:2 When In Balance
The Helper (2) with the Peacemaker (9) make a warm, loving, accepting and nurturing couple who enjoy each other's company and create a supportive, healing space for others. Both are other-referencing and place a high value on harmony so this a relationship with little direct conflict. Both can be accommodating, low-key and compassionate, seeing the pain in others and wanting to help alleviate suffering. With these foundational similarities, there are also some balancing differences.

Helper (2)s are generally more social, engaging, decisive and extroverted. They bring energy and initiative to the dynamic, and they may drive the social calendar of the couple. Relationships are important to them, and they gain a lot of happiness from their interactions with other people. With this consistent drive to connect, they need less alone time than their Peacemaker (9).

The Peacemaker (9) offers steadiness, uncomplicated directness and a relaxed, easygoing attitude. They are adaptable and can be comfortable in a lot of different environments and situations. More low energy and less decisive than their Helper (2) partner, they take more time to putter, process their feelings and just generally relax.

Together, this can be an easygoing, sensitive, kind and altruistic pair. They support each other in a variety of ways ranging from affirmation, acts of service, physical presence and kind gestures. Both strive to be sensitive to the needs of the other and harmony and support are top priorities for both partners.

9:2: The Downward Spiral

This couple's avoidant tendencies and confusion around personal boundaries can be the trigger for the downward spiral. With tightening defenses, both Helper (2)s and Peacemaker (9)s can avoid bringing up difficult subjects relating to the relationship, and may instead make unspoken agreements to let difficult issues go unaddressed. This means important problems go unresolved, building walls of unhappiness and resentment setting the stage for the downward spiral.

Alternatively, weak boundary awareness can be an issue in this couple. Both types have a tendency to merge, and in the case of the Helper (2), this can manifest as a desire to get overly engaged in the issues of their Peacemaker (9) partner. The Helper (2) leans in to help as a way of expressing love and a subconscious strategy to gain appreciation. However, the Peacemaker (9) may resent these efforts, experiencing their Helper (2) as bossy and controlling. Both partners are triggered but their reaction moves in different directions. The Peacemaker (9) becomes more withdrawn and disengaged, and the Helper (2) gets more demanding and involved. Thus begins a repeating toxic loop of help and withdrawal.

As the defenses tighten, so does the intensity of the polarization. The Helper (2) seeks appreciation, and as this need goes unmet, their increase their efforts. The Peacemaker (9) numbs out and can feel internal confusion. Because both types avoid conflict, the relationship may continue but both types may fall into a depression or experience other physical manifestations of an unhappy relationship. Eventually one or both partners may decide to get their needs met elsewhere or end the relationship.

9:2 The Lighthouse

Indirect communication and a lack of clarity around their own needs and desires mark the beginning of the downward spiral for this pair, so becoming clearer on both fronts is the way to break the downward momentum. A strong navel point and a powerful Kundalini Yoga breathwork practice will help these types.

9:2 The Kundalini Yoga Connection

Energetically, confusion around personal boundaries is an issue this couple needs to address. Both partners may have difficulting identifying where each individual starts and ends. Developing a strong self-awareness is helpful for both.

Helper (2)s need to manage their impulse to speak for the Peacemaker (9) and to instead refocus on their own needs. Kundalini Yoga kriyas that increase body awareness, self-care and self-acceptance are helpful for Helper (2)s. And cultivating stillness is helpful for the dynamic so the Peacemaker (9) feels less of an urge to withdraw.

Peacemaker (9)s need to connect to their own power and learn to be direct instead of passive-aggressive. This starts with them understanding their needs and desires. They need to cultivate a sense of themselves and to develop their power center. Kundalini Yoga kriyas and meditations to build a strong navel center, a strong nervous system and to raise their energy are helpful for Peacemaker (9)s.

See the appendix for Helper (2) and Peacemaker (9) recommended Kundalini Yoga kriyas and meditations.

9:3 Peacemaker (9) with Achiever (3)

Anita, Achiever (3), formerly in a 30-year relationship with Donald, Peacemaker (9)

"The traits which attracted me to Donald were his wonderful sense of humor, his intelligence, his unflappable sense of calm, his ability to "not sweat the small stuff," his support and his stability.

I met Donald very young – we went to the same elementary school and were about one year apart academically. We began dating when he was in high school.

Energetically, we were opposites. The notation under my picture as student body president in our school's yearbook read, "Rushing madly and incessantly about, she is always doing something for someone sometime." Donald was the oasis of calm in this caldron of frenzied activity. He was the voice of reason, the unflappable companion who could help me put things in perspective, my anchor in a turbulent sea.

I could count on his support. When I had been in the professional world for four years and discovered that the company was paying me less than my male co-workers for the same position, with the same responsibilities, I wrote a letter stating that I would resign my position rather than accept this inequality. This was in the 1960s when it was less common for a woman to stand her ground. My husband was very supportive of this decision and encouraged me to be assertive with management. He was the wind beneath my wings.

In our relationship, I brought drive and sense of adventure to the dynamic. During our marriage, we moved to Germany for four years and traveled extensively during that time. My happy-to-stay-home husband said if it hadn't been for me, we would never have left the United States and that if he had accepted the job in Germany without me, he would have done little traveling. But in the end, he admitted he appreciated all the travel we did and all the experiences we had together.

Donald was a loving and caring dad and a good provider who ensured his children had a stable home. We both agreed on child-rearing, so when the children tried to play the one-parent-against-the-other game, we were a united team.

However, communication around sensitive topics was not a strong point in our relationship. When Donald had problems that annoyed him or made him angry, he would simply clam up. He felt little was worth arguing about and would say "if I'm still angry in three days, we can talk about it." Of course, we never did. This stonewalling led to a wall of undiscussed hurts, wounds and resentments.

During the relationship, our different energy levels also became an issue. After our three children were born, we decided to build our own house on several acres of land. This was a huge undertaking and introduced an unprecedented amount of stress, both emotional and financial, into our relationship. When we moved into the house, we still had many tasks to complete. With my Type A drive, I wanted to aggressively attack the list of tasks. My lower energy husband was intimidated by the breadth of the work and would often take time out to relax in his familiar reclining chair, beer in hand, watching sports. He once said "I used to feel guilty when I wanted to watch a football game, and you were working, but I don't anymore. I don't have your energy and can't keep up with you."

The marriage never recovered from this period, but as we weren't good at openly discussing our issues, many years passed quietly as the relationship deteriorated. We both avoided the situation and crafted independent lives for ourselves. To the outside world, the marriage looked intact, but this was not, in fact, the case. During this period, my husband's occasional drink developed into full-blown alcoholism. Eventually, a medical issue, exacerbated by Donald's alcoholism, brought the entire reality into the light and shortly after we divorced."

9:3 The Theory

9:3 When In Balance
The Achiever (3) and the Peacemaker (9) can make a very supportive and balancing match bringing each other important personality traits the other generally lacks.

Peacemaker (9)s bring support, acceptance, encouragement and an unflappable sense of calm. Because they are less image-conscious and less concerned about the opinion of others, they offer the Achiever (3) a firm base from which to jump. The Achiever (3) correctly senses the Peacemaker (9) will support them through thick and thin, and this gives the Achiever (3) greater self-confidence to pursue their goals. Peacemaker (9)s enjoy the simple things in life and can help remind their Achiever (3) to slow down and smell the roses. Achiever (3)s like to be admired, and the Peacemaker (9) finds it easy to be proud of their Achiever (3).

In return, Achiever (3)s help the Peacemaker (9) to wake up to all that life has to offer. Achiever (3)s bring a high energy, drive, ambition and a fast-paced, "can do" attitude that helps motivate and focus the Peacemaker (9). With their Achiever (3) at their side, Peacemaker (9)s may stretch themselves to try new things, go places they haven't been and to break out of their comfortable routine. They sparkle in the face of their new experiences and enjoy a broader worldview.

Energetically, this couple has the potential to be balancing. The Peacemaker (9) gives the Achiever (3) permission to relax, and the Achiever (3) helps the Peacemaker (9) to get going. The easy acceptance of the Peacemaker (9) and the enthusiastic drive of the Achiever (3) can be healing for both partners. When self-aware and in balance, this can be a successful and enduring match.

9:3 The Downward Spiral

This couple can run into trouble by being too conflict avoidant. Peacemaker (9)s feel threatened by conflict, and Achiever (3)s feel threatened by a negative image, so both people tend to sweep issues under the rug. With tightening defenses, the Achiever (3) gets more attached to the image of a perfect relationship, and the Peacemaker (9) gets more withdrawn to maintain harmony.

Peacemaker (9)s feel extreme anxiety in the face of conflict and will often stonewall or shut down to avoid the related stress they feel from a loss of harmony. They prefer to wait, hoping that time passing will somehow resolve the issue.

Achiever (3)s are very interested in maintaining a positive image. Love is fused with the appearance of wellness, and it is hard for them to separate the two. To feel stable, they want the image of the "perfect marriage" and to honestly deal with an issue might shatter that image.

As both people polarize into their corner of denial the relationship weakens, though to the outside world everything may appear fine. Dinner parties continue, holidays seem bright and happy to outsiders, school functions have both parents in attendance, but behind closed doors, the relationship is cold and distant. Both partners are unhappy but unwilling to face reality. Instead, they craft separate lives for themselves and continue down their path of avoidance.

The downward spiral gains momentum. The Achiever (3) has many unmet needs of being admired and appreciated. They may fall into a depression or go outside of the relationship to get their needs met. The Peacemaker (9) may start to resent the falseness of the Achiever (3) and the mask that is presented to the outside world. They experience the Achiever (3) as attention seeking, self-centered and phony. The lives may continue to drift apart as the couple becomes like distant housemates.

Often, some life crisis such as an affair or a major health challenge brings the deterioration of the relationship into awareness. If the core issues remain unaddressed and unresolved, the relationship may collapse.

9:3 The Lighthouse

Issue avoidance is the root of the downward spiral for this couple. Feelings of shame and anxiety trigger avoidance, so dealing with these two issues on a somatic level can help break the momentum of the downward crash.

In addition, the Achiever (3) needs to recognize how anxiety-provoking conflict is for a Peacemaker (9). Stonewalling is often a way to avoid anxiety, so unthreatening ways to address issues are the most effective. And Peacemaker (9)s need to acknowledge how image conscious their Achiever (3) is. Achiever (3)s are better able to address sensitive issues when they are feeling very safe, secure and their image is not in jeopardy.

9:3 The Kundalini Yoga Connection

Feelings of shame result in the Achiever (3) sacrificing reality for an image. Achiever (3)s can cut off from their emotions, leaving them often with a polished external world but a sad and unfulfilling inner world. Kundalini Yoga kriyas and meditations that cultivate heart opening, self-acceptance and self-love are beneficial for Achiever (3)s.

Peacemaker (9)s need to strengthen their nervous system and their navel center/third chakra to activate their power center. The anxiety of conflict feels less overwhelming with a strong nervous system. A strong navel point gets the Peacemaker (9) in touch with their needs allowing them to advocate for themselves better. Kundalini Yoga kriyas and meditations to build their nervous system and the navel center are highly beneficial for Peacemaker (9)s.

See the appendix for Achiever (3) and Peacemaker (9) recommended Kundalini Yoga kriyas and meditations.

9:4 Peacemaker (9) with Individualist (4)

Marianna, Individualist (4) married in a 28-year relationship with Tony, Peacemaker (9)

"My husband is steadfast, reliable, solid, dependable and a person of integrity. He is kind, inclusive and accepting, but he has a strong backbone and doesn't suffer fools. He can advocate for himself quite powerfully when he sees someone trying to control him or do something he doesn't like.

I appreciate that he doesn't get blown off course by my emotional ups and downs. The fact he doesn't take my moods personally means I can be free to have my feelings which is important to me. I find the emotional storms pass much more quickly when they have the space they need to come and go.

I am grateful for his self-awareness. He realizes when things are getting boring or if we are stuck in a rut. In 28 years together, of course this has come up, and his willingness to try new things with me has been a blessing to our relationship.

Our relationship is based on trust and giving each other space to be individuals while still supporting each other and the partnership. I trust him completely. I can leave my journals lying around, and I know he would never read them - he would be bored by them anyway!

He supports me in pursuing what matters to me, including innumerable Enneagram trainings and other personal development workshops that take me away from our home and three children for days at a time. He doesn't need to know what I'm doing as long as he knows I feel it's important. I encourage him to pursue his own interests as well; recently he went to do trail work in Oregon and Washington without me. Our relationship thrives on a combination of togetherness and separate interests.

When we are together, I feel like we're a pair of cats. We just like to sleep next to each other and be in each other's presence without the need to talk a lot. We generally find each other's presence loving, accepting, relaxing and rejuvenating. We parent well together as our approach is the same, and our parenting style is very accepting, relaxed, loving but laissez-faire. We like it that way and so do our three boys, so we have a harmonious home.

As in all relationships, we've had our share of ups and downs, but we've been able to grow together as a couple. When I first started studying the Enneagram, I was upset that he wasn't interested in learning anything about this system that had become so important to me and that had upended my whole view of the world. I felt a strong pull from him to keep things the same, to resist growth and to refuse to recognize how I was changing. This triggered me, and I became more emotionally reactive and blaming, causing him to shut down even more. During this period, I was frustrated and began drinking excessively. I would pick fights with him while I was drunk or hungover. It was a difficult period, but we stuck together and got through it. I'm sober now, and we've learned how to work things through as a couple. I help him acknowledge and understand his emotions, and he helps me stay positive and connected to him while we are discussing difficult topics. We've come to appreciate our differences as gifts in each other instead of dismissing them or even disparaging them.

In our relationship dynamic, we have to be diligent about inertia and relationship drowsiness. Because we are so physically comfortable together, like two snoozing cats, we can be soothed into a kind of complacent trance where it seems like everything is great but really, we aren't sharing ourselves with each other, and we're growing apart emotionally. Our mutual need for independence and privacy can be a problem for the same reason. We can get into a rut of doing our own thing independently and then watching TV at night but not really talking. We've learned that we need to have physical adventures together, like hiking, backpacking, yoga and so forth, to bring in some sexual energy and spark into the relationship.

A big turning point in our relationship was realizing that it's okay for him to be mad at me. Neither of us could tolerate that for years which meant many issues weren't fully processed. He wouldn't let himself be mad so he would shut down, pretend things were fine or pout. I couldn't stand any anger from him, so I would endlessly try to explain and justify myself-or make myself so pitiful that he wouldn't dare be mad at me. It was so liberating when one day I said to him, "It's okay for you to be mad at me! I'm a pain in the ass, and I don't blame you!" These days it's ok for both of us to get mad, justified or not, talk about it, work it through, forgive.

If I hadn't learned the Enneagram, we'd still be where we were before, unless it got worse and we broke up, which was a distinct possibility. I'm so grateful for my husband, our relationship, our life together and that we have these tools to help us navigate our differences."

Nadia, Individualist (4) married in a 15-year relationship with Leo, Peacemaker (9)

"Leo is generous, easygoing, accepting and always up for an adventure. He is open and welcoming and makes others feel accepted just as they are. People love being around him. He has a wonderful sense of humor and laughs easily. We've been together 15 years, and as I watch him grow in self-awareness, he is more and more able to understand and articulate what he wants. When he reaches this point, he is mindful and clear in his responses.

In our relationship, he grounds me. If I'm feeling depressed and isolating myself, he'll say, "We're going to hang out with our friends!" It isn't a discussion – it's a statement and just what I need to get out of my emotional swirl and back into the real world.

Independence is one of the foundational values of our relationship. We've been married for 13 years, and over that time we've learned the importance of having our own independent activities, jobs, hobbies and friends. We do our things separately and come back together with renewed energy and excitement for the relationship. We both have professional work that feels meaningful and gives us a great basis of things to share. Leo is a music teacher, and I am a psychotherapist, so our jobs are both creative and relational. We really enjoy spending time with people and engaging in deep and meaningful conversations. Our favorite night of the year is when we host a Christmas Hootenanny and gather our friends and family for food, drinks and a sing-a-long. Leo leads us in song, and I create a beautiful and meaningful experience for our guests. This is when we are at our best individually and as a couple. Sometimes we joke that we should host a Hootenanny once a month because it is so fun for everyone and so good for our souls.

We balance each other, but it requires effort. When we first met, Leo was drawn to my emotional expressiveness after growing up in a home where feelings were repressed. While he was attracted to that part of me, he quickly learned that my constant focus on emotions might be too much for him. We had been dating a year when he took me to a choral concert. Halfway through the concert, I asked him "What are you feeling now?" He was really triggered because he just wanted to sit and enjoy the concert. He couldn't handle that I was so focused on his emotions, and he broke up with me that night because I was just "too much." We got back together a few days later, and he proposed a few months after that, but the theme of my emotions bordering on "too much" is an ongoing topic in our relationship years later.

We interpret conflict very differently. When I feel frustrated in our relationship, I start to idealize what it would be like to be with someone else. Mentally, I pull away from my husband and into my imagination. If this happens too much, I know we have an issue that needs to be addressed. I'm more proactive about initiating difficult conversations between us, and I am prone to want to "check in" about how we're doing. When I do, he eventually reveals that he's been frustrated for a while. During these difficult conversations, he will often say something like "I just feel like we don't have anything in common and are always in conflict." For me, conflict feels like it creates a deeper connection and brings me back to Leo.

While overall our relationship is good, I have to watch my habit of feeling dissatisfied and creating an internal fantasy in which someone rescues me and takes care of everything in my life. This is probably partly in response to my husband's lack of initiative and unwillingness to pursue what he wants. I know part of my wiring makes me always feel misunderstood. I know my internal work is to reveal myself rather than retreating into fantasy. I would like my husband to see how incredible of a man he is and how much he has to give the world. His inertia keeps him from taking right action and using his wisdom and talents to the fullest for himself and others.

In the balance, I'm very happy in my relationship. We share a deep bond, common values, and we are great partners on this personal growth journey we are on together. He supports me and pushes me at the same time. And I love him for it."

9:4 The Theory

9:4 When In Balance

The Individualist (4) and Peacemaker (9) can be an accepting, soothing, healing match who find a deep enjoyment from shared time together. The foundation of the relationship is a combination of support and allowing one another personal freedom to pursue their own goals and interests. Both enjoy the shared harmony they create together.

Peacemaker (9)s are steady, reliable, solid, dependable, inclusive and accepting. They don't get blown off course by the emotional storms of their Individualist (4), and this is very grounding for their partner.

Individualist (4)s bring rich expressiveness and intensity to the dynamic, helping to wake up the Peacemaker (9) and adding color to the dynamic. The Individualist (4) adds emotional electricity to the house ensuring issues gets discussed and important topics aren't swept under the rug. This is very balancing for the more avoidant Peacemaker (9).

This couple can share a deep, intense, intimate connection with each other.

9:4 The Downward Spiral
While their differences can be balancing, they can also be a source of frustration between these two partners. The mellow, easygoing Peacemaker (9) may experience the Individualist (4)'s focus on the emotional world as relentless and extreme, disrupting the harmonious environment the Peacemaker (9) strives hard to create. And the Peacemaker (9)'s tendency to resist change and maintain the status quo can be frustrating to the Individualist (4) who is on a never-ending quest in search of self. As defenses tighten, both partners polarize in opposite directions.

As the Individualist (4) demands more engagement and attention, the Peacemaker (9) begins to stonewall and withdraw. This further triggers the Individualist (4) who turns up the emotional volume and becomes more temperamental and explosive. As the downward spiral gains momentum, the Peacemaker (9) becomes more unresponsive, stubborn, disengaged and distant. Energetically, it is like an unstoppable force meets an immovable object.

Alternatively, the Individualist (4) may become frustrated with the Peacemaker (9)'s avoidant behavior and withdraw either physically or emotionally themselves, further weakening the bond. Unless something breaks the momentum of separation, the relationship may end.

9:4 The Lighthouse
Differing emotional reactions to stress and frustration mark the beginning of the downward spiral for this couple, so learning alternative stress responses can break the downward momentum. They need to recognize the pain in each other. Individualist (4)s feel wounded when they are misunderstood or feel unseen. Peacemaker (9)s become anxious in the face of conflict. Both are trying to alleviate their own pain rather than trigger the other. Both partners need to strengthen their nervous systems to accommodate changes in their own behavior as their resistance is their reactivity.

9:4 The Kundalini Yoga Connection
Individualist (4)s need to learn to manage the energy of their intense emotions. Cultivating

energy management and energetic stability are important in the quest to act and not react. Kundalini Yoga kriyas and meditations that strengthen the aura and cultivate stability, neutrality and balance are beneficial.

Peacemaker (9)s need to learn to resist the instinct to shut down in the face of potential conflict. They need to stand their ground and remain engaged and present. Nervous system work as well as Kundalini Yoga kriyas and meditations to strengthen the navel center, stay connected with the energy of emotion and to burn anger are helpful.

See the appendix for Individualist (4) and Peacemaker (9) recommended Kundalini Yoga kriyas and meditations.

9:5 Peacemaker (9) with Investigator (5)

Vladimir, Investigator (5) married in a 14-year relationship with Anastasyia, Peacemaker (9)

"I appreciate and admire my wife's ability to get into the mind of anyone else and see things their way. This isn't my strength, and her ability to see all sides of a conflict or of a situation has helped me to avoid trying to smash everything with logic. Her insight has helped me sit back and try to see things through a more emotional filter. I also consider her devotion to me a great strength, often because I have trouble seeing in myself those things which others might be attracted to or might appreciate. I feel lucky that she is devoted to me and looking out for me. I feel safe with her, knowing she has my back.

In our relationship, one of our core values is personal freedom. My wife gives me a great deal of latitude to do my own hobbies and pursue my own interests even though this sometimes means leaving her and our kids for an entire week away. Other people are surprised to hear I sometimes take my holidays this way, but this freedom is something that I need. We are committed to keeping each other happy, so we talk about what we want to do, individually and collectively, and find a way for both of us to do what we want.

She helps to balance me. My mind gravitates toward logic and reason, and my viewpoints can thus be a bit mechanical and dry. She brings a warmer, emotional perspective and can help bring me back on course if I start to lose myself to logic.

As it relates to issues, I am aware I am very much cut off from my feelings and only from time to time get flashes of understanding about how much I love my wife. Sometimes I worry that I don't show my love, I am too pedestrian and unromantic, focusing on the nuts and bolts and logistics of running a house and a family rather than letting her know how much she means to me.

Ironically, when I sat down to reflect on issues between the two of us, I couldn't think of any and had to ask my wife. And very kindly, she went through a list of things she imagined might annoy me about her. But I don't see these as challenges. I accept these parts of her character, and we go on. Maybe I am too superficial in emotional matters, but I believe that the relationship part of my life is the least challenging commitment I am in. If it were challenging, I really don't think we would have gone beyond the first few months let alone years. So, yes, it is annoying that she will not make her mind up about some things, sometimes, and it is annoying she has a disconnect from science and logic sometimes. But none of this is challenging. I love her, and it's crazy that she feels that her perceived flaws could create friction. It is part of who she is, and I love and accept her exactly as she is."

9:5 The Theory

9:5 When In Balance
Freedom and independence to pursue their personal goals are foundational elements of the Investigator (5) and Peacemaker (9) partnership. Both are committed to each other's happiness and dedicated to the relationship itself. From this base, this couple has a mix of balancing and similar traits.

Investigator (5)s are insightful, observant, resourceful, calm, objective and trustworthy. Their thinking is rational, logical and methodical, and these traits are useful to their Peacemaker (9) whose thinking can be more circular and emotionally-clouded. Their ability to focus and stay present is balancing for the Peacemaker (9) whose attention is more distractible and prone to wandering. All these traits make the Investigator (5) very grounding for their Peacemaker (9).

Peacemaker (9)s are undemanding, understanding, accepting and nonjudgmental. They accept their partner's desire for independence and time alone without taking it personally. They bring a warmer touch and a greater focus on human connection, and this is very balancing for the Investigator (5) who tends to isolate and relate more from the world of facts and data. Peacemaker (9)s offer easy companionship and nurturing, traits that can be deeply healing to their Investigator (5).

9:5 The Downward Spiral
Issues around too much space, feelings of neglect and relationship inertia can trigger

the downward spiral in this couple. Both types can operate independently, both can be distracted by their own pursuits and neither is overly eager to bring up thorny issues in the relationship. In this environment, interdependence suffers, and this couple can drift far apart without fully realizing it. Another potential trigger is if either partner puts their needs above the needs of the partnership. As both types are independent, it is important that they stay aligned with shared priorities.

A gradual awareness that their deeper needs are not being met may be the trigger for the downward spiral. With tightening defenses, Investigator (5)s isolate and Peacemaker (9)s withdraw and stonewall. As both raise their defensive gates, problems can go unaddressed, emotional wounds fester and tensions build, albeit a low simmering build rather than explosive expressions of frustration. The relationship may continue on this path for some time with more and more distance growing between the couple. Eventually, an outside event or an emotional outburst force the gap between this couple to be addressed.

9:5 The Lighthouse
The lack of a deep emotional connection and an emotional coolness are the roots of the downward spiral for this pair, so connecting from the heart is key to repairing the relationship. Both types can be avoidant about dealing with hard issues so finding a safe way to air grievances is important. In addition, finding ways to enjoy shared time is critical for this couple.

9:5 The Kundalini Yoga Connection
Staying present is important for both partners in this dynamic. Peacemaker (9)s must resist the urge to withdraw and avoid real issues. Investigator (5)s need to recognize and balance their drive to isolate. They need to work hard to stay connected.

Investigator (5)s need to connect with their heart and get their emotional energy moving. Engaging more deeply is easier with a strong nervous system. Kundalini Yoga kriyas and meditations for energy awareness, heart opening and to strengthen the nervous system are beneficial.

Peacemaker (9)s need to connect with suppressed anger and burn it out. They need to stay actively engaged and actively present. Kundalini Yoga kriyas and meditations that bring them into their body are helpful, as well as practices that burn anger and open the heart.

See the appendix for Investigator (5) and Peacemaker (9) recommended Kundalini Yoga kriyas and meditations.

THE NINE KEYS

9:6 Peacemaker (9) with Loyalist (6)

Simone, Loyalist (6) in a 7-year relationship with Gabriel, Peacemaker (9)

"Gabriel is one of the "easiest to get along with" people I have ever met in my life, and I love him insanely for that. It is nearly impossible to offend him. Because he is so tolerant, I feel safe to say what I need to say without the fear that I'm going to jeopardize our relationship. I'm pretty sure that I've annoyed him a couple of times, and I know that I've made him angry twice. But I cannot think of one time in our seven-plus year relationship that I've ever offended him. It's nice to be with someone who I don't have to walk on eggshells around.

Related to that, I love how emotionally stable he is. He reminds me of the eye of a hurricane: You can unleash a Category 5 storm around him. And it's terrible and devastating, and it rips someone like me to shreds. But then it passes after a time, and there he is…just standing there, firm as ever, same as ever, as if nothing terrible happened at all. He's literally like the human Stonehenge: no one knows where he came from, but he's there, and he's unchanging, and he's immovable, and we've all just come to trust that he's going to be there today and tomorrow just the same as he was yesterday. And I love that.

He's good at making room for other people while still being himself. He's really secure in who he is and that allows him to be with people who are very different from him without being threatened or becoming controlling. He's very adaptable, and he can fit in with any crowd. He molds to the people he's with. I know that when I'm with him, I can feel him molding to me; being what he knows he needs to be with me. It's not fake, and he's not pretending. He's just expressing the parts of him that fit me best. And those parts may not be the same parts that fit best when he's with his parents, for example. So, he expresses different parts when he's with them. He's like modeling clay: he can mold into any shape that you need him to, but he's never really changing the essence of who he is. Today he may take the shape of a bowl, but it's still a bowl made out of a clay. And tomorrow it may be taking the shape of a cylinder, but it's made with the same clay that made the bowl yesterday. His shape may change, but his substance is the same. He's also a person of surprisingly great depth. While initially, he comes across as very simple, the reality is that there is a lot of complexity beneath the surface.

Gabriel brings a sense of calm to our relationship which I appreciate because I'm a very anxious person on my own. I love that our relationship is drama free, emotionally safe and low maintenance. At the same time, he has a rebellious streak, and together we have a lot of fun – which I appreciate. I feel like it's easy to let my inhibitions go when I'm with him.

Another thing I like about our dynamic is how he is completely comfortable with me just as I am. He doesn't seem anxious about me being me and letting me live my life and do my thing. With him, I feel like I have room to explore myself and be my own person.

I would describe our relationship as stable, but it is an unconventional stability since, up until recently, we were both married to other people. Stability for us has been through a consistent connection. We've been together, we've been apart, we've stayed apart for months at a time, and none of it matters because every time we see each other again, we pick up from where we left off like it was yesterday. I have even deliberately tried to cut off this connection by avoiding him altogether. I've tried to focus on all the things I hate about him. None of it works. Our connection is always there. I know stability in his relationship is important to Gabriel. One of the things he disliked most about being married to his ex-wife is that she was always threatening to leave him and that put a constant stress on him. But he's complex and also has a great need to be independent too.

Communication between us can be a challenge, and it manifests in that we both hold back expressing our full genuine emotions. Despite how safe I feel with him, I worry that if I'm really honest with him about my thoughts and my feelings, he will feel smothered by me, and I don't want him to push me away because I'm overwhelming him. I try to self-calibrate when I'm with him and give just as much as he seems willing to receive. And I sense that he holds back his feelings a lot of the time too. With him, I wonder if it is because he feels he can't handle his feelings himself.

Overall, I feel very grateful for our relationship and the fact we have a very deep and rare connection. Our connection feels like an invisible cord that exists between the two of us... we can't see it, but one end is tied to him, and the other is tied to me. It's thick and well woven. Some days it's shorter in length, and we're closer together. Other days it's longer, and we're further apart then. But it's always there."

9:6 The Theory

9:6 When In Balance

The Loyalist (6) with the Peacemaker (9) build a relationship based on stability and a healthy mix of autonomy and teamwork. Both share a desire for a predictable, secure life centered on a committed relationship. Family, work life and routine take priority over adventure and risk-taking, and this couple share a fairly conventional life together.

The Loyalist (6) brings loyalty, curiosity, energy, and a drive to guard, protect and improve their environment and the relationship itself. Mentally active and vigilant, Loyalist (6)s can be endearing in their insecurity. They bring a warmth and a playfulness to the dynamic. Because they can be insecure and unsure of themselves, they make the Peacemaker (9) feel needed. Peacemaker (9)s readily step into this role, feeling they can offer their Loyalist (6) the unconditional acceptance they crave.

The Peacemaker (9) brings steadiness, commitment, nonjudgment, tolerance and a drive for peace and harmony. These traits are stabilizing and deeply healing for the Loyalist (6) who tends towards anxious thinking and who fears abandonment. Peacemaker (9)s are calm, grounded and collaborative but with a need for independence. This couple might be very tightly enmeshed in certain area of their lives but also have a great deal of autonomy in others.

Together, this is a balancing pair with the Peacemaker (9) offering the solid foundation and the Loyalist (6) bringing energy and vitality to the mix. This is a caring, committed couple who have a great deal of admiration for each other.

9:6 The Downward Spiral

There are several potential triggers for the downward spiral in this relationship. Inertia can be a factor as both partners are reluctant to question the status quo. The relationship can get rote and routine to the point where emotional connection suffers, and true intimacy is lost. Unfulfilling jobs may be maintained, dysfunctional financial situations continue and thorny problems go unaddressed far longer than they would with other couples. The relationship may march along but neither partner is truly happy, and there is a lack of alignment on future goals. Stalemates and unaired issues litter the environment threatening the core of the relationship.

Alternatively, differing stress responses can be a trigger. With tightening defenses, Loyalist (6)s become more anxious and more catastrophic in their thinking. If this is directed at their partner, the Peacemaker (9) reacts by withdrawing, shutting down or stonewalling. This further triggers the Loyalist (6) who becomes more reactive, demanding and hysterical. As the downward spiral gains momentum, both partners polarize into their corners without a clear path to reconciliation or healing. Without a break in the momentum, the relationship is at risk.

9:6 The Lighthouse

Issue avoidance, at a very deep level, and resistance to change can be the beginning of the downward spiral for this couple. Contrary to their nature, both partners need to work hard to stay alert to inertia and from the tendency to retreat from important issues. As this can be anxiety provoking for both, tools and techniques to lower anxiety are helpful. This couple also needs to periodically take time out to reconnect and reestablish life priorities. It can be easy for this couple to drift and not realize they are off course until they are very far off course.

9:6 The Kundalini Yoga Connection

Strengthening the nervous system helps both partners stay present and connected even in the face of uncomfortable conversations or situations. Connecting deeply to their body helps both partners get back in touch with their intuition and their sense of themselves.

Loyalist (6)s need to learn to manage their anxious thinking, which ultimately clouds their judgment. Anxious thinking leads to contraction so they cut off from the somatic information that would otherwise be useful. Loyalist (6)s have strong, useful instincts, but these can get lost in the face of anxiety. At an energetic level, they may lose touch with their inner guide and the voice of their soul as their mind and ego take over. Kundalini Yoga kriyas and meditations to release fear, to lower anxiety, to cultivate self-reliance and to develop trust are helpful.

Peacemaker (9)s energetically numb out as a strategy to avoid conflict. Despite the fact Peacemaker (9)s can be extremely powerful, they subconsciously cut off from their power as a mechanism to avoid the discomfort it would involve to step into it. Peacemaker (9)s need to wake up to their anger and discontent and learn healthier ways to engage in conflict. They need to get clear about their own ambitions, dreams, and desires. Kundalini Yoga kriyas and meditations to build the navel center (third chakra), to help them energetically wake up and to burn anger are helpful. Kundalini Yoga kriyas and meditations to build inner fire and resolve are also helpful.

See the appendix for Loyalist (6) and Peacemaker (9) recommended Kundalini Yoga kriyas and meditations.

9:7 Peacemaker (9) with Enthusiast (7)

Janice, Enthusiast (7) married in a 2.5-year relationship with Tom, Peacemaker (9)

"I'm attracted to Tom's stability, his kindness, his rational way of thinking and his openness to try new things. He accepts me just as I am which makes me feel very loved. I know I can be myself around him, and this gives me confidence. I appreciate how much he makes me a

priority and how dedicated he is to my happiness.

In our relationship, I'm often the one who comes up with the ideas, but he's almost always open to them. I've learned when Tom feels more secure and positive in our relationship, he is more open to new ideas and new things. It is important for him to feel wanted and not rejected. When I overcome any feelings of rejection he might have, he becomes an open source for all my new ideas and proposals. I love it because it means I have a steady partner in crime. We've had lots of adventures – a half marathon run, a Legion's race, a trip to Romania, travels to the UK, and now I'm pregnant, so we'll have a new chapter.

We are both "party" people, and we get joy from hosting parties, inviting people over and going out together. We like to motivate our friends to go to the movies, to the theatre or even start a new hobby. We both find it really uplifting.

A strength in our relationship is that my husband reads me really well, and I am also very aware that he has a hard time expressing himself. He instinctively understands me, and I work hard to get him to communicate with me. I think that awareness brings us balance.

As it relates to challenges, our communication style is very different. I'm more openly emotional and more likely to say directly how I am feeling. He's more contained, and if something is bothering him, he'll keep it to himself and try not to say anything. Of course, I can usually tell when he's upset, but I have to work hard, and in just the right way, to get him to talk about the issue. If I press too hard, he withdraws completely and gets stubborn. If I say nothing, I feel terrible because I know something is wrong. I've learned the best thing to do is to say that "I know there is something wrong and that not talking about it is making me unhappy" and then to leave him to bring it up when he feels ready. He cares so much about my happiness that he never lets it go too long. Underneath it all, I think Tom has a belief that talking will not solve anything. I feel the opposite, so this is a difference we work on.

Overall, I'm very happy in my relationship. I feel like I've found a life partner who loves me deeply and that together we're a great balance."

9:7 The Theory

9:7 When In Balance

The Enthusiast (7) with the Peacemaker (9) can make a loving, effective partnership helping to balance each other's nearly opposite energetic tendencies and compensating for each other's blind spots and weaknesses. The Enthusiast (7) helps to energize and wake up the Peacemaker (9). The Peacemaker (9) helps to ground and focus the Enthusiast (7). Foundational values of this partnership are mutual acceptance, the belief in a positive future and supportive, balancing companionship.

Enthusiast (7)s offer high energy, a positive outlook, curiosity and a nearly insatiable drive to try new things. Their extroverted drive for fun and their busy schedule help shake the Peacemaker (9) into action. Enthusiast (7)s are action-oriented without much fear of failure. This allows them to cheerfully charge into new environments and experiences without a lot of hesitation or deliberation. Any actual failure is reframed as positive, and they tend to be quite resilient. All of these characteristics are helpful and inspiring for the Peacemaker (9) whose approach to life is more slow-paced, hesitant and deliberate.

Peacemaker (9)s share a positive outlook about life but tend to be more grounded, calm, steady and reliable. They are considerate, good listeners focused on the needs of others and gifted at making outsiders feel welcomed and accepted. They model dependability, accommodation and a more relaxed laid-back approach to life that is very useful for the Enthusiast (7) to observe and mirror. They provide the Enthusiast (7) with easy companionship for the Enthusiast (7)'s wide range of adventures.

When in balance, this couple can be a wonderful balance of yin and yang energy, of high spirits and mellow acceptance.

9:7 The Downward Spiral
The downward spiral is usually triggered by the avoidance of negative topics or an imbalance of control.

Both types instinctively gravitate away from thorny issues and painful discussions. When fixated with tightening defenses, Enthusiast (7)s reframe negative events, focusing almost relentlessly on the positive. Processing negative emotions is extremely anxiety-provoking for most Enthusiast (7)s, and their attention instinctively moves to more positive topics. Likewise, addressing negative issues is challenging and anxiety-provoking for Peacemaker (9)s. Difficult discussions feel like a threat to the harmony Peacemaker (9)s seek to feel stable. Major issues may go unaddressed, but the anxiety surrounding the issues remains and in a fixated state, the partners may begin blaming each other, acting out or becoming directly or indirectly critical and frustrated with one another. Thus begins the downward spiral.

An imbalance of control can also be a trigger in this relationship. Enthusiast (7)s are self-referencing, and Peacemaker (9)s are other-referencing so it can be easy for the Enthusiast (7) to make demands, not realizing their Peacemaker (9) partner has different priorities and desires. The less verbal Peacemaker (9) may become passive-aggressive or start to numb out as an indirect strategy to stand their ground. The downward spiral is triggered and without fully realizing it, this couple can start to drift apart and may not consciously realize there is an issue until they have become quite distant.

The depth of the downward spiral has a lot to do with the partnership's level of awareness. In extreme cases, the Enthusiast (7) gets frustrated and anxious and begins attacking the Peacemaker (9), triggering more passive resistance and stonewalling. If the momentum isn't broken, this once joyous and balancing couple can polarize into respective corners of resentment, contempt, criticism and stonewalling until the relationship eventually ends.

9:7 The Lighthouse
Excessive avoidance of the negative and denial of reality mark the beginning of the downward spiral in this couple so learning to stay present and to address painful topics and issues directly is the key to breaking the downward momentum. The self-referencing Enthusiast (7) and the other-referencing Peacemaker (9) need to find a healthy balance of needs and priorities. Peacemaker (9)s need time and a receptive space to figure out what they really want. Enthusiast (7)s need to cultivate discernment and to learn that they will be ok even if they don't get everything they want.

9:7 The Kundalini Yoga Connection
Both partners will benefit from strengthening their nervous systems as they learn to address difficult topics.

Enthusiast (7)s need to identify and manage their anxiety instead of staying on the go and staying distracted. They need to learn to sit still, let feelings arise and stay present and focused in the face of discomfort. Kundalini Yoga kriyas and meditations to lower anxiety and to quiet the mind are beneficial. Because Enthusiast (7)s have such an active mind, a powerful physical practice can be helpful in slowing their noisy, anxious thoughts.

Peacemaker (9)s need to get in touch with their feelings and particularly their repressed anger. They need to change their relationship with conflict and learn to see it as part of a healthy relationship. Kundalini Yoga kriyas and meditations to burn anger, to get energy flowing in the body and to strengthen the navel center are all beneficial.

See the appendix for Enthusaist (7) and Peacemaker (9) recommended Kundalini Yoga kriyas and meditations.

9:8 Peacemaker (9) with Leader (8)

Cassandra, Leader (8) in a 7-year relationship with Mason, Peacemaker (9)

"Mason brings a sense of peace and calmness to my storm. While I can be moody and openly emotional, his temperament never seems to shift much. He is always in the same mood and the same mindset. He calms me down. He is stable, punctual and loves routine. I feel I can rely on him, and I know what to expect with him. I appreciate his practical thinking and the fact that he is an easygoing companion.

As it relates to challenges, he has what I would almost describe as mental laziness. If he can procrastinate, he does. His attitude is "if we can put it off until tomorrow, why do it today?"

I feel it is obvious that if he doesn't tell me what he needs, I can't help him. Yet, he can be quite closed and stubborn. This is a huge challenge for me, as I am more direct. I also see this behavior as selfish since he doesn't think things all the way through and doesn't seem to understand the damage being done by his stonewalling.

I'm 21 years old, and we've been together for 7 years. We'll see what the future holds."

Tamara, Leader (8) married in a 30-year relationship with Gordon, Peacemaker (9)

"Gordon is stable, calm, organized and wonderfully accepting. I feel like I can be my full self with him which makes me feel loved and helps me relax. In our dynamic, we balance each other. I am more the external leader, often off doing things in the outside world, while he holds down the homefront and takes care of things on a more practical, domestic level. He keeps the household running smoothly and is great at research and planning. I am the big picture person, and he brings the detail. For example, I had a friend move to Thailand, and she invited us to visit. I came home and told Gordon that we were going to go to Southeast Asia and that I wanted to see Vietnam. With no more direction from me, he researched the various countries and planned out a wonderful three-week trip. This included booking our flights and hotels, investigating visas and figuring out the best places for us to visit. We traveled to five countries in a part of the world that we had never been before. Amazing! I love this about him.

Like all couples, we have our challenges, and after over 30 years of marriage, our triggered reactions to each other are pretty well grooved. Our communication styles are different. In the face of a conflict, I seek an immediate resolution, and I get more aggressive if I don't get it. My husband withdraws in the face of conflict. With this as the backdrop, what seems like a simple question can turn into a full-blown argument in less than 30 seconds. This has happened so many times that we don't always hear what is being said or recognize the intent of each other in the heat of the moment. Something simple like me asking "Did you file the tax return yet?" can be interpreted as an attack which triggers him to withdraw and respond with "I'm really busy and don't have time to deal with this!" This leads me to escalate, and we're off to the races.

I have had to adjust my thinking around his sometimes passive-aggressive behavior. If Gordon doesn't agree with something that I thought we had agreed to, he will just do what he wants instead. He has even hidden things that he has done in an effort to get what he wants and avoid conflict. For example, he once booked a trip to Europe with his buddies and only told me after the plans were made, and tickets had been purchased. This was after when we agreed to limit our spending.

I wish he didn't feel so attacked by my communication style. I get very focused on conflict resolution because ambiguity feels extremely uncomfortable for me. He confuses my intensity as a personal attack. And I have come to realize him walking out of the room isn't dismissal or abandonment, but his way of processing and avoiding the anxiety that direct conflict provokes. We work on this difference.

Overall, I'm very happy with my husband. Our dynamic feels like a good balance, and we have over 30 years together creating and building a shared history. I'm grateful to have this man in my life."

Alexandra, Leader (8) married in a 25-year relationship with Troy, Peacemaker (9)

"My husband is amazing. He is strong and loyal to a fault. He is brilliant and humble. He is my best friend and has brought me countless gifts to assist me in my journey, my growth and in my healing. He is my rock through the challenges of life. He is the calm in my storm – my anchor. He balances me. There have been times when my need for control has been intense and beyond rational. I have felt almost a panic to fix things and help those close to me, usually my kids. And in the midst of this swirl, I have looked to my side and seen him there, calm, not reacting, just holding space and being strong. This calms me down.

We are at a transformative moment in our relationship. For many years, we were extremely reactive to each other. The more I tried to control everything, the more he retreated. I was intolerant of his passive-aggressive behavior, and he was intolerant of my impatience and forcefulness. As a person, I am very direct and like people to speak their mind. He feels that sometimes sharing his truth may hurt someone and therefore, he doesn't speak up. I like to get everything out in the open, so I know what I'm dealing with. Many times, this directness has been just too much for him.

Fortunately, despite our reactivity, I am still very much in love with him. I see past the protective gear he wears, and I understand how he came to rely on this emotional armor as my aggressiveness at times warranted it.

Previously, my biggest challenge in the relationship was not reacting to him shutting down. The more he ran, the more I pursued which created a very lose-lose situation.

We are now at a different point because I've had my own personal awakening. It might sound odd, but I had a clear realization that I didn't like being human. The "human" experiences were making me impatient, and I wanted to skip past them. Interestingly, when I realized that was my truth, everything seemed to fall into place. An almost indescribable peace came over me. I finally realized that I was missing the entire point. I am here to be a leader and to remind people of who they are, but because they were not "getting it" I was enraged. The peace that washed over me as I realized this was simply divine. I was able to see and feel my truth, and as the impatience and fear were released, suddenly my need to react to everything vanished. I am now more accepting of others. I can get past the façade they use to function or to survive in their environment.

This realization has helped me tremendously in my relationship with my husband. Prior to this realization, I was frustrated. I wished he would put a bit more effort into feeling better, into being more proactive and into moving in the direction he said he wanted to move toward. I wanted so much to help him, but it seemed the more I tried to help, the more he would bury himself in low energy and refuse any movement.

Now I know that his behavior gave me very priceless gifts to understand the depth of my dysfunction. I hope that I have done the same for him. And I hope that his desire to be whole will give him strength and direction. Anything that I could offer him right now would be to encourage him to follow his heart and his feelings and go where he feels peace. I have learned surrender."

9:8 The Theory

9:8 When In Balance
This pairing can be extremely balancing, inspiring and healing for one another. The Leader (8) shows the Peacemaker (9) how to behave with confidence and assertion, and the Peacemaker (9) shows the Leader (8) how to behave with acceptance, accommodation and receptivity to create a soothing, harmonious environment. Together, this pair can have a very supportive, satisfying and fulfilling relationship.

Leader (8)s bring directness, leadership, decisiveness and a bold "take charge" mentality to the dynamic. They can be brash, fierce and confident with big energy and a powerful life force. The more easygoing Peacemaker (9)s admire and are fascinated by these traits, finding the Leader (8) magnetic, attractive and alluring. They appreciate the Leader (8)'s spirit and vitality and can be energized by their Leader (8)'s presence. The Peacemaker (9) enjoys having someone to look up to, and the Leader (8) enjoys the admiration.

Peacemaker (9)s bring calm, stability, acceptance and a soothing, healing manner to the dynamic. They accept and appreciate the Leader (8) which gives the Leader (8) even more strength and encouragement to tackle life's challenges. Their peaceful, quiet energy balances the brashness of the Leader (8), and they offer a secure home, a safe harbor, a tranquil sanctuary for the Leader (8) to retreat to after life's daily battles.

When these two types are aligned in their goals and appreciative of their differences, they can be a dynamic, effective pair: a powerful mast and a durable sail.

9:8 The Downward Spiral
Under stress with tightening defenses, this couple polarizes. The Leader (8) seeks resolution of issues by adopting a strategy of direct confrontation. The Peacemaker (9) heads in the other direction, adopting an avoidant strategy of stonewalling and shutting down. These opposite strategies prompt a more intense reaction in the other, and the downward spiral is triggered.

The Leader (8)s almost can't relax until they understand where they stand so it can be hard to de-escalate a conflict with a Peacemaker (9) in retreat. As the Leader (8) becomes more direct and more aggressive, the Peacemaker (9) shuts down, stonewalls and numbs out even more to avoid conflict. The Leader (8) may interpret this withdrawal as rejection, triggering more anger and more intensity. The downward spiral gains momentum as the Leader (8)'s aggression prompts more withdrawal from the Peacemaker (9). The environment can get heated with verbal aggression, anger and threats.

From the Peacemaker (9)'s perspective, the Leader (8) has become too controlling, harsh and domineering. What before felt like leadership now feels like dictatorship. The depth and power of a Peacemaker (9)'s stubbornness are often miscalculated, and conflicts can continue in a simmering state with no path to resolution on the horizon. Eventually the Leader (8) may turn away in disgust, but at this point contempt has entered the picture, and the stability of the relationship is threatened.

9:8 The Lighthouse
Different stress responses trigger the downward spiral in this couple so learning to be energetically still under stress is important. Both Leader (8)s and Peacemaker (9)s are powerful people. When they move in opposite directions, they stubbornly polarize. To break the reactivity, both types need to strengthen their nervous system to allow for stillness.

9:8 The Kundalini Yoga Connection
Both need to change their relationship with their own power. Leader (8)s need to control their power, and Peacemaker (9)s need to activate their power.

Leader (8)s need to learn to act, not react and to manage the intense energy of their anger response. Their desire for direct confrontation triggers a response to shut down in the Peacemaker (9). Kundalini Yoga kriyas and meditations to burn out anger and to slow the anger response are helpful.

Peacemaker (9)s need to resist the urge to withdraw in the face of stress and potential conflict. They need to stand their ground and voice their feelings instead of withdrawing and relying on stubborn, passive-aggressive behavior. Kundalini Yoga kriyas and meditations to strengthen the aura, activate the throat (fifth) chakra and strengthen the core are beneficial.

See the appendix for Leader (8) and Peacemaker (9) recommended Kundalini Yoga kriyas and meditations.

9:9 Peacemaker (9) with Peacemaker (9)

Meadow, Peacemaker (9), formerly in a 9-year relationship with Kyle, Peacemaker (9)

"I would characterize the relationship as supportive, steady, comfortable and unpressured. It was the most even-keeled relationship I've ever experienced with very few ups and

downs. We were each other's best friend and had a high level of comfort with each other even if we didn't dig deeply into the other's motivations or psyche. We generally supported each other's outside activities – rock climbing, camping and travel to Thailand and India – and didn't place demands on the other's time. We fought very little, and when we did, it was generally over quickly. Even though we were together for nearly a decade, there was very little talk of getting married or even moving in together.

The central issue in the relationship was that we were both so eager to avoid conflict that important issues went unresolved or were even buried. I think we both subconsciously prioritized harmony above our own wants and needs in a way that was detrimental to the long-term health of the relationship. In retrospect, I was probably depressed for long spells while we were together but was good at hiding it.

I think my biggest challenge was to be really honest with Kyle about what I really wanted out of the relationship. We were too comfortable with each other, and with the lack of pressure we ended up in a long relationship where neither of us was unhappy, but neither were we truly happy."

9:9 The Theory

9:9 When In Balance
A double Peacemaker (9) couple is accepting, mellow and accommodating with a relationship characterized by low drama, routine and a lack of direct conflict. They naturally focus on the positive elements of their partner and the relationship itself. Peacemaker (9)s instinctively don't place lots of demands on their relationships and with a double Peacemaker (9) combination, this is multiplied. Both partners have a great deal of personal freedom to pursue their own interests, and the relationship itself may move at a slow, easygoing pace with little talk of a more formal commitment or change from the status quo. Harmony is paramount and is often fused with routine so this couple has a certain steadiness and regularity to it. They take pleasure in each other's company and may enjoy the simple things in life-cooking together, dining together, relaxing together and so forth. Peacemaker (9)s seek relationships in which they feel comfortable, and they can often find that sense of comfort in another Peacemaker (9).

This can be a stable, accepting pair who work hard to cultivate a predictable, harmonious future together.

TYPE NINE PEACEMAKER/MEDIATOR

9:9 The Downward Spiral
Conflict avoidance can trigger the downward spiral in this couple. Peacemaker (9)s instinctively withdraw in the face of conflict (or potential conflict) so it can be easy for this couple to avoid addressing difficult relationship issues. Frustrations build, tensions grow, but as the source of conflict goes unaired, resolution is never reached. Peacemaker (9)s can be out of touch with what they want so it can be hard for both partners to understand, much less express, their needs. Somatic issues may hint at a deeper problem with one or both Peacemaker (9)s becoming depressed or anxious without fully realizing it. As underlying tensions grow, the wall of denial thickens. Because Peacemaker (9)s are resistant to change, the relationship may continue in a zombie, low energy state for long periods of time before one partner finally decides to initiate change, often in the form of a split.

9:9 The Lighthouse
Issue avoidance and energetic sloth mark the beginning of the downward spiral in this couple. Both partners are eager to maintain harmony, so they sleepwalk through the relationship. Getting in touch with their deeper desires and higher purpose is the first step in healing this relationship. Recognizing there is an issue is a central first step as one or both partners may do mental gymnastics to convince themselves there is no problem. The ability to recognize their own energy, or lack thereof, and the somatic expressions of imbalance and discord are important tools in addressing issues in the relationship.

9:9 The Kundalini Yoga Connection
Sloth, sleepwalking and energetic and emotional narcotization are themes for Peacemaker (9)s so developing self-awareness of these issues is important. Because both are so avoidant, it can be hard for one or both partners to realize there is an issue.

Kundalini Yoga kriyas and meditations that build energy, burn anger and strengthen the nervous system and navel point are helpful. With increased energy through focused breathwork, the Peacemaker (9) may "breathe their way to clarity" about what they really want in life. Kundalini Yoga kriyas and meditations to strengthen the nervous system and the navel point are helpful so they can risk advocating for themselves and manage the discomfort of conflict.

See the appendix for Peacemaker (9) recommended Kundalini Yoga kriyas and meditations.

This book is a living document. We will be updating it periodically with new information. If you are or were in a relationship with a Peacemaker (9) and you would like to participate in the related relationship survey, please email me at lynn@lynnroulo.com.

THE BRIDGE BETWEEN THE ENNEAGRAM AND KUNDALINI YOGA

The Enneagram offers a powerful map of human psychology and provides an objective way to talk about perspective: our own and the perspective of others. In a detailed and impersonal way, it maps out how we see the world and how we interpret events.

While it does a great job describing our mental wiring through our habit of attention, it doesn't address the way we experience the world in our bodies, through anger, calmness, anxiety, joy, shame and love. It shows us the path to change and growth, but it doesn't hand us the tools we need to physically make the journey. It gives the map to awareness but stays silent on the somatic changes that are also necessary. It doesn't address the need to strengthen the nervous system to change our reactions or the need to rewire our brains to relax our habit of attention.

My experience

I came across the Enneagram when I was in my early 20s. Randomly I bought an Enneagram book in a bookstore and started reading. I went in numerical order of the nine types, and when I got to my type, the Enthusiast (7), it was eerie how accurately it described my behavior. It was like learning I was from a country I didn't know existed, and my behavior is a result of cultural biases I didn't know I had. Except the Enneagram isn't about countries, it is about the mind.

After I discovered my type, I learned my attention bias and how my mind is wired to interpret information. I was a classic, stereotypical young Enthusiast (7) staying on the go, running from event to event, confused about why my friends didn't want to go out as much as I did. My drive for new experiences and fun was almost insatiable. But I was also feeling restless and anxious. The Enneagram helped to explain all of this and more. It was like entering a whole new world. And the system was great because it showed not only how I behaved but also how my behavior was automatic – like a machine. It offered a roadmap to free choice and to break patterns.

As I learned more, I started taking small steps down this path to relax my habit of attention. But as an Enthusiast (7), my anxiety was so great, trying to make real changes in my daily life seemed impossible. I read the Enneagram advice: "As an Enthusiast (7) try to stay home quietly without having friends over or outside distractions around." But when I tried to stay home alone, I got so anxious; I would negotiate with myself that if I went out but stayed in the neighborhood, it was just like staying home. But I knew it wasn't, and I didn't understand why it was so hard to make these simple changes.

It wasn't until years later when I came to Kundalini Yoga through an entirely different set of life circumstances that I learned how to strengthen my nervous system enough to make uncomfortable changes. After about 6 months of a regular Kundalini Yoga practice, staying home suddenly didn't seem like such a big deal. I could do it. And while it was still uncomfortable, it was manageable.

I've been doing a daily Kundalini Yoga practice since 2009, and since that time, I've made many major life changes. After 15 years of living in San Francisco, California, I moved to Athens, Greece in 2012. I had no tangible reason to move, just a very clear feeling – like a calling – I should be in Athens. In 2015, once again I got a really clear feeling I needed to end my finance career, work that I had done for over 20 years. With more free time, I focused on teaching and writing about Kundalini Yoga and the Enneagram. I wrote my first book that year, even though I hadn't really been planning to write a book when I stopped my finance work. All of these changes I made with relative ease. I credit this ease to Kundalini Yoga.

KUNDALINI YOGA

The practice of Kundalini Yoga makes difficult moments more tolerable and gives you the tools to change your behavior. A simple yet powerful form of yoga, Kundalini Yoga rewires your brain for change. It makes you more "you". It is also gives you tools and methods to deal with stress.

7 quick facts about Kundalini Yoga

1. Kundalini Yoga is often referred to as the yoga of awareness. It is essentially a technology of energy and energy management. Unlike many forms of yoga, Kundalini Yoga places a large emphasis on the breath and the development of the nervous system. I often refer to it as the yoga for "people who think they can't do yoga" because the starting position is always the breath. If you can breathe, you can do Kundalini Yoga.

2. The first known references to Kundalini Yoga date back to the Upanishads, a sacred Vedic collection of writings written between 1,000 B.C. and 500 B.C.

3. For centuries, Kundalini Yoga was taught in secrecy, available only through a master-disciple relationship. In the late 1960s, a Punjabi master of Kundalini Yoga named Yogi Bhajan began teaching it publicly in the United States, breaking this ancient tradition. Now there are thousands of Kundalini Yoga teachers sharing the practice across the world.

4. The word "Kundalini" is an ancient Sanskrit word that literally means "coiled snake." It is also sometimes translated to mean "the curl of the lock of hair of the beloved." Kundalini energy is a creative energy of consciousness that resides at the base of the spine. Everyone has this energy, but for most people, it stays dormant their entire life. But it can be awakened. One of the goals of Kundalini Yoga is to activate this creative force and to simultaneously prepare your body for its awakening.

5. Kundalini Yoga has both physical and psychological benefits. Scientific studies report enhanced memory, weight loss, better focus and increased physical flexibility as well as psychological benefits such as lower anxiety, lower depression and decreased anger. Overall energy levels and immunity levels are also reported to increase with the regular practice of Kundalini Yoga. And less scientific but equally important, long time practitioners often report, "Kundalini Yoga has helped me be more me."

6. Kundalini Yoga is a science of angles and triangles. Every angle created with the body has a corresponding energetic effect. For example, lifting the legs 30 degrees affects the navel point. Lifting the arms 60 degrees affects the heart and lungs. Yogically, the body is thought of as a whole, energetic, vibrating, creative entity – a huge complex of energies on many different levels. Kundalini Yoga leverages this energy. [5]

7. Kundalini Yoga classes follow a standard structure as follows:
- Tuning in
- Warm up exercises (optional)
- Kriya
- Deep Relaxation
- Meditation
- Closing.

---

(5) Yogi Bhajan, Published 2007, "The Aquarian Teacher: KRI International Teacher Training in Kundalini Yoga as taught by Yogi Bhajan"

THE NINE KEYS

Your brain before Kundalini Yoga

Your brain after Kundalini Yoga

Why Practice Kundalini Yoga?

Ask any engineer, and they will tell you there is a huge difference in a data center with "rat's nest wiring" and "structured wiring." In an organized, structured wiring environment, outcomes are predictable, and changes can be made with minimum disruption. In a disorganized, rat's nest environment, outcomes are unpredictable, and changes can invite chaos.

Our brains are essentially the same. We all start off with our initial wiring, or in Enneagram terms, "our habit of attention." But through training, you can relax your habit. And when you relax your habit, your true self, your essence, comes forward. The fastest, most effective method I know to relax your habit of attention is Kundalini Yoga. It helps you rewire your brain.

This rewiring is the result of the combination of physical exercises (asanas), mudra, mantra and focused breathwork. Combined, these elements strengthen the nervous system and rewire the brain.

Another benefit of Kundalini Yoga is that it develops your nervous system. The nervous system, a combination of your spinal cord, your brain and your nerve endings, is like the control center for your body. It dictates much of how you experience the world. You can think of it like the postal system of your body.

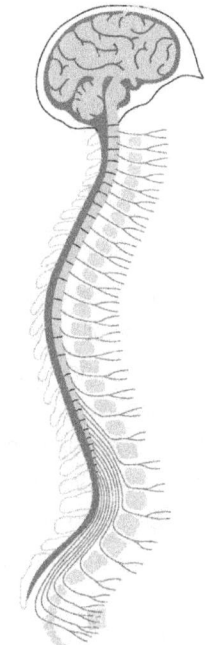

Your brain acts as the central control center, taking in all the information and sending instructions. In the post office analogy, it would be like the central computer system connecting all the post offices across the country.

The spinal cord, a bundle of nerves running down your spine, is constantly getting and sending messages from your body. It is like the mail truck system of the postal office, delivering information in both directions.

When this system is well-developed, the messages from the body can be more accurately received and interpreted. When the nervous system is weak or underdeveloped, the person gets trapped in their fixation, their reality distortion. The data is misinterpreted, and the resulting behavior is based on a reality distortion.

For example, a Loyalist (6) might see a missed call on his wife's phone from a number he doesn't recognize. And his brain starts to tell him he is being threatened, a stranger is calling, maybe his wife is having an affair, his marriage is ending and so forth. With a more developed nervous system, this same missed call might be interpreted as an open question, instead of a projected outcome: Who is calling? And when it turns out to be a telemarketer, he accepts this information and quickly moves on with his day.

As a practice, Kundalini Yoga places a large emphasis on strengthening the nervous system. In Enneagram terms, a strong nervous system means that when you are trying to relax your habit of attention, it doesn't feel as uncomfortable to make changes. You can begin to choose your behavior.

What are the Tools of Kundalini Yoga?

1. Kriya
2. Mantra
3. Mudra
4. Body Locks
5. The Breath and Pranayama
6. Relaxation

1. Kriya [5]

The word "kriya" means action. A kriya in Kundalini Yoga is a sequence of postures and physical exercises (asanas), breath and sound that are integrated together for a particular effect. It is the combination of posture, breath and sound in specific sequence and duration that create the effect. There are literally hundreds of Kundalini Yoga kriyas for different outcomes. There are kriyas for the navel center, for the aura, for depression, for anger and so forth. If you have a specific issue you are trying to resolve, Kundalini Yoga likely has a kriya for it. We are trained these kriyas should never be altered or modified. They are passed down purely through the generations, and the purity of Kundalini Yoga is one of its strengths.

2. Mantra [5]

Mantra is a mind projection created in either a spoken or mental manner. Mantras can be a word, phrase, syllable or sound. They can be recited, sung or repeated silently in the mind. They are a technique for regulating the mind.

There are many mantras, and each one has its own quality, rhythm and effect. Every thought or feeling that we have is on a vibratory frequency. By using mantras, we direct the mind into a higher vibratory frequency.

It doesn't matter if you know what the mantra means. And it doesn't matter if you believe that mantra works. It is like calling 911 in an emergency. It doesn't matter if you believe it or not, the connection still goes through. This is the power of mantra. It tunes you into a specific energetic frequency while it simultaneously quiets the thoughts in your mind, as it takes some of your mental energy to recite the mantra.

---

(5) Yogi Bhajan, Published 2007, "The Aquarian Teacher: KRI International Teacher Training in Kundalini Yoga as taught by Yogi Bhajan"

Kundalini Yoga mantras are generally in Gurmukhi, a language from the Punjab region of India. Below are five common mantras used in Kundalini Yoga.

1. ONG NAMO GURU DEV NAMO

Ong Namo: I bow to the subtle divine wisdom

Guru Dev Namo: I bow to the divine teacher within.

2. AAD GURAY NAMEH
JUGAAD GURAY NAMEH
SAT GURAY NAMEH
SIRI GUROO DAYVAY NAMEH

I bow to the primal Guru

I bow to the truth that has existed throughout the ages

I bow to True Wisdom

I bow to the Great Divine Wisdom.

3. SA TA NA MA

SA is birth, the beginning, infinity, the totality of everything that ever was, is or will be.

TA is life, existence and creativity which manifests from infinity.

NA is death, change and the transformation of consciousness.

MA is rebirth, regeneration and resurrection which allows us to consciously experience the joy of the infinite.

4. HAR

Creative infinity.

5. SAT KAR TAR

The divine is the doer, the Universe is the doer, God is the doer.

3. Mudra [5]

A mudra is a position of the hands that locks or seals and guides energy flow and reflexes to the brain. The hands are an energy map of our consciousness and health. Each area of the hand connects to a certain part of the body or brain. Each area represents different emotions and behavior. The hands become a keyboard for input to our mind-body energy system.

The following are five common mudras in Kundalini Yoga.

1. Gyan Mudra (Seal of Knowledge) ("passive")

To form Gyan Mudra, put the tip of the thumb together with the tip of the index finger. This stimulates knowledge, wisdom and the power to compute. The energy of the index finger represents expansion. This is a commonly used mudra that gives receptivity and calmness.

2. Gyan Mudra (Seal of Knowledge) ("active")

This mudra is the same as Gyan Mudra passive except that you bend the index finger under the thumb, so the fingernail presses against the back of the second joint of the thumb.

3. Buddhi Mudra (Seal of Mental Clarity)

To form Buddhi Mudra, place the tip of the little finger on the tip of the thumb. Practicing this opens the capacity to communicate clearly and intuitively. It also stimulates psychic development.

4. Shuni Mudra (Seal of Patience)

To form Shuni Mudra, place the tip of the middle finger on the tip of the thumb. This mudra is said to give patience, discernment and commitment.

5. Surya or Ravi Mudra (Seal of the Sun, Seal of Life)

This mudra is formed by placing the tip of the ring finger on the tip of the thumb. Practicing it gives revitalizing energy, nervous system strength, good health and the power to win.

---

[5] Yogi Bhajan, Published 2007, "The Aquarian Teacher: KRI International Teacher Training in Kundalini Yoga as taught by Yogi Bhajan"

4. Body Locks (Bandhas) [5]

Body locks or bandhas are basic techniques to contract and align specific parts of the body to manage energy. They are a key element in the science of Kundalini Yoga. There are three main body locks:

- Neck Lock (Jalandhar Bandh)
- Diaphragm Lock (Uddiyana Bandh)
- Root Lock (Mulbandh).

When all three body locks are applied simultaneously, it is called the Great Lock or Mahabandh.

Neck Lock (Jalandhar Bandh)

This is the most basic and generally applied body lock. To apply Neck Lock:

- Sit comfortably with a straight spine.
- Lift the chest and sternum upward.
- At the same time, gently stretch the back of the neck straight by pulling the chin towards the back of the neck.
- Keep the head level and centered. Do not tilt it forward or to either side.
- Keep the muscles of the neck and throat relaxed. Keep the muscles of the face and brow relaxed.
- The stretch is automatically applied by the shift of relative position between the chin and the chest. Do not force the head forward or down.

Diaphragm Lock (Uddiyana Bandh)

To apply Diaphragm Lock:

- Sit comfortably. Inhale deeply, then exhale completely expelling all the breath out.

---

[5] Yogi Bhajan, Published 2007, *"The Aquarian Teacher: KRI International Teacher Training in Kundalini Yoga as taught by Yogi Bhajan"*

- Pull the entire abdominal region, especially the area above the Navel Point, upward and back towards the spine. The Navel Point itself does not contract, though it is pulled upward from above.
- Do not collapse the chest downward when you apply this lock.
- Lift the chest. Never collapse the chest downward when you apply this lock.
- Gently press the lower thoracic and lumbar spine forward.
- Keep the lift strongly applied for 10-60 seconds according to your endurance. Do not strain.
- Release the lock by relaxing the abdomen and gradually inhaling. At this time, do not raise the chin.

Extras:
- You can practice this body lock in a standing position. For many people, this makes it easier to isolate the muscles that are involved. Stand straight with the feet spread shoulder-width apart. Bend forward slightly with the hands on the knees. Lift the chest and slightly apply Diaphragm Lock. Feel the full upward pull of the abdomen from below as well as from above to the navel.
- Never do Diaphragm Lock on an empty stomach.
- Apply this body lock only with the breath completely expelled.

Root Lock (Mulbandh)

The Root Lock is a smooth motion that consists of three parts. To apply the Root Lock:

- First contract the sphincter. Feel the muscles lift upward and inward.
- Once these muscles tighten and move, contract the area around the sex organs. This is experienced as a slight lift and rotation inward of the pubic bone.
- Then contract the lower abdominal muscles and the Navel Point toward the spine.
- These three actions applied together in a smooth, rapid flowing motion are the Root Lock.

Extras:
- This body lock can be applied when the breath is retained in or out.
- Root Lock differs from Diaphragm Lock in that the navel area is not contracted while in Root Lock.

5. The Breath and Pranayam

The breath is essentially the steering wheel for your thoughts. As you change your breath, you start to rewire your brain. Most of us breathe between 16 to 20 breaths per minute as we go throughout our day. We're having a fairly rapid, fairly shallow breathing experience. As you become more trained, you can breathe as little as one to two breaths per minute. And when you slow your breathing down to 4 cycles or fewer per minute, you automatically change the way your brain processes information. You become more positive in your thinking, more relaxed and expansive, more receptive to information, and you feel more in control.

The quantity, quality and circulation of the breath creates the foundation of a vital and creative life. It is a barometer of how much energy we normally run on and how much reserve capacity we have created for emergencies. The breath is both gross and subtle. The gross aspect is the blend of oxygen, nitrogen and other elements that chemically constitute air. The subtle aspect is the prana or vital force that energizes the mind, body and consciousness.[5]

Your breath has a relationship to your character. This relationship works both ways so if you learn to change your breath, you can also make adjustments to your character. For example, if you struggle with impatience, lengthening your inhale will help cultivate patience. If you struggle with depression, shortening your exhale can help lift your mood and increase your energy. Every person has a different temperament, character and a unique breath rhythm. Energetic people have a shorter inhale than exhale. Easygoing people typically have a long exhale. It is when the inhale is too short, the exhale too long or the breath is out of rhythm that problems begin.

Yogically, the deeper the breath, the more activated the chakras energy centers in the body become.

- 6 breaths per minute or fewer activates the heart
- 4 breaths per minute or fewer activates the third eye
- 2 breaths per minute or fewer activates the crown chakra
- 1 breath per minute activates the whole system. This is a very healing breath.

Deepening your daily breath pattern gives you much more energy in daily life. Deep complete breathing is one of the most effective tools for increasing health, vitality and connectedness in one's life. It has the following effects:

Physical: Stress occurs when the muscular or mental tension cannot return freely to an uncontracted or relaxed state. Stress causes poor breathing. Poor breathing includes shallow, erratic upper-chest breathing with a faster breath rate. This leads to chaotic tension and weak nerves. And poor breathing increases the susceptibility to more stress. This sets the scene for illness and breakdown in the body's various systems.[5]

Emotional: We hold a tremendous amount of tension and emotional trauma in our muscular structure in the form of emotional armor. Proper breathing, which changes our breath signature, allows the release of armoring. As we increase the general flexibility of the body and expand the lungs, our sensitivity increases because the armor decreases.[5]

Vitality: Breathing correctly frees up the flow of prana and as our armoring and tension release, our vitality increases.[5]

Feelings of connection: When our vitality is increased, our prana is flowing, we feel emotionally secure, and our physical bodies are strong. A deep sense of connection results.[5]

Pranayam[5]

Prana: life force

Pran: first unit

Ayam: expansion.

Pranayam is the science of breath and controlling the movement of prana through the use of breath techniques.

Kundalini Yoga uses a wide range of pranayam techniques, using rhythm and the depth of the breath to effect and manage different energy states of health, consciousness and emotion. Some of the most common and widely used pranayama are long deep breathing and breath of fire.

Long Deep Breathing
Long deep breathing uses the full capacity of the lungs by utilizing the three chambers of the lungs: the lower/abdominal chamber, the middle/chest chamber and the upper/clavicular chamber.

---

(5) Yogi Bhajan, Published 2007, "The Aquarian Teacher: KRI International Teacher Training in Kundalini Yoga as taught by Yogi Bhajan"

Long deep breathing starts by filling the abdomen, then expanding the chest and finally lifting the upper ribs and clavicle. The exhale is the reverse: first, the upper chamber deflates, then the middle and finally the abdomen pulls in and up, as the Navel Point pulls back toward the spine.

There are three distinct parts to long deep breathing: abdominal breath, chest breath, and clavicular breath. When all three parts of combined, you have long deep breathing.

Abdominal Breath

Let the breath relax to a normal pace and depth. Bring your attention to the Navel Point area. Take a slow deep breath by letting the belly relax and expand. As you exhale, gently pull the navel in and up toward the spine. Keep the chest relaxed and focus on breathing entirely with the lower abdomen.

In the beginning, to help learn the breath, you can place one hand on the Navel Point and one on the center of the chest. On the inhale, raise the hand on the navel toward the ceiling by using your breath. On the exhale, lower it steadily. With your other hand, monitor the chest to stay still and relaxed.

Chest Breath

Sit straight and keep the diaphragm still. Do not let the abdomen extend. Inhale slowly using the chest muscles. Focus on the sensation of expansion. Exhale completely but do not use the abdomen. If you place your hands on the top and bottom part of the ribs, you should feel how the bottom ribs move more than the top ones.

Clavicular Breath

Sit straight. Contract the navel in and keep the abdomen tight. Lift the chest without inhaling. Then inhale slowly expanding the shoulders and the collarbone. Keep the chest lifted as you exhale.

The steps to long deep breathing are below.

1. Sit straight. When the spine is in a balanced position, the ribs and muscles can move more freely.
2. Begin the inhale with an Abdominal Breath. Then add the Chest Breath. Finish with the Clavicular Breath. All three are done as one smooth motion.
3. Start the exhale by releasing the clavicle. Then slowly empty the chest. Finally, pull in the abdomen to force out any remaining air.

The benefits of long deep breathing include:

- Increases the flow of prana.
- Reduces the buildup of toxins in the lungs by encouraging the clearing of the small air sacs.
- Stimulates the brain chemicals – endorphins – that help fight depression.
- Brings the brain to a new level of alertness.
- Pumps the spinal fluid to the brain, giving greater energy.
- Filling the lungs to capacity revitalizes and readjusts the magnetic field.
- Cleanses the blood.
- Regulates the body's pH (acid to alkaline balance).
- Energizes the body and increases vitality.
- Relaxes and calms the mind.
- Activates and clears the nerve channels.
- Aids in the acceleration of emotional and physical healing.
- Aids in breaking subconscious habit patterns such as insecurities and fears.
- Aids in fighting addictions.
- Re-channels previous mental conditioning on pain so as to reduce or eliminate pain.

Breath of Fire

Breath of fire is one of the foundational breath techniques used in Kundalini Yoga. It is a rapid, rhythmic and continuous breath through the nose while you pump your navel point. Breath of Fire is powered from the navel point and solar plexus.

- To exhale, the air is expelled powerfully through the nose by pressing the navel point and solar plexus back towards the spine. This feels automatic if you contract the diaphragm rapidly.
- To inhale, the upper abdominal muscles relax, the diaphragm extends down, and the breath seems to come in as part of relaxation rather than through effort.

Notes to do Breath of Fire:
- The breath is equal on the inhale and exhale with no pause in between.

- It is always practiced through the nostrils with the mouth closed unless specified otherwise.
- The chest stays relaxed and slightly lifted throughout the breathing cycle.
- When done correctly, there should be no rigidity of hands, feet, face or abdomen.
- Begin practicing Breath of Fire for 1-3 minutes. If the breath creates a dizziness or giddiness, take a break. Some tingling, traveling sensations and lightheadedness are normal as your body adjusts to the new breath and new stimulation of nerves.
- Women: If you are pregnant or having your period, don't do Breath of Fire. Instead do Long Deep Breathing.

Benefits of Breath of Fire
- Expands the lung capacity and increases vital strength.
- Strengthens the nervous system.
- Strengthens the navel center/third chakra.
- Increases physical endurance.
- Reduces addictive impulses for drugs, smoking and unhealthy foods.
- Increases oxygen delivery to the brain facilitating a focused, intelligent and neutral state of mind.
- Boosts the immune system.

6. Relaxation [5]

"Total harmonious relaxation cures the body.
To achieve this, there must be a coordination between
the three facets of ourselves: body, mind and soul."
~Yogi Bhajan

Relaxation is difficult for most people because of a subliminal level of emotional conflict or turmoil. We each have an inner dialogue, largely subconscious, that generates patterns of anxiety, anger, hopelessness and other self-defeating emotions. This drains a person's energy, taxes the nervous system and weakens immunity.

---

(5) Yogi Bhajan, Published 2007, "The Aquarian Teacher: KRI International Teacher Training in Kundalini Yoga as taught by Yogi Bhajan"

A deep relaxation that releases these patterns and that opens us to a new inner organization is essential to vibrant living. To effectively relax, we need to change the distribution of prana – vital life force – in the body and to activate systems of nerves that allow the self to reorganize patterns of being and acting.

Tips for a deep relaxation:
- Lie on the back with your arms at your side.
- Palms face up.
- Feet are uncrossed.
- Close your eyes.
- Relax the breath. Let the belly naturally rise and fall.
- Let everything go. Prepare to heal, rejuvenate and relax.

General guidelines

General guidelines for a Kundalini Yoga practice are as follows:

1. Tune in
We chant "Ong Namo, Guru Dev Namo" three times at the beginning of each Kundalini Yoga class. The purpose of tuning in is threefold:

- It sets the intention that the class is beginning.
- Chanting this mantra has a specific physiological effect. It triggers the pituitary gland and changes the secretions of this gland in the endocrine system.
- It tunes you into the Golden Chain of teachers, an entire body of consciousness that guides and protects your practice.

Even when doing a Kundalini Yoga practice on your own, it is highly recommended you tune in using this mantra as you will get much more out of the practice.

2. Follow the kriya precisely
Follow the kriya as it is described. Kriyas should never be altered or modified. They have been passed down, in very specific and pure form, for thousands of years. The purity of Kundalini Yoga is one of its strengths.

3. Take a deep relaxation

As described earlier, a deep relaxation is one of the most critical parts of a Kundalini Yoga practice. During relaxation, you rejuvenate your parasympathetic nervous system, distribute the energy you have built up during the kriya, help muscles release rigid patterning and adopt a more neutral state, promoting glandular shifts, centering yourself emotionally, releasing stress and assisting the body and mind in developing an understanding of its own 'natural state' so that it relaxes automatically throughout your day. To do deep relaxation, lie on your back with your arms at your side, palms facing up and relax completely. In a typical class, this relaxation lasts eleven minutes, but it can be shortened down to lower amounts of time as well.

4. Do the meditation

The meditation at the end of the Kundalini Yoga practice is really the heart of the practice. The meditations are as varied as the kriyas for different effects and goals. Meditations generally include breathwork and may or may not include mantra.

5. Close the practice

> *"May the long time sun*
>
> *Shine upon you.*
>
> *All love surround you,*
>
> *And the pure light within you*
>
> *Guide your way on."*

Each Kundalini Yoga class ends with two verses of "May the Long Time Sun Shine Upon You." This song has been the closing of Kundalini Yoga classes since the day in 1969 when Yogi Bhajan heard it being played by some of his students. He liked the song and decided to incorporate it into Kundalini Yoga classes as the closing. I like it because it is uplifting and creates a nice finish to the class. The song is sung in two verses.
To close at the very end, we chant Sat Nam. Sat Nam is a phrase used commonly throughout Kundalini Yoga. Literally translated, Sat means truth and Nam means name. Loosely translated it can mean "truth is my name." It can also be a simple acknowledgement that the Great Mystery is who we are. As a greeting, saying Sat Nam is like saying "I see your true nature" or "I acknowledge the divine in you."

You can follow these guidelines as you start a Kundalini Yoga practice based on the kriyas and meditations in the following chapter.

The next chapter introduces four Kundalini Yoga kriyas and meditations. The first kriya and meditation are general purpose options and a great way to begin. The following three kriyas and meditations are mapped more specifically to the Enneagram types and central issues the different types need to address to relax their habit of attention. This mapping was done by me based on my knowledge, training and personal experience.

You gain more benefit from a regular, daily Kundalini Yoga practice, and the key to a consistent, daily practice of any type is to keep the expectations reasonable.

With that in mind, I recommend everyone start with a three-minute minimum daily commitment. On those days when you can do more, this chapter has something for you too.

There are a few key concepts to keep in mind as you embark on your daily yoga practice:

- Daily exercise in small amounts is far more powerful than single, intense workout sessions. The key to success is consistency over intensity, especially in the beginning.

- Create goals that are too small to fail, yet not too small to make a difference. Three minutes of an exercise will begin to make some changes in your body. In general, for Kundalini Yoga exercises and meditations, three minutes is enough to affect the electromagnetic field, the circulation and stability of the blood. The three minutes also often gives you enough energy to do more.

- Willpower is essential in maintaining a regular practice. Willpower means you do your practice regardless of your emotional state. Willpower is a limited resource (which is why we set the bar low), but it can be strengthened. You strengthen willpower by being consistent with your habits.

Kriya for Elevation

This easy set of exercises is excellent as a tune-up. This is a great starter kriya for all Enneagram types. The Kriya for Elevation systematically exercises the spine and aids in the circulation of prana to balance the chakras. This set includes twelve exercises, and the times have ranges so you can start at one minute for most exercises and work up to the higher range (usually three minutes per exercise).

What are the goals of a regular practice of this kriya?
- Lower stress
- Increased energy
- Increased flexibility
- Stronger nervous system.

Exercise 1:
Ego Eradicator

Posture/Mudra	Breath	Full Time	Short Time
Sit in Easy Pose.	Breath of Fire	3:00	1:00
Raise the arms to a 60 degree angle. Curl the fingertips onto the pads at the base of the fingers. Plug the thumbs into the sky.			
Eyes closed, concentrate above the head.			
To End: Inhale and touch the thumb tips together overhead. Exhale and apply mulbandh. Inhale and relax.			
Comments: This exercise opens the lungs, brings the hemispheres of the brain to a state of alertness and consolidates the magnetic field.			

THE NINE KEYS

Exercise 2:
Spinal Flex

Posture/Mudra	Breath	Full Time	Short Time
Sitting in Easy Pose, grasp the shins with both hands. To End: Inhale, exhale, relax.	As you inhale, flex the spine forward and lift the chest. As you exhale, flex the spine back, keeping the shoulders relaxed and the head straight. Continue rhythmically with deep breaths.	3:00	1:00
Comments: This exercise stimulates and stretches the lower and mid spine.			

Exercise 3:
Spinal Twist

Posture/Mudra	Breath	Full Time	Short Time
In Easy Pose, grab the shoulders with the thumbs in back and the fingers in front. Keep the elbows high with the arms parallel to the ground. To End: Inhale, facing straight forward. Exhale and relax.	Inhale as you twist the head and torso to the left. Exhale as you twist to the right.	4:00	1:00
Comments: This exercise stimulates and stretches the lower and mid spine.			

Exercise 4:
Front Life Nerve Stretch

Posture/Mudra	Breath	Full Time	Short Time
Stretch both legs straight out in front. Grab the toes in finger lock (Index finger and middle finger pull the toe, and the thumb presses the nail of the big toe). To End: Inhale up and hold the breath briefly. Stay up and exhale completely, holding the breath out briefly. Inhale and relax.	Exhale, as you lengthen the core of the spine, bending forward from the navel, continuing to lengthen the spine. The head follows last. Inhale, use the legs to push up. The head comes up last. Continue with deep, powerful breathing.	3:00	1:00

THE NINE KEYS

Exercise 5:
Modified Maha Mudra

Posture/Mudra	Breath	Full Time	Short Time
Sit with the right heel tucked into the perineum and the left leg extended forward. Grasp the big toe of the left foot with both hands, applying a pressure against the toenail. Pull Neck Lock. Exhale, bring the elbows to the ground as you lengthen the spine, bending forward from the navel, continuing to lengthen the spine, bringing the head to the knee. Spine stays straight. Hold, with Breath of Fire. To End: Inhale. Exhale and stretch the head and torso forward and down. Hold the breath out briefly	Breath of Fire	2:00	1:00
Comments: This exercise helps elimination, stretches the sciatic nerve and brings circulation to the upper torso.			

Exercise 6:
Modified Maha Mudra (Switch Legs)

Posture/Mudra	Breath	Full Time	Short Time
See #5 with opposite leg. To End: Relax.	Breath of Fire	2:00	1:00

Exercise 7:
Life Nerve Stretch

Posture/Mudra	Breath	Full Time	Short Time
Spread the legs wide, grasping the toes as in Front Life Nerve Stretch.	Inhale and stretch the spine straight, pulling back on the toes. Exhale and, bending at the waist, bring the head down to the left knee. Inhale up in the center position and exhale down, bringing up the head to the right knee. Continue with powerful breathing.	2:00	1:00
Comments: This exercise develops flexibility of the lower spine and sacrum and charges the magnetic field.			

THE NINE KEYS

Exercise 8:
Center Stretch

Posture/Mudra	Breath	Full Time	Short Time
Inhale up in the center position and exhale, bending straight forward from the waist touching the forehead to the floor. Continue this up and down motion.	Continue with powerful breathing.	3:00	1:00
To End: Inhale up, stretching the spine straight. Exhale, bringing the forehead to the floor. Hold the breath out briefly as you stretch forward and down. Inhale and relax.			

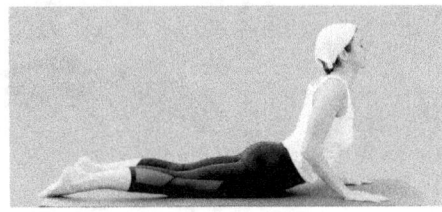 

Exercise 9:
Cobra Pose

Posture/Mudra	Breath	Full Time	Short Time
Lie on the stomach with the palms flat on the floor under the shoulders. The heels are together with the soles of the feet facing up.	Breath of Fire	3:00	1:00
To End: Inhale, arching the spine to the maximum. Exhale and hold the breath out briefly, apply mulbandh. Inhale. Exhaling slowly, lower the arms and relax the spine, vertebra by vertebra, from the base of the spine to the top. Relax, lying on the stomach with the chin in the floor and the arms by the sides.			

Exercise 10:
Shoulder Shrugs

Posture/Mudra	Breath	Full Time	Short Time
Sit in Easy Pose. Place the hands on the knees. To End: Inhale. Exhale and relax.	Inhale and shrug the shoulders up toward the ears. Exhale and drop the shoulders down. Continue rhythmically with powerful breathing.	2:00	1:00

Comments: This exercise balances the upper chakras and opens the hormonal gate to the higher brain centers.

Exercise 11:
Neck Rolls

Posture/Mudra	Breath	Full Time	Short Time
Sit in Easy Pose. To the Right: Begin rolling the neck clockwise in a circular motion, bringing the right ear toward the right shoulder, the back of the head toward the back of the neck, the left ear toward the left shoulder and the chin toward the chest. Left: Reverse the direction of the neck rolls and continue. To End: Bring the head to a central position and relax.	Let the breath find its own rhythm.	4:00 (2:00 min. each side)	2:00 (1:00 min. each side)

Comments: The shoulders remain relaxed and motionless. The neck should be allowed to gently stretch as the head circles around.

THE NINE KEYS

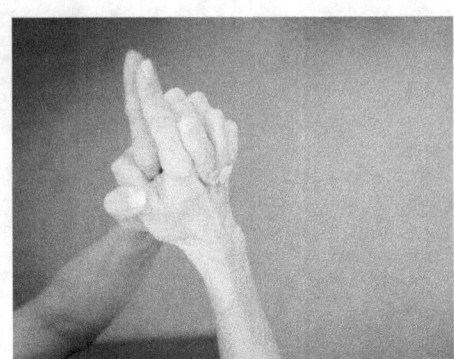

Exercise 12:
Sat Kriya

Posture/Mudra	Breath	Full Time	Short Time
Sit on the heels with the arms overhead and the palms together. Interlace the fingers except for the index fingers, which point straight up. Men cross the right thumb over the left thumb; women cross the left thumb over the right. Begin to chant Sat Nam emphatically in a constant rhythm about 8 times per 10 seconds. Chant the sound Sat from the navel point and solar plexus, and pull the navel all the way in and up. On Nam relax the navel. To End: Inhale and squeeze the muscles tight from the buttocks all the way up the back past the shoulders. Mentally allow the energy to flow through the top of the skull. Exhale. Inhale deeply. Exhale completely and apply the mulbandh with the breath held out. Inhale and relax.	Let the breath find its own rhythm.	7:00	2:20
Total Kriya		38:00	14:20

Comments: Sat Kriya circulates the Kundalini energy through the cycle of the chakras, aids in digestion and strengthens the nervous system.

Deep Relaxation

After you complete a Kundalini Yoga kriya, take a deep relaxation. This is when your body does its deep healing and incorporates some of the energy you have generated through the exercises. The relaxation can last anywhere from two to eleven minutes. To take a deep relaxation, lie on your back with your arms at your sides, palms facing up and relax completely.

Meditation for Gurprasaad

Gurprasaad means the "gift of the Guru," the universal teacher. As you practice this meditation, feel yourself being showered by all of the blessings of heaven—health, wealth, happiness, your ultimate caliber and capacity. Fill your heart and soul with all the bounties of nature. This is a very restful posture.

The subtle pressure against the meridian points on the rib cage brings immediate relaxation. No time restrictions were indicated. Recommended practice time is for 3, 11, 22, 31, 62 minutes or up to 2.5 hours.

Instructions:

Posture/Mudra	Breath	Eyes	Full Time	Short Time
Sit in a comfortable meditative position. Cup the hands together with the palms facing up at the level of the Heart Center. Press the upper arms against the rib cage, and feel that you are asking for a blessing from God (or the Universe or any equivalent that makes sense for you).	Let the breath find its own rhythm.	Start with eyes 1/10th open; allow the eyes to close as the meditation progresses.	11:00	3:00

Comments: Meditate on the boundless flow of the Universal Soul. Feel a deep inflow of spirit.

Heart's Delight: Kriya for the Heart Center

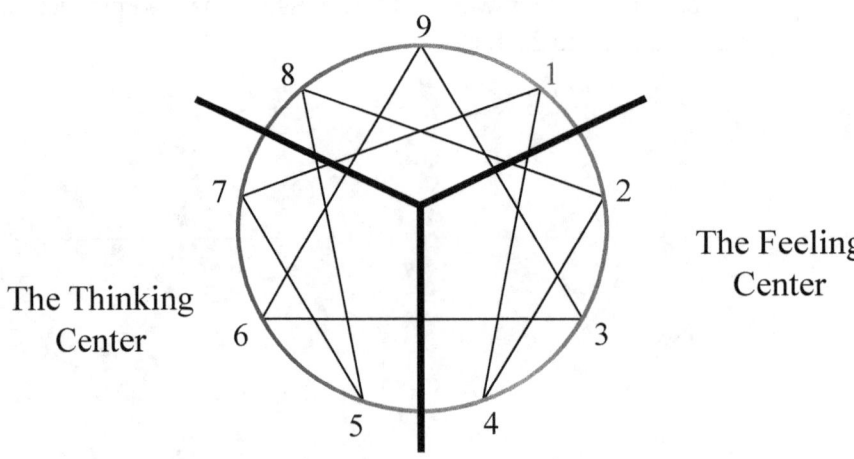

*«You have to know your strengths and your weaknesses.
Between your strengths and your weaknesses is you.»*
~Yogi Bhajan

In the Enneagram, the nine personality types are divided into three groups or centers: the Heart Types in the Feeling Center, the Head Types in the Thinking Center and the Body Types in the Instinctive Center. This chapter addresses the Heart Types in the Feeling Center.

**The Heart Types in the Feeling Center
Enneagram Type Two: Helper/Giver/Lover
Enneagram Type Three: Achiever/Motivator
Enneagram Type Four: Individualist/Artist**

These three types experience the world first through the energy of emotion (and afterward in their body and mind). They have gifts and issues entwined in the emotional world. All types also deal, either consciously or subconsciously, with a sensitive issue running deep in the background of the personality. For the heart types, the sensitive issue is shame. Because of this issue of shame, all three of these types also have a complicated relationship with their image.

SHAME: A painful feeling about oneself as a person.
Shame is essentially a rejection of some aspect or element of yourself. The opposite of shame is self-acceptance. To move from shame to self-acceptance is to accept all elements of yourself, even your weaknesses, your faults, the parts you don't like or that you would like to change. And the path to self-acceptance is a connection back to the heart so that self-love can be developed. In moving from shame to self-acceptance, you can share your unique gifts with the world.

Type Two, the Helper/Giver/Lover, under expresses their feelings of shame. In Helper (2)s, shame can manifest as a distortion of their own needs. While highly aware of the needs of others, these are people who are often very disconnected from their own needs. Subconsciously, they may feel a certain sense of pride in the idea that they can support many while needing very little themselves. For Helper (2)s to come back into balance, they need to connect with their hearts and accept their own needs. The path to balance in Helper (2)s is self-nurturing and self-care.

Type Three, the Achiever/Motivator, represses shame. In these people, shame can manifest as an extreme fear of failure and a complete rejection of their human weaknesses. Shame can also show up as an almost pathological competitiveness and need to win. For Achiever (3)s, to be associated with something that fails can feel like annihilation. The path to balance for this type is stop over-identifying with the opinions of other people and to start to tune into their own genuine essence and sense of self. At the core of this is self-acceptance, which includes flaws and weaknesses as well as strengths.

Type Four, the Individualist/Artist, over expresses shame. Individualist (4)s feel defined by their deficiencies and imperfections. These people may have a very difficult time seeing the good in themselves, even when friends and family remind them of their strengths regularly. The path to balance for an Individualist (4) is the development of neutral mind, an environment in which emotions are acknowledged but not overemphasized. In neutral mind, Individualist (4)s can also recognize their strengths.

The Kundalini Yoga Kriya Heart's Delight
In yogic philosophy, the fourth chakra is the Heart Chakra or Heart Center. It is called Anahata. It represents the opening of feelings, compassion and the capacity to love, including self-love.

THE NINE KEYS

This kriya works to open the heart at a core level, allowing for self-love. It is a wonderful kriya to help dissolve the energy of shame.

What are the goals of a regular practice of this kriya?
- Enhanced mood, decreased anxious and/or depressive thoughts
- The calming effect of the kriya allows you to eliminate unnecessary thoughts and feelings, so you can be more in the present and experience your feelings more clearly.

Exercise 1:
Prayer Pose

Posture/Mudra	Breath	Full Time	Short Time
Sit in easy pose with hands pressed together in Prayer Pose at the Heart Center.	Long, deep breathing	3:00	1:00

Exercise 2:
Back Platform on Elbows

Posture/Mudra	Breath	Full Time	Short Time
Support a straight body on the elbows and heels. Hold position with long, deep breathing.	Long, deep breathing	3:00	1:00

Exercise 3:
Sternum Rotation

Posture/Mudra	Breath	Full Time	Short Time
Circle the chest only, forward, right, left and back while keeping the head and hips in place (To understand the motion, practice this isolation lying on the back: lift the chest only several times. Then slide the chest left and right a few times to understand the motion).	Let the breath find its own rhythm.	3:00	1:00

THE NINE KEYS

Exercise 4:
Bear Grip

Posture/Mudra	Breath	Full Time	Short Time
Grip fingers together with the left palm facing out and the right palm facing in at the Heart Center. The palms don't touch.	Inhale and pull hands with maximum force, exhale, then pull hands. Apply Mulbhand.	4 repetitions (approximately 2 minutes)	2 repetitions (approximately 1 minute)

Exercise 5:
Raised Left Arm

Posture/Mudra	Breath	Full Time	Short Time
Bring both hands in Gyan Mudra. Raise the left arm to 60 degrees at the side, palm facing down. Bring the right arm to 30 degrees, palm facing down so that the arms almost form a straight line. Keep the eyes open and focused on a point straight ahead. Try not to blink. Apply the Mulbhand.	Long, deep breathing	5:00	1:40

KRIYA FOR THE HEART CENTER

Exercise 6:
Heart Connection

Posture/Mudra	Breath	Full Time	Short Time
Place the left hand at the center of the back, palm facing out. Place the right hand on the heart. Feel the flow of energy between the hands and meditate.	Long, deep breathing	5:00	1:40
Total Kriya		21:00	7:20

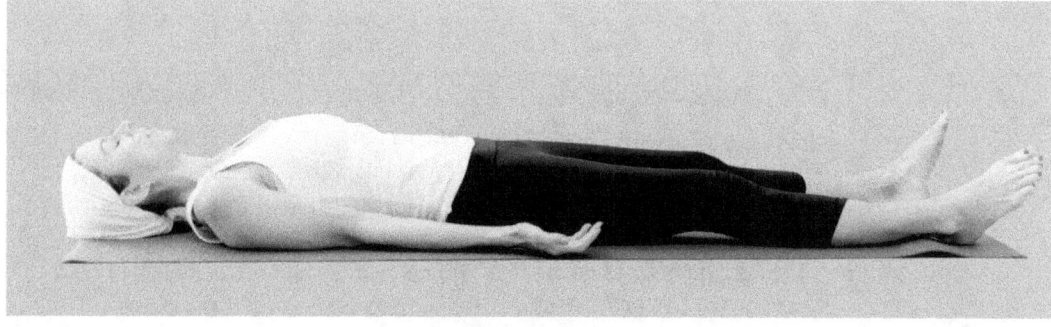

Deep Relaxation

After you complete a Kundalini Yoga kriya, take a deep relaxation. This is when your body does its deep healing and incorporates some of the energy you have generated through the exercises. The relaxation can last anywhere from two to eleven minutes. To take a deep relaxation, lie on your back with your arms at your sides, palms facing up and relax completely.

Meditation for Creating Self-Love

"Love doesn't rule you. What rules you is fear, phenomenal fear. Through this kriya, love can be invoked and fear can be reduced."
~Yogi Bhajan

This meditation has three parts. The first exercise is called Reverse Adi Shakti Kriya in which you are mentally and hypnotically blessing yourself. This self-blessing affects and corrects the magnetic field. Doing this exercise will hurt if you are an angry person. Self-help is very difficult for those who are angry. After doing this exercise for five minutes, your muscles will also start hurting if your diet is improper. The taste in your mouth will change if you are breathing correctly.

The second exercise will benefit everything between the neck and navel. It will give strength to the heart and will open up the Heart Center.

Exercise 1:
Self-Blessing

Posture/Mudra	Breath	Eyes	Full Time	Short Time
Sit in Easy Pose with a straight spine. Hold the right palm 6 to 9 inches/15 to 23 cm above the top center of the head. The right palm faces down, blessing you. This self-blessing corrects the aura. The left elbow is bent with the upper arm near the rib cage. The left palm faces forward and blesses the world.	Breathe long, slow and deep with a feeling of self-affection. Try to breathe only one breath per minute: Inhale 20 seconds, hold 20 seconds, exhale 20 seconds.	The eyes are closed and focused at the lunar center in the middle of the chin.	11:00	3:40

MEDITATION FOR CREATING SELF LOVE

Exercise 2:
Arm Stretch

Posture/Mudra	Breath	Eyes	Full Time	Short Time
Extend the arms straight out in front, parallel to the ground, palms facing down. Stretch out to your maximum. To end: Inhale deeply and move slowly and directly into position for next exercise.	The breath is long, slow and deep.	The eyes are closed and focused at the lunar center in the center of the chin.	3:00	1:00

Exercise 3:
Upward Stretch

Posture/Mudra	Breath	Eyes	Full Time	Short Time
Stretch the arms straight up with the palms facing forward. There is no bend in the elbows. To end: 1) Inhale, hold the breath for 10 seconds while you stretch the arms upward (try to stretch so much that your buttocks are lifted) and tighten all the muscles of the body. 2) Exhale. Repeat this sequence two more times.	Long, deep breathing	The eyes are focused at the lunar center, and the breath continues to be long, slow and deep.	3:00	1:00

Kriya For Relaxation and To Release Fear

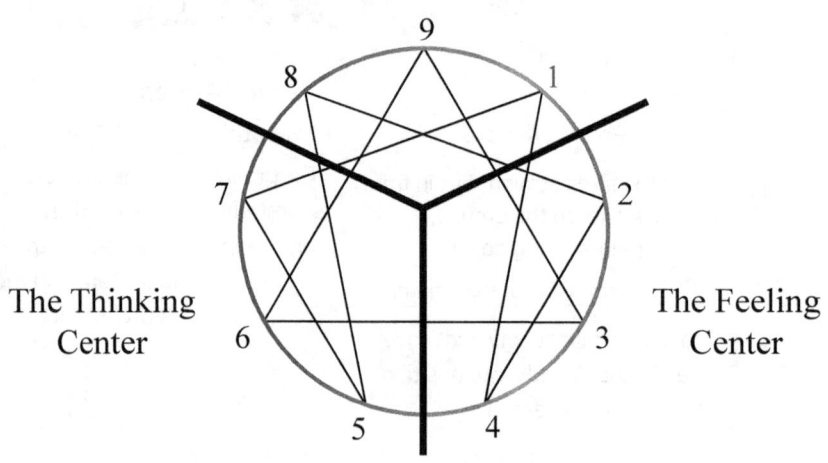

"One of the best actions we can take, with courage, is to relax."
~Yogi Bhajan

In the Enneagram, the nine personality types are divided into three groups or centers: the Heart Types in the Feeling Center, the Head Types in the Thinking Center and the Body Types in the Instinctive Center. This chapter addresses the Head Types in the Thinking Center.

The Head Types in the Thinking Center
Enneagram Type Five: Investigator/Observer
Enneagram Type Six: Loyalist/Skeptic
Enneagram Type Seven: Enthusiast/Generalist

These three types experience the world first through their thoughts (and afterward in their body and the energy of emotion). They have gifts and issues entwined in the mental world. These types also deal, either consciously or subconsciously, with a sensitive issue running deep in the background of the personality. For the head types, the sensitive issue is anxiety. Because of this anxiety, all three of these types also have a complicated relationship with time as it relates to the past, present and future. They have difficulty staying in the present moment due to concerns about the future.

ANXIETY: A feeling of worry, nervousness or unease about something in the future with an uncertain outcome.

Anxiety relates to the future. It doesn't exist if your mind is focused on the present moment. But a lack of confidence in a positive future can lead to anxious thinking that takes you out of the present moment.

Anxiety shows up differently in the three head types.

Type Five, the Investigator/Observer, underexpresses their anxiety by adopting a boundaried approach to life to manage these concerns. In Investigator (5)s, anxiety is controlled by a strict management of outside influences. Investigator (5)s use their mental facilities to try and outthink an uncertain future. They gain as much information as possible before committing to future obligations and tend to keep their future obligations as limited as possible.

In Type Six, the Loyalist/Skeptic, anxiety is over expressed. This is someone who feels anxiety fully and regularly. Loyalist (6)s try to manage their anxiety by imagining the worst-case scenario and then planning for it. Loyalist (6)s use their mental facilities to try to imagine everything that could go wrong, so they aren't caught off guard. Paradoxically, when an actual catastrophe occurs, this type is usually grace under pressure, as if to say "I've been waiting for this moment all my life…"

In Type Seven, the Enthusiast/Generalist, anxiety is repressed by staying on the go. Enthusiast (7)s are often unaware they have an issue with anxiety. With them, it often shows up as boredom, a desire for new experiences or an almost pathological drive to maintain a full calendar of events. Enthusiast (7)s deal with their anxiety by working hard never to let it surface, adopting a strategy of "it's hard to hit a moving target."

The path to balance for all of the head types is to come into the present moment. The first step is to relax so the mind can drop into the present moment.

The Kriya for Relaxation and to Release Fear
This kriya dissolves tension throughout the body and brings you to a state of calm, where you can feel a deep sense of peace, presence and of connectedness.

What are the goals of a regular practice of this kriya?
- Lower stress
- Increased energy
- Increased feeling of presence and being in the present moment
- Stronger nervous system.

THE NINE KEYS

Exercise 1:
Standing Cat-Cow

Posture/Mudra	Breath	Full Time	Short Time
Stand Up. Grab the calves or behind the knees. Begin to flex the spine as in Cat-Cow Posture.	Inhale and flex the spine downwards as if someone were sitting on your back. When the spine is pressed downwards the neck is arched up.	7:00	1:45
Use the hands and feet as a firm base of support for the spine.	Exhale and flex the spine in the opposite direction, bringing the chin to the chest.		
The legs remain straight.	Continue with a steady rhythm, coordinating the movement with the breath.		

KRIYA FOR RELAXATION AND TO RELEASE FEAR

Exercise 2:
Standing Torso Twist

Posture/Mudra	Breath	Full Time	Short Time
Remain standing and place the hands on the hips. Rapidly rotate the torso in large circles from the waist.	Let the breath find its own rhythm.	9:00	2:15

Comments: This exercise rejuvenates the spleen and liver. You may feel nauseous as the liver releases toxins.

THE NINE KEYS

Exercise 3:
Torso Turn

Posture/Mudra	Breath	Full Time	Short Time
Sit in Easy Pose. Make fists and place them in front of you as if grasping a steering wheel. Begin twisting the body powerfully from side to side. Twist to your maximum. Keep the elbows up and let the neck move also.	Inhale left, exhale right, with a powerful breath.	4:00	1:00

Comments: This exercise works on the kidneys. The neck must move in order to release the blood supply to the brain.

Exercise 4:
Extended Arm Wave

Posture/Mudra	Breath	Full Time	Short Time
Remain sitting in Easy Pose. Extend the arms up at a 60 degree angle, palms facing up, fingers straight and thumbs extended out. Begin to open and close the hands rapidly, bringing the tips of the fingers to the base of the palms.	Let the breath find its own rhythm.	7:00	1:45

Comments: This exercise breaks up deposits in the fingers and prevents arthritis. If you already have arthritis, it may work on improving it.

KRIYA FOR RELAXATION AND TO RELEASE FEAR

Exercise 5:
Sideways Arm Pumps

Posture/Mudra	Breath	Full Time	Short Time
Sit in Easy Pose. Extend the arms out to the sides parallel to the ground. Make fists of the hands with the thumbs tucked inside the hands touching the fleshy mound below the little finger.	Inhale through the mouth and flex the elbows, bringing the fists to the shoulders. As you exhale through the mouth, straighten the arms out to the sides. Move rapidly and breathe powerfully. Stiffen the mouth into an "O" as you inhale and exhale. Continue rhythmically, coordinating the movement with the breath. The breath is powerful.	6:00	1:30

Comments: This exercise removes tension from the neck and purifies the blood. In this exercise your fears will leave you when you powerfully project out on the exhale.

Exercise 6:
Fist Rolls

Posture/Mudra	Breath	Full Time	Short Time
Still in Easy Pose, begin rotating the fists in small circles at the level of the Heart Center. Roll the left fist counter clockwise and the right fist clockwise. Keep the elbows straight and fists tight. Move the shoulder blades and the muscles underneath the shoulder area.	Let the breath find its own rhythm.	2:00	1:00

Comments: This exercise adjusts the muscles under the breasts. If this area is tight, it makes you very uptight.

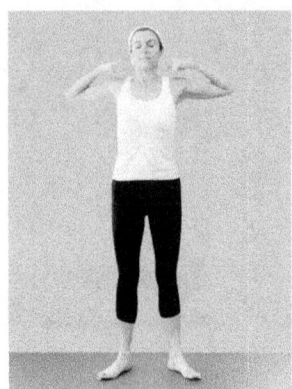

Exercise 7:
Crow Pose

Posture/Mudra	Breath	Full Time	Short Time
Crouch in Crow Pose, soles of the feet flat on the floor, with the knees wide, and drawn up towards the chest. Keep the spine straight. Make fists of the hands with the thumbs out, and place them near your neck just above the shoulders. Fists stay in this position as you inhale and stand up.	Inhale up, exhale and lower yourself back down to Crow Pose.	3:00	1:00

Exercise 8:
Sitali Pranayam

Posture/Mudra	Breath	Full Time	Short Time
Sit in Easy Pose and relax the hands on the knees. Keep the spine straight. Curl the tongue and protrude it slightly past the lips.	Inhale deeply and smoothly through the tongue and mouth. Exhale through the nose. Make the breath long and heavy.	5:00	1:15
Comments: Sitali Pranayam is effective against anger, bad moods and temperament. If your mouth becomes bitter, it means you have bad breath, but it is being cleaned out as you do this pranayam.			

KRIYA FOR RELAXATION AND TO RELEASE FEAR

Exercise 9:
Listening Sitali Pranayam

Posture/Mudra	Breath	Full Time	Short Time
Play the Dukh Bhanjan recording if available, and meditate on the healing vibrations of the Golden Temple and the shabd (sound current of the words). Continue Sitali Pranayam, breathing rhythmically, coordinating the breath to the music. Continue.	Breathe Sitali Pranayam.	2:00	1:00

Exercise 10:
Sitting Dance

Posture/Mudra	Breath	Full Time	Short Time
Continue listening to the recording. Sit in Easy Pose and raise the arms, curving them upwards. Move as your body feels. Stop thinking and move with the beat.	Let the breath find its own rhythm.	10:00	2:30

467

Exercise 11:
Bowing Jaap Sahib

Posture/Mudra	Breath	Full Time	Short Time
Sit on the heels in Rock Pose, with hands on thighs. Listen to a recording of Jaap Sahib and begin bowing the forehead to the floor to the Namastang rhythm, bowing 4 counts resting 1 cont with the music (touching the forehead to the ground and rising up is 1 count). Without the recording, the movement is done to 10 beats as follows: Bow down and come up 4 times (to the count of 8) and rest in the upward position, on counts 9 and 10. Mantra: Jaap Sahib	Let the breath find its own rhythm	8:00	2:00
Comments: This exercise done in Rock Pose has been known to heal any mineral formations in the body such as kidney stones and gallstones.			

KRIYA FOR RELAXATION AND TO RELEASE FEAR

Exercise 12:
Venus Lock Meditation

Posture/Mudra	Breath	Full Time	Short Time
Sit in a meditative posture. Lock the hands behind the back of the head in Venus Lock, elbows out to the sides and apply pressure, keeping the spine straight. Close your eyes and begin chanting aloud with the Jaap Sahib recording. Copy the very essence of it and feel the vibrations going through your hands to the back of the head as you chant. If the recording is not available, breathe long and gently in this position.	Long, gentle breathing	8:00	2:00
Total Kriya		71 min	19 min

Yogi Bhajan's Comments: "Relax. Let yourself become calm and together. Feel that you are going to achieve God's Light in you. Totally remove any difference between yourself and God."

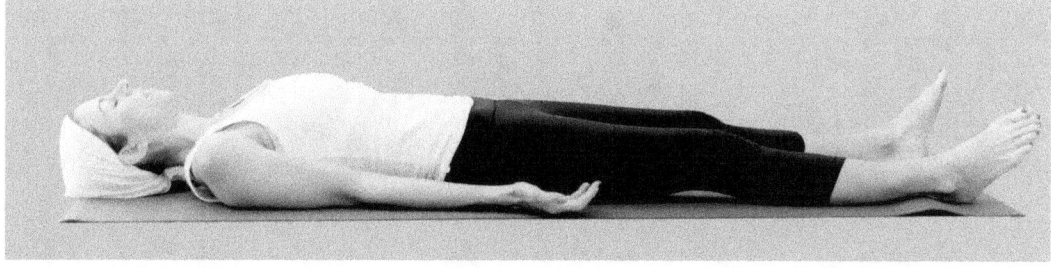

Deep Relaxation:

After you complete a Kundalini Yoga kriya, take a deep relaxation. This is when your body does its deep healing and incorporates some of the energy you have generated through the exercises. The relaxation can last anywhere from two to eleven minutes. To take a deep relaxation, lie on your back with your arms at your sides, palms facing up and relax completely.

Meditation to Remove Fear of the Future

"The beauty in you is your spirit. The strength in you is your endurance. The intelligence in you is your vastness."
~Yogi Bhajan

This meditation clears the fear of the future which has been created by your subconscious memories of the past. It connects you to the flow of life through your Heart Center.

"The crossed thumbs help neutralize your mind's frantic calculations to avoid fear and pain. It is the calculations themselves that produce anxiety and get you out of touch with the resources of your intuition and heart."—Gurucharan Singh Khalsa, Director of Training, Kundalini Research Institute

You can start with 11 minutes and gradually work up to 31 minutes of practice.

Meditation to Remove Fear of the Future

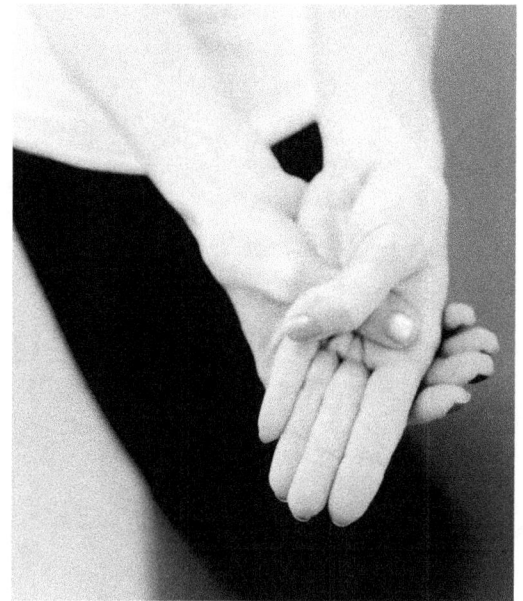

Instructions:

Posture/Mudra	Breath	Eyes	Full Time	Short Time
Sit comfortably in Easy Pose. Begin by resting the back of the left hand in the palm of the right hand. Grab the left hand with the right, so that the right thumb nestles in the left palm. Cross the left thumb over the right. The fingers of the right hand curve around the outside of the left hand and hold it gently. Place this mudra at the Heart Center, resting against the chest. Holding your hands in this way will give you a peaceful, secure feeling. Meditate to your favorite version of the shabd: Dhan Dhan Ram Das Gur. To End: Inhale deeply and relax.	Let the breath find its own rhythm.	The eyes are closed.	11:00	3:00

Kriya for Relieving Inner Anger

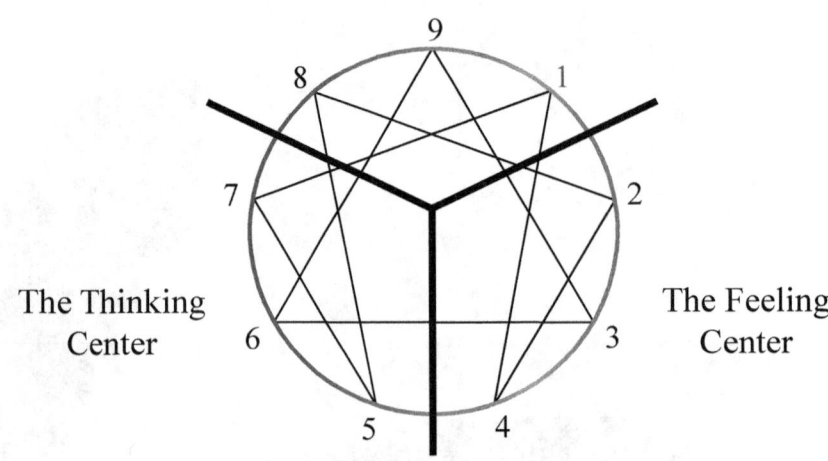

"You cannot make your life a reaction to others, you must make your life your own."
~Yogi Bhajan

In the Enneagram the nine personality types are divided into three groups or centers: the Heart Types in the Feeling Center, the Head Types in the Thinking Center and the Body Types in the Instinctive Center. This chapter addresses the Body Types in the Instinctive Center.

The Body Types in the Instinctive Center
Enneagram Type Eight: Leader/Challenger
Enneagram Type Nine: Peacemaker/Mediator
Enneagram Type One: Perfectionist/Reformer

These three types experience the world first through their bodies and afterward in their mind and the energy of emotion. They have gifts and issues entwined in the somatic world. All types deal, either consciously or subconsciously, with a sensitive issue running deep in the background of the personality. For the body types, the sensitive issue is anger. Because of this anger, all three of these types also have a complicated relationship with action and reaction. They have difficulty with the appropriate expression of aggression.

ANGER: An uncomfortable and hostile response to a perceived provocation, hurt or threat.

Anger generally occurs when a person feels their personal boundaries are being or are going to be violated.

Anger shows up differently in the three body types in the instinctive center.

Type Eight, the Leader/Challenger/Protector, over expresses anger, usually in response to feeling vulnerable. Leader (8)s generally have easy access to anger and maintain strong (sometimes too strong) boundaries around the softer emotions. Leader (8)s can have difficulty managing their anger and expressing vulnerability.

In Type Nine, the Peacemaker/Mediator, anger is under expressed. This is a person who often has an avoidant relationship with anger and usually has a delayed expression of anger. Peacemaker (9)s experience and process anger slowly – it may take days, weeks, months or even years for them to realize they are angry. This repression is a subconscious strategy to maintain a harmonious environment, one their top priorities.

In Type One, the Perfectionist/Reformer, anger is repressed and instead expressed as frustration, irritation or annoyance. Perfectionist (1)s can feel "tightly wound," as though there is tension just below the surface but not directly expressed. This is a subconscious attempt not to lose control and to "stay above it." However, the energy of anger stays in their body.

The key to coming back into balance with the body types is to get in touch with their anger, express it appropriately and to release it physically from their body.

Kriya for Relieving Inner Anger

Taught on September 21, 1988

"When the inverted anger becomes part of the body, the simple effect is that you have absolutely no relationship with your Self... Inferiority complex or superiority complex is a cover-up of inner anger. Manipulation and lying are parts of inner anger. Not being self sustaining or having a foundation to work it out is an inner anger. Misbehavior, wrong calculation, self-destruction, destroying the business, destroying the relationship are all inner anger...On the other hand, anger comes from the place of the Agaan Granthi. It is the area of the heart; it is the blood, it is the circulation, it is the diaphragm, it is the heart pumping. The whole life depends on it. So in the center of the heart is a furnace. Either it can cook for you, or it can burn down your house, and there is nothing in between. That is the tragedy of it."

-Yogi Bhajan

Kriya for Relieving Inner Anger

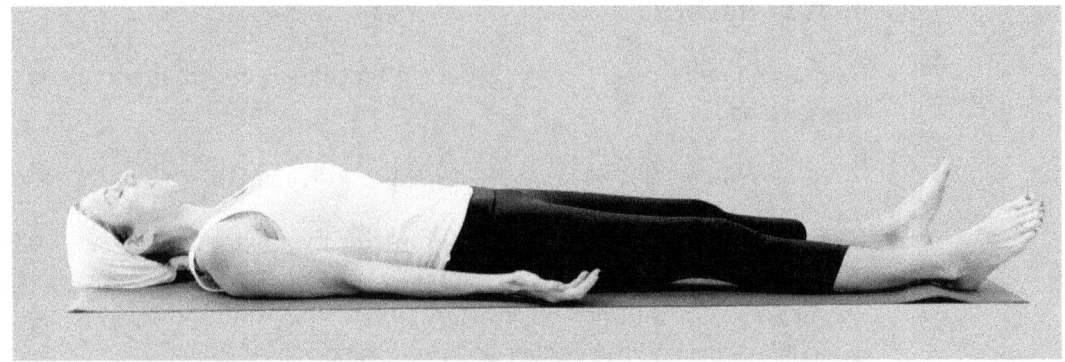

Exercise 1:
Snoring

Posture/Mudra	Breath	Full Time	Short Time
Lie down flat on the back in a relaxed posture with arms at the sides, palms open and legs slightly apart. Pretend to snore.	Let the breath find its own rhythm.	1:30	1:00

Exercise 2:
Toe Point

Posture/Mudra	Breath	Full Time	Short Time
Still lying on the back, straighten the legs, point the toes and raise them both up to 6 inches/15 centimeters.	Let the breath find its own rhythm.	2:00	1:00

Comments: This exercise balances anger. It puts pressure on the Navel Point in order to balance the entire system.

Exercise 3:
Tongue Breathing

Posture/Mudra	Breath	Full Time	Short Time
Remaining in the posture, stick out the tongue and do Breath of Fire through the mouth.	Breath of Fire	1:30	1:00

Exercise 4:
Anger Release

Posture/Mudra	Breath	Full Time	Short Time
Still on the back, lift the legs up to 90 degrees. Keep the arms on the ground by your sides. Begin to beat the ground with all the anger you can achieve. Beat hard and fast, keeping the arms stiff and straight.	Let the breath find its own rhythm.	2:30	1:15

THE NINE KEYS

Exercise 5:
Knees to Chest

Posture/Mudra	Breath	Full Time	Short Time
Still on the back, bring the knees into the chest and stick the tongue out.	Inhale through the open mouth and exhale through the nose.	3:00	1:30

Exercise 6:
Celibate Bowing

Posture/Mudra	Breath	Full Time	Short Time
Sit in Celibate Pose, buttocks on the floor between the heels. Cross the arms over the chest and press them hard against the rib cage. Bend forward and touch the forehead to the floor as if you are bowing. Move at a pace of approximately 30 bows per minute. To End: For the last 30 seconds speed up and move as fast as you can.	Let the breath find its own rhythm.	3:00	1:30

KRIYA FOR RELIEVING INNER ANGER

Exercise 7:
Body Beat

Posture/Mudra	Breath	Full Time	Short Time
Sitting with the legs straight out in front, begin to beat all parts of your body with open palms. Move fast.	Let the breath find its own rhythm.	2:00	1:00

Exercise 8:
Forward Bend

Posture/Mudra	Breath	Full Time	Short Time
Stand up. Bend forward, keeping the back parallel to the ground, and let the arms and hands hang loose. Remain in this posture and sing.	Let the breath find its own rhythm.	3:00	1:30
Comments: In class, Yogi Bhajan played a recording of Guru Guru Wahe Guru, Guru Ram Das Guru.			

THE NINE KEYS

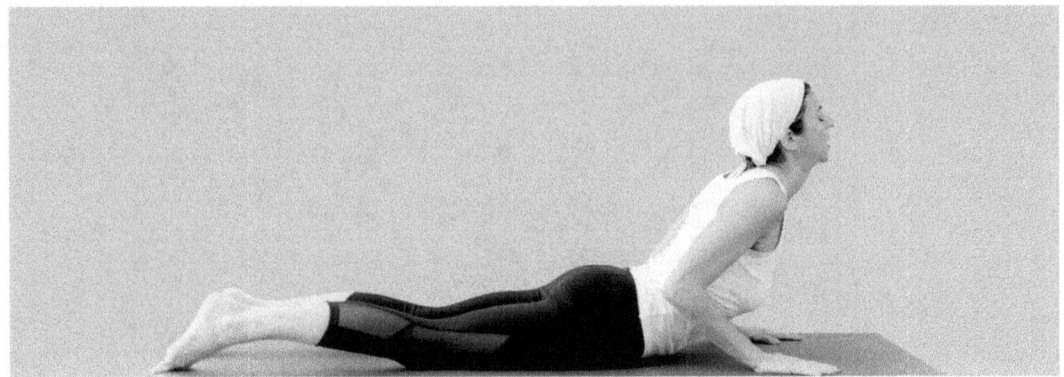

Exercise 9:
Singing Cobra Pose

Posture/Mudra	Breath	Full Time	Short Time
Continue singing and come into Cobra Pose. Lying on the stomach, place hands under the shoulders with palms flat. Elongate the spine, lift the chest and heart up, drop the shoulders and stretch the head back. Straighten the arms. Continue singing in this posture. To End: For the last 30 seconds, circle the neck and continue to sing.	Let the breath find its own rhythm.	1:30	1:00

Exercise 10:
Kicking Cobra

Posture/Mudra	Breath	Full Time	Short Time
Still in Cobra Pose begin kicking the ground with alternate feet.	Let the breath find its own rhythm.	:30	:30

KRIYA FOR RELIEVING INNER ANGER

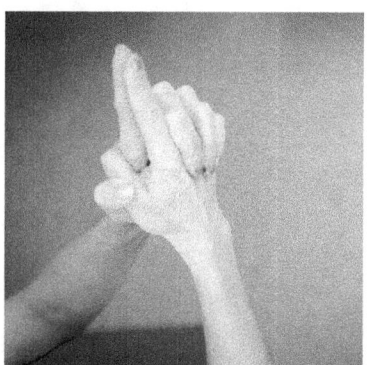

Exercise 11:
Sat Kriya in Easy Pose

Posture/Mudra	Breath	Full Time	Short Time
Sit in Easy Pose and close the eyes. Stretch the arms overhead, keeping the elbows straight. Interlace the fingers with the Jupiter (index) fingers extended and pointing straight up. Squeeze the Navel Point in and up as you say Sat (rhymes with "but"). Release as you chant Naam (rhymes with "mom"). Continue. To End: Inhale and squeeze the muscles tightly from the buttocks all the way up the back. Mentally allow the energy to flow through the top of the skull. Exhale and relax.	Let the breath find its own rhythm.	3:00	1:30

Comments: When chanting a mantra the breath will self regulate.

Deep Relaxation

Posture/Mudra	Breath	Full Time	Short Time
In this kriya, the deep relaxation is incorporated as an exercise. This is when your body does its deep healing and incorporates some of the energy you have generated through the exercises. To take a deep relaxation, lie on your back with your arms at your sides, palms facing up and relax completely.	Let the breath find its own rhythm.	5:00	5:00
Total Kriya		28:30	17:45

Meditation:
To Conquer Inner Anger and Burn It Out

March 8, 1999

"This meditation can be done either in the morning or the evening. If you do this eleven minutes every day, your entire life will change. This will give you a new life. Do this for forty days, it will change your personality from A to Z."
~Yogi Bhajan

Instructions:

Posture/Mudra	Breath	Eyes	Full Time	Short Time
Sit in easy pose with your arms stretched out straight to the sides. There is no bend in the elbows. The Jupiter (Index) finger points upward, and the thumb locks down the other fingers. The power of Jupiter, the knowledge, should be tough, stiff and straight. Close your eyes and concentrate on your spine. To End: Inhale deeply, hold the breath for ten seconds while you stretch your arms out to the sides as far as possible, exhale. Repeat this sequence two more times.	Inhale deeply through the rolled tongue (Sitali Breath) and exhale through the nose.	Closed.	11:00	3:00

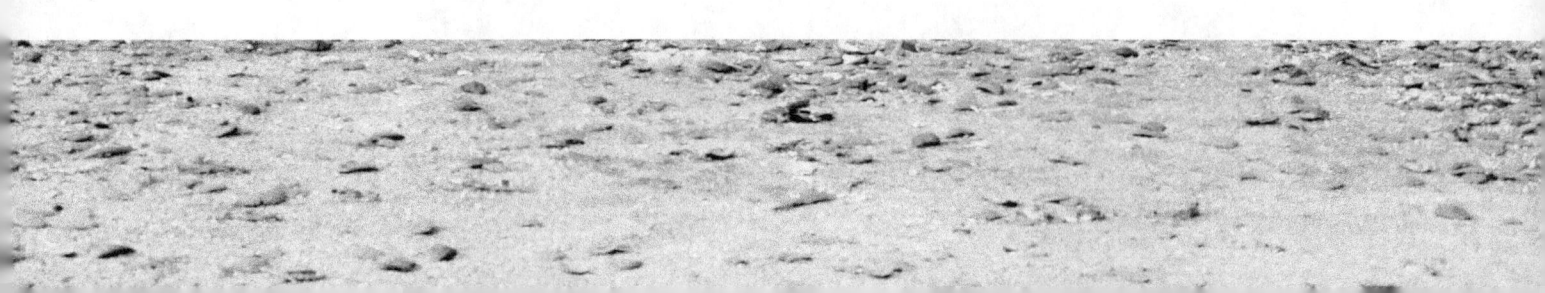

"Life is simple. Life is not complicated. Life is only one thing: Identify yourself."
~Yogi Bhajan

Closing

The Obstacles Don't Block the Path.
The Obstacles are the Path.

"What Enneagram types go well together as a couple?"
"Whom should I be with?"
"Will we be happy?"

These are some of the most common questions after someone learns their own Enneagram type. But the answer is both simple and complicated.

The answer is that all type combinations can be happy together if both partners have high levels of self-awareness. And the reverse is true. All combinations may struggle if both people lack self-awareness. And if one partner is self-aware and the other isn't, it can be like oil and water, and usually, at some point, the relationship just stops making sense.

Type compatibility is more about similar levels of self-awareness than it is about personality type. And success is more about both partners being highly self-aware. With awareness, you don't take your partner's behavior personally. They aren't doing "it" to you. They just do "it."

Self-awareness: Focusing your awareness on yourself. This includes your ability to notice your feelings and emotions, your physical sensations, your reactions, your habits, your behavior, your thoughts and your motivations. It is the ability to observe all of those different aspects of yourself as if you were another person observing you. It is cultivating your "inner observer." It is about seeing these elements honestly and objectively. It is about focusing on the reality of your behavior and not on the story you tell yourself about yourself. Self-awareness isn't about being spiritual. It is about observing yourself objectively.

Most of the couples in this book who have stayed together for decades with relative success talk about how they approach the relationship as a key component in their personal growth. They use their relationship as a way to understand themselves better. Indirectly, you have read this in the 100+ testimonials in this book.

THE NINE KEYS

In yogic philosophy, everything that happens in our lives is for our soul's growth and benefit. We are here to learn lessons, and people come into our lives to help us master those lessons. The lessons are many: tolerance, unconditional love, forgiveness, self-esteem, self-care, surrender and so forth. Yogically, life isn't good, life isn't bad, life is just raw material and how you interpret the events. With perspective, painful experiences can be transformed into gifts.

"This relationship has been a non-stop lesson in letting go of ego and loving without cause. Despite the fact it isn't logical, my husband doesn't fully trust me. In earlier years, this used to make me really sad, but I have learned it isn't personal. Being in a relationship for such a long time is a great way to learn unconditional love." Amelia, Enthusiast (7) married in a 26-year relationship with Jan, Loyalist (6)

"Anything that I could offer my husband right now would be to encourage him to follow his heart and his feelings and go where he feels peace. I have learned surrender." Alexandra, Leader (8) married in a 25-year relationship with Troy, Peacemaker (9)

"We've been together for 40 years, so of course along the way, our way of relating to each other has grown and changed. We've learned to respect our differences." Simon, Investigator (5) married in a 40-year relationship with Mary, Loyalist (6)

"One of the biggest challenges in our relationship is that we aren't able to get all of our needs met with each other. For example, I need more emotional support than Kate can provide. With some couples, these issues might drive them apart. Interestingly, however, with us, the differences actually hold us together. We both understand we need people outside our relationship to get some of our needs met. And we both understand we need real space away from each other at times. But we also know that doesn't mean we don't enjoy spending time together. Even after 36 years of being together, Kate and I are still intrigued by each other. Simon, Individualist (4) married in a 36-year relationship with Kate, Enthusiast (7)

The obstacles don't block the path. The obstacles are the path. These couples found a way to use their hurdles as a personal growth opportunity. They used the challenge as a way to understand themselves better. And couples who split apart use the relationship as a growth opportunity, just with a different outcome. They learned to leave an unhealthy situation or to see themselves more clearly.

"Coming to terms with the fact that we needed to divorce was one of the hardest things I've ever done. But I began to see that the alternative would be enormously detrimental to my

health on top of everything else. This was 15 years ago, and I now see the situation much more clearly." Cynthia, Peacemaker (9) formerly in a 25-year relationship with Douglas, Loyalist (6)

"With perspective and the knowledge of the Enneagram, I now see that we were operating from a level of being unevolved and unaware when under stress. I was always seeking authenticity, regardless of appearances and image. He was always trying to maintain the look of success, regardless of authenticity. I was undermining his stability, and without his stability, expressions of my strength felt threatening to him. 10 years have passed, and I now understand why things broke down. I also appreciate that we really were good partners and achieved some amazing things." Margaret, Leader (8) formerly married in a 29-year relationship with Stanley, Achiever (3)

"I credit her with turning my life upside-down in a good way after I had come out of a divorce from an unhappy 9-year marriage. She helped me to understand who I really was and who I wasn't." Doran, Individualist (4) formerly in a 2-year relationship with Gala, Individualist (4)

Fulfilling, supportive, intimate, harmonious relationships equate to a happy life and good health. This is the biggest single conclusion of the Harvard Study of Adult Development, a 75-year study conducted by Robert Waldinger, a clinical professor of psychiatry at Harvard Medical School. The biggest factor in your long-term happiness isn't money, professional success or fame. It's your relationships. And your relationships improve dramatically with heightened self-awareness. With this in mind, the investment in developing self-awareness is an obvious one.

Self-awareness is cultivated, and systems like the Enneagram and Kundalini Yoga offer powerful tools to accelerate this process. The Enneagram gives you the mental map of your internal wiring. It helps you understand where your attention goes and how you interpret events. Kundalini Yoga offers a somatic understanding of yourself. It helps you identify, develop and ultimately direct your energetic response to situations. When woven together and used consistently, these two systems offer a rapid, effective way to identify yourself. You are no longer lost. You are found. And once you are found, you can accept others in your life more readily.

Appendix Of Kundalini Yoga Kriyas And Meditations Recommended For Each Enneagram Type

Enneagram Type 1: Perfectionist/Reformer
Kriya For Heart Connection[6]
Kriya For Elevation .... page 443
Kriya For Relieving Inner Anger .... page 474
Meditation To Burn Out Inner Anger[6]
Meditation For Gurprasaad .... page 451
Meditation To Conquer Inner Anger And Burn It Out .... page 480

Enneagram Type 2: Helper/Giver/Lover
Kriya For Balancing Prana And Apana[6]
Kriya For Elevation .... page 443
Heart's Delight Kriya .... page 454
Meditation For A Calm Heart[6]
Meditation For Gurprasaad .... page 451
Meditation For Creating Self-Love .... page 458

Enneagram Type 3: Achiever/Motivator
Kriya For Balancing The Head And Heart[6]
Kriya for Elevation .... page 443
Heart's Delight Kriya .... page 454
Meditation To Change The Ego[6]
Meditation For Gurprasaad .... page 451
Meditation For Creating Self-Love .... page 458

Enneagram Type 4: Individualist/Artist
Kriya To Strengthen The Aura[6]
Kriya For Elevation .... page 443
Heart's Delight Kriya .... page 454
Meditation For Inner Conflict Resolve[6]
Meditation For Gurprasaad .... page 451
Meditation For Creating Self-Love .... page 458

---

(6) See Kundalini Yoga Kriyas and Meditations in "Headstart for Happiness: A Guide Book Combining Kundalini Yoga and the Enneagram" by Lynn Roulo, published 2016.

APPENDIX OF KUNDALINI YOGA KRIYAS AND MEDITATIONS RECOMMENDED FOR EACH ENNEAGRAM TYPE

Enneagram Type 5: Investigator/Observer
Kriya To Balance And Recharge The Nervous And Immune System[6]
Kriya For Elevation .... page 443
Kriya For Relaxation And To Release Fear .... page 462
Wahe Guru Meditation[6]
Meditation For Gurprasaad .... page 451
Meditation To Release Fear Of The Future .... page 471

Enneagram Type 6: Loyalist/Skeptic
Kriya For Emotional And Mental Balance[6]
Kriya For Elevation .... page 443
Kriya For Relaxation And To Release Fear .... page 462
Meditation For Self Authority[6]
Meditation For Gurprasaad .... page 451
Meditation To Release Fear Of The Future .... page 471

Enneagram Type 7: Enthusiast/Generalist
Kriya To Purify The Self[6]
Kriya For Elevation .... page 443
Kriya For Relaxation And To Release Fear .... page 462
Meditation For Caliber Of Life[6]
Meditation For Gurprasaad .... page 451
Meditation To Release Fear Of The Future .... page 471

Enneagram Type 8: Leader/Challenger/Protector
Kriya To Open The Heart Center[6]
Kriya For Elevation .... page 443
Kriya For Relieving Inner Anger .... page 474
Meditation For One Minute Breath[6]
Meditation For Gurprasaad .... page 451
Meditation To Conquer Inner Anger And Burn It Out .... page 480

Enneagram Type 9: Peacemaker/Mediator
Wake Up Series Kriya[6]
Kriya for Elevation .... page 443
Kriya For Relieving Inner Anger .... page 474
Breath Of Fire Meditation[6]
Meditation for Gurprasaad .... page 451
Meditation To Conquer Inner Anger And Burn It Out .... page 480

---

(6) See Kundalini Yoga Kriyas and Meditations in "Headstart for Happiness: A Guide Book Combining Kundalini Yoga and the Enneagram" by Lynn Roulo, published 2016.

Kundalini Yoga Summary of Terms

Bear Grip
Place the left palm facing out from the chest with the thumb down. Place the palm of the right hand facing the chest. Bring the fingers together. Curl the fingers of both hands so the hands form a fist. This mudra is used to stimulate the heart and to intensify concentration. It is more effective if the hands are pulled strongly.

Cat-Cow Posture
Begin on the hands and knees. The hands are shoulder width apart with the fingers facing forward. The knees are directly under the hips. Inhale and tilt the pelvis forward, arching the spine down (cow position), with the head and neck stretched back. Do not scrunch the neck. Open the heart and raise the chin as far back as you can without collapsing the neck. Exhale and tilt the pelvis the opposite way, arching the spine up (cat position) pressing the chin into the chest.

Crow Pose
Begin in a standing position. Squat down. Knees and feet are wide apart with heels flat on the ground. Apply Neck Lock. The back should be perpendicular to the ground. If you are having difficulty getting down or keeping your balance, try widening your feet and knees more. If you can't get your heels down, you may use something underneath your feet.

Easy Pose
Sit and cross the legs comfortably at the ankles. Pull the spine up straight and press the lower spine slightly forward.

Ego Eradicator
Sit on the heels or in Easy Pose. Apply a neck lock. Lift the arms to a 60 degree angle. Then draw the shoulder blades down over the back of the ribs so the shoulders are away from the ears. Curl the fingertips into the pads of the palms at the base of the fingertips. Stretch the thumbs towards the sky. Close the eyes and begin Breath of fire. To end, touch the thumbs above the head and open the fingers.

Rock Pose
Start by kneeling on both knees with the top of the feet on the ground. Sit with the heels under the sitting bones. The heels will press the two nerves that run into the lower center of each buttock. Keep the spine pulled straight.

Stretch Pose
Lie on the back and push the base of the spine into the ground. Bring the feet together and raise the heels 6 inches/15 centimeters off the ground. Raise the head and shoulders 6 inches/15 centimeters off the ground. Stare at the toes with the arms stretched out pointing towards the toes. Palms should face down, and arms angle slightly out from the body.

Third Eye
The Third Eye is an energy center located at center of the forehead a little above the eyebrows. Mental focus at this location stimulates the pituitary gland and sushmuna (the central nerve channel of the spine).

Venus Lock
To form Venus Lock, interlace fingers with left little finger on the bottom, with the right index finger on top for men and the left for women. The fleshy mounds at the base of the thumbs are pressed together. This mudra brings the ability to focus and concentrate.

Recommended Resources In Alphabetical Order

Enneagram:
Books

"The Complete Enneagram: 27 Paths to Greater Self-Knowledge"
by Beatrice Chestnut, PhD., copyright 213

"The Enneagram in Love and Work"
by Helen Palmer, copyright 1995

"The Enneagram: Understanding Yourself and Others in Your Life"
by Helen Palmer, copyright 1991

"Personality Types: Using the Enneagram for Self-Discovery"
by Don Riso and Russ Hudson, copyright 1996

"Understanding the Enneagram" by Don Riso and Russ Hudson,
copyright 2000

Online resources
www.enneagraminstitute.com

Kundalini Yoga:
Books

"Meditation as Medicine" by Dharma Singh Khalsa,
copyright 2001

"Waves of Healing" by Siri Atma Khalsa,
copyright 2009

"Transitions to a Heart-Centered World" by Guru Rattana,
copyright 2014

Online resources
www.libraryofteachings.com
www.3ho.org

Thank you

Thank you to all the people who made this book possible including:

- The hundreds of people who came together
from all over the world to share their personal testimonials.
This book is dedicated to you.

- All of my Kundalini Yoga teachers who have helped,
shaped, influenced and supported me since I first discovered
Kundalini Yoga in 2007.

- My friends, family and community who participated in the creation
of this book in numerous and far reaching ways.

- To my editor, who prefers to remain anonymous.

- To Michalis Kafetzis and Krav Maga Kolonaki-IKMF
for the use of their studio for this project.

- To the whole team at Copyland.

- Photo Credit for the Kundalini Yoga images: Dimitris Pantidos.

- Photo Credit for About the Author Photos: Sakis Androutsopoulos.

- Graphic Design, Book Design and Cover Art: Ioulia Kirikou.

About the Author

Lynn Roulo is an American Kundalini Yoga and Enneagram instructor living in Athens, Greece. She teaches a unique combination of the two systems, combining the physical benefits of Kundalini Yoga with the psychological growth tools of the Enneagram. Her first book, Headstart for Happiness: A Guide Book Using Kundalini Yoga and the Enneagram was published in 2016.

She received her Kundalini Yoga teaching certification from the Guru Ram Das Ashram in San Francisco, California and began her teaching experience in 2009 at homeless shelters throughout San Francisco. In February of 2012, she relocated to Athens, Greece. She currently teaches throughout Europe and the United States.

Her study of the Enneagram System of Personality began in 1995. She is certified as an Enneagram Professional Trainer (EPTP program), and her training includes the Enneagram Intensive, Foundations of Spiritual Method, Subtypes, and the Enneagram Typing Process. While living in San Francisco, California, she participated in numerous narrative tradition panels with facilitators including Helen Palmer and Peter O'Hanrahan.

About Kundalini Yoga:

"I like Kundalini Yoga because everyone can do it. I usually refer to it as the yoga for people who think they can't do yoga. The starting position is always the breath, so if you can breathe, you can do Kundalini Yoga."

About the Enneagram:

"I think of it as a tool for compassion. When you start to understand yourself and your own behavior, you can start to break the patterns that don't serve you and choose you actions instead of just acting out your habit. And when you begin to understand what is going on in other people's minds, all that crazy behavior doesn't seem so crazy."

My Story

I spent most of my adult life as a Certified Public Accountant (US CPA) working in the Silicon Valley/San Francisco technology start up and venture capital industries. In 2012, I decided to move to Athens, Greece.

My reasons for moving were purely intuitive. I'm not Greek by heritage, I had no job here, I didn't speak any Greek, and there was no Greek man in the picture. I just had this really clear feeling, almost like a calling, that I should go to Greece.

And so I came.

I remember getting on the plane to leave San Francisco. My dog and two cats were in cargo below, and I had packed a suitcase full of clothes. Almost everything else I had sold or given away. There wasn't anyone to meet me in Athens because I didn't really know anyone. But it was one of the calmest moments of my life. I was totally sure I was making the right choice. And I haven't regretted it at all. I love Greece.

To learn more about the Enneagram or Kundalini Yoga or to schedule an Enneagram Typing interview, contact Lynn at lynn@lynnroulo.com.

References
Yogi Bhajan Quotes

Quote	Reference
"You have to know your strengths and your weaknesses. Between your strengths and your weaknesses is you."	Waves of Healing, page 24 by Siri Atma Khalsa
"Love doesn't rule you. What rules you in fear, phenomenal fear. Through this kriya, love can be invoked and fear can be reduced."	Yogi Bhajan lecture, April 4, 1994
"Total harmonious relaxation cures the body. To achieve this there must be a coordination between the three facets of ourselves: body, mind and soul."	Library of the Teachings, Aquarian Teacher Level One Instructor Yoga Manual, page 115
"The beauty in you is your spirit. The strength in you is your endurance. The intelligence in you is in your vastness."	Yogi Bhajan lecture, October 26 1988
"You cannot make your life a reaction to others, you must make your life your own."	Yogi Bhajan lecture, July 21, 1981

Kundalini Yoga Kriya and Meditation References

Kriya	Author	Reference	Date
Kriya for Elevation	Yogi Bhajan	Library of the Teachings	no date given
Kriya for Relaxation and To Release Fear	Yogi Bhajan	Library of the Teachings	no date given
Kriya for Relieving Inner Anger	Yogi Bhajan	Library of the Teachings	September 21, 1988
Heart's Delight Kriya	Guru Rattana	Transitions to a Heart Centered World, Second Edition, copyright 2014, page 58	no date given
Meditation for Gurprasaad	Yogi Bhajan	Kriya: Yoga Sets, Meditations and Classic Kriyas, page 186	no date given
Meditation to Remove Fear of the Future	Yogi Bhajan	Library of the Teachings	October 26, 1988
Meditation to Conquer Anger and Burn It Out	Yogi Bhajan	Library of the Teachings	March 8, 1999
Meditation for Creating Self-Love	Yogi Bhajan	Library of the Teachings	April 4, 1994

Lynn
enneagram & kundalini yoga

www.ingramcontent.com/pod-product-compliance
Lightning Source LLC
Chambersburg PA
CBHW060456010526
44118CB00018B/2437